China's New Voices

China's New Voices

*Popular Music, Ethnicity, Gender,
and Politics, 1978–1997*

NIMROD BARANOVITCH

University of California Press

BERKELEY   LOS ANGELES   LONDON

Chapter 2 of this book was previously published in different form:
Nimrod Baranovitch, "Between Alterity and Identity: New Voices of
Minority People in China," *Modern China* 27 (3), copyright © 2001
by Sage Publications, Inc. Reprinted by permission of Sage Publications, Inc.

University of California Press
Berkeley and Los Angeles, California

University of California Press, Ltd.
London, England

Library of Congress Cataloging-in-Publication Data

Baranovitch, Nimrod, 1965–.
China's new voices : popular music, ethnicity, gender, and politics,
1978–1997 / Nimrod Baranovitch.
        p.   cm.
Includes bibliographical references (p.) and index.
    ISBN 0-520-23449-9 (cloth : alk. paper).—ISBN 0-520-23450-2
(pbk. : alk. paper)
    1. Popular music—Social aspects—China.   2. Popular music—
Political aspects—China.   3. China—Civilization—1976–   I. Title.

ML3918.P67 B36   2003
306.4'84—dc21   2002068452

Manufactured in the United States of America

12   11   10   09   08   07   06   05   04   03
10   9   8   7   6   5   4   3   2   1

The paper used in this publication is both acid-free and totally chlorine-
free (TCF). It meets the minimum requirements of ANSI/NISO Z39.48–
1992 (R 1997) *(Permanence of Paper)*. ⊗

In memory of my father,
Avigdor Baranovitch (1937–1998),
and dedicated to my mother, Yulia Keile

Contents

Illustrations

Preface

Adopting an interdisciplinary approach that combines theories and methods from anthropology, musicology, literary criticism, and cultural studies, this book aims to provide an ethnography of popular music culture in contemporary urban China, one that pays equal attention to both descriptive and interpretive aspects. Focusing on the city of Beijing, the capital of the People's Republic of China (PRC) and one of its largest cities, the study examines three dimensions of the so-called pop and rock music culture: ethnicity, gender, and state politics.

The book is based on two field trips to China and Hong Kong that I carried out in January–August 1995 and March–June 1996. During these two periods I established contacts with many individuals: some of China's most prominent pop and rock musicians and music critics, ordinary people who provided me with lay perspectives on popular music culture, and other people involved in the music industry and academia who offered me their professional and academic perspectives. With some of these individuals I sustained close relationships and had frequent lengthy conversations, while with others I conducted formal extensive interviews. Many spontaneous occasional conversations with people on the street and in the marketplace, shops, bars, and university campuses also provided me with a considerable amount of important information. Conversations, interviews, and two open-question questionnaires that I distributed covered people belonging to different social groups, including both sexes, various age groups, different ethnic groups, as well as urbanites and newcomers from the countryside.

Much of the information on which this study is based came also from participation and observation in musical events. These included lengthy recording sessions (as an observer), live concerts of popular music, dance parties, and visits to discos and karaoke bars. Another source of information was television and radio programs that included popular music, and commercially released audiocassettes, CDs, and videocassettes. Various publications in Chinese about music and related subjects also constituted a major source. These included scholarly and nonscholarly writings in various newspapers, magazines, and books. Publications in English about China as well as general writings about popular culture provided me with important information as well as important theoretical insights.

Popular music is a multimedia phenomenon and a composite art. It includes sound, text, and visual aspects, and it may also be performed. My descriptions and analysis in this study draw upon all of these expressive domains in pursuit of both factual data and meanings.

NOTE ON ROMANIZATION AND TRANSLATION

Except for names of places and individuals that are widely known in the West in other transliterated forms, all transliterations of Chinese names, terms, and other words into English in this study follow the *pinyin* romanization system, which is used in the People's Republic of China. Unless otherwise noted, all translations in the text are mine.

Acknowledgments

This book derives from a dissertation that I submitted to the Music Department at the University of Pittsburgh in 1997 (see under Bernoviz in the References). The research for this dissertation was made possible by the generous financial support of the Asian Studies Program and the Music Department of that university. I would also like to thank the Pacific Cultural Foundation for providing me with a writing fellowship that helped me through the last phase of completing the dissertation. The writing of the book was supported by a generous grant from the Harry S. Truman Research Institute for the Advancement of Peace, at the Hebrew University of Jerusalem. I gratefully acknowledge this support.

Many individuals have contributed to this project, some in direct ways and some indirectly, and to all of them I owe a debt of gratitude: to the late Dora Schikman, who opened the door to China for me more than two and a half decades ago, for her patience, vision, and encouragement; to Dalia Cohen for initiating me into the field of musicology; to Mercedes Dujunco for introducing me to the possibility of combining my two major areas of interest; to Linda Penkower for her encouragement and help while I was at Pitt; to Rene Lysloff for introducing me to important theories and for commenting on an early draft of the introduction; to Akin Euba for introducing me in his seminar to the enormous scholarly potential that lies in popular music and for commenting on an early draft of the dissertation; to David Brodbeck for agreeing to join my committee at the last minute and for commenting on the dissertation; and to Nicole Constable for her thorough and constructive criticism of an early draft of the dissertation, which considerably improved it, and for opening the door to new domains in China scholarship for me.

In 1997 I returned to Israel and started to revise the dissertation into a book. Since then a number of people have read parts or all of the dissertation and its revised versions and offered invaluable comments and suggestions for improvement, and I thank them all. Sheldon Hsiao-peng Lu, Irene Eber, and Evelyn Rawski read the completed dissertation and offered valuable feedback. Special thanks go to Helen Rees, Susan Brownell, and Mercedes Dujunco, who read two versions of the entire manuscript and offered constructive criticism and pages upon pages of comments and detailed suggestions for improvement. My gratitude also goes to Stevan Harrell and one anonymous reader for their comments on the brief version of chapter 2, on ethnicity, which was published recently as an article in *Modern China*. Thanks also go to Agnes Wen of the Hillman Library at the University of Pittsburgh for searching for and sending me articles that I could not find in Israel, and to Iris Wachs for her important proofreading.

This study would not have been possible without the help of many people in China. I am grateful to the following individuals for sharing with me their knowledge, experience, thoughts, and feelings, all of which constitute the essence of this book: Zang Tianshuo, Li Tong, and the other members of Black Panther *(Hei bao);* Wayhwa, Wang Xiaofeng, Huang Liaoyuan, Dai Jinhua, Zheng Jun, Lolo, Lao Ying, and the other members of Mountain Eagle *(Shan ying);* Teng Ge'er, Cheng Jin, Wu Tong, Feng Jun, and the other members of *Lunhui*/Again; and Gao Feng, Zhang Guangtian, Chen Xiaolong, Huang Haibing, Wang Feng, Cui Yongqiang, Shen Yongge, Jin Ping, Gu Ping, A Tai, Dong Dong, and Liang Maochun. I owe a special debt of gratitude to Jin Zhaojun for his numerous articles (which provided me with an invaluable reference and a source of inspiration), for lengthy stimulating conversations, for helping me to contact many people, and for patiently answering my endless questions through email between my visits to China. My gratitude is also extended to Erez and Abigail Cohen and their children and to Pnina Zelcer for making my stay in Beijing in 1995 and 1996 more pleasant.

Special thanks are reserved for Bell Yung, who since I first arrived at the University of Pittsburgh to study with him in 1992 has provided me with guidance, inspiration, and continuous assistance and encouragement.

Finally, I would like to express my deepest gratitude to my wife, Leung Kwai-tung, and our three children, Avshalom, Zohar, and Ma'ayan, for their patience, help, and love. I dedicate this study to them and to my parents, Yulia Keile and Avigdor Baranovitch, to whom I owe everything.

Introduction

For close to three decades in China after 1949, one could hear in public a single voice, that of the party-state.[1] The government dictated much of culture and imposed unity in almost every domain. The new revolutionary trend extended from suppression of political views that did not agree with those of Chairman Mao Zedong as far as the attempt to eliminate regional, ethnic, class, and even gender differences. Beginning in the late 1950s and continuing through the 1960s and 1970s, for instance, millions of urbanites were sent to the countryside to become workers and peasants. During the Great Leap Forward, with its adjacent campaign against "local nationalism," and once again during the Cultural Revolution, attempts were also made to forcefully assimilate the many ethnic minorities who inhabit China into the new Han-dominated socialist order. In the domain of gender, the Communists' striving for equality between the sexes led to the emergence of a unisex ideal. This ideal, however, was masculine in essence. Thus, women were supposed to become like men, and many qualities and practices that traditionally were considered feminine were now viewed as feudal and decadent, and efforts were made to eliminate them. The realm of music was no exception. During the decade of the Cultural Revolution in particular, only militant revolutionary songs that praised the leadership and a handful of revolutionary operas and ballets were allowed to be performed in public.

Much has changed, however, since the death of Mao in 1976 and the rise to power of Deng Xiaoping in the late 1970s. Although since then state control has still been relatively tight compared to that in democratic states, it became significantly looser than it had been in the revolutionary period. For the last twenty years culture has no longer been dictated or imposed unilaterally from above. Attempts to dictate culture are still made by the government, but success is more limited than before. The significant liberalization since the late 1970s, the shift to a free-market economy, and the opening of the country to outside influence have all led to the resurgence of social, cultural, and even political diversity. It is within this diversity that culture is constructed and transformed through a process of constant public negotiation, in which multiple forces play active roles. It is against this general background that this book aims to shed light on some of the new agencies and voices that are emerging in China today and to illuminate the plurality of relationships and interactions between them.

China's New Voices focuses on the domain of popular music culture. There are several advantages in exploring social change and state politics specifically in this domain. Popular music culture is one of the largest and richest public spheres in China today. Popular music is almost everywhere: broadcast daily for many hours on local and national television and radio, sold on CDs, cassettes, and videotapes, discussed in newspapers and magazines, and sung and danced to by diverse people in karaoke bars, discos, and live concerts. A related feature of popular music culture is its polyphonic nature. As it is directed toward and enjoyed by a wide audience, popular music often crosses sociocultural and political lines and constitutes a site where intense interaction between different sociocultural and political forces takes place and multiple voices are heard. Different social, cultural, and political forces—such as the state, dissidents, and supporters of the system, peasants and urbanites, Han and non-Han, men and women, people from Beijing and people from Guangzhou and Shanghai, nouveaux riches and intellectuals, elite and nonelite—all use popular music to express and communicate different beliefs, aspirations, feelings, and identities and to interact with one another. As such, popular music culture provides the scholar who aims to understand contemporary China with a unique opportunity to find out what large numbers of different people—individuals and groups— think, feel, experience, like and dislike, do and want to do. It also allows him or her to identify old and new forces and groups and to analyze the relationships and interactions between them, such as power hierarchies and negotiation of power, conflicts and allegiances, influences, unity and diversity, and the articulation and negotiation of different identities.

The tight control that the Chinese Communist Party practiced over the content and style of public culture during large portions of the Maoist era and its ability to create, at least for a while, one national public culture that was relatively homogenous, transcending the diversity of the population, were closely linked to its control over the production and dissemination of culture. Similarly, the polyphonic nature of popular music culture in China in the last two decades is closely connected with important transformations in the domain of culture production and dissemination. The introduction since the late 1970s of new, simple, and low-cost technologies, like cassette and video recording, for example, has enabled people to escape the centralized and homogenizing control of the state. It also enabled many heretofore voiceless people to speak publicly in new voices and to articulate new subjectivities. One very recognizable feature of the first decade of the post-Mao era was the fact that people started to speak publicly in voices that did not always correspond to the voice of the state, sometimes even in oppositional voices.

The newly introduced market economy also contributed a significant share to this process of decentralization and diversification, as laws of supply and demand replaced unidirectional dictation by the state. The process of pluralization equally benefited from new values and practices, such as preference for innovation, diversity and free choice, free competition, nonconformism, personal freedom, and political resistance. These were linked to the renewed exposure to Western culture and to modern capitalism but also to the revival of prerevolutionary native practices and realities. The resurgence of regional differences is one such revival. The new ideologies, technologies, and mode of economy challenged not only the state. They equally challenged dominant social groups that traditionally have had more access to and control over the means of cultural production and dissemination—dominant groups such as men, members of the Han majority, and the intellectual elite.

Another feature that makes popular music highly suitable for a project that focuses on a period of radical transformation and aims to explore changes in various cultural domains is popular music's own changing nature and its close relationship with many other cultural domains. Compared to folk and classical music and culture, in which continuity and transcending a particular time and space often constitute the ideal, popular music and culture change frequently and are linked more closely to changes in values and behavior, politics, economics, and society. Popular music both mirrors and shapes society and culture as they change. The recent history of China provides multiple examples of this dialectical relationship and of the power of music to shape reality, and not just to reflect or "anticipate" it (Attali 1985) in some kind of prophetic sense. In his study of popular spoken dramas, cartoons, and newspapers during the Sino-Japanese war, for instance, Hung Chang-tai suggests that the Communists' "ingenious use of popular culture . . . contribute[d] to their ultimate seizure of power" (1994, 7). This argument, of course, applies also to popular music. It was partially through songs that the Communists penetrated the masses, associated themselves from very early on with the anti-Japanese struggle, mobilized the masses to join the war, and then credited themselves with the victory. It was also partially through songs that they were able to disseminate their new ideology among the masses, transform socioeconomic conditions, and credit themselves with the achievements. Songs also helped the Communists to discredit the Nationalist government, propagate the vision of a new, bright socioeconomic and political future under their control, and ultimately gain the massive support that led to their victory.

The Cultural Revolution, with its "model plays" *(yangbanxi)*, provides us with another important example of the formative role of music in shaping reality. As Lois Wheeler-Snow has written: "The Cultural Revolution brought about the new 'model' theater, [but that] theater also played a crucial part in bringing about the Cultural Revolution, just as it played a role in the Communist revolution itself" (1972, 101–2). Disseminated through every possible medium—film, radio, recordings, television, live performances, and public address systems—and heard and seen "everywhere" and "at all times," as many people testify, the model operas, together with numerous revolutionary songs, were part of the fuel that inspired people to actually make the revolution and sustain it for a whole decade.

Similarly, one cannot gain full understanding of the 1989 democracy movement without understanding the role that rock music played in shaping the minds of the students who led it in the years that preceded the movement, as well as during the movement itself. The relationship between rock music and the Tiananmen movement will be discussed in detail in the next chapter.

There are, of course, other popular cultural domains and expressions that both reflect and shape society, such as television, journalism, and film. Nonetheless, there is something that is distinctive about popular music as a form of communication. Popular music is a multimedia phenomenon and a composite expressive art that not only combines sound, text, and visual aspects—in the form of cassette covers and video clips, for example—but that also can be performed, and not only by professionals but also by the so-called audiences. Popular music culture is a highly participatory domain, in which large numbers of people actively interact with one another and express themselves through words and also through song and dance.

This participatory nature of popular music culture is enhanced by the important role played in it by low-cost, simple media, like cassettes, video, and karaoke. Whereas television and film, which also play important roles in popular music culture, have traditionally been controlled by the rich and powerful because of their complex and expensive technologies, popular music culture, with its newer media, is accessible to even the most marginal and peripheral groups in society.[2] In short, popular music culture is a site of particularly intense and powerful interaction because it involves multiple forms of communication, more active participation, and more people.

The academic concept of popular culture has been a subject of much discussion and debate, and the student of this phenomenon faces multiple definitions that are often very different from one another, and sometimes even contradictory. Two compilations of essays on popular culture in China that were published in the 1980s can serve as a good illustration of the wide range of definitions and understandings of the popular. Although lacking an explicit definition of popular culture, *Popular Chinese Literature and Performing Arts in the People's Republic of China 1949–1979* (McDougall 1984) is obviously based on the understanding that the popular is that which is the most widespread. The essays in that volume deal with official revolutionary cultural products: revolutionary mass songs, the model operas of the Cultural Revolution, and so on, all of which were produced and disseminated by the Chinese Communist Party during the revolutionary period. By contrast, *Unofficial China: Popular Culture and Thought in the People's Republic* (Link, Madsen, and Pickowicz 1989) identifies the popular with the unofficial. Despite the fact that the latter volume at least partially overlaps in time and scope with the earlier compilation, its authors define the popular as "distinct from official culture, that is, the official ideology of the Chinese state" (5). Thus, whereas in the earlier volume we are introduced, under the title "popular culture," to official revolutionary model literature, the more recent compilation introduces us, under the same title, to underground literature from the Cultural Revolution, literature that included pornographic and detective stories as well as Western romances (see Link's essay in that volume).

The difference with regard to the understanding of the popular between these two compilations on popular Chinese culture reflects an ongoing debate that is embedded in the general study of popular culture worldwide. Three major models dominate this debate. The first model views popular culture as something imposed from above on the passive masses, an instrument whose main purpose or use is to advance the interests of those in power and maintain their hegemony.[3] The second model, by contrast, even when it acknowledges the control exerted by powerful forces in society over the production of culture, nevertheless emphasizes the active role of the disempowered and subordinated people in their selective consumption and active reception of popular culture and the way they use it to promote their interests. While the former model stresses the uses of popular culture by dominant groups, the latter stresses the way the people use popular culture to resist and subvert the dominance and hegemony of powerful forces.[4] The third approach to the subject integrates the first two contradicting models. This model acknowledges the active role that both dominant and subordinated forces play in popular culture, and views the latter as an arena of constant struggle.[5]

In this study I utilize the above-mentioned three models as analytical tools rather than definitions. Popular culture cannot be essentialized, as its qualities, except for the more neutral quantitative one—namely, that it appeals to a wide audience and is widely distributed (a quality that most scholars take for granted)—may change from time to time and from one place to another.[6] The first model no doubt best describes popular culture in China during the revolutionary period, although it should be modified to accommodate political motivations rather than material ones as its main driving force. This model, however, is only partially useful in understanding popular culture when it comes to the post-Mao era. The second model, and certainly the third one, are more appropriate to explain the complex dynamics in this latter period. Nevertheless, they also have serious limitations. Both, like the first one, are bound by a Marxist theoretical framework that is conflict-oriented, privileges class relationships, and assumes a binary, structurally fixed, hierarchical dominant/subordinate power relationship.[7]

In the few studies that specifically explored popular culture in post-Mao China in a coherent theoretical framework that aimed to tackle the concept and meaning of the popular, the subject has usually been discussed within a similarly simplistic binary framework that basically recognizes the existence of two major forces and highlights only one type of relationship between these forces, a relationship that is always conflict-oriented. One example is *Unofficial China*, mentioned earlier. In this volume Link and his coauthors study popular Chinese culture in the framework of official versus unofficial dichotomy. It is in the context of this framework that they define popular culture as unofficial culture. In the introduction to their volume the editors relate this dichotomy to that of the state versus society, and argue that "popular culture includes any kind of culture that has its origins in the social side of the tension between state and society" (1989, 5). Tension thus becomes a privileged type of relationship in this compilation. Another example is Andrew Jones's pioneering study of popular music in the 1980s, *Like a Knife: Ideology and Genre in Contemporary Chinese Popular Music* (1992a). Although Jones avoids divorcing the state from the popular as Link et al. do, he nevertheless follows a similar approach when he divides the popular music scene into two main categories—official pop and nonofficial rock—and explores the relationship between the two in terms of the popular dichotomy of hegemony versus resistance.

In this book I expand and somewhat complicate these theoretical frameworks by introducing a more nuanced and less structural approach, which I believe is more appropriate for describing and understanding any reality. In my view popular culture is a complex and dynamic sphere, a web of interwoven relations and axes in which multiple forces (rather than just two) interact and negotiate, creating a plurality of relationships between them (rather than just one, which is always conflict-oriented). The main contribution of this book lies in its treatment of ethnicity and gender in the context of popular culture. Although informing a significant portion of social interaction and serving as essential resources for the creation of many cultural meanings, these two domains have surprisingly received little attention in previous studies of popular culture in China, which have tended to treat Chinese society as a single, undifferentiated whole. The book adheres to the idea of a multiplicity of forces also in recognizing that even in each of these domains the interaction involves more than just two forces. Thus, in chapter 2, on the negotiation of minority/majority identities and representation in popular music, for example, I dedicate a lengthy discussion to two minority musicians who have very different ethnic backgrounds. The chapter also explores different Han subjectivities and the role of the state in the negotiation of ethnic identities, which is complex in its own right. Similarly, the discussion in chapter 3 on the negotiation of manhood and womanhood in popular music refers to several male musicians, several female musicians, and the state. One of the main purposes of this chapter is precisely to show that there are today in the popular music scene in China multiple male and female agencies that are very different from one another.

The binary framework adopted in many studies on popular culture is problematic, not only because it basically allows for the existence of only two forces but also because it often assumes clear-cut categories that are often difficult to substantiate. Indeed, one of the characteristic features of the post-Mao era has been the "greying" (Barmé 1992a) of culture. This greying applies especially to the official versus unofficial dichotomy. In the 1990s in particular it became increasingly difficult and often impossible to determine what or who was official and what or who was unofficial. Different spheres often overlapped, and individuals often participated in more than just one subculture, thus acquiring multiple allegiances. Jin Zhaojun,

China's most prominent popular music critic, for instance, has been writing for years in the *People's Daily (Renmin ribao)* and *People's Music (Renmin yinyue)*, the most politicized official newspaper and music magazine, respectively. His articles nevertheless often expressed sympathy for rock-and-roll, a style that has been officially banned in China since it became popular in the late 1980s.[8] Another example is the nihilistic writer Wang Shuo. Wang started as an unofficial, rebellious writer in the late 1970s and early 1980s. In the late 1980s and early 1990s, however, he became increasingly involved in numerous productions for the state-run Central Chinese Television (CCTV), thus becoming very much associated with officialdom. But the situation changed once again in 1996, when Wang became one of the major victims of the new "spiritual civilization" campaign, during which his works were officially denounced once again.

The dynamism and complexity embodied in these two examples apply equally to power and influence. My book approaches all sociopolitical relationships with the understanding that "power is everywhere" (Foucault 1980) rather than "above" (or "below"), and that there are many kinds of power, rather than total power and total powerlessness or just domination and subordination.

It is the move beyond the well-established fixed and binary hierarchies of dominance and subordination that enabled me to shed light in this book on new, important agencies and voices previously unheard. It is also by making this move that I hope to show here how general culture in China today is constructed through constant and complex negotiation between multiple forces rather than dictated or prescribed unilaterally by a single force, be it an imagined omnipotent and uncompromising Chinese state or any other privileged group or force, such as Han Chinese in the domain of ethnicity or Chinese men in the domain of gender. In chapter 1, where I survey the main developments in the popular music scene since the late 1970s, I show, for example, how the popularity of *liuxing/tongsu* music (literally meaning "popular" music, but in practice suggesting soft pop) forced the state to recognize it as a legitimate style. Another example is found in chapter 2, on popular music and ethnicity, where I challenge the widely held view according to which when we move beyond local contexts to the general culture in China, minority people are passive, voiceless, and powerless. The chapter suggests not only that minority people have a voice in the general culture but also that they are able to exert significant influence on Han-produced minority representations and even on state-sponsored ones. A similar argument is presented in chapter 3, on popular music and gender. There I challenge the widespread tendency in writings on women in post-Mao China to depict them almost as total victims. Contrary to this view, chapter 3 proposes that though the commercialization of the 1990s in particular had indeed damaged the status of women in many respects, it nevertheless enabled some women to achieve an independent public voice that is unprecedented in its scope and nature.

The hegemony-resistance framework has too often led scholars of popular culture to focus exclusively on conflict or struggle. This book aims to expand this focus by adhering to the idea of plurality of relationships. Expanding this traditional focus on hegemony, resistance, and struggle is done partially through exploring the "ambivalences and ambiguities of resistance [and domination]" (Ortner 1995, 190). The book, however, achieves this aim also by moving beyond the domination-resistance scheme altogether. After all, human beings are engaged in a "multiplicity of projects" (191), not only in attempts to dominate or resist domination.

Forces or subcultures that appear to be in conflict with one another in every aspect may nevertheless simultaneously share certain ideologies, interests, and practices. Thus, in chapter 4, on popular music and state politics, for example, in addition to examining how the state uses popular music to consolidate its hegemony and control and how rockers use popular music to resist this control and hegemony, two important aspects that have been explored in the past and on which I elaborate here, I also show that there are significant points of convergence and unity. The chapter also proposes that between forces in the popular music scene that previously have been dealt with only in terms of conflict and opposition, there also exists an important symbiotic relationship. Other important types of relationships dealt with in this study are difference and integration. Difference plays an important role in the construction of identities and is examined in the chapters on ethnicity and gender. Integration is discussed in the chapter on ethnicity.

This book is about ethnicity, gender, and state politics as much as it is about popular music culture. In other words, besides offering a new perspective on popular Chinese culture, I hope equally to benefit the study of gender, ethnicity, and politics in China, academic fields in which, with few exceptions, popular music culture has traditionally received little attention. The distinctive qualities of popular music culture that I listed above—the fact that it is widespread and that it often crosses sociocultural lines, and its polyphonic, interactive, and participatory nature—all make it a very important lens that proves extremely useful for illuminating new aspects related to each of these fields.

1 China Diversified: An Overview of Popular Music in the Reform Era, 1978–1997

The rise of Deng Xiaoping to power in the late 1970s and the series of reforms that he initiated marked the beginning of a new era in Chinese history. One of the immediate consequences of the opening of China to the outside world, a reform that was labeled the "open door policy," was the flooding into the country of foreign cultural products, among which was popular music. As foreigners could now move into and out of China more freely, cassettes and records of contemporary pop started to be smuggled in and soon swept the entire mainland. The earliest foreign popular music to penetrate China came from Hong Kong and Taiwan. This music has been labeled *gangtai* music, a label that combines the Chinese names of these two neighboring Chinese polities (*Xianggang* and *Taiwan*, respectively). "The Moon Represents My Heart" *(Yueliang daibiao wo de xin)* was one of the first *gangtai* songs to arrive in the mainland in the late 1970s:

THE MOON REPRESENTS MY HEART
(lyrics and music by Anonymous; performance by Deng Lijun)

You asked me how deep is my love for you
How strong is my love for you?
My feelings are true
My love is also true
The moon represents my heart . . .

One gentle kiss
Already moved my heart
A short time of deep emotions
Made me long until now . . .

Like most *gangtai* songs, "The Moon Represents My Heart" was the antithesis of the songs that people on the mainland had been listening to and singing in the previous thirty years or so. The lyrics were about love, not love for the homeland, the party, or Chairman Mao, but rather romantic love between a man and a woman, a theme that had almost disappeared from the popular music scene on the mainland after 1949 because of its association with "decadent" "bourgeois individualism."[1] The mere expression of individual personal feelings, too, was something new and in complete contrast to the official, collective, political, and didactic ethos that prevailed in the popular songs of the revolutionary period.

Many of the most famous *gangtai* songs that were introduced to the mainland in the late 1970s and early 1980s were sung by the famous Taiwanese female singer Deng Lijun. The following statement by the mainland songwriter Jia Ding provides some clue to what Deng Lijun's songs and *gangtai* music in general meant for many mainland Chinese during the early years of the reform period:

> The first time I heard Deng Lijun's songs was in 1978. I just stood there listening for a whole afternoon. I never knew before that the world had such good music. I felt such pain. I cried. I was really very excited and touched, and suddenly realized that my work in the past had no emotional force. (Quoted in Jones 1992a, 16)

Deng's singing, considered the ideal in *gangtai* music at that time, was soft, sweet, often whispery and restrained. The sweet flavor of her voice was enhanced by gentle vibratos, coquettish nasal slides, and a moderate, relaxed tempo. Most of her songs were based on Western harmonies, while the melodies often retained the traditional Chinese pentatonism. A Chinese flavor was also created in some of the songs through the use of traditional Chinese instruments, like the *dizi* (bamboo flute), *erhu* (two-string fiddle), *sanxian* (three-string lute), and various gongs. The more common accompaniment, however, featured Western instruments, the most important of which were electric guitars, bass, drum set, electric organ, and violins. A Western influence manifested itself in many *gangtai* songs also in the use of Western popular dance rhythms. It is commonly agreed upon among mainland music scholars and critics that *gangtai* music of the 1970s descended from pre-1949 *liuxing* music, that is, the Western-influenced popular music that emerged in Shanghai and other cosmopolitan cities in China during the 1920s and 1930s in the context of the new modern, urban leisure culture of nightclubs, cabarets, and dance halls.

Jin Zhaojun, one of China's most prominent popular music critics (see

Figure 1.   Jin Zhaojun in his office. Photograph by Nimrod Baranovitch.

figure 1) characterized the musical style on the mainland during the revolutionary period as "lacking in *yin* and abundant in *yang*" (1988), meaning overly masculine and lacking in femininity. The fact that during large parts of the revolutionary period only militant music circulated publicly both reflected and created a reality in which people were denied a whole range of basic human emotions and modes of expression. This extreme situation created an extreme thirst for soft and slow songs. China was like a dry field in which a match had been thrown. So strong, fast, and comprehensive was the reaction that within months the country was literally flooded with Deng Lijun's songs. The Chinese composer Wen Zhongjia recalled hearing sometime in the late 1970s the sounds of Deng's songs coming even from "a small hut owned by a Kazak" in the remote Xinjiang Autonomous Region in northwest China (Wen Zhongjia, public lecture, Beijing, 23 May 1996).

The popularity of Deng Lijun, whose songs are still cherished by a whole generation, was also the result of the long isolation from much of the rest of the world that people on the mainland had experienced. Deng's and other *gangtai* songs were among the earliest samples of life coming from the outside world to which people were also able to relate because they used the same language. The popularity of the songs reflected the strong desire that many people on the mainland harbored, as they still do, to reach out after decades of isolation.

The speed and scope of the dissemination of *gangtai* music during the late 1970s and early 1980s marked the end of the extremely tight control exercised in the preceding three decades by the Communist Party over Chinese society and culture. The weakening of party control was closely related to new technologies that entered the mainland when China opened itself to the outside world. In music it was cassette technology that challenged most powerfully the tight control of the party. Tape recorders and cassettes had a decentralizing and democratizing effect, empowering people through the ability to choose and listen to the music they liked. People no longer depended exclusively on state-controlled radio, television, films, performances, and other official channels of dissemination to get their music. The simple technology and low cost involved in cassette recording made the mass production and dissemination of alternative, unofficial culture easier than ever before. As state-controlled media ceased to monopolize the cultural sphere, their homogenizing effect, too, lost much of its previous impact.

The introduction of cassette technology and the general liberalization also led to the emergence of a new mode of listening. With the growing private ownership of tape recorders, people's reception of music was no longer confined to public areas and mass gatherings, since now individuals could create an intimate sonic space with their privately owned tape machines:

> Looking back to those years, [I remember how] with other youngsters I took the risk of being criticized by the leaders, [and] in the dark dormitory, holding a bottle of beer, [we] listened secretly to that "decadent music" [*mimi zhi yin*] by the compatriots from Hong Kong and Taiwan that was transmitted from a cheap smuggled cassette which I don't know how many times was already dubbed. . . . At that time I felt it was the paradise of music. . . . (Xu 1996)

The late 1970s and early 1980s are remembered in music circles on the mainland as a period of imitation and study. Deng Lijun was the most popular model for imitation, and many new singers built their own careers by imitating her. Cheng Lin, one of China's most famous female pop stars, was labeled at that time "little Deng Lijun," and many newly emerging nightclubs in southern China had their own "little Deng Lijun." Completely ignorant of the developments in popular music that had taken place around the globe in the previous decades and determined to learn, mainland musicians plunged into what was labeled "stripping off cassettes" *(ba daizi)*, which meant studying the music of the newly introduced foreign cassettes simply through close and repeated listening (Jin 1996c). After "stripping off" imported cassettes, mainland musicians started to reproduce the new arrangements that they heard. Part of the problem faced by these musicians was that, due to China's long isolation, they were not even familiar with many of the instruments used in the original arrangements.

As China was now officially headed toward modernization, *gangtai* music came to symbolize for many on the mainland a desired Chinese modernity (Brace 1992, 144–45). The new rush to catch up, however, did not proceed without resistance. The relationship between the new *gangtai* songs that flooded the mainland and pre-1949 *liuxing* songs was too obvious to be ignored, and these had a long history of condemnation on the mainland.

Since the 1930s, *liuxing* songs were seen in leftist circles, especially after the Japanese invaded Manchuria in 1931, as decadent and escapist, and were accused of distracting the attention of urbanites from the nationalistic cause. The sentimental, romantic content, and soft, sweet, slow delivery of the songs were blamed for softening people's hearts and weakening their will for struggle and sacrifice. Xian Xinghai, one of China's best-known revolutionary composers, for instance, wrote in 1940 that the music by Li Jinhui, the father of *liuxing* music, "anaesthetized many urbanites of the time" (Sun Ji'nan 1993, 21).[2] *Liuxing* music was labeled in leftist, patriotic circles "yellow," meaning pornographic, and it eventually came to represent Western and Japanese imperialism, the corrupted Nationalists, and the Chinese bourgeois, who were seen as seeking leisure, careless about the national crisis, imitating Western decadent culture, and, above all, exploiting China's workers and peasants. Half a century later this view of *liuxing* music was very much alive on the mainland:

> Under the circumstances of that time, some popular [*liuxing*] songs with themes that had to do with love really had the side-effect of lulling people's fighting will and relaxing their morale. Although based upon reason one may admit that the existence of these songs was inevitable, emotionally speaking it is difficult to accept the fact that at that specific period, while revolutionary people were sacrificing their lives, there were others who were "choosing the plump and picking the slender" in "the peach blossom river" and "the place of beautiful women." (Zhang Zhentao 1990, 3)

"Peach Blossom River" *(Taohua jiang)* is the title of a famous popular song by Li Jinhui that was written in 1927–28. "The place of beautiful women" *(meiren wo)* and "choosing the plump and picking the slender" *(tiao fei jian shou)* are quotations from the lyrics of the song, in which a young man and a young woman discuss how the former picks his lovers. It was this view of *liuxing* music that led eventually to its disappearance from the mainland. The style disappeared together with the urban leisure culture of nightclubs and dance halls a few years after the Communist victory in 1949.

The term *liuxing* itself, which is one of the words in Chinese for "popular," carried with it such negative connotations that in order to overcome the opposition, a new term, *tongsu*, was coined instead to denote "popular" in the combination "popular music."[3] A friend of mine who was a young teenager in the early 1980s recalled how her teachers in high school warned her and her fellow students to stay away from *gangtai* songs, which they labeled "yellow" and "decadent," using the same loaded terminology that was coined more than half a century earlier. An official of the Ministry of Culture interviewed in 1982 was asked about popular songs from Hong Kong and Taiwan. The official classified *gangtai* songs into three categories: "low-class and filthy, pure love songs, and songs about ordinary life and homesickness for the mainland," and regarded only the last category as completely acceptable (Honig and Hershatter 1988, 59–60). Around that time, in the midst of an anti-pornography campaign, high schools "began music classes to teach revolutionary songs, presumably so that young people could satisfy their desire to sing without resorting to licentious tunes" (61). In the summer of 1985, a year and a half after the end of the 1983 large-scale campaign against "spiritual pollution," the State Council issued updated "Regulations Strictly Forbidding Obscene Goods." The regulations forbade, among other things, the importation, reproduction, sale, and broadcast of audiotapes that concretely described sexual activity (62).

However, despite the opposition, mainland musicians soon started to produce songs that were modeled after the newly introduced *gangtai* songs. One of the earliest *liuxing/tongsu* songs produced on the mainland following the initiation of reforms was "Longing for Home" *(Xiang lian)*. The song was first performed in 1980 and immediately triggered a hot public debate:

LONGING FOR HOME
(lyrics by Ma Jinghua; music by Zhang Piji; performance by Li Guyi)

The shape of your body
Your voice
Are printed forever in my heart

Although yesterday is already gone
And it will be hard to meet again after we separate
How can I forget your deep love? . . .

"Longing for Home" became a target of vigorous attacks, not so much because of its lyrical content, which, based at least on its title, still dealt with love for one's native land rather than with "decadent" romantic love, but rather because of its music. Some critics did not like the song's tango rhythm or Li Guyi's soft, breathy singing *(qi sheng)*, which reflected the influence of the newly introduced *gangtai* songs. Li Guyi was the first mainland singer to use breathy singing after decades in which only two types of singing, Western heroic bel canto singing *(meisheng changfa)* and artistic folk/national singing *(min'ge/minzu changfa)* were permissible. For these critics, the rhythms of Western popular dances and soft, breathy singing still symbolized all the evil that was associated with *liuxing* music of the 1930s and 1940s. So strong was the distaste that some even labeled the song "the sounds of a subjugated nation" *(wangguo zhi yin)* (Yang Xiaolu 1990, 225).

The criticism and attacks, however, did not result in the disappearance of "Longing for Home" and other controversial songs.[4] Instead, in sharp contrast to previous decades, these songs were soon hits, and the singers who sang them became the first stars in post-revolution China.[5] The survival and popularity of these controversial songs marked the termination of the cultural monophony that had prevailed in China for several decades, and the beginning of a more polyphonic era. The fact that these songs became popular despite the lack of official sanction reflected the new liberal atmosphere and the fact that the forces that strove for change and reform were now stronger than hard-line and more conservative forces. It also indicated that a new political dynamic had emerged in China, namely, that large portions of society were now taking the liberty of not following official prescriptions. The popularity of *liuxing* music despite official disapproval reflected the negative effect that the catastrophic experience of the Cultural Revolution had on the hegemony of the Communist Party, being among the earliest manifestations of the new post-revolutionary ethos of disillusionment and political cynicism that emerged as a result of this traumatic experience.

The loosening of official control, the move to a semicapitalist economic system in selected parts of China, and the increase in cultural exchange with Western and Western-influenced countries during the early 1980s soon led to the reappearance of nightclubs and dance halls in which music played a central role. The most important center for the revival of modern urban leisure culture in China in the early 1980s was Guangdong Province in southern China. The pioneering role of Guangdong was related to its geographical proximity to Hong Kong, from which large portions of the foreign cultural products came, its remoteness from the more conservative capital, and the fact that part of this province was now enjoying the new status of "a special economic zone," which meant a higher degree of liberalization and autonomy.

The transformation of Guangdong serves as a good example of the close relationship between economic and political reforms and cultural change. The new emphasis on economics and the move to a semicapitalist market system meant that money and profit replaced, at least to a certain extent, the privileged position that political ideology had enjoyed during the revolutionary era. With the officially encouraged emergence of market dynamics, which were intended to increase initiative and productivity and thus to accelerate the modernization that was the main target of the reforms, the likes and dislikes of society became more influential and powerful than ever, as now they were translated into market demand. Catering to public taste, which did not always conform to official prescriptions, became in turn an important goal for many governmental production units, which by the early and mid-1980s gradually ceased to enjoy governmental subsidies and had to rely on their own profits. The rise of a new sector of private entrepreneurs called *getihu* was yet another factor in the process that gradually led to the emergence of unofficial, alternative mechanisms of culture production and dissemination, mechanisms that Orville Schell has named the "second channel" (1994, 293–310). It was through these second channels that Deng Lijun's and other *gangtai* songs, as well as controversial native *tongsu* songs, managed to be popularized despite the lack of official sanction or support, and sometimes even despite official disapproval.

Against this background there also emerged a new kind of musical activity called *zouxue* (literally meaning "going to the caves"). This activity, which also started in Guangdong (Jin 1996b) was part of the new general trend of people moonlighting outside their *danwei* (governmental work units) to make extra money in an emerging free-market economy. While hitherto all musicians in China, like most other individuals, had belonged to governmental work units, which supported them but at the same time also controlled them and dictated official norms of behavior, musicians could now, partially at least, escape state control. This meant, among other things, that musicians were not obliged anymore to produce and perform only officially sanctioned music. *Zouxue*, simply meaning gigs, or temporary contract jobs, were a significant breakthrough; musicians now had much more freedom in choosing where, what, and how to perform, as neither they nor their performances were necessarily controlled by the state. *Zouxue* became yet another important alternative channel that helped in the dissemination of unofficial songs. Parallel to the emergence of this practice in the early and mid-1980s, some singers and musicians also began leaving their governmental units altogether, embarking on private careers in the hope of becoming richer and gaining more personal and artistic freedom. One such musician was Cui Jian, China's first rocker, who left his work unit, the Beijing Philharmonic, in 1987 (Jaivin 1988, 84).

It took nearly a decade after *liuxing/tongsu* music was first introduced on the mainland for the state to officially recognize it. The new style was officially recognized in 1986, when it became for the first time an acknowledged, legitimate singing category in the annual state-run CCTV singing competition (Yang Xiaolu 1990, 226; see also Jin 1990b, 1996d). Until 1986 all the participating songs in officially organized competitions and other musical events had to be sung in either bel canto style or artistic folk/national singing style. The year 1986 is also remembered for the large-scale officially organized *tongsu* concert that took place in Beijing in May of that year. It was the first of its kind and another indication of the full official recognition of *liuxing/tongsu* music. It is because of these two events that 1986 is also considered the year of the birth of mainland pop.[6] The incorporation of *liuxing/tongsu* music by the state reflected the fact that even official culture was now constructed through negotiation and not dictated unilaterally from above, as it was during the revolutionary period. The reintroduction of *liuxing* music into Chinese public culture was not initiated by the state. The style existed for almost a decade outside of the official sphere. The state had little choice but to accept and incorporate it in order to communicate with China's youngsters, who were the main patrons of this music.

The sweet, romantic character of *gangtai* songs and their mainland counterparts have too often led scholars to ignore their subversive role in the context of the late 1970s and early to mid-1980s. When scholars began to seriously study popular Chinese music in the late 1980s and early 1990s, it was mainly if not exclusively rock music that they associated with unofficial, alternative and subversive culture in post-Mao China and with liberating functions. Quite in contrast to this view, the discussion above suggests that long before rock music appeared in China, sweet, romantic *liuxing/tongsu* songs played an important role in challenging officially sanctioned discourse, practices, and ideologies, and in changing Chinese culture.

THE NORTHWEST WIND *(XIBEIFENG),* 1986–1989

In 1986 there emerged in the popular music scene on the mainland a new style called *xibeifeng* (Northwest Wind). The rise of this new style was triggered by two new songs, "Xintianyou" and "Having Nothing" *(Yiwu-*

suoyou), which appeared that year in Guangzhou and Beijing respectively (Jin 1988). The two songs, the latter of which is also considered the first Chinese rock song, were significantly different from the prevailing slow, soft, romantic *gangtai* songs and their mainland counterparts, and they soon led to a nationwide "wind," or fad, which reached its peak in late 1988 and early 1989.

XINTIANYOU
(lyrics by Liu Zhiwen and Hou Dejian; music by Xie Chengqiang)

I raise my head
Facing the blue sky
Searching for the far gone past
Carefree white clouds travel as they wish
Nothing has changed

Wild geese heard my song
Small stream kissed my face
The red flowers of the mountain lily open and then fall
Time and again . . .

Xintianyou is the generic name of a folksong type associated mainly with northern Shaanxi Province. The 1986 song was named after this regional folksong type because it adopted some of its major musical characteristics, including certain melodic patterns, its unique vocal delivery, and the use of the folksy *suona,* a double reed oboe also found in other locations in China. Since these musical characteristics, which were also used in "Having Nothing," came from China's northwest, the new style was accordingly labeled Northwest Wind. *Xibeifeng* songs combined the folksy characteristics of the northwest with a strong, fast modern disco/rock beat. The incorporation of this beat reflected the enormous popularity that disco (*diseke* in Chinese) enjoyed in large cities and small towns all over China in the mid-1980s, not only among the younger generation but also among elderly people (Chiu 1985; Brownell 1995, 277–88). The fast tempo and strong beat of Northwest Wind songs, which were enhanced by an aggressive bass line, were the opposite of the slow beat that was found in most *gangtai* songs and their mainland counterparts. The difference, however, was not limited to rhythm and tempo. In contrast to the stepwise melodies and the soft, sweet, restrained, and highly polished singing style of most *liuxing/tongsu* songs of the time, *xibeifeng* songs had large leaps in their melodic line, and they were sung loudly and forcefully, almost like yelling, in what many Chinese writings describe as a bold, unconstrained, rough, and primitive voice. The new style was a kind of musical reaction against the style of songs from Taiwan and Hong Kong introduced on the mainland almost a decade earlier.

The musical stylistic reaction symbolized for many the reassertion of mainland cultural independence. *Xibeifeng* was the first indigenous, popular style to emerge on the mainland since the beginning of the reform era, after nearly a decade in which China was flooded by cultural products from outside the country. The new style combined the most primordial elements of the backward, desolate rural areas of northwest China with the most modern rhythm. It was a combination of something quintessentially Chinese with something very modern. In this, it represented the revival of mainland creativity in the new modern, cosmopolitan era.

The popularity of *xibeifeng* songs also reflected the aspiration harbored by many in China to resume the mainland's historic cultural hegemony over Hong Kong and Taiwan. The struggle for cultural hegemony between China on the one hand and Hong Kong and Taiwan on the other has been, at least since the early 1980s, an inseparable part of popular music culture and discourse on the mainland. Northern Shaanxi Province, the geographical location associated with the new style, was significant in the context of this power struggle, since it is considered to be, by all Chinese, both in and outside of China, the cradle of Chinese civilization. Thus, the incorporation into the new style of what was seen as primitive, primordial musical elements was in a sense an attempt to reestablish the status of the mainland as the ancestral land and ancestral culture, a status that China lost after 1949, especially after the Cultural Revolution, during which Chinese traditional culture suffered the most severe attack ever. Many *xibeifeng* songs articulated in both music and lyrics a sense of pride in the power of the northwest's peasantry, who came to represent the entire people of the mainland, to endure and overcome the worst kind of hardships. If the soft, sweet, slow, restrained, polished urban *gangtai* style represented for people on the mainland a longed-for femininity, *xibeifeng*'s loud and rough vocal delivery, fast and forceful beat, powerful bass line, and bold melodic leaps, along with the screaming sound of the folksy *suona*, constructed the desired powerful, earthy, primordial masculine image of the mainland.

Xibeifeng was the musical branch of the large-scale Root-Seeking *(xungen)* cultural movement that swept China during the early and mid-1980s, and which manifested itself also in literature and in film. For many Chinese, songs belonging to this style were instrumental in reestablishing a connection with China's lost past and in regaining a new sense of collective identity. Like the lyrics of "Xintianyou," many *xibeifeng* songs articulated feelings of loss and longing, and a desire to go back and reconnect with authentic China, with its remote past and primordial earth. In contrast to the personal romance that was celebrated in *gangtai* songs, *xibeifeng* songs were the expression of a search for the collective past. For some, this search was more than just an artistic journey. Hou Dejian, the Taiwanese musician who wrote the lyrics for "Xintianyou," actually left Taiwan and moved to the mainland.[7]

The Root-Seeking movement was closely tied to an identity crisis that overtook China's intellectuals in the early 1980s. It was an attempt to reestablish a renewed sense of identity and to mediate the conflict that many Chinese intellectuals faced in the post-revolutionary era, being deprived of history and tradition after the Cultural Revolution, cynical about communism and the whole revolutionary ethos, and suddenly flooded with Western culture. It was against this background that China's almost mythic Yellow Earth Plateau *(huangtu gaoyuan)*, the cradle of Chinese civilization, became the theme for many literary works and films. *Yellow Earth* (*Huang tudi;* directed by Chen Kaige, 1984) was one such film. It told the story of a Red Army soldier engaged during the Yan'an period in the collection of folksongs in a primitive village in this region. Like the songs in this movie, *xibeifeng* songs represented the roots that people were searching for. The folksy tunes offered a tangible bridge to a geographical location that came to symbolize a desired imaginary past and a longed-for collective existence.

However, like *Yellow Earth* and other expressions of the Root-Seeking movement, the *xibeifeng* fad was not without ambiguities and contradictions. Despite the nationalistic sense of pride and love for the homeland, *xibeifeng* songs were also filled with tragic overtones and articulated a sense of dissatisfaction and a strong desire to change things. The contradictory nature of the style is illustrated in "My Beloved Homeland" *(Wo relian de guxiang)*, which became a hit in 1987:

MY BELOVED HOMELAND
(lyrics by Guang Zheng; music by Xu Peidong; performance by Tian Zhen)

My homeland is definitely not beautiful
Low straw huts, bitter well water
One small stream that often gets dry . . .
On a barren soil
Harvesting a meager hope
Staying year after year

Living generation after generation
Oh! Oh! Oh! Oh! Oh! Homeland! Homeland! . . .
I want to use my true feelings and sweat
To make you change into a fertile land, yah . . .

If earlier I suggested that *xibeifeng* songs' rough vocal delivery, strong beat, aggressive bass line, bold melodic leaps, and screaming *suona* constructed a desired masculine image of China as a nationalistic reaction against the flooding of the mainland by *gangtai* culture, then the very same musical features paradoxically perhaps also articulated challenge and resistance to the Chinese government. The lyrics of "My Beloved Homeland" gain much of their oppositional political meaning if they are examined in the context of the recent history of public discourse on the mainland. Below is a translation of several excerpts from a communist classic from 1943 named "Nanniwan." This song is especially suitable for comparison because it also talks about the yellow earth of northwest China, where Nanniwan is found. It does so, however, not so much because of the association of this location with the origins of Chinese civilization but rather because it was there that the Communists established their now mythical red capital of Yan'an following the Long March.

NANNIWAN
(lyrics by He Jingzhi; music by Ma Ke)

. . . We arrived in Nanniwan, Nanniwan is a beautiful place . . .
Everywhere there are crops, everywhere there are cattle and sheep
Nanniwan of former years was barren hills, yah, uninhabited, yah . . .
Today in Nanniwan everywhere, yah, is Jiangnan, Jiangnan, yah.[8]
Study and produce,[9] Brigade 359 is a model
We move forward, and offer flowers to our model.

Both "Nanniwan" and "My Beloved Homeland" mention the arid conditions and other not-so-pleasant features that are associated with the backward rural area of China's Loess Plateau. However, in sharp contrast to "Nanniwan," where these characteristics are associated with the bitter past, in "My Beloved Homeland" they are associated with the present. Whereas "Nanniwan" highlights the transformation of the barren hills under the Communists and suggests that they have turned them into Jiangnan, the fertile and rich region south of the Yangtze River, "My Beloved Homeland" suggests that nothing in fact has really changed and that the promise embodied in "Nanniwan"—and in general Communist official discourse—has not been fulfilled. For more than thirty years most popular songs in China followed the principle of socialist realism. Like

"Nanniwan," they conformed to Mao's prescription, in his Talks at the Yan'an Forum on Literature and Art of 1942, that art and literature should present reality (under the Communists) in a "more idealized" light.[10] Artists and writers who worked under the Communists were supposed to depict reality not as it was but rather as the Communists thought it should be. Accordingly, revolutionary songs were all optimistic and positive, always negating the past and presenting the present and future under the praised Communist Party as bright and promising. No room was left for criticism and pessimism. It is against this background that the full meaning of the lyrical content of some of the most important *xibeifeng* songs can be fully understood. The mere nostalgic stance of these songs reversed the Chinese Communist Party's prescribed order. It turned the past into a desired object, and that in itself implied dissatisfaction with the present, which in communist China translates immediately into political criticism directed at the party. But there are also statements in *xibeifeng* songs that articulate a more explicit criticism. Examples of such statements are found in the line "nothing has changed" in "Xintianyou," and in the line "my homeland is definitely not beautiful," which opens "My Beloved Homeland." Such lines trivialized the communist revolution and challenged the communist myth of great and positive transformation that songs like "Nanniwan" and other revolutionary cultural expressions established and perpetuated for over three decades.

The very same messages were also articulated in Chen Kaige's film *Yellow Earth*. The Red Army soldier in the film is very enthusiastic about the revolution, but not only is he unable to change anything in the primitive village to which he is sent, despite its proximity to Yan'an, but he even ends up being at least partially responsible for the death of the girl protagonist, whose expectations and hopes he raises with unfulfilled promises of liberation (Barmé and Minford 1988, 251–69).[11] The statements "nothing has changed" and "my homeland is definitely not beautiful," together with Cui Jian's "Having Nothing" (which I discuss later), suggest an important aspect in the Northwest Wind fad that has received little attention: namely, that it was one of the earliest public artistic articulations of discontent and criticism directed at the government since the rise to power of the Communist Party in 1949.[12]

The Root-Seeking movement was filled with ambiguities and ambivalences. The major ambivalence involved the treatment of tradition and China's peasantry. Although nostalgia for some kind of primitive and authentic "Chineseness" was an important component in many artistic expressions, there were also embedded in the movement articulations of criticism of and desire to escape from this same sought-for Chinese essence. This ambivalence manifested itself most clearly in one of the best-known films from the period, *Red Sorghum* (*Hong gaoliang;* directed by Zhang Yimou, 1987–88), which was also the direct source of one of the most popular *xibeifeng* songs, "Young Sister Go Boldly Forward" (*Meimei ni dadan de wang qian zou,* also referred to as *Meimei qu,* meaning "Young Sister's Tune").[13] Some suggest that the movie was also the trigger behind the whole *xibeifeng* fad (see Ling Xuan 1989, 37). *Red Sorghum* will be remembered, among other things, as the film that introduced sexuality into the mainland's cinema. With its music and its two protagonists it constructed an image of China that is full of force, vitality, and freedom, the image that many Root-Seeking writers, like Mo Yan, were trying to construct in their works.[14] The important thing about this construction, however, was its implied criticism and challenge, as it was a reaction against what these artists perceived as the loss of power, vitality, and virility in Chinese culture due to long lasting sociocultural and political oppression. It was within this context that "Young Sister Go Boldly Forward" gained much of its meaning. The song is sung in the film after its two protagonists (a strongly built rustic male worker and a young woman whom he is originally hired to carry in a sedan chair to a forced marriage) make love in the middle of a field in a celebration of a primitive, wild outburst of pure physical desire and challenge to the traditional order, both past and present. Following this act, hidden from view, the male protagonist shouts the song while running in the field parallel to a road on which the female protagonist is now riding a donkey, accompanied by her father, who does not understand where the shouts are coming from. Yelled in a coarse, masculine voice in unconstrained, carefree, and wild fashion, "Young Sister Go Boldly Forward" was generally interpreted in China as embodying "the rise of a real man who is under profound oppression" (Luo Yuan in Yang Xiaolu and Zhang Zhentao 1990, 410). The last quotation offers a vivid illustration of the less positive attitude toward tradition that was an integral part of the Root-Seeking movement.

Xibeifeng both reflected and shaped the intense public cultural and political negotiation that was taking place on the mainland during the 1980s. This public negotiation was unprecedented in its scope in the history of the People's Republic. The negotiation reached one early peak in June 1988, when the series *River Elegy (He shang)* was broadcast on national television. Like *xibeifeng* songs and Root-Seeking literature and films, the series was an artistic reflective journey to the origins of Chinese civilization. The actual journey of exploration to the Yellow River area documented in this series was a fierce attack on traditional Chinese culture. The series called for greater Westernization and modernization in order for China to become a strong modern nation, and triggered a fierce public debate that resulted in a revised version of the series, which was broadcast in August, this time without sections that explicitly challenged the Communist Party and its policies (Su and Wang 1991; De Jong 1989–90). Like many *xibeifeng* songs, *River Elegy* communicated a sense of tragedy, suggested rather explicitly in the title of the series, and reflected the growing sense of crisis among Chinese intellectuals and others during the late 1980s. Like "My Beloved Homeland," it articulated a strong sense of dissatisfaction but simultaneously an idealistic, patriotic desire to shake off the shackles of tradition and change things. The relationship between *River Elegy* and *xibeifeng* has been drawn even closer by Su Xiaokang, one of the script writers of the series, who in his account of its creation mentions "Young Sister Go Boldly Forward" and "Having Nothing" as having inspired him to write the script (Chong 1989–90, 46).

River Elegy was broadcast in the midst of the *xibeifeng* fad and less than one year before the 1989 protest movement started. In August 1988, Jin Zhaojun published an article in the *People's Daily* arguing that *xibeifeng* articulated "all the dissatisfaction and even disgust and rejection felt by the new generation of young people" (1988). Jin further pointed in this article to the emerging critical attitude among youngsters in China and their aspiration for independence. He noted that Chinese youngsters experienced enormous pressure, mental conflict, and confusion due to the rapid change in values and the transition from the old to the new, and suggested that *xibeifeng* emerged because it satisfied the youngsters' need to "release their feelings of oppression." In this article Jin fulfilled the role that officials responsible for music in traditional China had often fulfilled, namely, to sense the general atmosphere among the people by carefully listening to their songs. Moreover, his article also predicted in a sense what was about to happen the following year. In 1995, six years after the 1989 June 4 incident, Jin tied the incident more closely than ever before to the Root-Seeking movement and the *xibeifeng* fad, suggesting that the incident was actually the climax of both (Jin, interview with the author, 16 August 1995). The protesters who stormed Tiananmen Square in April 1989 were driven by the same sense of self-empowerment that is communicated in "Young Sister Go Boldly Forward," and they expressed the same sense of dissatisfaction articulated in "My Beloved Homeland." The latter also articulated the collective and idealistic sense of mission and patriotism and the desire to change things that many of the protesters shared.

The violent crackdown on the movement that took place in the night of June 3–4 was a significant turning point in China's post-revolutionary history. It redefined the negotiated space, reducing it again significantly, and signaled that the government was no longer going to tolerate too overt and direct a political challenge. The crackdown also resulted in a dramatic cultural transformation that has been manifested in post-1989 popular music culture, among other things, in the disappearance of much of the idealism and overt criticism that were articulated in *xibeifeng*.

PRISON SONGS *(QIU GE)*, 1988–1989

In 1988 and early 1989, parallel to the climax in the *xibeifeng* tide, China was stormed by a second fad, labeled "prison songs." The simultaneous spread of these two fads, at least for a while, was another indication of the emerging social and cultural diversity on the mainland. The prison song fad was initiated by Chi Zhiqiang, a famous actor who had spent some time in jail because of his involvement in criminal activity and who upon release started to set folk melodies from northeast China to lyrics that depicted his experience as an ex-convict (Wang Xiaofeng, interview with the author, Beijing, 18 June 1996).[15] The style eventually came to comprise songs by other ex-convicts and old songs by *zhiqing*, educated urban youth who were sent during the Cultural Revolution to the countryside for reeducation through hard labor. One important characteristic feature that these different songs had in common was the articulation of nonmainstream sentiments and worldview, and the fact that the subcultures with which they were associated constituted what Jin Zhaojun has labeled a "counter-culture" (1989a). In sharp contrast to *xibeifeng* songs, prison songs were usually slow and lyrical, or "weepy" (Zeng 1988), and whereas the former communicated an highbrow, collective, idealistic sense of mission, the latter invoked negative role models, often used vulgar language, and articulated a new ethos of dark realism, despair, cynicism, and social alienation and antagonism, which in many respects were similar to those found in much of early American blues. In their nonheroic and nonidealistic sentimentalism, vulgar colloquial language, "unhealthy" themes, and celebration of nonconformist values—which manifested themselves also in titles like "Mother Is Very Muddle-Headed" *(Mama hao hutu)*, "There Is Not a Drop of Oil in the Dish" *(Cai li meiyou yi di you)*, "Bachelor/Hooligan's Happiness" *(Guanggun le)* (Zeng 1988), and "I Want to Drink Beer" *(Wo yao he pijiu)* (Ling Xuan 1989, 38)—prison songs celebrated both nonofficialdom and anti-intellectualism. So annoying were these songs to some that one distinguished editor of a recent compilation of popular songs suggests that they embodied a "deformed social mentality" (Ling Ruilan 1994, 6) and simply ignores them in the compilation's lengthy introduction, despite the fact that these songs sold more than what songs belonging to most other styles have ever sold in China (Wang Xiaofeng, interview with the author, 18 June 1996).[16]

"Song of an Educated Youth from Changchun" is a representative prison song belonging to the subcategory of old songs by rusticated youth:

SONG OF AN EDUCATED YOUTH FROM CHANGCHUN
(lyrics by Duzi; music by Anonymous)

I'm an educated youth
I was sent down to the country, to Jiutai County
All day I swung a pickax, digging shit for fertilizer
"Transforming the earth!" and "Changing the sky!"
Made me so tired my back and legs ached
After a year I was sent home
But I didn't even have any traveling money[17]

Prison songs shared many of their characteristics with a new type of literature that emerged in China around the mid-1980s and that has been mainly associated with the young writer Wang Shuo. Wang was the first contemporary writer on the mainland since at least 1949 to write on "small-time ex-cons, drifters, pimps, good-girls-turned-bad . . . and the perennially bored *liumang*, or hooligans" (Wong Yu 1996, 46). His literature has been labeled in highbrow intellectual circles on the mainland "ruffian" or "riffraff" *(pizi)* literature, and it has actually been viewed in those circles as nonliterature. In contrast to the Root-Seeking intellectual writers who were engaged in highbrow cultural self-reflection, and who looked for inspiration, comfort, and refuge to the remote primitive rural areas of China, Wang Shuo's stories depict in great detail, simplicity, and colloquial language the dark realities of China's emerging post-revolutionary complex urban life. Like prison songs, his stories marked a radical break from official discourse both in their themes and their sardonic, nihilistic worldview, the kind of view that many in China adopted after the Cultural Revolution.

Like the extreme popularity of Wang's stories, the popularity of prison songs reflected the fact that many people in China during the 1980s became tired of official artistic representations and discourse, which back then were always "healthy," "positive," straight, monophonic, didactic, full of political propaganda, idealized, and far from the real life that people actually experienced. Prison songs, by contrast, like Wang Shuo's stories, depicted a life that was closer to that which many people experienced in the sense that they included defects and evil, even if some of the songs, like the stories, focused on rather extreme and marginal cases.

Despite his generally negative view of the style, Jin Zhaojun nevertheless notes in his article on the new fad that prison songs have a "strong character" (1989a), a comment that suggests that, in contrast to the revolutionary period and its oppressive conformism, the style's nonconformism in itself was now not only tolerated but welcomed. The dissemination and popularization of prison songs were yet another manifestation of the state's loss of its absolute hegemony and near monopoly over cultural production and dissemination, and of the emergence of new sociocultural diversity. These meanings were also clear to many people on the mainland, who reacted with obvious delight by patronizing the style, and also verbally. One verbal expression of such delight is found in the following paragraph taken from a 1988 article on the fad, one of the few that have ever been published:

> The secret of the commercial success of the cassettes lies in the fact that they understand the needs of the public. The lesson that we can learn from this is that the days in which professional [official] composers create on order and certain songs or kinds of songs are forcefully popularized are gone forever. . . . The popularity of "prison songs" . . . shows that . . . people of different social strata and mentalities can choose the cultural products that they like, similar to the way people freely choose their clothing. . . . Allow the people to decide themselves what they like, after all, our society is progressing. (Zeng 1988)

The prison songs fad was not only initiated and created by marginal and even negative role models like Chi Zhiqiang, and not only depicted nonorthodox life, but was also patronized mainly by two nonorthodox social groups, private entrepreneurs (getihu) and China's youngsters (Jin 1989b). The getihu emerged in China in the late 1970s and early 1980s, following the economic reforms, and symbolized the beginning of privatization. In contrast to the 1990s, when private enterprise was widespread and more acceptable socially, during the 1980s those who practiced it were considered socially marginal and had a strong negative image attached to them.[18] At that time many of the getihu were themselves ex-convicts, dropouts, petty criminals, and those who had been sent to the country during the Cultural Revolution and had now returned to the city and did not belong to any governmental unit. Being outside governmental units, these people were the first to open small private businesses and to become engaged in unofficial activities. Prison songs were patronized by the *getihu* because these songs told their own story. Jones notes that the appropriation of the style by the *getihu* went beyond consumption, reporting that "privately owned beauty parlors and restaurants effectively promoted 'jail songs' [same as "prison songs"] by pouring them out into the streets on their stereo systems" (1992a, 45). Prison songs thus articulated the experience, worldview, and emotions of the marginal *getihu* and provided them with both a sense of identity and a voice.

The soft and slow melodies of the style, however, also provided the *getihu* with an escape from their experience and public identity. In a 1987 article about Shanghai's emerging nightclubs, of which the main patrons at that time were the *getihu* who had gotten rich thanks to their private businesses, and who were among the few who could afford the new form of entertainment, the authors note that the nightclub allowed the *getihu* a kind of desired experience that was exactly the opposite of what they experienced during the day. The *getihu* are quoted in the article as saying: "During the day [we are] demons, at night we become human beings" (Song He and Tie Cheng 1987, 14–15). Thus, like the sentimental music that was played in Shanghai's nightclubs during the late 1980s, prison songs provided the *getihu* with a way out of their "demonic" existence and image.

The popularity of prison songs among China's urban youth, on the other hand, reflected the emerging post-revolutionary general fascination with alternative, nonconformist, marginal, and less idealized ways of life and experiences, which understandably was stronger among this social segment. The shared experience of oppression and conflicting values make youngsters in China, as in many other places in the world, a distinct social group, and by patronizing prison songs this group was articulating their marginality in relation to, and antagonism toward, oppressive mainstream culture.

Prison songs were banned from the state-run television station (Wang Xiaofeng, interview with the author, 18 June 1996) and, at least according to rumor, the state eventually even banned the sales of the cassettes that carried them (Ling Xuan 1989, 38). The ban, however, had the opposite result, at least for a while, leading to the intensification of the fad and to a boom in sales (38). The prison songs fad and especially the reaction of the public to rumors that the government had banned the style were indications of the growing split between the state and significant portions of society, and of the increasingly cynical attitude of the latter toward official culture and policies. The popularity of the style not only despite, but even because of official ban, was a clear manifestation of popular self-empowerment, protest, and resistance to the party-state. In the 1990s these new political dynamics became so well established in China that merchants even started to fake announcements of possible official bans in order to promote sales of controversial artistic works (Zha 1995, 137).

Despite all the differences between them, prison songs and *xibeifeng* songs shared one important element, namely a strong sense of dissatisfaction. A few weeks before the 1989 protest movement started in Tiananmen, and exactly three months before the violent crackdown that ended it, Jin Zhaojun wrote in the *People's Daily* that the popularity of prison songs "clearly shows the imperfect emotional state of society and the low morale among the people" (1989b). Several weeks later, in May, one writer drew the connection between the popularity of the style and popular dissatisfaction in more concrete terms:

> There has always been a gap in society between the ideal and the real, and society in a period of transformation is even less perfect. The contradictions between the poor and the rich, between what people invest and what they get in return, between their hopes and success, the disastrous effect that a bad social atmosphere creates, and the economic difficulties that the rise in market prices create for people . . . cause many people to feel dissatisfied and pessimistic. . . . "Prison songs" evoke a sympathetic response and cater to the tastes of these people. Consequently, the more this wind blows, the fiercer it becomes. (Ling Xuan 1989, 38)

In the very beginning of their 1989 book on popular culture in China (*Unofficial China: Popular Culture and Thought in the People's Republic*), Link et al. make the following statement:

> Few foreigners anticipated the Beijing Spring of 1989 and the massacre of protesting workers and students that so tragically ended it. Western sinologists were not generally aware that many citizens of China were so profoundly discontented with their government. . . . The Beijing Spring taught us how little we knew about the most important aspects of life in China. (1989, 1)

In retrospect, it seems that if China scholars had treated pop culture more seriously in the 1980s, perhaps none of us would have been so surprised when the 1989 protest movement broke out with such a force. The 1989 movement was obviously the result of the feelings of dissatisfaction, disillusionment, despair, bitterness, idealism, self-empowerment, and the desire to change things that were articulated in *xibeifeng* songs and prison songs long before the movement started.

THE RISE OF CHINESE ROCK AND ROLL (*YAOGUN*)

Chinese rock is associated primarily with Beijing. Some explain this association by relating it to the compatibility between rock and the musical style of northern China, which in contrast to the southern style tends to be rough, hard, and percussive. Another explanation, which was suggested to me by several informants during my stay in China, is that Beijing, being the most politicized city in China, was the most natural place for rock, with its highly politicized ethos, to emerge and develop. To support their argument, informants pointed out that the 1989 democracy movement was launched by students in Beijing and not in Guangzhou. Other people suggested that the reason for the association lies in the fact that people in Beijing are more bold and idealistic than people in the south, who tend to be more timid, pragmatic, and materialistic.

Another explanation of the relationship between Beijing and Chinese rock has to do with the presence of foreigners in China and the fact that most of them reside in the capital (Zhou 1994, 10–11). This explanation certainly accounts for the early years of rock in China. Until late 1989 and early 1990 rock music on the mainland was extremely marginal, and it was performed mainly in small nightclubs, bars, and hotels patronized by foreigners. Most of these venues were located in Beijing's northeast foreign-embassies region, where most of the foreigners work and live. Also associated with the emergence of rock in China were Chinese universities, which during the 1980s saw increasing numbers of foreign students. Most of these students resided in Beijing. Foreigners, mainly but not exclusively Westerners, played a central role in the introduction of rock to China. They not only introduced foreign cassettes and patronized emerging local rock, but also participated in the performance and production of this early rock. One of the earliest rock bands in China was formed by foreigners, and many others included foreign members. Peter Micic suggests that the participation of foreigners in early Chinese rock was important because it "lent a degree of credibility" to the nascent local bands, as rock was itself a foreign import (1995, 89). Mainland rockers were also influenced by live performances of famous musicians visiting from abroad. It is often suggested, for example, that the emergence of rock in China was influenced by the 1985 visit to the country of the British duo Wham!

Chinese rock made its first large-scale public appearance in China with the large-scale 1986 *tongsu* concert mentioned earlier. Among the one hundred *tongsu* musicians who were invited to participate in this huge concert was China's first rock star, Cui Jian. It was also in this concert that many Chinese heard for the first time Cui's "Having Nothing," a song that came to symbolize China's new revolution of the reform era:

HAVING NOTHING
(lyrics, music, and performance by Cui Jian)

I have endlessly asked when you will go with me
But you always laugh at me having nothing
I want to give you my aspirations and also my freedom
But you always laugh at me having nothing . . .

The soil under my feet is moving, the water beside me is flowing
But you always laugh at me having nothing
Why do you always laugh, why do I always have to chase
Do you really mean to say that before you I will always have nothing
Oh oh oh oh oh oh, when will you go with me . . .

"Having Nothing" introduced into post-revolutionary China a whole new ethos that combined individualism, nonconformism, personal freedom, authenticity, direct and bold expression, and protest and rebellion, in short, the essence of Western rock culture. Authenticity and individualism were embodied in the fact that Cui Jian sang a song he had written about his own personal experience. The practice of musicians singing their own songs and expressing personal feelings was completely strange to most Chinese at that time. Both in orthodox, official songs and in unofficial *liuxing* music, singers only sang; they did not write songs or talk about themselves. Even songs by Deng Lijun, which did celebrate individual feelings, still expressed general, objectified personal feelings rather than a personal, subjective voice. But in singing his own song Cui Jian was mainly challenging the official practice in which singers are expected to serve as the voice of the state or the people. "Having Nothing" trivialized the state, ignored most bluntly Maoist prescriptions concerning art, and empowered the individual self, asserting its independent value. Direct and bold expression as well as protest were embodied in the statement "I have nothing," which is repeated over and over again in the song. In this statement Cui Jian articulated what many people felt in China but few have ever dared to say in public. He was publicly saying the truth in the most direct way after decades during which idealized official discourse silenced all other voices.

Because of all these innovations "Having Nothing" had a shocking impact on the audience in the 1986 concert. This impact also derived from the physicality of Cui Jian's performance. Many recall how, in what was then an unprecedented sight, the musician came on stage with his "pants unevenly rolled up, wearing the once-fashionable loose yellow army shirt, which was completely out of date now, and with a guitar hung on his neck" (Yang Xiaolu and Zhang Zhentao 1990, 368–69). Like Western rockers in the 1960s and 1970s, the first Chinese rocker publicly challenged the dominant mainstream culture, with its highly choreographed aesthetics and ethos. Challenge was also embodied in the sound of the music: the strong stimulating beat, the coarse, rough, loud vocal delivery, the wild singing of nonsense syllables, and the music's direct, unrestrained, and liberating quality. "Having Nothing" was a celebration of lack of control. It was the antithesis of both the traditional Confucian aesthetics of moderation and restraint, whose best modern musical manifestation is found in the moderate, tame style of mainstream *liuxing/tongsu* music, as well as the antithesis of the official communist aesthetics of polished and disciplined professionalism. In other words, it was the antithesis of everything that the mainland audience had been familiar with until then. So strong was the impact of Cui Jian's first performance that following the concert one journalist wrote, "After Cui Jian's 'Having Nothing' Chinese popular music will not be 'having nothing' anymore" (quoted in Jin 1996d).

Despite its personal quality, "Having Nothing" soon came to symbolize the frustration and the sense of loss harbored by a disillusioned generation of young intellectuals, who, following the Cultural Revolution and the sudden exposure to Western modern culture, grew cynical about communism and increasingly critical of China's traditional and contemporary culture, which seemed more irrelevant than ever. In its emphasis on the words "having nothing," Cui Jian's song articulated the sense of spiritual and material impoverishment of this disillusioned social segment. In stating publicly that he had nothing, however, Cui Jian also posed an unprecedented public artistic challenge to the idealized, self-legitimizing official discourse, and thus also to the legitimacy of the Communist Party. The challenge did not go unnoticed. In his book on Cui Jian, the journalist Zhao Jianwei reports that when the latter sang his song in the 1986 *tongsu* concert, a high official who was present at the concert hall left angrily (1992, 257). Zhao also quotes the reaction of another high official, who said on another occasion: "What having nothing? Isn't it a slander directed at our socialist homeland? Is it possible that he is saying that we have nothing now?" (258). These two reactions were the earliest manifestations of official disapproval of rock on the mainland. Since its first large-scale public appearance, Chinese rock has been officially banned from state-run television and has often been subjected to official restrictions where live concerts are concerned. As for Cui Jian, he was not allowed to give another large-scale live performance until 1989 (Jones 1992b, 83).[19]

Cui Jian's next large-scale performance, which was also his first major solo concert, took place in Beijing Exhibition Hall in March 1989, a few weeks before the outbreak of the 1989 demonstrations. The concert featured songs from his new album *Rock and Roll of the New Long March (Xin changzheng lu shang de yaogun)*, which was released around that time. Cui Jian's audience consisted mainly of students, students like those who only a few weeks later stormed Tiananmen Square (Jones 1992b, 83). The relationship between rock and the Tiananmen movement became even clearer during the movement itself. Cui Jian's songs were sung by students in the square during the demonstrations, and his "Having Nothing" became one of the anthems of the protesting students all over China (Jones 1992b, 83).[20]

On May 19, one day before martial law was declared in Beijing, Cui Jian visited the square and sang "Opportunists" *(Toujifenzi)* (Schell 1994, 317), a song in which he directly addressed the protesters:

OPPORTUNISTS
(lyrics, music, and performance by Cui Jian)

All of a sudden an opportunity arrived, empty without an aim . . .
After all, what does an opportunity mean, for a short while it's not
    so clear . . .
The truth is always in a distant place, girls are always beside you
But when you face them you always compete with them for power . . .
Friend, please come over and help, there is no need for you to have too
    much knowledge
Because the work here only requires feelings and courage
Friend, you are given an opportunity, have a try in handling affairs for
    the first time
Like when you are eighteen years old and you are given a girl
Oh . . . we have an opportunity, let's demonstrate our desires
Oh . . . we have an opportunity, let's demonstrate our power

Like most of Cui Jian's songs, "Opportunists" is sung to a forceful beat, in a fast tempo, and in a shouting, challenging, liberating coarse voice. Resistance and subversion are also articulated through the pronunciation of the song's lyrics, which are often completely unintelligible. This deliberate obscurity challenges the orthodox communist aesthetics of clarity, which aimed at communicating with and indoctrinating the masses. Cui Jian's singing not only creates a sense of alienation but also implies a subversive, illicit agenda.

"Opportunists" is one of the most overt and direct articulations of self-empowerment and political challenge found in Cui Jian's songs and in Chinese rock in general, as it is so intimately connected with the 1989 democracy movement. The refrain of the song ("Oh . . . we have an opportunity, let's demonstrate our desires, oh . . . we have an opportunity, let's demonstrate our power") is a forceful call for action. Thus, after half a century in which the power of music to mobilize the masses was utilized in China exclusively by the Communist Party to establish its hegemony and control, rock music introduced into the country an alternative way to use music politically.

The musician and music critic Zhang Guangtian surely has a point when he labels rock "a weapon" (1996, 51).[21] Rock not only reflected the atmosphere of discontent that took over China in the late 1980s, and not only helped Chinese youth to express artistically their aspiration for change. It also shaped the attitudes of these youth and inspired them to action, introducing a new ethos of personal freedom and rebellion and providing them with a strong sense of self-empowerment. This new ethos and this sense of self-empowerment were major factors influencing the democracy movement. The link between rock and the 1989 movement was also acknowledged by Wu'er Kaixi, one of the most prominent student leaders of the movement, who in a scholarly conference in Boston in the fall of 1989 suggested that "Chinese rock and roll influenced students' ideas more than any of the theories of aging intellectuals on democracy" (quoted in Feigon 1994, 127).

The year 1989 was not the first time rock and student protests were linked. The link between the two was already in evidence three years earlier, during the student demonstrations of late 1986 and early 1987. Unrest among students in Shanghai during that period came right after a series of concerts given by the American surf-rock band Jan and Dean. This was the first well-known American rock group to tour China. Some members of the audience started to dance in the aisles, and some even jumped onto the stage. The security people present at the concert, who were completely unfamiliar with this kind of spontaneous and "undisciplined" audience participation, tried to arrest one of those who took part in the dancing. The youth, a student from Jiaotong University, resisted arrest and was beaten. This incident led to a face-to-face dialogue between Shanghai students and Jiang Zemin, then mayor of Shanghai, and the failure of this dialogue marked the beginning of active student demonstrations in Shanghai in December 1986 (Schell 1988, 223–24).[22]

Despite this, however, "Opportunists" is not unambiguous. As one informant suggested to me, while Cui Jian obviously expresses in the song his support for the student movement as a whole, he nevertheless simultaneously mocks, perhaps even criticizes in it certain participants in the movement whom he calls *toujifenzi,* a word that carries negative connotations in Chinese, just as "opportunists" does in English. The mocking or criticism, according to the above-mentioned informant, was mainly directed at the student leaders who attempted to take advantage of the movement to gain personal political profit. But it was also directed at the general blindness, naiveté, and immaturity of the participants in the movement. This aspect is implied in the lines: "All of a sudden an opportunity arrived, empty without an aim. . . . What does an opportunity mean, for a short while it's not so clear. . . . Like when you are eighteen years old and you are given a girl." It is not clear if in "Opportunists" Cui Jian was predicting the failure of the movement or just diagnosing its problems. His ambivalence toward and criticism of certain aspects of the movement, however, were articulated explicitly through his behavior during his visit to the square. According to several sources, the rocker left the square in disgust after several competing student factions attempted to manipulate him and claim ownership over him. The contradicting messages in "Opportunists," nevertheless, may also be read as strategic. After all, especially in China, ambiguity is always safer.

ROCK BECOMES A FAD

Whereas before the Tiananmen movement rock was patronized almost exclusively by university students and small, marginal, "underground" *(dixia)* bohemian circles, after Tiananmen it became yet another fad and part and parcel of general urban youth culture in China. This change was in part a coincidence, but it was also related to the movement itself and particularly to the way it ended. The rock fad began in the euphoric and carnivalistic spring of 1989, during which it rose to the surface and achieved popularity in the most general public sphere. The intensification of the fad during the early 1990s was a continuation of the process that had started just before and during the movement, but it was also a backlash, a popular expression of anger, defiance, and perhaps a kind of compensation for the failure of the movement. The link between the birth of the rock fad and the 1989 democracy movement revealed itself first and foremost in the fact that whereas prior to the movement there were only a handful of rock bands in Beijing, "in the later half of 1989 [that is, right after the crackdown] rock bands were already found everywhere in [the city]" (Jin 1990a). It was also between May and July of 1989 that three of China's earliest and most famous rock bands were established: Breathing *(Huxi),* which according to Wayhwa,[23] the lead singer of the band, was "formally" established right after the violent crackdown and as a reaction to it (Wayhwa, interview with the author, Beijing, 25 June 1996), the Females Rock Band (*Nüzi yaogun yuedui,* also known as Cobra), which was established in May (Zhou 1994, 102), and Zang Tianshuo's 1989, which was established in July (Zang Tianshuo, interview with the author, Beijing, 16 August 1995). Wayhwa, who pointed out to me the relationship between the establishment of her band (now disbanded) and the 1989 movement, further suggested that the name "Breathing" reflected the strong sense of suffocation that many in China felt in the late 1980s. The relationship between the birth of the rock fad in China and the democracy movement is also embodied in the name of Zang's rock band, "1989." Despite Zang's insistence that there is no relationship between the name of his band and the movement (interview, ibid.), the name cannot escape invoking the movement.

The rise of rock from its underground, marginal position into the general public sphere was celebrated a few months after the crackdown on 17 and 18 February 1990, when Beijing's largest ever all-rock concert was held two nights in a row in the Capital Gymnasium, one of the city's largest halls with close to 20,000 seats. The meaning of the event was not lost on those who had followed rock from the time it was first introduced into the mainland. And so, just a little more than a month following the concert, Jin Zhaojun joyfully declared in an article published in *Beijing Youth Paper (Beijing qingnian bao)* that rock ceased to be a "ghost" in China and that China ceased to be a "rock desert" (1990a). The rock concert was entitled "The 1990 Modern Music Concert," "modern" being the politically correct substitute for the word "rock," which by then was already regarded by officials as a synonym for subversion. Now that Beijing had several rock bands, the concert featured six of them, among which were Cui Jian's Ado, Tang Dynasty *(Tang chao),* and the above-mentioned Breathing, the Females Rock Band, and 1989. I was told that the concert took place due to a lack of clear policy toward rock in the period following the Tiananmen incident. The official permission to hold the concert, however, may also have been a deliberate attempt on the part of the party to ease tension and to regain credibility among the youth of Beijing.

The 1990 all-rock concert played an important role in publicizing and consolidating the Western values that Cui Jian first introduced a few years earlier with his "Having Nothing." The major criterion that the organizers set as a qualification to participate in the concert was originality *(yuanchuang).* In other words, only bands that performed original songs were invited to participate. This criterion resulted in the exclusion of at least one rock band, Black Panther *(Hei bao),* which at that time did not perform any original material but which later became one of China's most successful rock bands. Although inter-band politics probably played a significant role in deciding which bands could participate, setting forth such a criterion was significant in itself, as it reflected the fact that an increasing number of Chinese musicians were adopting not only Western music but also the Western artistic ethos of originality and innovation. In the 1990 rock concert rockers reacted against traditional Chinese artistic values, in which reorganization of old material as opposed to invention is the dominant mode of artistic creativity. They also reacted against *gangtai* and official pop, in which performers still rarely perform their own music and, in the case of the latter, creativity is channeled into officially prescribed propaganda purposes. Finally, the concert also challenged the practice of imitation that with a few exceptions dominated the popular music scene in China during the 1980s. This practice manifested itself, for example, in the setting of Chinese texts to Western melodies, a practice that was very popular at that time.

The criteria for participation set by the organizers of the 1990 rock concert were also important in what they excluded. In contrast to politicized, officially organized large-scale concerts and music contests, the purely artistic criteria were an overt celebration of depoliticization. In other words, the concert was a celebration of art for art's sake, a notion dismissed by Mao Zedong in his authoritative Yan'an Talks of 1942. Nevertheless, in the Chinese context, where officially art is still hardly divorced from politics, even this celebration of the autonomy of art had political meanings, not to mention that many of the songs sung at the event carried political messages.

The 1989 movement not only triggered the rock fad but was also reflected in it. This relationship is best illustrated by the many references to the June 4 incident in early post-Tiananmen rock songs. One such song is entitled "New World" *(Xin shijie):*[24]

NEW WORLD
(lyrics by Cao Jun and Wayhwa; music by Cao Jun; performance by Breathing)

Recited: I know everyone needs a new world. If you want freedom, here
    I am, ready to give you everything.

I need a new world . . .
I've lost my old dreams all through the night . . .
I need a place where I can cry
Cry out for love and justice

I need a sky where I can fly
Fly out for right and freedom
I am too lonely
Unable to endure
I want to hold your hand
To call aloud for help, how much longer . . .[25]

"New World" also contains many themes that are commonly featured in early post-Tiananmen rock songs, including disappointment, loneliness, disillusionment, and a strong desire to escape. The sentiments invoked in the lyrics of the song are also articulated in its music. The song starts in a ballad style, with low, restrained singing accompanied by slow keyboard arpeggios and long crooning notes played on the electric guitar, all of which enhance the sense of loneliness, sadness, helplessness, and disillusionment that is articulated in the lyrics. The last lines of the song (starting from "I need a place where I can cry"), however, which are sung in high register and loud voice to the same repeated melody and accompanied by a forceful rhythmic drive, are more like a powerful cry of despair combined with anger, resistance, and defiance. The dual nature of this cry is well represented by the Chinese word *nahan*, which was often used in the early 1990s when reference to rock was made.[26] Meaning both a cry for help and a cry of despair, but at the same time a war whoop or shout, *nahan* encapsulates the wide spectrum of feelings that were articulated in rock songs during the late 1980s and early 1990s.[27]

Another recurring theme found in many early post-Tiananmen rock songs is a strong desire for self-empowerment, which reflects the strong sense of helplessness and disempowerment that many youngsters in China experienced when the democracy movement failed. Examples of this desire are found in song titles and lines such as "Let me stand up," "Give me the courage of lightning" (from "Let Me Stand Up" [*Rang wo zhanliqi*] by Breathing), and "Sun god, I need you to give me unlimited power" (from "God of Light" [*Guangmang zhi shen*] by Black Panther).

Chinese rock reached a peak of creativity and popularity between 1990 and 1993. Dozens of rock bands were established and rock music was performed on a regular basis. The main venue for rock performances, nevertheless, was still informal, small-scale, underground rock parties, called "party(s)" in English, which enabled musicians to perform, earn some money, socialize, and establish a rock community that provided the individuals who participated a desired identity of exclusive anti-mainstream and anti-officialdom fraternity.

The core participants in the rock subculture not only performed rock

music but also adopted characteristic nonconformist appearance and behavior. These included long hair for males, jeans, silver metal ornaments
and black leather coats, and a carefree, hippie-style behavior. Rock paraphernalia was sold in Beijing in several rock shops where, in addition to
"rock clothes" *(yaogun fuzhuang)* and ornaments, one could also find cassettes and CDs of rock music.

Most important, however, was the "rock spirit" *(yaogun jingshen)*, a
loaded term that basically meant a rebellious attitude. The introductory
notes from a 1995 cassette album by a rock band called *Lunhui*/Again illustrate some aspects of the worldview and experience that many rockers
in China shared (and which some continue to share), among which is the
notion of "rock spirit": [28]

> Being a rock band of a newly born generation, *Lunhui* almost doesn't
> have any perceptual knowledge of the turbulence that our country went
> through during the 1960s and 1970s. [Because] from the time they
> were capable of remembering things China already stretched out both
> arms in a cry of openness and embraced thought, culture, art, and even
> lifestyle that came from the outside world, they received much more
> foreign influence than their seniors. What they came into contact with
> since they were young was not revolutionary songs and traditional
> music, but rather pop and rock music from abroad. In order to achieve
> their music ideal and express their knowledge of world outlook they
> are much more fearless than their seniors, and despise authority much
> more. In other words, they have more of a rock spirit [*yaogun
> jingshen*].

In addition to offering a concise definition of "rock spirit," equating it with
fearlessness and spite for authority and thus encapsulating the political
significance of rock in authoritarian China, the notes also suggest another
important element in rock ideology, which is a strong desire to reach out
and adopt a cosmopolitan, Western attitude. The admiration for foreign,
specifically Western, culture went almost to the point of fetishization
among significant portions of Chinese intellectuals and youth during the
1980s and early 1990s. This fetishization manifested itself in rock culture
most clearly through the adoption of the musical style itself and a whole
set of Western values. Another important manifestation was the relatively
extensive use of English. For many young Chinese intellectuals, among
them rockers, Westernization was synonymous with modernization and
rock represented both. An example of this view is found in an article dedicated to the Beijing all-rock concert of 1990 that was written by Jin Zhaojun right after the concert. In this article the critic suggests that the con-

cert was an indication that "China had moved rapidly beyond Li Jinhui . . . quickly caught up with *gangtai* . . . and some [Chinese musicians] . . . are already casting their eyes on the remote popular music of Europe and America" (1990a). The evolutionist tone of this statement is quite common in general discourse on the mainland. The important point in relation to rock, however, is that during the late 1980s and early 1990s this music was seen by many as the most progressive and modern type of music.

The desire to reach out and to adopt modern Western culture reflected a strong reaction among China's intellectuals to their long experience of enclosure *(fengbi)* and against traditional Chinese culture. Indeed, one of the major characteristics of rock in China during the late 1980s and early 1990s was the celebrated negation of traditional Chinese culture, especially of traditional Confucian values and morals, such as hierarchy, obedience, restraint, moderation, the privileged position of the collective (the state, society, and the family), and the suppression of the individual self and his/her desires and personal freedom. One example of a fierce and comprehensive attack on traditional Chinese culture in general and on Confucianism in particular in the context of rock subculture is found in Zhao Jianwei's book on Cui Jian, in which the author elaborates on, among other things, Lu Xun's famous equation of Confucianism with cannibalism. The repeated references to Lu Xun in rock discourse during the late 1980s and early 1990s are not incidental. Many students and young intellectuals during this period consciously connected themselves with the May Fourth iconoclastic tradition. Indeed, the fetishization of the West in the rock subculture reminds one of similar radical attitudes expressed in the May Fourth movement of the 1920s and 1930s.

The iconoclastic negation of tradition in rock and the simultaneous highbrow, Root-Seeking embrace of folk tradition in *xibeifeng*, which like rock also had precedents in the early decades of the twentieth century (see Hung 1985), represented the century-long ambivalence in Chinese culture, particularly among China's intellectuals, with regard to Chineseness and tradition on one hand and Westernization and modernity on the other. This ambivalence, however, was temporarily solved in the late 1980s.

The decline of *xibeifeng* in the late 1980s and the simultaneous rise of the rock fad represented a shift in the attitude of many of China's intellectuals. Nostalgia and the romantic embrace of folk tradition—found in many Root-Seeking expressions since the early 1980s and ambivalent to begin with—changed in the late 1980s into an unequivocally fierce negation, as if during the journey of exploration China's intellectuals became disillusioned with the peasant culture they had romanticized for a while.[29]

This disillusionment was vividly illustrated in *River Elegy*. In sharp contrast to the treatment of China's peasants in *Yellow Earth*, which though ambivalent was nevertheless filled with sympathy, and which represented the early phase of the Root-Seeking movement, the treatment of China's peasants and traditional culture in *River Elegy* was overtly derogatory. Part 4 in the documentary goes so far as to explicitly blame the "low human quality" of China's peasants for preventing China from achieving Westernization and modernization. Like *River Elegy*, the popularity of rock in Chinese cities in the late 1980s and early 1990s reflected a peak in the sense of alienation of China's intellectuals vis-à-vis China's traditional culture and peasants, an alienation that had a devastating impact on the movement they led in the spring of 1989, and consequently also on their position in the 1990s.[30]

THE DECLINE OF ROCK:
TIANANMEN, COMMERCIALIZATION,
KARAOKE, AND NATIONALISM

In 1994, despite the release of numerous rock cassettes, Chinese rock was obviously in decline. Gao Feng, whose song "Open the Door" *(Ba men dakai)* was included in one of the many rock collections released around that time[31] and who one year later changed direction and became one of China's most famous pop stars after he wrote a folksy patriotic song called "Great China" *(Da Zhongguo)*, offered the following explanation of why he decided to give up rock:

> Rock had no future. It reached a dead end, and it wasn't going to develop anywhere. I needed to survive, and I also wanted to become a star, so there was no other choice but to change direction. (Gao, interview with the author, Beijing, 8 June 1996)

Many rockers blame the state for the decline, suggesting that by adopting a harsh policy toward it starting in late 1993 it eventually strangled rock. While the banning of rock from television, the most powerful medium in China, was almost always enforced, the state started in late 1993 and early 1994 to place more restrictions on rock performances, especially in Beijing. The stricter attitude of the government toward rock performances, however, can account only in part for the decline of the style. On 18 July 1993, Cui Jian gave a concert in Shanghai despite the restrictions mentioned above. In drastic contrast to the enormous popularity the star had enjoyed in the past, however, only one third of the seats in the concert hall were occupied, and the ticket price for the event dropped from 80 *yuan* to 3.5 *yuan*. By contrast, a month later, Hong Kong pop star Andy Lau (Liu Dehua in Mandarin), who sings mostly soft, sweet, sentimental pop songs, filled the same 18,000-seat concert hall to full capacity. The cheapest ticket for his concert was 180 *yuan*, and on the black market tickets even sold for 700 *yuan* (He 1996). Some qualifications are in order here: first, that rock never enjoyed in Shanghai the popularity that it enjoyed in Beijing; second, that *gangtai* music has always been the "dominant" style (Brace 1992, 137) on the mainland since the beginning of the reform era; and third, that in 1993 Cui Jian was already considered by many to be an "old" musician. Nonetheless, the fact that Cui Jian was not able to fill a whole concert hall in a major Chinese city indicated that the decline of rock was due not only to official restrictions on rock performances.

In the article from which the data on Cui Jian's performance in Shanghai was taken, the author notes in a mocking tone:

> The angry youth seem to have grown up overnight. Well behaved and obedient [*guaiguai de*], they returned to their home, which although full of rules and vexation is nevertheless a warm, sweet home. (He 1996)

Talking in 1996 to students at Beijing University, formerly one of the strongholds of rock music, I found that there, too, rock had lost much of its past appeal. Instead of Cui Jian or other rockers, young students now listed sweet, soft mainstream *gangtai* singers like Zhou Huajian and the Hong Kong superstar Jacky Cheung (Zhang Xueyou in Mandarin) as their favorite idols. In a routine survey that I conducted at the giant McDonald's in Beijing's Wangfujing central shopping district, a survey in which I asked people to say what they thought of certain songs and to list their favorite songs, I found youngsters who had not even heard of "Having Nothing," while others marked it as one of their least favorite songs. In the mid-1990s rock was obviously returning to the marginal social enclaves from which it first emerged.

The decline of rock, very much like its rise, was closely related to the June 4 incident. If the rock boom, which started in late 1989 and early 1990, was at least in part a result of the euphoric movement that celebrated, like rock, freedom and self-empowerment, as well as an immediate reaction to its outcome, then the decline of rock a few years later was the long-term consequence. The violent crackdown and the failure of the democracy movement marked a significant turning point in the recent history of Chinese culture, and the decline of rock was one manifestation of the cultural transformation that took place on the mainland as a result of this failure.

The decline of rock reflects the fact that young people and others lost much of their past idealism and their will to change things. "Back then," one friend told me, "I really cared about the country. I went to the square because I hoped I could change things. But the government didn't want my help. So I don't care anymore. There is nothing I can do." After the immediate anger disappeared, the ethos of conscious resistance and rebellion that was embodied in rock lost much of its appeal, as it proved useless. Rock, in other words, became associated with yet another false promise, and its loss of appeal reflected yet another disillusionment. Many people today seem to want to get the best of whatever there is and are trying to use positive thinking as an alternative way to cope with reality. Several people associated with rock even expressed the view that "the youngsters today have nothing to complain about." Some of them, who participated in the student demonstrations in 1989 and were in Tiananmen Square on the night of the crackdown, seem to be cynical even about their own behavior during the movement. Several of these people suggested that the students were too naive and too radical, and that they were manipulated by a few student leaders who wanted to gain political power for themselves. One intellectual musician who participated in the demonstrations even went so far as to express the view that intellectuals and rockers in China are just putting on airs, asking cynically: "Can they really perform better than this government?" It was obvious in the mid-1990s that the success of the regime in suppressing the movement and maintaining stability, order, and economic progress had caused many to reevaluate the movement, and many saw it now in different light. When I asked one famous rocker about the political power of rock, he replied in a skeptical tone: "Did rock really change anything in the West?" and after a short pause added: "First you need to feed the people, and only when everyone has enough to eat can you really start to talk about politics." Although there is no doubt that at least some of these statements have resulted from self-suppression of previous antagonism, rationalization, and a wish to avoid clashes with officialdom, they nevertheless clearly reflect the loss of hope of bringing about radical change and the general decline of active and overt resistance to the government.

The decline of rock reflected the general lack of interest in China of the 1990s in stimulating politicized cultural products, thoughts, or behavior, let alone political activity. People seemed to be interested mainly in material comfort: in making money and improving their living standard. As for music, there is no doubt that listening to nonpolitical, sweet, romantic music was the dominant practice in the mid-1990s, even among intellectuals. If past revolutionary songs, like some of the more recent rock songs, aimed to stir people up and mobilize them to struggle and action, then, in contrast, the dominant practice and both official and unofficial discourse about music in the mid-1990s placed music in the context of "relaxation" *(qingsong)*.

The victory of the state over the idealism that challenged its hegemony in 1989 was also the victory of materialism. Many individuals in China with whom I spoke shared the view that materialism and practicality have taken over in the 1990s and that there was little spirituality *(jingshen)* or culture *(wenhua)* left. The radical commercialization of the 1990s was another factor blamed by many rockers and rock fans for the decline of rock. In one interview I conducted with Wang Xiaofeng, the famous vocal music critic lamented the passing of the 1980s:

> Between 1984 and 1989 culture flourished, there was the *menglong* [obscure or hazy] poetry and people read Freud and Nietzsche. Nowadays bookstands sell only future-telling books, and all that people are thinking about is how to make money. (Wang Xiaofeng, interview with the author, 15 April 1996)

The radical commercialization of the 1990s is not only the result of the government's attempts to divert public attention and emphasis from the political to the economic. It is equally related to global economical trends in the post–Cold War era. The economy became increasingly important in China of the 1990s, just as the economy became increasingly important in many other developed and developing countries around the globe. As money and profit became increasingly valued and sought after, commercialization led many rockers to temper their past alienation and antagonism to the mainstream in an attempt to reach larger audiences. Because the state still controlled all television stations, the most effective promotional media in China (as in most other places in the world), rockers also started to temper their political criticism to avoid clashes with the state, clashes that could have a devastating impact on their income and career. Maintaining a good relationship with officialdom was important because the state also controlled most of the large-scale pop concerts, which were the most important source of income for musicians on the mainland, where pirating has been prevalent.[32] It was in this context that the distinction between rock and pop that was so important in the late 1980s (see Jones 1992a) started to blur, and rock lost much of its distinctive flavor.[33]

Another, related cause for the decline of rock was the intensified influence of *gangtai* culture. Because record companies from Hong Kong and Taiwan were much better equipped than local companies and had more experience operating in a free-market economy and commodifying music and musicians, the increase in free-market activity in the 1990s meant that such companies could now also expand their activity. Although some of these foreign companies started to patronize native rock and other kinds of music, their main investment was naturally in mainstream *gangtai* music. It was against such a background that *gangtai* music started to dominate to an unprecedented extent the mainland's musical landscape. One record company executive has offered the following estimation:

> The total value of the music market is about RMB [*yuan*] 1 billion, of which popular music accounts for 80 percent; and of the pop music market, Taiwan and Hong Kong products take four-fifths of that. For ten years now, this structure has changed little. (Coral Lee 2000, 44)

The rapid spread of karaoke technology in China during the 1990s also contributed to this transformation. As the spread of karaoke increased, music was used not so much to be listened or danced to, but rather to be sung with. The popularity of the new practice caused music producers to favor music that could be easily reproduced. *Shangkou*, meaning something that could be easily learned and sung, became an important aesthetic principle. Equally important were a moderate, regular tempo, clear and predictable melodies, and clearly articulated words. Needless to say, these new karaoke-inspired musical preferences were the very antithesis of rock.

If the decline of rock reflected a bankruptcy of idealism and a decline in overt resistance to the state and to traditional Chinese culture (this is not to say that resistance completely disappeared, as it still existed in many other, less explicit forms), the return of the highly commercialized sweet, soft, slow, relaxing *gangtai* pop to many of the social pockets that once patronized rock reflected the overwhelming dominance of a new worldview in the China of the 1990s. Zha Jianying has suggested that despite the political takeover of Hong Kong by the mainland, it is actually Hong Kong culture that has been taking over the mainland (1995, 164; see also Gold 1993, 907). Indeed, the extreme popularity that Hong Kong pop songs enjoyed in the mid-1990s in Beijing, the last stronghold of resistance to the southern "colonial" and "meaningless" culture, supported such a view. Nothing illustrated this situation more vividly than the fact that an increasing number of youngsters in Beijing in the mid-1990s could sing pop songs from Hong Kong in perfect Cantonese. The popularity of songs from Hong Kong among social groups that previously looked down upon on this kind of music suggested that the traditional Hong Kong model of political stability, materialistic prosperity, extreme commercialization, pragmatism, disinterest in politics—at least when the average person is concerned—social harmony, and light entertainment culture has replaced idealism, the spirit of resistance and protest, and the aspiration for radical change.[34]

The waning of the revolutionary idealism of rock, however, does not mean that all idealism in China is dead. A hallmark of the 1990s in China is the revival of nationalism and the concomitant popularity of the notion of "distinctive national character" *(minzu tese)*, which has long been propagated by the Chinese government. Both may be seen as additional reasons for the decline of rock. Li Tong, the leader of Black Panther, has tied the decline of rock specifically to a 1994 official campaign to promote classical and national *(minzu)* music (personal communication, Beijing, 19 July 1995). Nationalism, however, is not something that rockers necessarily resisted. Several disillusioned rockers told me in 1996 that they had become less enthusiastic about rock because, after all, rock was not their own music.

This shift in attitude tells us something important about the role and status of intellectuals and Westernization in post-Tiananmen China. Many intellectuals in the 1990s became disillusioned about Westernization after realizing that it was not suitable for the great majority of China's population. The failure of China's intellectuals to communicate with the great majority of China's population during the 1989 movement, to mobilize them and to get their support, contributed significantly to this shift. In addition, by the mid-1990s more than a decade and a half had passed since China first opened itself to the West, and many intellectuals simply had gotten to know the West better, including its less admirable aspects. China's economic boom also constituted a cause for a new pride. And against this pride many saw now the United States in particular as a competitor looking to block China's advance. The United States was blamed for the rejection of China's bid to host the Olympic Games in the year 2000, and its involvement in the conflict with Taiwan in the mid-1990s led to even greater anti-American and anti-Western nationalistic sentiments. If the rock fad reflected a climax in the status of China's intellectuals, in their fetishization of the West and their alienation vis-à-vis the regime, China's peasants, and Chinese tradition, its decline indicated the weakening of all these trends. Similarly, the unprecedented popularity of *gangtai* music in China in the 1990s was a signifier of the resurgence of more traditional aesthetics and values such as restraint, moderation, and sociopolitical stability and harmony.

Ironically perhaps, the commercialization of the 1990s had a democratizing effect, not only by weakening the orthodox authoritarianism of the state but also, and perhaps even more, by weakening the cultural hegemony of China's intellectuals. *Red Sorghum, River Elegy,* rock, and even *xibeifeng,* did not really cater to the taste of the great majority of China's population. The popularity of these cultural products reflected rather the power of China's intellectuals and the fact that during the 1980s they dominated cultural production. This highbrow, intellectual trend suffered a serious setback once culture became a commodity. In the radical consumerism of the 1990s the dormant subjectivities in Chinese society started to awaken, as average people now exerted an important influence on cultural production with their buying power.

The Chinese rock movement differed from its Western counterpart in that it never made it into mainstream culture. The marginality of rock in China seems to point above all to the significant cultural, political, and social differences that exist between China and the West, and to the fact that, despite its recent modernization and Westernization, China is nevertheless developing on a different track from that on which Western countries have been developing. An increasing number of intellectuals in China expressed similar views in the early and mid-1990s, some with delight, others with obvious disappointment. One journalist wrote in 1996, for instance, that "rock in China is [like] a ship in the ocean. It is [like] an orphan that does not have the blood veins of traditional culture" (He 1996). And as early as 1993, only three years after he joyfully suggested that China is not a "rock desert" any more, Jin Zhaojun, too, soberly acknowledged that "there is, after all, a considerably big distance in style and musical concept between rock music and the traditional appreciation habits of mainland listeners." Jin was now predicting that "the influence of rock in the mainland will be very limited . . . and [it] will not become too big a tide" (Jin 1993).

The impact of rock, nevertheless, should not be underestimated. It still constitutes a viable subculture in urban China, especially in Beijing, and although marginal, still exerts, even if only indirectly, some degree of influence on the wider culture.[35] More important, in the years in which the style enjoyed a wider popularity, it played a significant role in introducing Western values into Chinese culture, some of which at least, like individualism and nonconformism, have become an integral part of urban daily life practices, thought, and discourse, and are articulated and celebrated today in a wide range of sociocultural circles.[36]

THE MAO FAD (MAO RE)

In 1990, following a series of precursors, such as the mid-1980s revival of arias from modern revolutionary operas, several renewed renditions of old revolutionary songs, and Cui Jian's large-scale appropriation of several revolutionary symbols in his 1989 album *Rock and Roll of the New Long March,* a Mao Zedong fad swept the mainland.[37] The earliest manifestations of the fad were Mao images on amulets, busts, badges, posters, cups, buttons, and other objects, which began popping up all over the country in enormous quantities. The fad was enhanced when the Xinhua publishing house issued ten million copies of a new four-volume edition of Mao's collected works (Schell 1994, 283).[38] Finally, beginning in late 1991 and early 1992, a series of cassettes of old revolutionary praise songs for Mao, entitled *The Red Sun (Hong taiyang),* were released all over the country, marking the climax of the fad.[39] The songs were performed by some of the most popular pop singers of the time, who sang them to a modern disco and rock beat and modern arrangement.

Like many other fads in and outside of China, it was not clear who initiated and sustained this fad. Some suggested that the revival of Mao was the result of government efforts to give people a sense of security after the June 4 incident (Hertz 1998, 79). By contrast, Jin Zhaojun holds that the fad was initiated from "below by the common people" (Jin, interview with the author, 8 June 1996; see also Jin 1992). Following one of my main arguments in this book, however, I believe that, like many phenomena in China during the 1990s, the "Mao craze" cannot be attributed to a single force. It was, rather, the result of a complex and changing dialectical interaction between multiple forces, which also cannot be easily placed in a neat binary top-bottom dichotomy. Another reasonable suggestion—that the fad was initiated by party hard-liners and was directed against Deng and the reformist faction (Schell 1994, 280–82; Hertz 1998, 79)—in itself defies the simplistic top-bottom dichotomy.[40]

The Mao fad reflected, among other things, the continuing sense of crisis in China during the early 1990s, dissatisfaction with the economic instability, continuing popular resentment of the widespread corruption among high officials, and the general sense of insecurity that was shared by many amid the rapid transformation. The fad was an unprecedented burst of popular nostalgia. Through the revival of the great leader, it constructed an idealized, stable, euphoric past, which provided both comfort in the context of an opposite reality and a way to comment on this reality. The latter function was also alluded to by Sun Guoqing, the pop star who revived a revolutionary praise song back in the late 1980s and was now one of the major figures in the new fad. As Sun said, "I can't say clearly whether it is the recollection of the past or a reflection on the present."

As suggested earlier in relation to the *xibeifeng* fad, nostalgia can often be understood in communist China as a form of resistance to the party because it suggests the undoing of the official practice of negating the past to legitimize the present regime and its current policies. In other words, if the party's hegemony and legitimacy have always been based on a negation of the past, then nostalgia implies the negation of the hegemony and legitimacy of the party. Thus, singing songs of praise to the leader and period that Deng Xiaoping and his followers had reacted against for more than a decade meant challenging and delegitimizing the present leadership. Three years after the fad was over, people continued to note with nostalgia that "unlike the current leaders, Mao was as poor as anyone else," that he really "served the people," and that "he knew how to handle things."

It is no wonder, then, that reform-minded party officials eventually decided to suppress the fad. The musician and critic Zhang Guangtian, whose 1993 album included songs of praise and longing for the late leader that he composed during that period, attributed the failure of his album to an official ban imposed on it because of these songs. In an interview, the musician recalled how all of a sudden the media stopped broadcasting his songs, and how this change in policy directly affected the sales of his album (Zhang Guangtian, interview with the author, 24 June 1996). Zhang's album opens with a song titled "Mao Zedong":

MAO ZEDONG
(lyrics, music, and performance by Zhang Guangtian)

. . . Every morning the sun is still bright red like fire
I can see you standing alone in the distance
Your finger is pointing at my soul
I move forward with you, Mao Zedong . . .
Mao Zedong, Mao Zedong, with you I charge a hail of bullets . . .
Mao Zedong, Mao Zedong, with you I walk forward cheerfully and
    humorously . . .
When love and battle have become the same today
Give me, ah, give me power, Mao Zedong
When the sounds of the bells of New Year rumble again
Can you get burned by the short piece of cigarette that is left in
    your hand?
Let me light for you a red string of firecrackers
So, ah, so loud, Mao Zedong . . .

The song opens with a sweet, soft, and slow singing, to the accompaniment of piano, violin, and acoustic guitar. A small drum provides a gentle rhythmic line similar to that found in traditional storytelling. In the second stanza, however, the style begins to change gradually. Snare drums play a marchlike rhythm, the tempo becomes faster, and the singing becomes more powerful and accentuated. This heroic drive, strengthened by the singing of a choir in the background, reaches its peak in the refrain, where a drum set forcefully joins in. Following the refrain, the two styles are mixed to invoke both romantic nostalgia and militant revolutionary fervor.

Zhang's album ends with another song dedicated to Mao, entitled "Please Stay" *(Qing ni liuxia),* in which he sings: "Chairman Mao, please answer . . . talk about love, talk about the true qualities of heroes. . . . Chairman Mao, please stay . . . talk about truth, talk about the profound mysteries of the soul. . . . Chairman Mao, turn back your head . . . talk about revolution, talk about ideology, talk about the history of the past, talk about the direction from now on."

Orville Schell lends support to Zhang Guangtian's claims concerning the official ban on his music, noting that "Li Ruihuan, a reform-minded vice-premier with responsibility for overseeing culture, was reported to have circulated a document in the name of the Central Committee's Secretariat arguing that the broadcast of these reconstituted songs from the Cultural Revolution should be suspended" (1994, 287). Schell further reports that in "February [1993] the Shanghai newspaper *Wenhui Daily* convened a scholarly gathering to discuss the significance of the Mao phenomenon, and one of the conclusions of the conferees was that the Mao craze showed that efforts 'to negate' the Cultural Revolution had been 'insufficient' and that the Party had 'failed to approach its harmfulness to the entire nation from the high plane of reason.'" Schell finally adds: "It was not long before even Deng himself weighed in. 'In my view the campaign is abnormal,' he said of the Mao craze. 'Young people today who do not understand the last forty years of our country's history may be given the wrong impression'" (287).

The different official responses to the Mao fad—encouragement first, and then an attempt to suppress it—provide a vivid testimony to the political meanings and power that memory in general and nostalgia in particular have in communist China. In the omnipresent and often indirect state politics in revolutionary and post-revolutionary China, present-day battles are often launched symbolically over the past. Moreover, as the Mao fad illustrates, these struggles, whether between party hard-liners and party reformers or between the party and parts of society, are often fought in every possible realm, including pop culture and music.

The struggle over Mao, the past, and their meaning, and thus also over the present and the future, started, as noted earlier, several years before the Mao fad. One of the more significant earlier manifestations of this subversive nostalgia was embodied in Cui Jian's 1987 revival of "Nanniwan," the communist hymn from the Yan'an period, which he performed in a rock style. According to Wang Xiaofeng, it was because of this performance that Cui Jian was banned from giving any public performances until 1989. Officials labeled Cui's rendition "red [communist] song sung in yellow [pornographic] fashion" *(hong ge huang chang)*, meaning that Cui's rock version of the song was a contamination of a sacred symbol (Wang Xiaofeng, interview with the author, 1 June 1996). Claire Huot points out that the problem with Cui Jian's rendition was not only the fact that he transformed the original song into a rock song but also that he turned what was a cheerful, optimistic song that praises the party into a "blues" song that "sounds like a funeral hymn" (Huot 2000, 160).[41]

Two years later, in 1989, the rocker named his new album *Rock and Roll of the New Long March,* which was also the title of the first song in the album. The revival of the revolutionary past reached its peak in Cui Jian's concerts, in which the past was actually reenacted. Since his first large-scale performance in 1986, Cui Jian habitually performed wearing an old-style army shirt that immediately invoked the revolutionary period. The musician explained that the uniforms make him feel "comfortable and self-confident" (Zhao 1992, 39). In 1990 Cui Jian turned his benefit concert tour (which I discuss in chapter 4) into a revived Long March. In Henan Province, where the first concert in the tour took place, the musician stated: "This is our first base area in the new Long March of rock and roll" (26). Throughout the tour, which was cut off halfway (Jaivin 1990a, 47), Cui also habitually appeared on stage at the opening of his performance with a large flag on which was written: "Rock of the New Long March" (71). Cui Jian's appropriation of revolutionary songs and symbols from the 1930s and 1940s expressed a strong desire, shared by many in China during the late 1980s and early 1990s, to revive the idealist ethos of the golden age of revolutionary China. This revival aimed to fill the spiritual vacuum that many experienced amid the loss of faith and ideology and the emergent radical commercialism of the 1980s and 1990s. For many students and other urban youth who constituted the majority of Cui Jian's audience, Mao symbolized a desired revolution similar to that in which they themselves were involved in 1989. If the Cultural Revolution was for Deng Xiaoping a period of unprecedented disempowerment, which he understandably wanted to forget and make others forget as well, for Chinese students and youth, who never experienced it, it was a period in which young people like themselves, namely the Red Guards, had an unprecedented amount of power and were called on by Mao himself to revolt and take over China. Even an ex–Red Guard with whom I spoke in 1997 in the United States still felt nostalgic about the Cultural Revolution: "We could do everything we wanted back then," he said to me, "it was a 'Great Democracy' [*daminzhu*]." In the 1989 student movement it was probably more tempting than ever before for Chinese youth to read the past in this way and consequently to try to revive it. This nostalgia, however, was not an idle wish. It also aimed to communicate a message to the party by "reminding the authorities of forsaken ideals" (Gregory Lee 1995, 104).

Nostalgia and ideals, however, were only two of the many meanings embodied in the Mao fad. Wang Xiaofeng suggested to me that the fad, paradoxically perhaps, was also closely related to Deng Xiaoping's retirement from public life right after the June 4 incident, and that it reflected the Chinese people's need for a strong leader who would straighten things up. Singing old revolutionary songs to a contemporary disco and rock beat and turning the almighty Mao into a pop icon also gave many people the "carnivalistic" (c.f. Bakhtin 1984) pleasure of self-empowerment so rare in China. Even in Cui Jian's early revival of "Nanniwan" and other revolutionary symbols it was not clear whether the musician was articulating an idealist nostalgia or parodying both the communist past and the present by transforming them into part of his contemporary rebellious pop/rock culture. The Mao fad created an ironic hybrid, and hybridity in itself, as Gregory Lee observes, "contests, challenges, weakens, and ultimately invalidates the authority and legitimacy of dominant monolithic . . . cultures" (1995, 105). Orville Schell suggests that transforming Mao into a pop commodity was equivalent to "transforming the sacred into the profane" (1994, 291), an act that had a trivializing effect (289). This act in turn functioned "as a form of exorcism" that enabled many also to "break the psychological authority that Mao as an image continues to hold over all Chinese" (289).[42]

Finally, despite everything that is said above about subversive nostalgia, parody of Mao, and challenge to Deng's regime, the Mao craze could also be interpreted as one of the earliest manifestations of the wave of nationalism that swept the mainland in the 1990s. Both Gregory Lee (1995) and Jeroen De Kloet (2000, 250) suggest that even Cui Jian's appropriation of Maoist symbols could be read as a way to stress Chineseness and as an expression of popular nationalism. Such interpretation provides another explanation of why certain elements in the party supported the craze, at least for a while. It also implies that rock should not always be perceived as being in opposition to official ideology, a point on which I elaborate in the last section of chapter 4.

2   The Negotiation of Minority/ Majority Identities and Representation in Popular Music Culture

The late 1970s saw a resurgence of ethnicity and ethnic nationalism in China. This resurgence, which has intensified ever since, came about as a result of several interrelated factors, among which were the general liberalization, similar trends around the globe, and the traumatic experience of the Cultural Revolution. The brutal suppression of China's minority traditions during the latter period had the effect of awakening minority ethnic consciousness and led the minorities to reaffirm their ethnicity with greater determination than ever before. Another factor that became increasingly important was the market. As market activity intensified, there was an increasing demand for minority otherness, which in the cosmopolitan and consumerist environment was transformed into an exotic commodity.

The ethnic revival in China in the last two decades has led to a significant increase in studies that focus on China's minorities. One important theme dealt with in many of these recent studies is the negotiation of minority identities and their representation. Several studies have studied the subject in local contexts. Others have focused on culture and art on the national level. In few studies, however, has attention been paid to the role that music—and popular music in particular—played in this process of negotiation, and it is the purpose of this chapter to fill this gap.[1]

Explicit and sometimes implicit in many of the recent studies on minority identities in the People's Republic has been the recognition of the privileged and dominant role of the Chinese state in their construction and representation. Several studies have demonstrated how the state controls the definition of minority identities and their public representation in the general culture (Clark 1987a; Harrell 1990; Gladney 1994a). Others have even demonstrated how the state influences perceptions and practices of certain minority people that concern their own ethnic identity (Diamond

1995; Harrell 1996b; Hansen 1999; Kaup 2000). Since the revival of scholarly interest in ethnicity in China, nevertheless, it has also been repeatedly suggested that minority people have some degree of agency. This agency has been demonstrated most vividly in several studies that point out the existence among certain minorities of perceptions, narratives, and practices related to their ethnic identity that fail to conform to, and sometimes even contest, those constructed by the state (Harrell 1990; Gladney 1991; Litzinger 1995, 1998; Cheung 1996; Schein 1997; Hansen 1999).

Previous studies that highlighted the agency of China's non-Han peoples in the construction, definition, and representation of their ethnic identity have done so, however, mostly in relation to local context.[2] By contrast, the general view has been that, where nationally distributed media and culture are concerned, minority representation is still monopolized by the state and the Han majority, and that minorities themselves are passive, powerless, and voiceless.[3] Contrary to this widely held view, this chapter will suggest that after nearly four decades in which minorities indeed always occupied in the general culture the position of gazed-upon objects, today some minority individuals are achieving a new voice in the national public sphere and are actively participating in the public representation of their ethnic identity. The chapter suggests, in other words, that minorities in China today not only have alternative conceptions and narratives concerning their ethnic identity—a fact that has already been pointed out in several studies—but that these also inform and contribute to the construction and reconstruction of their public identity in the general culture.

These new arguments concerning the changing role of China's minorities, the state, and the Han majority in the negotiation of ethnicity in China are closely linked with the fact that this negotiation is examined here in the domain of popular music culture. The main contribution that this neglected domain offers us is related to the unique nature of two important mass media that are closely associated with it, namely, cassette and video recording. China's minorities were previously denied access to more expensive and technologically complex media, like television and film, because these were—and still are—tightly controlled by the Han elite and the Han-dominated Chinese state. Since the 1980s, however, the low cost and the ease of production and dissemination of cassettes and videos have turned these media into an important alternative vehicle through which ethnic minorities have achieved a public voice despite their disadvantaged position in terms of control over the "old" media (Manuel 1993). The widely held view that minorities in China have no voice in the general culture is closely connected with the fact that previous studies that explored the negotiation of minority identities and representation in this sphere concentrated mainly on film and television (Clark 1987a, 1987b; Rayns 1991; Gladney 1994a, 1995; Yau 1994; Yingjin Zhang 1997). Such studies could not hear any minority voice because these media communicated the voice of the forces that controlled them: the state and the Han elite. The distinction between the two types of media, nevertheless, should not be overstated. This chapter will also show that some minority individuals were able recently to gain access to some of the old media after being popularized through the newer ones.

MINORITIES, HANS, AND THE STATE UP TO THE END OF THE REVOLUTIONARY ERA: A GENERAL BACKGROUND

There are in China today fifty-six officially recognized ethnic groups, referred to on the mainland as "nationalities" *(minzu)*. Approximately 92 percent of the country's population is made up of the Han majority, whereas the remaining 8 percent is made up of fifty-five national minorities. This large number of nationalities, however, still does not fully reflect the enormous ethnic diversity on the mainland. Not only are there groups in China who do not consider themselves to be part of any officially recognized minority and who still seek separate official recognition, but there is also the Han majority, which some insist actually consists of different ethnic groups (Gladney 1994b).[4]

China's fifty-five minorities differ significantly from one another in population size, size of territory, location, culture, and history.[5] They also differ in their relationships both past and present with the majority Han population and the Chinese state. Some of the minorities have maintained a culture that is distinct from Han culture while others have been almost fully assimilated. Some of the minorities have developed close and positive relationships with the Han majority and the Chinese state, whereas others have had a long history of antagonistic relationships, manifested in repeated rebellions and other violent conflicts. Other minorities have had minimal interaction either with the Han or the Chinese state. Although the majority of China's minorities have at least partially integrated into the Chinese state, ethnic-related tension is in some cases still very high. This tension reveals itself most forcefully in the fact that there are some ethnic groups, most notably the Uyghurs in the Xinjiang Uyghur Autonomous Region and the Tibetans in Tibet, with strong aspirations to secede and achieve full political independence. Violence has been an inseparable part in the interaction between these two minority groups and Han China both in the past and in the present.

It is well known that with few exceptions the Han have always seen their culture as superior to that of any other culture in the region. This view was shared by some of the ethnic groups who lived among the Han. Traditionally the Han viewed their relationship with neighboring non-Han ethnic groups as a core-periphery relationship. In this view Han culture was perceived as the dominant radiating center influencing all the non-Han, peripheral others. In reality, however, the relationship was far more complex, and the influence was far from unidirectional, a fact that has recently been acknowledged by a growing number of Han Chinese scholars. The domain of music offers one example of the dialectical relationship between the Han and the non-Han. Suffice it to say that many of the musical instruments that we today consider to be traditionally Chinese, like the *erhu* (a two-string fiddle) and the *pipa* (a four-string lute), have non-Han origins. No less important is the fact that China was not always ruled by the Han majority. In the last millennium alone, two major dynasties controlling all of China were established by non-Han ethnic groups that today hold the status of national minorities: the Mongols, who established the Yuan Dynasty in the thirteenth century, and the Manchus, who established the Qing Dynasty, the last dynasty in Chinese history, which lasted from 1644 until 1911.[6]

The traditional derogatory Han view of minorities has been documented extensively (see Lin 1961; Eberhard 1982; Diamond 1988; Thierry 1989; Harrell 1990). The Han have always seen themselves as civilized, while minorities have traditionally been perceived as barbarians. An example of this view is the following contemporary account given by a Shanghainese Han man who was sent during the Cultural Revolution to Qinghai Province, where he encountered Tibetans for the first time:

> The Tibetans are a warm and friendly people, and my experience with them was a happy one. . . . I even ate that stinking mutton with them, using my bare hands, drinking tea mixed with salt and sheep fat and poured into a bowl that had been specially "cleaned" for me. Later I found out that the bowl had been cleaned with dried sheep dung and then dried with my host's dirty shirt, "as a mark of respect." . . . Tibetans living in towns are more "Hanized," that is, more like us with respect to clothing, food, and hygiene. . . . [The Tibetans] like to eat their mutton almost raw . . . with their hands and not with chopsticks. They don't normally eat pork and they don't like to speak Mandarin Chinese. . . . Given that there were so many modern Chinese around, I found it surprising how much of the Tibetan lifestyle and customs still

reflected their feudal past. I expected that they would be imitating our customs. . . . Some of their customs were quite surprising to me—for example, the way in which they bury their dead. Actually they don't bury them at all. . . . The corpse is hacked into small pieces and then scattered in all directions as food for the vultures. . . . In the old days they sometimes dumped the corpse into their river and let it decompose there, but we don't allow that anymore because it can cause disease. I couldn't understand such a barbaric custom. . . . Tibetan women enjoy sex and consider it as natural as eating or sleeping. . . . As a result of this promiscuity . . . there is a high rate of venereal disease in the area. (Quoted in Frolic 1980, 152–54)

This account illustrates many of the images that have typically been embodied in the public identity of minorities in China. To begin with, the Han narrator constructs a clear-cut distinction between the Han ("us") and the Tibetans ("them") that comprehends almost every domain of life. The dichotomies posed by him, namely raw versus cooked food, use of hands versus use of chopsticks in eating, "stinking" mutton versus pork, and so on, have always been part of the discourse concerning the differences between Han and non-Han. As is also the case in this account, this traditional discourse often leads eventually to the ultimate dichotomy of the Han being civilized versus all others being barbarians. The emphasis on cleanliness is telling. The narrator associates the Han with hygiene, and the Tibetans, except for those who have become sinicized, with dirt. This categorization, too, fits traditional discourse and attitude; the more "Hanized" *(Hanhua)* non-Han people became, the more civilized they are thought to be. We are also told by the Han narrator that he expected the Tibetans to imitate Han customs, an expectation that derives from the traditional view that the Han are superior, and that others, once given the opportunity, would certainly do their best to become like them. The inferiority of non-Han people has traditionally also been perceived in terms of morality. An example of this is found in the references to the alleged promiscuous sexual practices of Tibetan women.

However, as is also the case in many past and present Western depictions of non-Westerners, the attitude toward the Tibetans in this account is not totally negative or necessarily antagonistic. The statements about the Tibetans being warm and friendly are representative of a more complex attitude on the part of the Han, the kind that we label today orientalism (c.f. Said 1978).[7] Though not very developed in this particular account, there have been times when this orientalist attitude included not only real fascination but also strong desire. In other words, non-Han people sometimes became the exotic other believed to possess desirable features that the Hans were thought to lack (Khan 1996, 127–28; Diamond 1988). Freedom, eroticism, and virility have been some of these desirable features.

Like Western orientalism, the above account cannot be separated from the context of colonization, that is, from the fact that the control of the Han-dominated Chinese state was more often than not imposed upon ethnic minorities in China. But whereas for centuries the Chinese empire "aimed at no more than control," which was often nominal (Dreyer 1976, 14), the situation changed when modern Western nationalism was introduced into China. The statement "we don't allow that anymore" in the above account suggests a typical tension in modern China between the state and China's minorities, and implies that more than just control has been at stake in the last century. The modern concept of nation-state required a higher degree of integration and unity than was deemed necessary in previous centuries. Thus, soon after the fall of the Qing empire, Sun Yat-sen, who was greatly influenced by Western concepts, declared: "We must facilitate the dying out of all names of individual peoples inhabiting China, i.e., Manchus, Tibetan, etc. . . . We must satisfy the demands of all races and unite them in a single cultural and political whole" (quoted in Dreyer 1976, 16.). The assimilationist agenda set forth in this statement became most obvious under Chiang Kai-shek. It was under his leadership that the governor of Guizhou Province, for example, declared in the mid-1940s that "no nationality may have different clothes, scripts, or spoken languages" (quoted in Mackerras 1994, 60).[8]

The situation under the Chinese Communist Party has been somewhat more complex. The Communist Party recognized many more minorities than the Nationalist government has and repeatedly declared its commitment to protecting their minority rights.[9] In the first PRC constitution, adopted by the First National People's Congress in 1954, it is stated that minorities shall have the "freedom to use and develop their own spoken and written languages, and to preserve or reform their own customs and ways" (quoted in Mackerras 1994, 145). It is also stated in the 1954 constitution that the "People's Republic of China is a unitary multinational state. All the nationalities are equal. Discrimination against or oppression of any nationality and acts which undermine the unity of the nationalities are prohibited" (ibid.).[10] Nevertheless, despite these clear attempts, and others on the rhetorical level, to abolish "Han chauvinism," the Communist Party simultaneously established a new official discourse that not only did not abolish the traditional patronizing attitude but in fact systematized it and added a sort of scientific justification to it. The new official discourse drew upon Marxist unilinear evolutionary theory and depicted the Hans as more progressive economically, technologically, politically, and culturally. One example of the use of this discourse was provided by Liu Shaoqi, who stated in 1954 that the Hans should assist minorities because they have "a comparatively higher political, economic, and cultural level" (quoted in Mackerras 1994, 147). This new discourse, with its emphasis on Han assistance, was created at least partially to legitimize the control of the Hans and the Chinese state over China's minorities.

In practice the situation was no less complex. During the years prior to 1949 in the Communist-controlled areas and the years following 1949 in the rest of China, the Communist Party's treatment of China's minorities was rather favorable. The party sponsored various ethnic cultural projects, and minorities were granted a considerable amount of autonomy to maintain their differences. Several autonomous regions were established in areas inhabited by compact minority populations. The initial tolerance, however, did not last for long. As China moved to the radical left, first in the late 1950s, during the Great Leap Forward with its associated campaign against "local nationalism," and later during the Cultural Revolution, pressure was put on minorities to conform to the general revolutionary order. China's minorities were now practically forced to assimilate. During the Cultural Revolution in particular, in the prevailing atmosphere of political paranoia and as part of the brutal suppression of diversity, many ethnic practices, especially those related to religion, were abolished. Related objects were destroyed, and many minority individuals came under physical attack because of their ethnicity. Referring to one of the most extreme cases of attacks on minorities during the Cultural Revolution, William Jankowiak quotes an estimation by Mongolian scholars according to which between 300,000 and 400,000 Mongols were arrested, and between 10,000 and 100,000 died of wounds inflicted during that period. He also notes that much of the ethnic heritage in Huhhot, the capital of Inner Mongolia, including Tibetan-Buddhist temples and other ethnic symbols, were destroyed by Red Guards (1993, 19).[11] So brutal was the persecution in some instances that it even led many minority individuals not only to give up their traditional practices and customs but even to hide their minority identity.

REVOLUTIONARY MINORITY SONGS AND ORTHODOX MINORITY REPRESENTATION IN THE PRC

One of the most significant changes in the cultural landscape on the mainland following the establishment of the PRC in 1949 was the emergence of a massive new body of artistic minority representations. This was not the first time in modern Chinese history that minority culture was represented in the general culture, but from 1949 on such representation became a well-organized, party-sponsored project. Among the new artistic minority representations were songs about minorities. Like numerous new films, paintings, and literary works that took China's minorities as their main theme, the minority songs were intended by the new government to advance ideologies of solidarity, equality, and unity among the different ethnic groups in the country. They were also intended to propagate and legitimize the new regime among minority populations, to foster their loyalty to the new state, and no less importantly, to assert control over them and their territories.

Minority songs from the revolutionary period and the processes involved in their production reveal much about relations during these three decades between the Han and minorities on the one hand and the state and minorities on the other. They tell us about the power relations involved, the complex and ambivalent agendas of the party, and its changing attitudes toward minorities. They also tell us how minority identities were constructed in the general culture and about the nature of these identities. Below are translations of four representative revolutionary minority songs. The first song, composed in the early 1950s, concerns the Mongols and Inner Mongolia. The second, also composed in the early 1950s, is about Xinjiang; it combines references to at least the two major ethnic groups who live there, the Uyghurs and the Kazaks. The third, composed in the early 1960s, is about Tibet and the Tibetans. The fourth, composed in the early 1970s, is about the Was (Va), a small minority group who live in southwest China.

THE SUN IN THE GRASSLAND RISES NEVER TO GO DOWN
(lyrics and music by Meiliqige)[12]

White clouds float in blue sky, under the white clouds horses gallop . . .
I proudly tell [people]: this is our home . . .
People here . . . sing about their new lives, they sing about the
    Communist Party[13]
Chairman Mao, ah! The Communist Party! They are bringing us up to
    maturity . . .

XINJIANG IS GOOD
(lyrics by Ma Hanbing; music by Liu Chi)

Our Xinjiang is a good place, ah! . . .
Come, come, come . . .
to our beautiful countryside, our lovely home . . .
The grapes, melons, and fruits are so sweet

Coal, iron, gold, and silver hide everywhere . . .
Pluck your *dongbula*,[14] yah! Dance and sing songs
for the great unity of the people of all ethnic groups
Praise in song the leader Mao Zedong . . .

ON BEIJING'S GOLDEN MOUNTAIN
(referred to in printed and recorded collections as a "Tibetan folksong"
without any attribution of lyrics or music)

. . . The rays of light of Beijing's golden mountain illuminate all four
    directions
Nurtured by Mao Zedong's thought we grow up
The emancipated serfs have good morale, new Xizang [Tibet] is
    building socialism
Praise songs are offered to Chairman Mao, praise songs are offered to
    the Chinese Communist Party, *hei ba za hai!*

A WA PEOPLE SING A NEW SONG
(lyrics by a collective; music by Yang Zhengren)

. . . Beat the drums, strike the gongs, A Wa sing a new song . . .
The mountains smile, the water laughs, and the people are happy . . .
Tightly united, the people of all ethnic groups advance forward . . .
Whatever Chairman Mao says the A Wa people do . . .
Follow Chairman Mao ai! Follow the Communist Party ai! . . . *Jiang*
    san mu luo!

An important characteristic feature of revolutionary minority songs, taken
as a whole or individually, is their ambivalent and contradictory nature.
This nature reflects the general ambivalence embodied both in minority
identity in China and in the attitude of the state toward minorities. On one
hand the songs celebrate difference and diversity, but often, sometimes
simultaneously, they also prescribe uniformity and conformity with the
general socialist order. The celebration of difference and diversity is articulated in the songs through various means: the music, the lyrics, the minority dances that often accompany the songs, and the minority costumes that
are usually worn by the performers who performed them. These distinguish the songs and identify them as minority songs. "The Sun in the
Grassland Rises Never to Go Down," for example, uses a characteristic
Mongolian mode and is sung in a characteristically Mongolian slow tempo,
which replicates the strong sense of free rhythm that is found in much of
traditional Mongolian music. "Xinjiang is Good," to give another example,
is based on a Xinjiang folksong. It introduces local Uyghur dance rhythms
and the heptatonic scale used in Uyghur music, which includes the fourth
and the seventh degrees that are usually absent from the predominantly

pentatonic songs of the Han majority (Yang Xiaolu and Zhang Zhentao 1990, 100–1). Minority songs are easily identifiable also because of the references in their lyrics to well-known minority images. In the Mongolian song, for instance, reference is made to the grassland and the horses, images that in the Chinese mind have symbolized Mongolia for centuries (Khan 1996). In the Xinjiang song it is the grapes, melons, and the local *dongbula* lute that help to construct the song's minority identity. In many minority songs this identity is enhanced through use of vocables and words in the minority language. Examples of this are found in the Tibetan song in the phrase *"ba za hai"* and in the Wa song in the phrase *"jiang san mu luo."*

The otherness constructed in these four songs is of different degrees and it bears different meanings. In the Mongolian song and the Xinjiang song there is a relatively strong tolerance for diversity. This is enhanced because of the more detailed description of minority culture, and more importantly, the explicit pride in the minority homeland and in being a minority people. The situation, however, is quite different in the Wa song, and more so in the Tibetan song. Here little is actually said about minority culture. Whereas the Mongolian and Xinjiang songs pay at least some symbolic tribute to minority culture and homeland, the Tibetan song is dedicated entirely to the praise of Mao, the party, socialism, and the capital, which is thousands of miles away. In this song, not only is pride in being a Tibetan absent, what little otherness is articulated is also entirely negative. The Tibetans are referred to in the song twice as "emancipated serfs" *(fanshen nongnu)*, a term that did nothing to obliterate traditional Han pejorative attitudes and in fact officially stigmatized all Tibetans as primitive people of a slave society. Otherness is constructed in the Tibetan song, in other words, to be negated and to justify change. The song also suggests that identity with the majority group is the change that is needed.[15]

With its emphasis on emancipation, the Tibetan song not only legitimizes the control by the Communist Party but also establishes the superiority of the Han majority, who had always dominated the party, because after all "salvation, be it Christian, socialist, or revolutionary, implies a hierarchy" (Lu 1993, 3). In short, the Tibetans in "On Beijing's Golden Mountain" (like other minorities in many other songs) are allowed to maintain otherness only where melodies and colorful costumes are concerned. And even these still have to undergo sinification to fit Chinese taste. More significant expressions of otherness, by contrast, are negated and symbolically neutralized.

The influence of songs like "On Beijing's Golden Mountain" in the PRC was tremendous. Such songs were popularized all over the mainland and, together with numerous new minority films and other artistic expressions, played a vital role in constructing and disseminating new, officially sponsored public identities for many minorities in China. As minority songs became part and parcel of China's omnipresent new revolutionary mass culture, it is not surprising that many personal Han accounts about minorities feature attitudes and terminology similar to those found in the new official discourse. This influence manifests itself also in the above-quoted report by the Han man who was sent to Qinghai Province during the Cultural Revolution, both in his general attitude and particularly in his reference to the Tibetan "feudal past."

The differences between the Mongolian and Xinjiang songs on one hand and the Tibetan and Wa songs on the other reflect the change in the official attitude toward minorities in the PRC during the Maoist period—that is, the move from a relatively tolerant line in the early 1950s to a less tolerant one in the 1960s and early 1970s. The differences, however, also have to do with the minorities involved. The aggressive assertion of control and the unflattering depiction of local minority culture and population that are found in "On Beijing's Golden Mountain," although found also in songs about other minorities written during the 1960s and 1970s, are nevertheless more common in songs about Tibet from the 1960s on. There are several interrelated reasons for this unique treatment of Tibetans, including their radical cultural differences vis-à-vis the Hans, Tibet's geographical distance, and most importantly, Tibetans' longstanding desire to achieve independence from China, which revealed itself in repeated revolts, the most severe of which took place in 1959.

The aggressive assertion of control and the unflattering depiction of Tibetans are perpetuated in many present-day, officially produced representations of Tibet. One example can be found in a song entitled "Ode to the Public Servant" (Gongpu zan; lyrics by Gao Zhanxiang, music by Guan Xia; performed by the female singer Wan Shanhong), which was broadcast on Chinese Music Television in early 1996.[16] Sung in Chinese in Westernized professional style, the song eulogizes Kong Fansen, a Han party cadre who worked in Tibet and died in a car accident in 1994, for devoting many years of his life to the service of the Tibetan people. Like minority songs of the revolutionary period, the lyrics are dedicated to praising the party. They assert its role in serving the local population and thus, as in earlier songs, imply Han superiority and legitimize their control over Tibet. The messages are also communicated visually in the clip that accompanies the song. Dressed in a bright red dress, the female singer, who appears both as a savior and a superior sovereign and who represents China, the party, and the Han majority, is shown surrounded by an anonymous group of voiceless Tibetans. In sharp contrast to the singer, they are depicted almost as half-human, with dirty faces and wearing dark, dirty, torn cloths. This hierarchical relationship is articulated once again, this time with explicit assertions of control, at the very end of the clip, when Chinese soldiers are shown unfolding the Chinese flag in front of Potala Palace, Tibet's national symbol.

"Ode to the Public Servant" and similar present-day representations of Tibet reflect the continuing tension between the Chinese state and the Hans on one hand and the Tibetans on the other. Like "On Beijing's Golden Mountain," such representations constitute an offensive official reaction to the threatening antagonism that many Tibetans continue to feel toward the Chinese state and the Hans, an antagonism that manifested itself in the unrest of 1987–89 and 1993. They also reflect the persistence of radical cultural differences, the fact that the Chinese government has not (yet) been able to change the demographic proportions in Tibet to create a Han majority, and the wide international sympathy for the cause of Tibetan independence.

The decrease in tolerance is obvious in minority songs since the late 1950s, but an undermining of alterity and equality is also suggested, albeit much less overtly, in earlier minority songs from the 1950s, which otherwise seem to celebrate diversity and pluralism. This contradiction is revealed most vividly in "The Sun in the Grassland." Despite the sense of equality that this song aims to communicate, one can also find in it traces of a hierarchical order in which the minority population is positioned in an inferior position vis-à-vis the Han majority and the Chinese state. The line "Chairman Mao, ah! The Communist Party! They are bringing us up to maturity" *(Mao zhuxi ah! gongchandang! fuyu women chengzhang),* for instance, reveals the oft-mentioned patronizing and "infantilizing" (Schein 1997, 75) attitude of the Hans and the Han-dominated state toward China's minorities. This line depicts all Mongols as children who depend for guidance on Mao, a leader of Han origin, and on the Han-dominated party. The child metaphor is also found in nonminority revolutionary songs, but in minority songs and other artistic minority representations it is used much more frequently and indiscriminately to refer to the entire ethnic group. The hierarchical order suggested in the lyrics of the song is communicated visually in a video collection of old popular songs that was released in the mid-1990s. In the clip that accompanies the song in this collection there is an excerpt from a documentary that shows minority representatives dressed in their traditional-style costumes paying tribute to Chairman Mao. Young and somewhat embarrassed, they move in a row in front of the old and confident Han patriarch, presenting him with token presents while bowing submissively; not unlike their ancestors who came to the capital to offer homage and tribute to the Chinese emperor in premodern times.[17]

The tolerance for diversity and the apparent celebration of Mongolian alterity that is suggested in "The Sun in the Grassland" are not without significant qualifications too. Despite the positive depictions of the familiar Mongolian images of horses and grassland at the very beginning of the song, the rest of the song nevertheless suggests clear limits to Mongolian otherness and implies a significant identification with the Han majority and the rest of Chinese society. The song prescribes loyalty to Mao, the party, and socialism, all of which, particularly the last, imply that limited room is actually left for significant cultural diversity. Similarly, the idealization of the present and the future under the new Han-constructed socialist order suggests a negation of the Mongolian past, which also implies giving up important markers of alterity. The negation of the past and the idealization of the present and future under the Communist Party are characteristics that are found in literature and art not only about minorities. In the case of ethnic minorities, however, such trend significantly endangers the distinctive group identity of the minority population.

The above-mentioned ambiguities and contradictions are intimately connected to the fact that orthodox representations of minorities in the PRC have always been controlled more by the Chinese state and the Han majority than by the minority people whose voice they often claimed to represent. In this sense, most officially produced minority songs have always been more about minorities than by or even for minorities. Control by the state and the Hans is manifested in the process by which most of these songs were produced. It was common practice, starting before 1949 in the Communist-controlled areas and throughout the mainland after 1949, to send Han musicians to minority areas to conduct politically oriented artistic work. The artists' aim was to familiarize themselves with local musical idiom, to compose new songs that combined local ethnic musical idiom with socialist messages, and to train local artists in the new revolutionary artistic practices. Parallel to this activity, minority artists and intellectuals were brought into official institutions, where they acquired politically correct knowledge about their ethnic identity and learned how to represent it artistically in politically accepted venues.[18] These two related practices explain why, despite the fact that "The Sun in the Grassland" was written by a composer of Inner Mongolian origin, one can still find in it clear traces of the subjectivity of the state and its privileged Han agents. Another manifestation of nonminority subjectivity in minority songs is the typical objectifying gaze upon minorities and minority culture. In many minority songs, minority identity is reduced to a limited number of symbols, like grassland and horses in the case of many Mongolian songs, but often also to trivial symbols like the sweet watermelons, grapes, and *dongbula* lute in the case of the Xinjiang song, which lumps together the Uyghurs and the Kazaks. There is also, of course, the socialist realist tone in these songs; minorities are always happy and smiling and their life is always idyllic. This suggests the political reality within which the songs were produced and the omnipresent subjectivity of the Han-dominated party-state.

Another manifestation of the control of the state and the Hans over orthodox minority songs is the fact that most of them were composed in Mandarin Chinese and performed in the professional Westernized style that started to influence Han Chinese musicians in major cities several decades before the revolution. Officially organized competitions constituted an important form of control and an incentive for the creation of new minority songs. Songs that conformed to official prescriptions and helped propagate correct political attitudes have often been rewarded through officially granted prizes and officially sponsored popularization. "The Sun in the Grassland" is a case in point, wining first prize in a national song contest in 1954 (Yang Xiaolu and Zhang Zhentao 1990, 99).[19] Like most officially sponsored cultural and artistic expressions from the revolutionary period, orthodox minority songs have always aimed first and foremost at propagating national unity and confirming and legitimizing state and party control and ideology. Alterity has always been celebrated to serve these agendas.

Many minority songs from the revolutionary period are referred to in printed and recorded collections as "folksongs" (*min'ge;* e.g., "Xinjiang folksong," "Tibetan folksong," etc.). The label "folksong" appears sometimes in addition to a more specific attribution that identifies particular individuals or a group as responsible for the creation of the song, but sometimes it is the only attribution, as in the case of "On Beijing's Golden Mountain." Although some of these songs were composed by minority musicians and popularized among the minority group, in many cases these songs actually had very little to do with the minority people to whom they were attributed and whose voice they claimed to be. In other words, the label "folksongs" was more of an attempt by the party and its Han and minority agents to claim authenticity for these musical representations than a spontaneous, collective voice, the *vox populi* of the masses of the minority population involved. A firsthand account of the revolutionary folksong phenomenon in communist China that addresses the issue of authenticity has been provided by Yang Mu, a mainland Chinese musicologist who resides today in Australia and who has conducted extensive studies of folksongs on the mainland. In his account Yang Mu refers to the Li minority of south China:

> In my field work it has often happened that, after asking the local singers to sing all types of their folksongs, and having listened to them singing for many hours, I never heard a single song that could be considered "revolutionary." For instance, one day in 1981, in a village of the Li people in Xifanxiang, Dongfang County, on Hainan Island, I spent eight hours recording the best singers of the village singing a variety of types of their folksongs; and none of the songs I heard were "revolutionary folksongs." At my request, a male singer eventually sang two such songs and a female singer sang one. However, the male singer stated that those two songs had been composed and sung when he was involved in government-organized broadcasting and folk arts performance tours some years ago; they were never sung by anyone else in their actual daily life. And the female singer said that the one she sang was actually not even a local song, but one she had learned in the early 1950s from the People's Liberation Army soldiers garrisoned in their village. (1994, 308)

Party-state sponsorship should also be assumed in those songs where attribution is made to an anonymous "collective" *(jiti)*, as is the case, for example, in "A Wa People Sing a New Song." "Anonymous collective" may be erroneously understood, at least by Western readers, as something similar to a folk community. In the revolutionary Chinese context, however, it suggests some kind of government-sponsored project. Such attribution is common, especially in the case of artistic expressions from the 1960s and 1970s when collective creativity, as opposed to that of an individual, became common practice. The famous Xinjiang song "Chairman Mao's Words Are Written in the Bottom of Our Hearts" *(Mao zhuxi de huar ji zai women xinkan li)*, for example, is attributed in many sources to an anonymous collective. One source, however, is more specific in its attribution, attributing it to the Xinjiang Military Region Creativity Team.[20]

MINORITY REPRESENTATION AND STATUS IN THE POST-MAO ERA: INTRODUCTORY REMARKS

In the late 1970s, after a decade of forced assimilation during which the subtext of conformity found in many early minority songs rose to the surface and was put into practice in rather extreme fashion, there was a radical shift in official policy toward minorities. As if to compensate for the brutality of the past decade, ethnic minority identity was not only tolerated but even encouraged. The shift in official policy toward minorities revealed itself, among other ways, in a wave of minority representation in television programs and officially organized events. In many of these events, minorities became visible and audible to an unprecedented extent, both through minority songs and through lively minority dances, which became more colorful than ever before.

The dominant style of minority representation in the post-Mao era has been similar in many ways to the tolerant orthodox minority representation of the early and mid-1950s. A large-scale officially organized May 1 pop concert that I attended in Beijing in 1995 provides a vivid illustration of this continuity. The evening ended with a popular patriotic praise song for the Chinese homeland, entitled "Great China" *(Da Zhongguo)*, which was performed in Chinese by the Han musician Gao Feng, who also composed the lyrics and tune. The performance of the song, which among other things asserts Chinese sovereignty over Tibet, was accompanied by several dozen dancers dressed in the traditional-style costumes of China's fifty-five minority nationalities. They danced while unfolding a huge Chinese flag with which they covered themselves like a roof. Although lacking the revolutionary prescriptions regarding loyalty to Mao, the party, and socialism, this post-Maoist minority representation was nevertheless orthodox in many respects. The objectification of minorities, which manifested itself in the use of the old stereotypical images of "neutralized alterity" (Khan 1996, 144), still suggested Han subjectivity. Gao Feng, who obviously represented the Hans, was the only one of those present on stage who had a voice. By contrast, the fifty-five minorities, who were not even necessarily impersonated by minority individuals and who always stood to the rear of the stage, were only allowed to dance. Colorful and smiling, they reaffirmed the legitimacy of the party-state in the old revolutionary socialist-realist fashion.

This May 1 concert also contained a folksy minority song devoid of overt political content; it was sung by the famous Yi female singer Qubi Awu, who when appearing on television and in officially organized concerts always wears traditional-style Yi costumes. Qubi Awu's song belongs to a particular variety of orthodox minority songs in which state ideology is merely implicit; such lack of politics made these songs unacceptable during the Cultural Revolution (Mackerras 1984, 198), but they reappeared with renewed vigor in the 1980s. Many of these songs have romantic love as their main theme; others describe festivities and other customs of minorities. Although devoid of overt political content, the subjectivity of the Hans and the state is nevertheless obvious in these songs too, manifesting itself in the same objectified, stereotypical, exotic, and often trivialized images found in the more politicized songs. Moreover, the songs never mention customs that might appear problematic (e.g., certain religious practices) or any antagonism or discontent; they only portray smiling, happy, colorful, but often primitive "natives." Thus, like the old revolutionary minority songs, this May 1 performance did celebrate diversity, but did so only superficially and only to serve the main purpose of the evening, which was to pay homage to the state, to legitimize its control and to confirm national unity.

This obvious continuity notwithstanding, the post-Mao era nonetheless has also seen a significant change in minority representation, the essence of which is the emergence of new representations that contest the orthodox style. This change is intimately linked to the new atmosphere in China. The opening to the world, the general liberalization, the introduction of a free-market economy, and the resurgence of ethnicity all contributed to the emergence of a new cosmopolitan milieu on the mainland. It is this milieu that I would like to highlight in this section.

The transformation of Beijing in the last decade or so is representative of this new cosmopolitanism. The city has been flooded in recent years with foreigners and foreign cultural products (Pizza Hut and McDonald's are only two examples). These came not only from outside the country but also from within, as the last two decades saw not only the opening of China to the outside world but also an increased interaction and mobility within China between people of diverse ethnic groups.

The new cultural exchange within China manifested itself in Beijing of the mid-1990s in many everyday practices. Mutton, for example, which Han Chinese traditionally associated with barbarian nomads, was now sold on many street corners by minority people from Xinjiang who could barely speak Chinese. It was common to see, especially in the late afternoon, people lining up in front of a shish-kebab *(yangrouchuan)* stand, waiting impatiently to buy several sticks of what they previously regarded as "stinking" meat, covered with a mixture of spices that are never used in Chinese cuisine. There were also Xinjiang Villages *(Xinjiang cun)* in the capital, where minority people from Xinjiang and other minority areas ran restaurants that served characteristic minority foods and where the dominant spoken language was not Chinese. The Uyghur-language pop that was blasted in the Xinjiang Villages through loudspeakers placed outside of restaurants and shops was also very different from the mainstream Han

Chinese pop that was played in a similar way in other parts of the city. Although this music sounded more like the revolutionary Xinjiang folksong discussed earlier, it was still very different even from this song, which after all is a sinified version of Xinjiang music. Besides the sonic manifestations of minority-ness, the Villages were filled with visual ethnic symbols such as replicas of the tops of mosques and examples of Arabic script, which decorated many of the restaurants and shops.[21]

Plenty of neon signs in Korean in another part of Beijing were yet another conspicuous manifestation of the city's emergent cosmopolitanism. While the expensive karaoke bars and restaurants on which such signs appeared were patronized mainly by rich Korean businessmen and their Chinese partners, the new small carts that offered Korean cold dishes *(Chaoxian xiaochi)*, were patronized even by poor newcomers from the countryside who sold fruits and vegetables in the same market places where these traditional Korean dishes were offered for sale.

This new cultural exchange, in which minority people moved with their culture into the heart of China, combined with the general sense of self-criticism and disillusionment that overtook many Chinese as a result of the traumatic experience of the Cultural Revolution, led to a significant change in Han attitudes toward minorities and their cultures. Many of the traditional stereotypes and images of minorities in China continued to exist in the mid-1990s, but due to the change in atmosphere they were often loaded with different meanings from those that they had carried in the past. This was particularly true in large urban centers, and especially where intellectuals and the younger generation were concerned. For example, a common characterization of the difference between the Han majority and its minority others was based on the binary opposition *hanxu* versus *shuanglang*, which respectively mean "reserved" ("restrained," "subtle," or "indirect") and "straightforward" ("candid," "hearty," "frank," or "open"). There is no doubt that *hanxu* was still associated by many in China with being civilized, whereas the stereotypical straightforwardness of minorities was associated with a lack of culture. But it was also obvious that in the new cosmopolitan and liberal era many turned this dichotomy upside down in terms of value. Such people no longer considered *hanxu* an ideal mode of behavior and thinking, but rather the manifestation of a long and continuous cultural and political oppression. Similarly, like *shuanglang*, everything that contrasts with *hanxu*, like *ziyou, ziran, ye*, and so on ("free," "natural," and "wild," respectively), was viewed by many as a welcome alternative.[22]

In the context of this cosmopolitan atmosphere and the shift in the official attitude toward minorities—which manifested itself also in concrete benefits and privileges such as the right in many areas to have more than one child—it was not surprising to find many minority individuals who again felt confident and proud in their minority identity. A Tujia (a minority from central China) friend of mine, for example, recalled how as late as the mid-1980s he felt uncomfortable with his minority identity. By the mid-1990s, however, he was proud of belonging to a minority: "I am Chinese like anyone else," he said to me one day, "but I also have something unique about me, which most Chinese don't have." The new sense of pride and confidence, as well as more practical benefits of minority status in China, also revealed themselves statistically; after many years in which many chose to conceal their minority identity, a vast number of minority people started since the early 1980s to identify themselves once again as members of minority groups. In 1978, for instance, 2.6 million people were registered as Manchus. This figure had grown to 9.8 million by 1988 (Gladney 1991, 317).

It is against this background that contending minority representations started to appear in China at least as early as the mid-1980s. These representations not only caused the state to lose its traditional monopoly over the representation of minorities in nationally distributed media, but also forced it to make significant concessions in its own officially sponsored minority representations. The following sections explore this change, with an emphasis on the new role that minority people played in it.

TENG GE'ER AND HIS CHALLENGE
TO ORTHODOX MINORITY REPRESENTATION

The following statement was made by Teng Ge'er, a famous Mongolian musician from the PRC. It was published in 1993 in *Audio and Video World (Yinxiang shijie)*, a popular music magazine published in Beijing and distributed nationwide:

> I can't sing anymore the kind of songs that deceive oneself as well as others, like "The Beautiful Grassland Is My Home" *(Meili de caoyuan wo de jia)*. My elders and my fellow people will not forgive. . . . In my native land, Ordos grassland, the herding people live year after year in drought and poverty. The lushness of the grassland belongs only to the past. (Quoted in Zheng 1993, 2)

The critical attitude in this statement and the challenge expressed in it are not new. Students of ethnicity in China are well aware that at least among some minorities it is quite common to find people who are discontented with their present position and in particular with the way their minority group is represented in mainstream culture. What is relatively new here, however, is the fact that such an attitude is publicly and directly expressed by a minority individual in nationally distributed media. Teng Ge'er's statement provides one example of the significant shift that took place recently in the role that minority people play in the general culture in the PRC, and particularly in the representation of their ethnic identity in this sphere.

In his statement that he "can't sing anymore the kind of songs that deceive oneself as well as others," Teng Ge'er presents a general critique of the orthodox official representation of Inner Mongolia and the Mongols in the PRC. "The Beautiful Grassland is My Home," the song he mentions, is a famous popular song from the revolutionary period about Mongolia, which is similar in style and content to "The Sun in the Grassland." Teng Ge'er suggests that the main problem with orthodox minority songs about Mongolia is the gap between their idealized depictions of minority life and the actual experience of many of his fellow Mongols. The challenge in this statement is, however, not only directed at official rhetoric. If, by idealizing the present and negating the past, old minority songs aimed to legitimize the party-state—whose presence, they claimed, turned the heretofore miserable minority existence into a sweet life—then the minority musician's rejection of this song and his nostalgia for the past challenge the legitimacy of the party-state. The critique is powerful because the musician not only criticizes the unfaithfulness of orthodox minority songs but goes on to describe in concrete terms the current misery of the Mongolian people.

Teng Ge'er's challenge finds another, more poetic but not less powerful, expression in a song entitled "The Land of the Blue Wolf" *(Canglang dadi)*, which has circulated nationwide since 1994 on a solo cassette entitled *Dreams Float with the Wind.* In this song, whose title invokes the image of the legendary ancestor of the Mongolian people, Teng Ge'er articulates a tragic nostalgia for the remote past, when Mongolian rulers, rather than Han Chinese, ruled the mainland and when the Mongols had a viable and distinctive way of life and identity:

THE LAND OF THE BLUE WOLF
(lyrics by Teng Ge'er and Buhe'aosi'er; music and performance by Teng Ge'er)

> . . . I once heard that the nomadic people were the masters of the
> mainland . . .
> My ruler[s] of former days, where are you now? . . .

The steeds have lost their masters
The hunting dogs have lost their steeds
The land of the blue wolf is yellow sand
How lonely is the grassland in the wind . . .

It has been suggested by several scholars that in the ethnic revival in the PRC in the post-Mao era, the non-Han elite who claim to represent their ethnic groups often essentialize their minority identity very much along the lines of their traditional identity in mainstream culture. Stevan Harrell, for example, has observed that these non-Han elites are a "small coterie of urban intellectuals who are much more part of the general Chinese culture than are the people they are representing" (1996a, 14). Almaz Khan provides some support to this observation, pointing to how the Mongolian elite today, in their construction of Mongolian identity, ignore agriculturalist and urban Mongols, very much like the state and the Han majority do in their representations of Mongolian identity, despite the fact that these groups constitute the majority of the Mongolian population. But Khan, himself a Mongol, also suggests that the shared symbols and images of Mongolian identity do not necessarily imply identical meanings. "For us," he writes, "the yearning and option for the pastoral is not simply a result of some innocent romanticism or nostalgia for the idyllic. In our efforts to resist socio-cultural subordination and assimilation, the imagery of pastoralism has inevitably became the most salient rallying point and identity marker because, as a mode of economy and way of life, pastoralism is not only the most effective distinguishing marker of opposition to Han Chinese, it is also intimately connected to the Mongol's proud past as a powerful nation that once ruled over the Middle Kingdom and beyond" (1996, 143).

Indeed, the symbols and images that Teng Ge'er uses in his songs to articulate Mongolian identity are not new. Galloping horses, endless grassland, a pastoral, nomadic way of life, and the historical figures of Chinggis Khan and his descendants ("my ruler[s] of former days") have all been part and parcel of public Mongolian identity in China for at least a century. But what makes Teng Ge'er's voice novel and challenging is the fact that he not only projects different meanings on these old images and symbols but goes a step further to deconstruct them, problematize their validity, and rearticulate them in a new way to offer an alternative narrative, which he communicates not only to other Mongols but also to people of other ethnic origins in and outside of China. When I asked the famous music critic Jin Zhaojun, who is a minority individual (a Manchu), about "The Land of the Blue Wolf," he commented: "A Han Chinese would certainly feel uncomfortable hearing this song" (Jin, interview with the author, 8 June 1996). A

Han woman with whom I discussed the song confirmed Jin's prediction: "It is clear," she said, "that he doesn't like us."

In the lines "I once heard that the nomadic people were the masters of the mainland," Teng Ge'er articulates resistance to Han dominance. Contesting Han dominance, however, does not necessarily imply a challenge to the state, which defines itself as multiethnic and which, theoretically at least, could be ruled by all politically qualified people regardless of their ethnic origin. Nevertheless the criticism in the song does not spare the state. Teng Ge'er's reference to Chinggis Khan, the most important Mongolian ruler of former days, to distinguish the Mongols from the Hans resists the attempts of the Chinese state to claim ownership over this historic figure by turning him into a national Chinese symbol (see Khan 1995, 267; 1996, 129). Another challenge to both the state and the Hans is articulated in the last four lines of the song. Here, as in his statement from the 1993 interview I quoted earlier, Teng Ge'er points to the gap between the orthodox idealized representation of Inner Mongolia and reality. In these lines Teng Ge'er refers not necessarily to the poor material condition of the Mongolian people, as he did in 1993, but rather to the poor condition of their identity. What Teng Ge'er suggests in this part of the song is that the traditional markers and symbols of Mongolian identity have lost their viability.

It would be surprising for most Chinese and many non-Chinese as well to find out that out of the 2,489,780 Mongols who inhabited Inner Mongolia in 1982, only 18.43 percent maintained a pastoral life, while most of the rest were agriculturalists. Not less surprising is the fact that in 1982, 84 percent of the total population in Inner Mongolia were Han (Khan 1996, 131, 138). These statistics are surprising precisely because there is almost nothing in the public image of Mongolian identity in the PRC that suggests this reality. The story that these statistics tell is of the aggressive colonization of Inner Mongolia by the Han majority and the resultant assimilation of the Mongolian minority. The officially encouraged migration of millions of Han Chinese into Inner Mongolia, which started decades ago, and new policies initiated by the central government since the late 1970s not only changed the demographic situation there but also destroyed the ecological basis for pastoralism; as Teng Ge'er's song suggests: "The land of the blue wolf is [now] yellow sand." [23] This situation stands in clear contradiction to the Chinese state's proclaimed policy of cultural autonomy for China's minorities. But this contradiction helps explain why, with few exceptions, the state has enthusiastically promoted the stereotypical symbols of Mongolian otherness in orthodox artistic representations of Mongolia, despite the obvious incompatibility between such otherness and the highest official concern for national unity and integration.

There are various explanations for this obvious contradiction between official fostering of symbolic minority otherness, which in the post-Mao era reached new heights, and official concern for national unity and integration. One reason is that this fostering of otherness is in fact a compromise that the state has had to make in face of increasing minority demands for maintaining otherness. Viewed in this way, the official fostering of minority otherness could be seen as an attempt to bolster loyalty to the Chinese state among minority populations by demonstrating that the state is committed to ethnic diversity. Another possible reason, which takes into account Han dominance in controlling official representations, is that the "othering" of minorities helps to assert Han modernity and superiority, because after all minority otherness often implies backwardness. This assertion in turn justifies Han dominance. Dru Gladney (1994a) provides another explanation, suggesting that official fostering of minority otherness in the PRC is in fact an attempt to advance the concept of a homogenous Han identity. Highlighting the differences between the Hans and other ethnic groups, according to Gladney, makes differences among the Han majority seem insignificant and therefore strengthens the state. The Mongolian case, however, presents another possible explanation, namely, that through the symbolic emphasis on minority otherness—the pastoral image in the case of the Mongols—the state is actually concealing or diverting attention from activity that aims to undermine and neutralize actual manifestations of this otherness. It is against such a background that another significant challenge in Teng Ge'er's song becomes clear. Teng Ge'er exposes a situation that the state, and probably many Han Chinese, would like to ignore or forget— namely, the colonization of Mongolia and the assimilation of the Mongols. "The Land of the Blue Wolf" is, then, simultaneously a tragic elegy, a cry of protest, and an attempt to raise the ethnic nationalistic consciousness of Teng Ge'er's fellow Mongols. The challenge in the song is communicated forcefully in its music. The first part of each stanza is sung softly to the accompaniment of an acoustic guitar, which provides a flowing, rhythmic drive. This folksy accompaniment enhances the images of grassland and horses found in the lyrics. This initial idyllic, pastoral atmosphere changes, however, in the second half. Here the singing is transformed into loud and angry cries sung in a higher register, which deliver the powerful lines that end each stanza ("I once heard that the nomadic people were the masters of the mainland," "My ruler[s] of former days, where are you now?" "The land of the blue wolf is yellow sand . . ."). The anger and challenge that these parts articulate is further enforced through the introduction of a powerful, war-like drumbeat. The idyllic opening is thus musically destroyed to convey the sense of tragedy embodied in the lyrics. The song ends with freely impro-vised vocables that gradually ascend in register until they are sung in fal-setto. This ending sounds very much like traditional Mongolian singing and articulates, in the context of this particular song, a strong sense of longing.

Another alternative representation of Mongolian identity is found in Teng Ge'er's 1996 album, *Black Steed (Hei junma)*. This album is the sound track of a 1995 Chinese-produced movie in Mongolian titled *Love in the Grassland's Sky (Ai zai caoyuan de tiankong)*, in which Teng Ge'er himself acted and for which he composed and arranged the music. *Black Steed*, the title of which is printed on the cassette cover in both Chinese and Mongo-lian, is sold in Beijing alongside hundreds of mainstream pop albums. It differs from most of these albums, however, in its strong ethnic flavor. Most of the pieces in the album are Mongolian folksongs sung by Mongo-lian singers in traditional singing styles. These songs are significantly dif-ferent from the standardized, sinicized Mongolian songs that have been popularized in China since the early 1950s, and it seems that by including them Teng Ge'er was hoping to articulate his otherness more forcefully, as well as to claim authenticity for his representation of Mongolian identity. The album, however, also includes modern, Westernized artistic elements and one song in Chinese. These reflect Teng Ge'er's urban elite background, his professional training in modern Western music, and his complex and ambiguous position vis-à-vis Mongolian tradition and Han China. Below are the lyrics of the above-mentioned song in Chinese. This song opens the album and is repeated later in Mongolian:

THE MONGOLS
("Menggu ren"; lyrics in Mongolian by Qimed; music and performance by Teng Ge'er)

Smoke of cooking rises from pure white yurts
I was born in a family of herding people
The vast grassland is the cradle that nurtures us . . .
This is what being a Mongol is all about . . .

"The Mongols" is accompanied by a *matouqin* (meaning in Chinese "horse-head fiddle"), one of the most characteristic Mongolian musical instru-ments, which adds a strong Mongolian sound. Teng Ge'er further enhances this sound by imitating some of the distinctive articulations of this instru-ment with his voice. The song also uses characteristic Mongolian melodic material and is sung in a typical Mongolian slow tempo.

The lyrics of "The Mongols" were originally written in Mongolian by Qimed, a poet from the Mongolian People's Republic (now Mongolia). The song's tune is one of Teng Ge'er's earliest compositions following his graduation in music theory and composition from the Music Conservatory in Tianjin in the mid-1980s. "The Mongols" was released in 1989 in Huhhot, the capital of Inner Mongolia, by the Inner Mongolia Audiovisual Publishing House as part of a locally produced cassette album in Mongolian entitled *My Blue Mongolian Homeland* (Khan 1996, 143). This song became a hit in Inner Mongolia in the context of the local ethnic revival movement that started in the late 1970s. The movement reached its climax in 1981 with a massive student protest that lasted a month and was imbued with a "sense of a highly self-conscious opposition to the dominant Chinese state and society" (142). Apparently, this ethnic revival movement is still alive, as two associates of mine who visited Inner Mongolia in 1995 reported that the song was still extremely popular there and was frequently sung on various occasions even in rural areas. Viewed from another angle, the popularity in Inner Mongolia of Teng Ge'er's song suggests that his alternative representation is accepted by a large portion of the people he claims to represent.

But how exactly does "The Mongols" articulate the opposition to the state and the Hans that was embedded in the Mongolian ethnic revival movement of the 1980s? Part of the answer may be found in the differences between this song and orthodox state-sponsored songs about Mongolia. The most obvious difference between "The Mongols" and such songs is the absence in the former of the Chinese party-state, its politics, its patronizing attitude, and its assertions of control over Inner Mongolia. This absence is characteristic of many post-Maoist songs, minority and nonminority alike, and is related to the less politicized atmosphere and the weakening of state control after 1978. "The Mongols," however, not only omits the state but also reacts against it and its assertions of control. The reaction becomes clear once the song is compared with "The Sun in the Grassland." Whereas the latter attributes the role of nurturing the Mongolian people to the party and Mao, "The Mongols," by contrast, attributes this role to the vast grassland. The use of nearly identical words in Chinese in the two songs (*fuyu women chengzhang* in the earlier song, and *buyu women chengzhang* in the later one, which I translate as "bringing up to maturity" and "nurture," respectively) suggests the possibility of a conscious parody. Another articulation of opposition is found in the proud statement concerning the Mongolian nomadic way of life. This statement contests the negative attitude of the Hans and the state toward this way of life and may be read as a protest against the state's successful pressure to change this traditional life pattern that in itself challenges state control.[24]

Until recently at least, pride in the traditional Mongolian nomadic way of life has been equally loaded politically in the non-Chinese Mongolian context from which the lyrics of the song derive. Many of the conflicts that the Mongols have had in China with the Han majority and the Chinese state have their parallel in the Mongolian People's Republic in the relationship Mongols there have had with Russians and the Soviet Union. This parallel helps to explain why "The Mongols" became popular across the border as well. The song was (re)introduced into Outer Mongolia as a theme song in a Mongolian film called *Tribe* (in Chinese, *buluo*), which was released several years before *Black Steed*. It became so popular in Mongolia that, according to several written and oral accounts, it is sung there regularly, even by children and elderly people (Zheng 1993, 2). It is this transnational pan-Mongolian solidarity between Mongols who live in China and Mongols who live across the border in Mongolia, a solidarity that is embodied in the production, content, and patronage of "The Mongols," that is perhaps the most serious challenge posed by Teng Ge'er to the Chinese state. This challenge was so serious that the state had to respond.

In 1992, Teng Ge'er was still not allowed to perform on Chinese television, presumably because of his association with rock music.[25] The minority musician protested against this official ban in an article from that period:

> [There is a need] to create a free space. Allow new people and new compositions . . . to compete freely. Reduce sectarian and ideological biases. There are always those [same] few people performing on television. . . . Create freely and only then will a hundred flowers blossom together.
> An opportunity to speak has to be given. (Quoted in Song Wei 1992, 4)

This ban, however, was lifted a few years later, and in 1995 and 1996 I saw Teng Ge'er performing on the Chinese Music Television channel quite regularly. One of the songs that the Mongolian musician performed was "The Mongols," which he sang in Mongolian. I believe that Teng Ge'er's victory is closely related to his minority identity and the political power that he gained through his artistic activity. In 1990 the musician won first prize with "The Mongols" in a popular song competition that took place in Ulaanbaatar (the capital of Mongolia), and in 1991 he was awarded the Golden Phoenix Prize by the Mongolian government for his contribution to the Mongolian people. In 1992, one year after winning this prize, Teng Ge'er traveled to Taiwan to perform two benefit concerts, the profits of which he contributed to the Taiwanese Mongolian-Tibetan Academic Foundation, which transferred the money to Mongolia (Zheng 1993, 3). These details suggest that Teng Ge'er has become an active and powerful representative of the Mongolian people and of Mongolian identity at large, so powerful that officials at CCTV could no longer afford to ignore him. When I asked the music critic Jin Zhaojun about this change in official policy, he commented:

> China's minorities have been suffering a lot of oppression. There is a limit to how much you can oppress them. If you go too far they will revolt. You have to let them speak. At least a little. . . . (Jin, interview with the author, 8 June 1996)

Allowing Teng Ge'er to perform on CCTV was a clear attempt to co-opt and contain his subversive voice. It is also quite understandable why officials at CCTV chose to broadcast this song and not "The Land of the Blue Wolf." In the context of the less politicized and less party-centered atmosphere in post-Mao China, the challenge in "The Mongols" could be considered moderate, even invisible from the point of view of most state officials and the Han majority. Broadcasting "The Mongols," in other words, provided officials with a way to respond positively to Mongolian nationalism and at the same time to neutralize the empowering and threatening qualities of the song through recontextualization, in which Mongolian nationalism is incorporated into Chinese nationalism. Nevertheless, the broadcast of "The Mongols" was evidently a compromise CCTV had to make, a compromise that reflects the limits of state control and power in the new liberal era.[26] Officials at CCTV may or may not succeed in this co-optation, but in any case they have given up their monopoly over the most important medium through which Mongolian identity is publicly constructed and represented today in the PRC. Similarly, Teng Ge'er may or may not be co-opted, but he has already succeeded in exerting significant influence over the representation of Mongolian identity in one of the most tightly controlled official media. The incorporation of Teng Ge'er by CCTV provides a vivid example of how lines between official and unofficial culture have become blurred in the 1990s and how minority individuals today are able to gain access with their alternative voices even to the most orthodox official media.

BETWEEN ALTERITY AND IDENTITY

Given the expressions of Mongolian nationalism that are embedded in Teng Ge'er's songs, it is quite understandable why he is so popular among

Mongols in Inner Mongolia and Outer Mongolia. But why should his music have the kind of appeal it does to mainstream Chinese audiences? The answer to this question lies in the long tradition of appropriation of minority culture in China. In the early decades of the twentieth century, after centuries in which non-Han groups constituted the other that helped to define the Han Chinese self, China's minority culture was appropriated for a new end. In the context of emerging modern Chinese nationalism, references to minority culture now provided the needed ingredient to legitimize China's claim over minority territories, as well as the primitive authenticity that is often required for constructing a national essence. It was in this context that China's minorities were appropriated to define Chineseness, not as the other anymore but rather as part of the Chinese self.

This paradoxical phenomenon started before 1949 but reached new heights afterward. Referring to films produced during the Maoist period, Paul Clark has written that "paradoxically, one of the most effective ways to make films with 'Chinese' style was to go to the most 'foreign' cultural areas in the nation. . . . Unlike steel mills and wheat fields, minorities' areas offered instant 'national style'" (1987a, 101). What makes minority culture so suitable to represent authentic Chineseness is ironically the fact that, after all, minorities are still the other. Starting from the Republican era (1912–49), authentic Chineseness was sought not only among minorities but also and primarily among Han peasants (see Hung 1985). The primitiveness of the Han self, however, naturally had its pitfalls. This became most obvious in the disillusionment of Root-Seeking intellectuals at the close of the 1980s. The Root-Seeking exploration of Chinese tradition ended up being too risky and too painful when the Han peasant culture celebrated by urban Chinese culturalists was found to be too much alive and too much their own, thus threatening their simultaneous claim to modernity.[27] It was against this disillusionment with the primitiveness of the Han self that China's minorities were rediscovered in the 1990s, generating much enthusiasm. Minority culture was remote enough not to hurt, but close enough to be considered Chinese. The increasing presence and influence of Western culture in the 1990s made the celebrated primitiveness of China's minorities more useful than ever before. It not only helped to assert a much-needed authentic mainland identity in the context of intensified globalization, but was also helpful in asserting the modernity of the Han self, which was now valued to an unprecedented extent but still difficult to assert vis-à-vis Hong Kong, Taiwan, Japan, or the West.[28] Thus, after Teng Ge'er's visit to Taiwan in 1992, one prominent mainland writer suggested that the popularity that Teng Ge'er enjoys in Taiwan has to do with his ability to provide his Taiwanese listeners with "homeland sound and homeland feelings" (Song Wei 1992, 4).

With the radical commercialization of the 1990s, the economic appropriation of minority culture, which started in the form of ethnic tourism to minority areas in the early and mid-1980s (Swain 1990, 1995; Oaks 1995), has also reached new heights. If heretofore the battle between the mainland and Hong Kong, Taiwan, Japan, and the West was mainly a cultural one that had to do with identity and claims of cultural hegemony, from now on economic considerations started to be just as important. With the unprecedented expansion of *gangtai* culture on the mainland, which was intimately tied to the increase in commercialization, mainland musicians found themselves unable to compete with the modern images and sounds that came from outside. Having less and less to offer in this direction for either local consumption, the transnational Chinese market, or other markets, many musicians started to use China's minorities as a source for new cultural economic enterprises. Minorities offered an attractive, colorful exoticism that with few exceptions was not to be found in Hong Kong, Taiwan, Japan, or the West. The old practice of Han musicians going to minority areas to study and collect local minority folksongs for political, artistic, or academic purposes has thus turned into an economic investment in the 1990s. A good example of this recent use of minority music is found in *Fire Hot Songs (Huo huo de geyao)*, a 1995 album by the pop singer Lin Yilun. This album was a result of a *caifeng* (the term in Chinese denoting folksong collection) that Zhang Quanfu, the major creative force behind the album, made to the Dai minority area in Yunnan Province ("Lin Yilun" 1995, 18). Several songs in this album show the conspicuous influence of minority music. A better-known appropriation internationally is the popular CD *Sister Drum (A jie gu)* from 1995, which appropriates Tibetan music and culture. This album became a top seller in China within months after its release and met with unprecedented success in East and Southeast Asia as well as in the West.[29] Bearing these trends in mind, it is perhaps not surprising that Teng Ge'er, a minority and not a Han musician, was in 1992 the first mainland pop star in recent history to set foot on Taiwanese soil and to give a concert there (Song Wei 1992, 4).

The commercial aspect of recent appropriations of minority culture differentiates them from orthodox minority representations. Another important difference, however, has to do with the amount and kind of agency that minority people themselves practice in some of these new representations. The contesting aspects of Teng Ge'er's artistic activity that I describe above indicate most clearly that he is an active agent and not a passive object. But Teng Ge'er's music and agency should not be understood exclusively in terms of contestation with the state or the Hans. The situation is much more complex than that. Teng Ge'er is completely aware of the symbolic value of his music as representing Chineseness rather than an exclusive Mongolian identity, and in much of his artistic activity he, too, plays an active and conscious role in stressing this value. Besides articulating a challenging, exclusive Mongolian voice, Teng Ge'er regularly sings songs that promote the mainland's Chinese identity. In the 1993 interview from which I quoted earlier, the Mongolian musician even goes as far as to criticize some Chinese composers for imitating Western music and giving up China's distinctive national character, while presenting himself as a guardian of this distinctive character (Zheng 1993, 3). The expressions of belonging to and identifying with China in Teng Ge'er's music and interviews suggest a complex sense of identity, which is not uncommon among minority people. But these expressions may also be calculated. In the highly commercialized atmosphere of the 1990s, Teng Ge'er may have decided that he has to balance the adversarial elements in his music if he wishes to sell any music to Han audiences, who after all constitute the majority of the buying public in China, as well as in Hong Kong and Taiwan. Another possible strategic reason for articulating a sense of belonging has to do with the political landscape within which Teng Ge'er operates. Despite the liberalization and reform in China in the last two decades, one can assume that Teng Ge'er is fully aware that going too far with his expressions of Mongolian nationalism may end in political persecution. It is mainly the political situation in China that leaves Teng Ge'er no choice but to maintain a delicate balance in his artistic activity between expressions of otherness and exclusiveness on the one hand, and expressions of belonging and identity on the other hand.

The similarities that some of Teng Ge'er's representations of Mongolian identity, like "The Mongols" for example, share with orthodox representations of this identity can be interpreted along similar lines. They may reflect the influence that official and mainstream practices and discourse since 1949 have exerted on him, and thus also his sense of belonging, a possibility that should not be underestimated, but they could equally be interpreted as a strategy the Mongolian musician employs to serve both his political and economical interests.

LOLO: THE AMBIVALENCE, CHALLENGE, AND APPROPRIATION OF A YI MUSICIAN

Another new minority voice that is heard loud and clear beyond local minority contexts and that challenges the orthodox representation of minorities in the PRC, but at the same time reveals much ambivalence, is that of a musician of Yi origin who calls himself Lolo. Lolo's ambivalence and challenge manifest themselves in the music that he composes, in his performances, in the lyrics that he writes, and also in the published interviews he gives to popular magazines. The most immediate expression of Lolo's challenge, nevertheless, is the name he chose. Lolo ("Luoluo" in *pinyin*) is one of the traditional names of the Yi minority of southwest China. When used by the Han majority, especially in southwest China, however, this name was and still is extremely pejorative, meaning "uncivilized human" or simply "a savage" (Lolo, interview with the author, Beijing, 4 June 1996; see also Harrell 1990, 520; 1995b, 63). This pejorative attitude is also embedded in the Chinese characters of the word, which like the written names of several other non-Han ethnic groups contain the radical that stands for "a dog": 猓猡.

Why, then, did a Yi musician choose a name that the Hans have been using as a synonym for "savage" and to entitle his first album *Lolo's Swing (Lolo yao)?* I learned about Lolo's sensitivities and intentions in a meeting I had with him in his home in Beijing in June 1996. "I am Yi first and Chinese second," stated Lolo with conspicuous pride. He then added: "Lolo is the traditional name of my people. The meaning of the name was originally good until the Hans turned it into a pejorative name. I want to show people that to be Lolo is respectable and that we also have a culture."[30] In our meeting Lolo told me that his official name is Zhang Jianhua, a typical Han name that reflects the sinification that he and his family went through in past generations. Zhang is a common Han surname and Jianhua, meaning "building up China" in Chinese, is a typical name given to children during the revolutionary period. The latter is a reminder, for Han and non-Han people alike, of the radical conformism and the politicized atmosphere that prevailed in China until less than two decades ago. But for Lolo both names also meant something that he is now trying to resist—namely, assimilation. Lolo's decision to do away with his sinicized patriotic given name and his Han surname, the latter being one of the most important indicators of Han identity,[31] and to adopt instead the traditional name of his ethnic group, which the Hans have turned into a synonym for "savage," is a clear expression of his struggle to redefine his identity. This name challenges most explicitly not only the deprecating attitude of the Han majority toward the Lolo, but also the repeated attempts of the Hans and the Chinese state to assimilate them. Because of the negative connotations associated with the name Lolo, this name almost disappeared from general culture in China after 1949. The disappearance of the name was the result of the efforts made by the Communist Party to promote solidarity and equality among the different nationalities on the mainland. As part of these efforts, many communist dictionaries omitted the name Lolo and started to identify the respective ethnic group exclusively by the name Yi or Yizu, which was more neutral.[32] The revival of the name Lolo in the general culture on the mainland by Lolo the musician, then, is a challenge to the dominant role of the Chinese state in the construction of Yi / Lolo public identity. This role has been a complex one, which though including efforts to protect the image of this minority group, has also been connected more than once with attempts to suppress, neutralize, and appropriate its otherness to advance the interests and agendas of the state and the Han majority.

In adopting the name Lolo, Lolo the musician is engaged in asserting his otherness, suggesting that he is neither ashamed of nor uncomfortable with his different ethnic origin, but rather proud of it. The minority musician's struggle to redefine and reinstate his minority identity manifests itself also in the way the name Lolo is written in his album. The two Chinese characters for Lolo are the first thing that catches one's eye when one looks at the album cover (see figure 2). These are, however, written in a modified way. Instead of using the dog radical that appears in the traditional characters, they are written with the radical that stands for a human being: 倮倮. Written in this way, the word "Lolo" can also mean "naked." This meaning certainly comes into mind when one reads the short statement printed on the album's cover: "Strip off showiness, expose the most real." In his explicit and implicit statements about stripping off and exposing the truth, statements directed mainly at the Hans, who constitute the majority of Lolo's audience, the minority musician constructs the essence of his otherness: truth, authenticity, purity, naturalness, freedom, and directness. Needless to say, the binary oppositions that Lolo constructs between himself and the Han majority also communicate an implied critique of mainstream Han culture. Thus, Lolo is an active participant not only in reconstructing his ethnic identity but also in reconstructing Han identity.

The cover of Lolo's album contains another challenge. In contrast to the typical, orthodox, objectifying minority representation in which minority people are usually depicted as happy, smiling natives who always wear their traditional, colorful costumes, Lolo appears on the cover of his album

Figure 2.   Lolo, *Lolo's Swing*, CD cover. Courtesy of Lolo.

not posing or smiling, and not dressed in the traditional-style, exotic Yi costume. Instead, he is shown directing a stern look at the viewer, the challenging look of someone who refuses to let others turn him into an object, of someone who struggles to have control over the construction and representation of his otherness, who struggles to protect his right to be different and to be a subject who speaks in his own voice. Resistance to the typical minority objectification is also manifested in the fact that the album features Lolo's address to his audience. This address is printed inside the cover next to another photograph of Lolo.

Lolo also celebrates his otherness in his songs. Many of the songs use distinctive minority musical elements rarely found in mainstream Chinese pop songs. These include distinctive melodic patterns and lively, stimulating rhythms, which are usually absent from mainstream Chinese pop, with the exception of rock. When I asked Lolo to compare Yi traditional music with Han folk and contemporary pop music, he noted: "The most important thing is that in Yi music, in contrast to Han music, there are almost always drums and percussion instruments involved, and the music always comes together with dance." The importance that Lolo attributes to the dance element in the music of his people reveals itself in the title of his album, *Lolo's Swing (Lolo yao)*. In our meeting the musician stressed that the word *yao*, which appears in the title of his album (which I translate as "swing" and which is also found in the Chinese word for rock and roll, *yao-gun*), is different from the *yao* that appears in many Han songs and which means "ballad." Whereas in the second *yao* the emphasis is on words, in the first the emphasis is on rhythm and body movement.

The lyrics in Lolo's album are inseparable from the sonic otherness that his songs establish. Following the poetic style used by several minorities in the southwest, many words come in pairs and there is an extensive use of characteristic nonsense syllables like *la, ma, li*, and so on. The vocal delivery of some of the songs also contributes to the articulation of otherness. "Putting Horses out to Pasture" *(Fang ma)*, for instance, which is based on a southwestern minority folksong, opens with a piercing, high-pitched, nasal female voice. "This is typical minority female singing," Lolo noted. "Han females can't sing like that. Listen to the female part in 'The Love of the Boat Tower' [*Qianfu de ai*; lyrics by Cui Zhiwen, music by Wan Shou, performed by Yu Wenhua and Yin Xiangjie], so sweet and restrained."[33] Here Lolo started to imitate and parody the female part in the latter song, and then added: "Minority female singers [in contrast] sing very high, with plenty of force. Eventually it is like screaming, crazy-like. . . ." When imitating this kind of singing, Lolo shook his head wildly as if out of control.

Several songs in Lolo's album create a light, silly, gamelike atmosphere by both their lyrics and music. One of these songs, entitled "Guess" *(Cai ma)*, is based on a southwest minority folksong that was popular years ago all over China. The original version of this song was mentioned to me while I was talking with a Han Chinese friend about the differences between Hans and minorities. My friend referred to the song to make the point that "minorities are more free than the Hans, and not as serious." He then added that he especially likes to hear this song sung by children. Lolo's rearrangement of this gamelike, childish song, however, is used not only to articulate the free and casual quality of his minority identity, but also to contrast it with Han restraint and seriousness and to satirize modern life, which in the Chinese context is associated more with the Hans than with any other ethnic group.

Below are excerpts from four reviews of Lolo's album, which give some idea of the complex context within which Lolo acts as an agent in the negotiation of his minority identity. These excerpts demonstrate how Lolo is appropriated in the general culture and how his subjectivity is still being resisted, but some of them also demonstrate that he is able to exert some control, albeit limited, even over his representation by others in the general media. The reviews were published in *The Circle of Performing Arts*

(Yanyiquan), a popular magazine published in Beijing and distributed nationwide:

> The lyrics of "The Moon in the Water Vat" are not the least bit urban. . . . There is a strong rustic flavor to it. . . . [The singing is] natural, warm, free, and it has a lingering charm. . . . The sound is very southern, very moist [as if] flowing from the mist in the Southwest mountains. . . . The melody is smooth like the flow of a clear spring, it flows naturally. . . . The two phrases "ao, my moon, ya my water vat," are the most folksy and the most enchanting. . . . The vocal accompaniment and the sound atmosphere have the flavor of a mountain forest. . . . (Song Xiaoming 1995a, 42)

> "A Village That Is Not Old," whose melody draws on materials from folksongs of the Dai nationality, is pure, fresh, and mysterious. . . . The song with the most beautiful lyrics and melody is "The Moon in the Water Vat." It's hard to believe that its pure melody, so rich in poetic flavor, and its rhythm actually come from a primitive dance of sex worship of the Wa and the Jingpo[34] nationalities. This is the nature of humans, their candidness, and the sublimity of beauty. At present, when China's mass music is almost annihilated by songs from Hong Kong and Taiwan, Lolo's songs give us a kind of unusual feeling, bestowing on ancient folksongs bright modern sensibilities, bestowing on modern songs an ancient cultural quality. In Lolo's words, "the objective that people run after hastily in fear is actually the past, which becomes more and more remote by their chase with each passing day and each step that is taken." . . . Returning to nature, returning to humanism, and finding the long-lost self in the desolate southwest *Man,*[35] which is far from modern civilization, this exactly is what Lolo seeks, and here also lies his value. . . . (Li Xi'an 1995, 43)

> We have fifty-six nationalities and several thousand years of folk music culture. It's a pity that they haven't started to develop yet in pop music. . . . The large quantities of artistic works that we listen to are too far from [our] folk and tradition, and much too close to pop music from Hong Kong and Taiwan, Europe and America. . . . Modern life is becoming impoverished. . . . All over the country we will find the same hotels and restaurants, and identical malls. . . . In the withering of nature our spirit also withers. . . . I hope our music people will return to the folk . . . to find power and truth. (Jin 1995a, 43)

> His music has a kind of sincerity and honesty. . . . The lyrics are plain, natural, candid, and heartfelt. . . . Lolo's voice is simple and sensual. . . . It expresses a primitive, pure, and good grasp of life and feelings. . . . (Guo 1995, 44)

These responses illustrate many of the points made earlier. The second and third reviews in particular illustrate the point made earlier with regard to the appropriation of minority music to assert authentic Chineseness vis-à-vis Hong Kong, Taiwan, and the West. In all the reviews Lolo's music is also referred to as an expression of primitiveness that is both desired and patronized, which is associated with qualities that the Hans are thought to lack, such as freedom, power, purity, and spirituality, but which simultaneously positions Lolo and his music in an inferior position. With the exception of the second review, Lolo is denied any relationship to modernity despite the fact that his music employs some of the most modern musical elements. Reading the reviews, one also gets the impression that the album is a collection of folksongs, and this not only denies Lolo's modernity but also diminishes his individuality as a composer and writer. This impression is strongest in the second review, where the author fails to acknowledge Lolo's originality and refers to his songs as "rearrangements" *(gaibianqu)* of existing folksongs. When I asked Lolo about this point, he replied that only two of the nine songs in the album are based on local southwest folksongs, whereas the rest are original songs (Lolo, interview with the author, 4 June 1996).

Nevertheless, Lolo is not denied individuality and subjectivity altogether, and he is able to articulate his voice even in these accounts. Many of the details in the full versions of these reviews were provided by Lolo himself, and he is even quoted in one of these reviews. Lolo's agency and voice are most conspicuous in the reference to the "primitive sex worship," which he claims inspired him when he created the song "The Moon in the Water Vat." A detailed description of this sexual context also came up when I interviewed him. Emphasizing this context is not incidental. Lolo is certainly conscious of the Han majority's renewed fascination with minority sexuality in the new liberal era, and by providing this extra-musical, exotic sexual framework for his songs, he no doubt hopes to attract attention. He also knows that in the new commercialized atmosphere of the 1990s, when "to be different from the crowd" *(yu zhong bu tong)* is one of the most popular slogans in commercials on television and radio, and in the printed media, as well as a celebrated value in public artistic reviews, his otherness, especially when it has to do with sexuality, is not only welcomed, but can also translate into hard cash.

Yet profit, important as it may be, is not the sole factor. Like many other Chinese today, Han and non-Han, Lolo is looking for his roots. Since issues related to sexuality have always been important for the Hans in marking social boundaries, reference to sexuality is also the most effective way for Lolo to regain his sense of identity and to articulate his otherness vis-à-vis the Hans. In his emphasis on the sexual aspect in minority identity, Lolo is obviously embracing an old Han-constructed minority stereotype, but the embrace is not without contestation because, after all, Lolo uses the image of sexuality to resist the assimilating power of the Han majority and the Chinese state. Lolo's contesting agency is revealed also in the alternative meanings he projects on the old image of minority sexuality. Traditionally, for most Han Chinese, the stereotypical sexuality of China's minorities signified either a detestable promiscuity or a desirable (though not necessarily legitimate) eroticism (Diamond 1988; Frolic 1980; Gladney 1994a; Schein 1997). Lolo embraces the symbol of sexuality but simultaneously extends the scope of meanings attached to it. The context of "primitive sex worship" within which he places his song turns the stereotypical minority sexuality into something spiritual, powerful, and holy. In the framework of his critique of mainstream culture Lolo's reference to sex worship is also a stance against values of restraint and concealment, which became synonymous with civilization in traditional Han culture. In short, Lolo is completely aware of the popular exotic images that are connected with minorities in China, and he actively and consciously participates in their construction and reconstruction.

Lolo's self-empowering struggle to gain subjectivity and control over the representation of his minority identity or that of other minority groups with whom he feels an affinity manifests itself also in the video clips that he created to accompany his songs. In contrast to many Han-produced films, which construct and perpetuate a sexual, feminine minority image, especially where the minorities of southwest China are concerned (as in, for example, the repeated shots of minority women, which in the case of the Dai minority are often shown bathing nude in the river), there is not a single woman in Lolo's video clips. Lolo explained to me that the absence of minority women from his clips was deliberate. Resisting the "superficial" minority stereotype, Lolo was determined to show the "deeper" qualities of minority existence. In the clip that accompanies the song "Dingdong on Top of the Bodhi Tree" (Putishu shang de dingdang), for example, Lolo decided to film the monks of Xishuangbanna in Yunnan Province with their shaved heads. The musician lived several years among the Dai minority in Xishuangbanna and was deeply influenced by their Buddhist practices, and it is this aspect of Dai minority life that he regarded as most representative and most suitable to accompany his song about the local holy Bodhi tree. In choosing to positively highlight in his songs and clips the religious life of the Dai minority, Lolo presents a challenge to the materialism that took over Han-dominated mainstream culture in the 1990s. These positive references to minority religious practices also contest the orthodox discourse in communist China, which attributes negative value to such practices and holds them responsible for minority backwardness. There is also a challenge here to past attempts made by the Chinese government to suppress these practices. Lolo suggested to me that he was the first to represent the Dai minority on the Chinese Music Television channel with images of Dai children and monks with shaved heads instead of images of beautiful local women. He then added that his clip significantly influenced later clips, to the point that soon after his clip was broadcast this image nearly turned into a cliché. This illustrates once again how minority individuals today are able to influence the construction of minority identity well beyond local contexts.

Although he is not as bold and straightforward in his comments as Teng Ge'er, Lolo nevertheless perceives his artistic activity very much like Teng Ge'er does, that is, as a reaction to the orthodox minority representation and to the Han dominance that is associated with it. When I asked him about the famous Yi female singer Qubi Awu, Lolo expressed appreciation for her technical skills. But he also expressed regret that she does not sing "her own songs . . . the songs of her own people, real Yi songs in Yi language," commenting that what she sings is "the high art that the Hans are writing for her" (Lolo, interview with the author, 4 June 1996). In this statement Lolo pointed out the essential difference, as he perceives it, between orthodox minority songs and his own songs. Whereas the former articulate mainly the voice of the Hans (and the state), his songs, his statements suggested, constitute an authentic Yi expression.

As in Teng Ge'er's case, however, Lolo's voice is not necessarily antagonistic or adversarial. In addition to the communication of otherness, Lolo also communicates in his music a strong desire to integrate into mainstream Han Chinese culture. This desire is illustrated first and foremost through his participation in the system and the fact that he caters mainly to Han Chinese audiences. Despite his criticism of Qubi Awu, which is important in revealing his intentions and sensibilities, Lolo does not sing in Yi language either. When I asked him about this paradox, he replied that his producer thought that at least in his first album he should use only Chinese, so people would not feel "too strange." It is also because of Lolo's wish to reach out to a Han audience that he generally avoids the use of local minority musical instruments, such as a rattle made of dried fruit, whose sound, he suggested to me, is too foreign for the Han Chinese.

Lolo's aspiration to be integrated and his desire to reach out from the boundaries of his own ethnic culture are also apparent in the fact that he lives and performs in Beijing. Unlike Qubi Awu's performances, Lolo's performances in 1995 and 1996 were not organized by the state. In the summer of 1996, for example, I saw Lolo perform in Beijing's Xinjiang Village in Weigongcun, one of the most cosmopolitan areas in the capital, at a private party for a newly opened pub. The party was organized by the owner of the pub, the famous music critic Huang Liaoyuan, who also owns a private recording company.[36] At the party, which hosted quite a number of famous musicians and music critics, some of the musicians started to perform in an informal jam session style. Among these musicians was Lolo, who sang a lively folksy Dai song in the original language. Though probably no one understood the lyrics or knew the song, it was nevertheless accepted with great enthusiasm.

Lolo's performances in Beijing are not limited to private parties in newly opened bars. In 1995 he participated in a much talked about large-scale concert that took place two nights in a row in Beijing's Exhibition Hall and was attended by hundreds of university students, young bohemians, workers, and other youngsters. The concert, which was called "China's First Unplugged Pop Concert" and celebrated acoustic pop music, was organized by several private organizations. The song that Lolo chose to perform on this occasion was a composition of his own entitled "*A Mo* Beijing." An explanatory note in the concert program explained: "*A mo!* is an exclamation that minorities in Yunnan use to describe someone, somewhere, something that is the most."

A MO BEIJING
(*lyrics, music, and performance by Lolo*)

I want to go to see Beijing
A ma [Mom] says that Beijing people are the most good-hearted . . .
A ba [Dad] says that Beijing [people] have good and honest
    expression . . .
A mo a mo Beijing, *a mo a mo* Beijing! . . .
Are there going to be stars over Beijing's mountains? . . .
Are there going to be sounds coming from the top of the trees in
    Beijing? . . .
I want to go to Beijing to count stars

In "*A Mo* Beijing" Lolo moves back and forth between expressions of alterity and expressions of belonging and the desire to integrate. A sense of otherness is established in the lyrics through the repeated use of the words "*a mo,*" through the footnote that explains this word, through the words "*a ma*" and "*a ba,*" which denote "mother" and "father," respectively, and locate the song and the individual who wrote it far away from Beijing, and through the narrative of the song, which emphasizes the remote origin of the narrator. Otherness was also articulated in the performance through body language. Lolo ended his performance with a bow while holding his palms against each other in front of his chest in the typical Buddhist greeting gesture, rarely used by Han Chinese.

These expressions of otherness notwithstanding, Lolo simultaneously expresses in the song admiration for Beijing and a strong wish to visit the city. The depictions of what he hears from his parents about the city turn the song into a praise song, similar to "On Beijing's Golden Mountain," which Lolo, like other Chinese, has heard and sung since childhood. And yet, even beneath this explicit expression of love for the capital, which may also reveal Lolo's present attachment to the city in which he has been living for the past several years, there are nonetheless also traces of cynicism and subtle criticism. The straightforward praise to Beijing in "*A Mo* Beijing" is subverted by the extreme naiveté of the narrative, the narrator, his parents, and by extension all the minority people of Yunnan. Despite the fact that goodness and candidness are indeed part of a popular image of people from Beijing, the opening lines actually tell more about the goodness, simplicity, and naiveté of the people of Yunnan, who think that all the people in Beijing have a good heart. The references later in the song to the singing birds, mountains, and stars of Beijing tell us again more about Yunnan than about Beijing. This time, however, the gap between Beijing as imagined by a man from Yunnan who expects to find what he knows, and the actual Beijing is unambiguous, resulting in a clear parody. Everyone in China is familiar with the beautiful natural scenes of Yunnan Province, and the audience is well aware of the fact that, in contrast to Yunnan, there are few birds singing on "the top of the trees in Beijing," there are few mountains in the city, and few stars can be seen at night because of the lights. The parody in "*A Mo* Beijing" could work in two ways. Nevertheless, in the context of Lolo's criticism of the modern and in the context of a concert that celebrated the rejection of modern electronic music, Lolo was obviously directing his parody at Beijing, and by implication also at the Hans. Thus, in this song as in many others, Lolo once again contrasts himself with Han modernity while associating himself with purity, simplicity, spirituality, and nature.

Another poetic expression of the desire to integrate into mainstream Chinese culture, this time without the cynicism that prevails in "*A Mo* Beijing," is communicated in "Over There" *(Na na bian)*. In this song from Lolo's 1995 album, *Lolo's Swing*, the minority musician articulates a subtle criticism of his own traditional culture, with its own ethnocentrist and isolationist attitude. When I interviewed Lolo, he told me that Yi elders have always perpetuated enclosure and isolation, warning the youngsters that everything beyond the Yi territory is bad. The song counteracts this traditional attitude by expressing the view that not all is bad "over there." The explicit integrationist attitude expressed in "Over There," is, of course, welcomed by the state, and may explain why Lolo's songs were broadcast on CCTV despite the close affinity of some of them to rock songs.

OVER THERE
(lyrics, music, and performance by Lolo)

In the past I used to sit in front of the door of the house watching the
moon moving slowly
Listening to Grandpa with his long beard saying: over there, where the
moon is
Wu wei,[37] over there the sky is endless
Wu wei, over there the land is desolate . . .
Today I know, over there the sky is not endless and the land is not
desolate
There are cattle and sheep there, and there are also girls, and there are
also bright sunny skies . . .

MOUNTAIN EAGLE

The tension between otherness and belonging is also found in a 1994 album by a group of three male Yi musicians who call themselves Mountain Eagle *(Shan ying).* The three musicians are shown on the cover of this album in traditional minority costumes. Inside, however, there are other photographs in which the three are shown dressed in a modern, Westernized outfit that includes American-style baseball caps worn backward (see figure 3). These photographs immediately articulate ambivalent messages, not only with regard to tradition and modernity but also with regard to the duality of Yi versus Han identity, because in the Chinese context modernity often implies sinification. Yi-Han duality is also articulated on the album's cover, where several characters in the traditional Yi script are printed alongside Chinese characters.

Otherness is articulated most forcefully at the very beginning of Mountain Eagle's album in a song entitled "The Torch Festival of the Seventh Month" *(Qiyue huobajie,* lyrics by Chen Xiaoqi, music by Jikequbu), where reference is made to the famous traditional Yi Torch Festival.[38] The song begins with a distinctive sonic image that distinguishes it from mainstream Chinese pop; the tempo is very fast, and it has a lively, stimulating, danceable rhythm that is enhanced by forceful solo percussion interludes. Throughout the song one can also hear wild shouts of vocables and words

Figure 3.   Mountain Eagle, *Getting Out of Daliangshan,* images from cassette cover. Courtesy of Pacific Audio & Video Co. (China) and Mountain Eagle.

in Yi. Although most of the lyrics in their songs are sung in Mandarin, Mountain Eagle makes extensive use of Yi in their songs compared with Lolo. They also make much more extensive use of local minority musical instruments, the most prominent of which is the *bawu*.[39] These traditional Yi elements notwithstanding, Mountain Eagle's album simultaneously celebrates mainstream modernity and thus also sinification. In the first song, for example, many of the phrases that are sung in Yi are performed in rap style. Moreover, the accompanying drumbeat in this song and others, as well as much of the melodic accompaniment, is produced using a midi synthesizer.

The lengthy introductory notes attached to Mountain Eagle's album provide another example of the complexity involved in the representation of minorities in China today:

> They come from the mysterious, remote, silent, and powerful and grand Daliangshan. This vast and boundless primeval forest bestowed on them a simple and honest, coarse and tough spirit. They belong to the Yi nationality, which worships the eagle and has a long history and its own unique cultural forms . . . and language. Therefore, their music is wild and simple, full of passion, and free. . . . Once seeping into our exhausted, dusty, and slow-to-react hearts, it certainly will make us experience an unprecedented shock and aesthetic awakening. . . . Their convergence with the modern record industry is a one-time, multifaceted, forceful collision of the classical and the modern, the Han nationality and the Yi nationality, mainstream music and alternative music. . . .

Unlike Lolo's album, where the musician personally addresses his audience, these introductory notes obviously do not leave much room for the subjectivity of the group members. They articulate a strong sense of Han ethnocentrism and an overtly patronizing and exoticizing attitude toward the Yis. The Yis, referred to as "they," turn into some kind of remote primitive tribe, while the Hans, "we," are depicted as modern, normal people. Nevertheless, if we examine these notes in historical context we need to acknowledge a significant change in the Han attitude toward minorities. This change includes the obvious desire to reach out to minorities, the appreciation of their otherness, the allowance for and appreciation of diversity in general, and the acknowledgment of minorities' ability to contribute to and enrich mainstream Chinese culture. The notes also illustrate how the construction of minority images is often inseparable from the articulation of Han self-criticism. The latter is articulated explicitly in the line "our exhausted, dusty, and slow-to-react hearts." But it is also suggested through the attribution to the music of the group, and by extension to the Yi minority in general, of such qualities as "powerful," "full of passion," and "free," qualities that the dichotomous discourse implies the Hans lack.

Like Lolo's album, Mountain Eagle's album reconciles a wish to assert otherness with the aspiration to integrate and participate in the larger system. The integrationist aspect suggested in the introductory notes is articulated in several statements on the back cover, all of which stress the group's Chineseness as well as their Yi origin. One of these statements, for example, states, "China's first album of original, Mandarin, Yi pop songs." The emphasis in this statement on originality and authenticity seems to be a reaction to orthodox minority songs and state-sponsored minority musicians, like Qubi Awu. This emphasis is more than a commercial gimmick. Unlike some of the minority folksongs that Yang Mu mentions in his article (1994, 308), Mountain Eagle is very popular in several minority areas in southwest China. Before releasing their 1994 Mandarin album, the group had already released several albums in the Yi language in southwest China (Mountain Eagle, interview with the author, Beijing, 27 February 2001). When I met them in Beijing in February 2001, they gave me one of their earlier albums, which is entirely in Yi.[40] Helen Rees mentioned to me that she has heard their music on several occasions in Yunnan (personal communication). And when I met Lolo in Beijing in February 2001, he too confirmed their popularity in southwest China, saying that nobody, including himself, has come close to being as popular as they have been in the last decade.

Mountain Eagle's album, like Lolo's, is not only about the abstract construction of identities and structural distinctions; it is also the embodiment of an actual interaction. The theme of integration should not be understood in the Chinese context today only in terms of the desire of the Hans or the state to incorporate the other, as the cover's emphasis on the group's Chineseness may imply, but also in terms of the will of the minorities themselves to be integrated without giving up their distinctive ethnic identity. Daliangshan, the region from which the group comes, is an autonomous region in Sichuan Province. It has been inhabited by the Yis since antiquity and is regarded as their homeland. The Yis who live in this region, in particular (there are Yi communities who live elsewhere) have traditionally been known for their isolation and their minimal interaction with the Chinese state and with the Hans, whose culture, according to Alan Winnington (who visited their territory in the late 1950s), they "violently hated" (quoted in Mackerras 1994, 63; see also Lin 1961, 1). The minority voice in Mountain Eagle's album is far from being absent, because they composed the music and the lyrics, and they sing on this album in Mandarin. By their participation in mainstream Chinese popular culture, Mountain Eagle reacts against the enclosure and isolation of their own ethnic group, similar to the way many Han Chinese, especially urban youth and intellectuals, wish to participate in the global transnational popular culture today as a reaction against their own experience of enclosure and isolation. Like Lolo, the members of Mountain Eagle express their wish to integrate not only through their use of Chinese and modern musical elements but also in

their lyrics. Although in none of their songs does the group criticize traditional Yi isolationist attitudes, as Lolo does in his song "Over There," they
nevertheless articulate a wish to reach out beyond Yi territory and culture
in several of their songs. The group's album is entitled *Getting Out of
Daliangshan (Zouchu Daliangshan)*, which is also the title of the last song
in the album. A similar message is also found in another song in the album,
"Parting Ballad" *(Libie yao)*, in which the group sings: "I want to see if the
outside world is really so exciting."

MINORITIES, ROCK, AND ALTERNATIVE
HAN-CONSTRUCTED MINORITY REPRESENTATIONS

Much of the discussion so far implied identity between the Han majority and
the Chinese state. This identity, however, should not be overstated. The
weakening control of the state in the post-Mao era not only enabled minority people to publicly challenge orthodox minority representations and their
official agenda but also allowed dissent from people who belong to the Han
majority. Challenging the official agenda in majority-produced minority
representations did not appear for the first time in post-revolutionary
China. Paul Clark has suggested that minority films during the revolutionary period, though officially produced, nevertheless provided Han audiences
with an escape to the exotic in times of oppressive politics, enclosure, and or-
thodoxy. He also suggests that some of the films were instrumental in exploring taboo subjects that were otherwise avoided (1987a, 19–20).[41] The
challenge, however, has grown much stronger in post-Mao China. The alternative agenda in some minority representations is not limited anymore
to implicit escape, although escape is still an important component; instead
they assume the form of explicit and direct criticism of mainstream culture
and the totalitarian state.

Several scholars have studied alternative Han-produced representations
of minorities that challenge orthodox minority representations and present
a cultural self-critique and political resistance. Most of these alternative
representations, however, although obviously different from orthodox representations in style and imbued with different meanings, were studied as
yet another objectification of minorities, in which minorities themselves
were denied all subjectivity and voice.[42] My discussion so far has pointed to
the agency of minority people mainly in their own minority representations. In what follows, however, I will argue that minority subjectivity and
agency are not limited to representations that they themselves produce, but

also influence Han-produced representations of minorities. The important point here is that minority people (and cultures) today are not only used by Han artists as vehicles or metaphors to present cultural and political criticism, but also actively inspire this criticism. The discussion below will illustrate this point by focusing on one rock song, "Return to Lhasa" *(Hui dao Lasa)*. This song about Tibet was composed by a Han musician, Zheng Jun, and was one of the most popular hits on the mainland in 1994 and 1995:

RETURN TO LHASA
(lyrics, music, and performance by Zheng Jun)

. . . Return to Lhasa, return to Potala Palace . . .
Washing my heart clean . . .
Awaken my soul . . .
Climbing the Tanggulu Mountain, I came across snow lotus . . .
She is going to teach you how to find yourself . . .
Singing endlessly, we dance endlessly
Lha ya yi ya yi . . . sa, feels like home . . .
Come, come, let's return together to Lhasa
Return to the home from which we've long been separated . . .

It was not long ago that some of China's minorities were brutally persecuted for their "superstitious" beliefs and practices.[43] In the post-Mao era, however, the very same minority religious practices that were violently suppressed during the Cultural Revolution, and in some cases even earlier, have not only been revived in minority territories but have also come to be associated in the general unofficial culture with a new desired spirituality that many Han Chinese, especially urban youth, are looking for.[44] Spirituality is also the main theme in Zheng Jun's song and his entire 1994 album. For him, as for many other Han and non-Han intellectuals and bohemian youngsters, Tibet has come recently to symbolize the ultimate in spirituality. Increasing numbers of urban Han youngsters visit Tibet today, no longer as missionary agents of state-sponsored "civilizing projects" (Harrell 1995a) in which they are expected to inspire and convert the other, but rather for the opposite purpose, namely, to "gain inspiration" and "search for themselves." This reversal is reflected in "Return to Lhasa" in the words "washing my heart clean," "awaken my soul," and "she is going to teach you how to find yourself." When I interviewed Zheng, he expressed regret that there is not enough spirituality in China and told me that for him Tibet represents all the beauty that is left in this world (Zheng Jun, interview with the author, Beijing, 19 August 1995).

Zheng entitled his album *Naked (Chiluoluo)*,[45] a title that according to him articulates his antagonism to the materialism, commercialization, and fakery that he believes, like many other Chinese today, has taken over China in recent years. The musician's criticism of the radical materialism and consumerism of the 1990s is a challenge directed at mainstream culture and perhaps also at the capitalist West, but not exclusively. It is equally a challenge to the state, which promotes economic prosperity and material progress but leaves little room for religion and spiritual freedom. Similar to Lolo's album, the image of nudity in the title of Zheng's album also challenges traditional and communist values and aesthetics of concealment, values that Zheng repeatedly criticized in our interview. The intertextuality between Zheng's album and Lolo's illustrates how Han and minority artists today form ideological allegiances that not only exclude mainstream culture and official ideology but also challenge them in the most direct manner.

It is interesting to compare Zheng's song with past and present orthodox representations that deal specifically with Tibet. As suggested earlier, such representations have usually tended, especially from the early 1960s on, to assert control in a more aggressive manner than was exercised in representations of other minorities, and to be less flattering to the local population. Zheng Jun's representation of Tibet is different from these orthodox representations in several significant points. The orthodox representations pull toward the center, assert state and Han control, and place the Han-Tibetan relationship within the context of a "civilizing project" in which the Han assist and enlighten the Tibetans, who are usually presented in a pejorative light. Zheng's representation, by contrast, pulls toward the periphery, asserts autonomy, and suggests that the "civilizing project" can work the other way around. Thus, for example, if "On Beijing's Golden Mountain" implied that the Tibetans should get rid of their old habits—the most important of which is, of course, religion—because these are the source of their backwardness, Zheng's song reverses this view in celebrating Tibetan spirituality. Another difference between Zheng's representation and orthodox representations of minorities concerns the conspicuous desire articulated in the former to cross the lines and become the other, at least symbolically. This desire manifests itself in the love affair with the native female other, whom Zheng treats as a teacher, and even more so in the statement that Tibet "feels like home."[46] By expressing his wish to cross the line and become the other, Zheng articulates the sense of alienation that many young people feel today in China regarding mainstream Chinese culture. The construction of minority freedom in particular implies a negation of the oppressive culture of the majority self with its emphasis on restraint and obedience. Zheng's use of a reference to minority culture to criticize contemporary and traditional mainstream Chinese culture has a strong parallel in the history of American popular music culture, as Trevor Wishart and Paul Virden have suggested:

> The music of those within the culture but not of it, the blacks, found resonance with the experiences of others who felt alienated from the established order. The black basis of today's "popular" music is the musical expression of a generation in conflict with the values of its elders. (Quoted in Middleton 1990, 77)

This parallel has also been echoed in an article by Chinese music critic Zhan Hao, who has written:

> The Hans have their own popular music, which is folksongs, but Han didacticism is too grave. Elements in [Han] folksongs that express feelings in a straightforward manner were suppressed; but there are plenty of folksongs in minority areas that are much less didactic. . . . Western pop music also has its basis and origin [elsewhere], namely, in black music. [Black] music is very free. . . . (1995a, 16)

The liberating aspect of Tibet is also communicated in Zheng's song through its music and its video. The song opens with slow, high-pitched singing accompanied by an acoustic guitar and a bell. These immediately construct the image of purity and spirituality that so many people in China today associate with Tibet. Later, this initial otherworldly atmosphere changes drastically when a faster tempo, an aggressive hard-rock beat provided by a Western drum set, fuzzy electric guitar line, and wild vocal delivery are introduced into the song. In this forceful, wild section, which accompanies the line "singing endlessly, we dance endlessly," Zheng celebrates another aspect of the desired spiritual and physical liberation that he finds in Tibet. This celebration of nonrestraint and lack of control is reinforced in the song's video, which in this part replaces shots of the serene scenery of Tibet and local people in worship with a staged hard-rock concert in which the musician is shown dancing wildly on stage.

The link between minorities and rock in Zheng's song is not uncommon in contemporary China. One early cinematic reference to rock, *Rock Youth* (*Yaogun qingnian*, 1988), for example, was directed by none other than Tian Zhuangzhuang, one of China's most prominent filmmakers, whose two minority films, *On the Hunting Ground* (*Liechang zhasa*, 1985) and *The Horse Thief* (*Dao ma zei*, 1986), have been acknowledged as marking a significant turning point in cinematic minority representation on the mainland.[47] A more obvious manifestation of this link, which suggests greater agency on the part of minorities, has to do with the patronage of rock. Prevented from giving large-scale concerts in Beijing, where the official ban on rock has been enforced strictly since 1993, rockers often performed in the mid-1990s in the peripheral hinterland. One week before flying to Lhasa to give a rock concert, Li Tong, the leader of Black Panther *(Hei bao)*, one of China's most famous rock bands, suggested to me that "minorities really like rock." To support his point, Li mentioned the band's frequent concerts in Kunming (the capital of Yunnan Province) where minority people, according to him, always constituted the majority of the audience and were always very responsive to rock. In a similar account, Lolo recalled how in one of Cui Jian's numerous concerts in Kunming, one Jingpo woman managed to climb onto the stage and started to dance on it while the famous rocker was singing:

> She danced so wildly, moving her head with her long hair up and down
> to the beat. No Han woman could ever dance like that. . . . Minorities
> are much more receptive to rock music because all the dance rhythms
> that are used in rock are already found in their own indigenous
> music. . . . [That's why] Kunming is a paradise for rockers. (Lolo, inter-
> view with the author, 4 June 1996)

Rock culture is probably the most viable and potent alternative culture that has existed in post-Mao China, being intimately tied since its emergence in the late 1980s to overt political and cultural resistance. The close relationship between alternative representations of minorities and rock music highlights the alternative agenda in the former and its implications of criticism and resistance. Both rock music, often perceived as synonymous with the West as a whole, and minority images constitute an alternative other in China, onto which members of the Han majority project their suppressed desires and fantasies. This parallel was apparent to me time and again in the similarity between statements that referred to the West and others that referred to China's minorities. On one occasion, for example, I was told by a Han woman that I should go to discos in Tibet because "there people can really dance. . . . They can get really crazy and free, not like the people here in Beijing, who are so reserved [*hanxu*]." This statement was strikingly similar to the following one, which I heard repeatedly from several individuals on different occasions, and which referred to the West: "You Westerners can dance and sing freely whenever and wherever you want, we Chinese [Han] can't!" It is also by combining these two related others, the officially banned, modern Western rock and the constructed minority freedom, that Zheng created in his song an alternative world that offered him and at least part of his audience spiritual and physical liberation.

However, like Western rock, minorities do more than just serve as empty bottles that the Hans use to contain and articulate their fantasies and criticism. The last decade has provided us with several examples of minority people who were able to initiate and inspire fantasies, criticism, and even action among the Han majority in the very heart of China. One example is Wu'er Kaixi, the Uyghur student from Xinjiang who was one of the most prominent leaders of the 1989 democracy movement. Gladney has noted that Wu'er Kaixi "frequently admits that it is his ethnic background that most made him aware of the oppression of the government in minority areas and the economic backwardness of his own people" (1991, 295). As suggested in the previous chapter, the 1989 movement was closely linked to the introduction of rock music and culture into China and the rise of indigenous Chinese rock. This link, which has also been acknowledged by Wu'er Kaixi, manifested itself most clearly in the fact that "Having Nothing," China's first rock song, became the anthem of the protesting students all over China. Much has been written on the creator of this song, Cui Jian, China's most famous and influential rock star, but it is rarely if ever mentioned that he is Korean *(Chaoxian)*. Although Cui Jian's music lacks any explicit reference to his ethnic minority background, his rock activity suggests once again that the link between ethnic minorities and rock culture in China is not only constructed by alienated musicians of Han origin, and not only at a symbolic or metaphoric level. Ethnic minority people link themselves with rock culture, consciously or unconsciously, because, as rock is associated with freedom and criticism of mainstream culture, it offers an outlet for their experience of alienation, oppression, and discrimination as minority people. Simultaneously, with its cosmopolitan, transnational character, rock offers minority people an escape from their inferior and marginal position in China. Indeed, rock music in China can be understood better as an important minority discourse that challenges the center once one acknowledges the active role that ethnic minority people play in it. Recognizing this active role would in turn increase our understanding of the position and role of minority people in the overall cultural and political transformation of post-Mao China, a role that has been neglected so far.

It is often difficult if not impossible to trace the exact origin of a particular trend and to point the direction in which it moves. New trends often emerge in complex contexts in which multiple forces interact with one another and influences move back and forth. Accordingly, the details above may not pinpoint the exact origin of the new trends in minority representation on the mainland in terms of timing and direction, but they nevertheless suggest a particular context, which implies that Zheng Jun's representation of Tibet was not another majority objectification of minorities over which the latter exerted no control, or in which they were denied any agency or voice. Zheng's activity has been part of a new transethnic subculture in which minority people and culture, perhaps for the first time in the history of the PRC, have played a central role, whether it be through encounters between minority people and Han rockers who come to minority regions to perform and travel—encounters that are much less hierarchical and missionary and therefore allow for more mutual influence than past and present state-sponsored encounters—or through the fact that many rockers and people who belong to the rock circle in big cities like Beijing are themselves minority people.[48] In this sense, Zheng Jun's voice, though not a minority voice itself, cannot be separated from the voices of Teng Ge'er, Lolo, and Cui Jian and the voices of other minority people who spoke around him and certainly influenced him.

"Return to Lhasa," nevertheless, also has its ambiguities. The song was, after all, part of an officially encouraged Tibet fever that swept the mainland in the mid-1990s, and although novel and challenging in its approach, it nevertheless still made quite explicit that Tibet was part of China. This perhaps helps to explain how it was broadcast in mid-1995 both by BTV (Beijing's local television channel) and CCTV. Despite the fact that the latter omitted the section in the song's video in which the musician is shown dancing wildly, the mere broadcast of this rock song on state-run national television was unprecedented and surprised everyone, including Zheng himself (Zheng Jun, personal communication, 1995). Later in 1995 Zheng also received an official invitation to participate in a television variety show that was about to be broadcast on the local Tibetan television station to mark the thirtieth anniversary of the establishment of the Tibetan Autonomous Region.[49] The decision to invite the rocker to participate in this highly politicized official television event and to broadcast his rock song nationwide was presumably motivated by the following line in the song: "[It] feels like home. . . . Come, come, let's return together to Lhasa, return to the home from which we've long been separated." This line is sung in the video while Zheng Jun is shown in front of Potala Palace. Officials must have interpreted this line as another expression of the official and Han majority claim for sovereignty over Tibet. What made Zheng's song so valuable in the eyes of the officials who decided to broadcast it despite its being a rock song was presumably the fact that this claim for sovereignty is combined in the song with an expression of appreciation for Tibetan culture and the fact that the song had been circulating for a while as an unofficial and nonpolitical song and had become very popular.

These facts made it eminently suitable for a sensitive occasion in which the party understandably wished to present itself and its politics as less oppressive.

This partial compatibility between "Return to Lhasa" and official ideology notwithstanding, Zheng's song contests many aspects of that ideology. Thus it provides another example of how alternative, unofficial representations of minorities are infiltrating today into the official sphere and expanding orthodox official discourse. Although still marginal, contending representations like "Return to Lhasa," with their evenhanded view of minorities, their genuine appreciation of minority culture (even if this culture is partly imagined), and most importantly, their allowance for significant autonomy and otherness, may have far-reaching implications. If such representations and the fact that they are able to penetrate official media do not already reflect a significant change in the state's attitude and general public opinion toward China's minorities, it is very likely that they will have some significant influence over them in the near future.[50]

IMPLICATIONS FOR INTERETHNIC AND STATE-MINORITIES RELATIONS IN CHINA

The facts that some of China's minorities today have direct access to nationally circulating media, that they actively participate as subjects in mainstream culture, and that they speak in an independent voice that is sometimes very different from the voices of the state and the Han majority all suggest a significant change in the cultural and political landscape in the domain of ethnicity in the PRC. The most obvious change, already implied by the data presented in this chapter, has to do with the dynamism of power relations between some of China's minorities and the Han majority, and between these minorities and the Chinese state, power relations that have too often been assumed to be static and of the clear dominance-subordination type. The data suggest that since the mid-1990s a significant amount of control over the construction and representation of the public identity of China's different ethnic groups (both minorities and the Han majority) has moved from the hands of the Chinese state and the Han majority to the hands of minority people. The fact that some minority individuals today can publicly present new alternative narratives about their ethnic identity, some of which are in opposition to the orthodox narratives, supports the idea that, at least in some respects, China has become more liberal and pluralistic in the 1990s and that the state today is often forced to make concessions to pressures

exerted on it from various groups. This chapter, nevertheless, simultaneously demonstrates the adaptive capabilities of the Chinese government.
These capabilities have been acknowledged by Susan Greenhalgh, who suggests the following in her study of the application of the one-child policy in
rural Shaanxi Province:

> State policy was slowly but surely altered to fit societal demands. . . .
> National level policy makers [are not] blind to the limits of their power.
> . . . State and society moved closer together, and state policy itself was
> altered to reflect fundamental societal need. (1993, 250)

The big question that now arises is to what extent the new minority subjectivities described here can affect future interethnic and state-minorities
relations in the PRC. No single answer can be given to this question, for two
reasons that are related to the voices themselves, leaving aside other important factors that are beyond the scope of this study. First, one has to acknowledge the diversity among the new voices. Teng Ge'er's Mongolian
subjectivity, for example, is much more politically challenging and adversarial than Lolo's Yi subjectivity. This difference is obviously related to the
different histories and the nature of the relationship that the two minorities
have had with the Chinese state and the Han majority. Whereas the Mongols have always made claims for an independent state, the Yis have not. Second, in the three voices described here there is much ambivalence and ambiguity. In Teng Ge'er's voice, for instance, there can be heard on one hand
certain elements that suggest something of the separatist ideology that has
always existed among the Mongolian minority (see Jankowiak 1993). Although this aspect of Teng Ge'er's activity should not be overestimated, we
should not ignore it either. Teng Ge'er's popularity among the Mongolian
population in China, his cross-border appeal, his ability to communicate
with his fellow Mongols through unofficial media and to speak in an independent voice, all make him powerful and potentially threatening to the
Chinese state and Han dominance. Like the role of Cui Jian's songs in the democracy movement of 1989, Teng Ge'er's songs can certainly inspire people
to develop alternative ideologies and help mobilize them to act against the
government. The fact that his voice circulates nationally and internationally
and not always through state-controlled media makes him potentially
influential and inspiring, not only among his fellow Mongols but also
among other minority populations who share similar experiences, as well as
among portions of the Han population and people outside China who may
develop a sympathetic attitude toward the plight of the Mongols and other
minorities. On the other hand, however, though certainly posing a chal-

lenge to the government and the dominant Hans, Teng Ge'er's voice (and certainly Lolo's and Mountain Eagle's) simultaneously suggests a significant degree of successful integration. The new minority voices described here therefore do not exclusively imply contestation or conflict. After all, the minority musicians mentioned here create and perform in Chinese, actively participate in mainstream culture, and are engaged in a significant peaceful cultural dialogue with Han China.

The two possibilities described above, that of increased tension or ethnic unrest because of the sense of empowerment that certain minority individuals have acquired recently and which they are now able to communicate to others, and that of increased integration, are not unrelated or necessarily contradictory. In other words, the threat embedded in their independent voices could be used by minority artists to advance equality, participation, and self-representation, as well as more integration in mainstream culture. It is after all this threat in Teng Ge'er's voice that forced CCTV to allow him the access to the officially controlled national media that he had been denied. If Teng Ge'er continues to speak in his new voice, he may eventually force the government to admit the gap between official rhetoric and the actual experience of many minority people and to act to correct the situation.

3   Negotiating Gender in Post-Revolutionary Popular Music Culture: Reconstructing Manhood, Womanhood, and Sexuality

One of the most conspicuous trends on the mainland in the last two decades has been an intense public effort to reconstruct gender differentiation and revive sexuality after close to three decades during which the government made every effort to eliminate both. Indeed, much of popular culture in post-Mao China is a reaction against the radical experiences of the revolutionary past, but there is probably no other domain in which the reaction is so visible as in the domain of gender and sexuality. The policy to eliminate gender differences during the Maoist years was part of the Communist Party's agenda to bring about equality between the sexes. Reaching its peak during the Cultural Revolution, this policy resulted in a unisex ethos, the most vivid manifestation of which was people's outer appearance. For years men and women in the PRC wore the same working uniforms—blue long pants and simple cotton shirts—which not only made them look alike, but also contributed significantly to the suppression of sexuality, as little of the body was left exposed and its shape was completely blurred (see Honig and Hershatter 1988, 42; Croll 1995, 71; Mayfair Yang 1999, 40–47).

The revolutionary period is remembered as a period of "gender erasure" (Mayfair Yang 1999). Yet it was mainly women who had to give up their gender identity and consciousness. The communist revolution aimed at, and indeed partially succeeded in, liberating Chinese women from their inferior position in traditional society, but it also denied them the right to be different. In the process of gaining their social equality, in the overwhelmingly militant and masculine period of the Cultural Revolution, model women were supposed to aspire to be like men both physically and mentally. This concept of womanhood revealed itself, among other ways, in the much-celebrated officially sponsored image of the Iron Girls *(tieguniang)*, which emerged right before the Cultural Revolution and depicted women doing traditionally male work, such as repairing electricity lines and drilling for oil. This superwoman-like, masculine image conformed to Mao's famous slogan that "women can do whatever men can do." During the Cultural Revolution, in addition to the masculine uniforms, women were also expected and often forced to wear their hair short like men. Dresses, makeup, and other traditional characteristics of femininity were regarded as bourgeois and counterrevolutionary, and were banned.

The traditional, "feudalistic" practice of binding women's feet, which more than anything else came to represent the oppressive, patriarchal nature of old China and its enslavement of women, had long been banned on the mainland when the Cultural Revolution broke out.[1] Yet, now, in the new asexual, masculine revolutionary order, the old practice of women binding their breasts gained increasing popularity, even among urbanites. "We were very shy," one woman in her mid-forties explained to me, describing how during the Cultural Revolution she, like many other young women, used a piece of cloth to bind her breasts tightly so it would appear as if she did not have any. "The ideal," she said, "was to be as flat as possible." Thus, ironically enough, it was once again women, not men, who had to alter their physical appearance to conform to yet another sociopolitical order.

As for the effort to eliminate sexuality, this started long before the establishment of the People's Republic in 1949. In his article on the *yangge* movement that was launched in Yan'an in 1943, David Holm describes how this folk art form, which combines dance, drama, and song and was originally filled with sexuality, was stripped by the Communists of all its sexual elements when they transformed it into one of their most important and effective propaganda and educational tools. Holm suggests that "the most important difference between old and new [*yangge*] . . . was the elimination of sexuality" (1984, 24). He also quotes two Chinese sources from the period that discuss the transformation of the *yangge* and illustrate the orthodox communist view of sexuality:

> [In the old *yangge*] there used to be many degenerate elements in performance, like sexual love, and the postures of the dance were also very lascivious, full of raised shoulders and flashing waists. We have thoroughly reformed these aspects of the dance. . . . In old *yangge* there is a heavy atmosphere of sexuality; here that cannot obtain. Old *yangge* was entertainment pure and simple, here we must have educational significance. . . . In order to drop the sexual element, we took the man and wife—a male-female relationship that could give rise to rather a lot of sexuality—and changed it into one that absolutely could not elicit sexual responses, the brother-sister relationship. (Holm 1984, 24–26)

Similarly, Hung Chang-tai notes that when party intellectual artists and cadres collected popular folksongs and refilled them with revolutionary lyrics to facilitate disseminating the party's ideology, they often ignored and excluded love and erotic songs, which they regarded as "old folksongs," emphasizing instead the collection of songs that suited the propaganda and educational function that the new songs were assigned to fulfill (1994, 257–58).

With few exceptions, romantic love was officially denounced by the party as an immoral, decadent, individualistic bourgeois practice that had to be eliminated and replaced by a puritanical, productive, collective, and militant revolutionary ethos. When the Communists took over the mainland in 1949, the elimination of artistic expressions of sexuality, which heretofore had been applied only to folk culture, was now extended to urban popular culture. One of the most vivid manifestations of this elimination was the disappearance from public spaces of the modern Westernized popular music that emerged in Shanghai and other large cities in the 1930s, in which romantic love was the main theme. Following 1949, romantic songs were gradually replaced in public culture by songs that articulated instead love for the country and the party (Evans 1997, 93–94).

This change not only affected the status of romance, but also contributed to the blurring of gender differences. Whereas many of the old popular songs celebrated male-female duality, with the exception of songs that referred to the liberation of women and were thus gender-specific, from the late 1950s women and men were basically singing the same mass songs, which paid little attention to their different experience and different physical, mental, and emotional qualities. Similar to the new unisex practices in society, the unisex aesthetics in music showed considerable preference for the masculine. The masculinization of music, like the masculinization of women, reached its peak during the Cultural Revolution. For a whole decade all music, with very few exceptions, was fast, loud, militant, and forceful, or as the music critic Jin Zhaojun characterized it, "lacking in *yin* [femininity] and abundant in *yang* [masculinity]" (1988). The soft, slow, gentle, and often coquettish lyrical *(shuqing)* style that has always been associated with the feminine disappeared from public culture even when divorced from its romantic content.

As in the revolutionary past, popular music in post-Mao China has been closely linked with developments in the domain of gender. So strong was the reaction in the 1980s and 1990s to the blurring of gender differences during the revolutionary period that today in many music shops cassettes and CDs, for instance, are divided not according to style, but rather according to the sex of the singer, thus creating a male section and a female section. Another example of the reversal of the revolutionary unisex and puritan ethos is found in "The Love of the Boat Tower" *(Qianfu de ai)*, which became one of the most popular hits on the mainland in 1993:[2]

THE LOVE OF THE BOAT TOWER
(lyrics by Cui Zhiwen; music by Wan Shou; performance by the female singer Yu Wenhua and the male singer Yin Xiangjie)

Male: Young sister, you sit on the bow of the boat
Elder brother walks on the riverbank
Love and rope arc swinging leisurely

Female: I, little young sister, sit on the bow of the boat
Elder brother, you walk on the riverbank
Our feelings
Our love
Swing leisurely on the towing rope . . .
You kowtow once in every step
Having no other hope
But to pull young sister's hand . . .
I only wait for the sunset
To let you kiss me until you have enough

"The Love of the Boat Tower" is a celebration of male-female dualism and contrast. The male part is fast and rhythmically accentuated. It is sung in a deep, coarse, yelling voice and is juxtaposed with the forceful sound of the *suona* (double-reed oboe) and the shouts of male workers. The female part, by contrast, is slow and soft. I⁺ is sung in the traditional high-pitched, nasal feminine singing style and is delivered in winding, coquettish singing to the accompaniment of a dotted rhythm. The video and the lyrics further enhance the contrast. The man pulls the boat and is often shown half naked. The woman, by contrast, sits motionless on the boat, dressed in a traditional feminine costume that leaves little of her body exposed. The result is a strong, rough, active, uninhibited male image as opposed to a weak, sweet, passive, restrained, chaste female image.

Nevertheless, it is the female singer who sings most of the lyrics in the song, and it is she who speaks about love and kisses. While this can be read as a way to invoke the traditional image of feminine talkativeness and seductiveness, it might also be read as an attempt to subvert and counteract the stereotypical image of feminine restraint and passivity that is constructed through the music, the lyrics, and the video. The message of this "new folksong" *(xin min'ge)* is thus far from unequivocal. The song may be interpreted as a nostalgic revival of gender binarism and traditional gender roles and images, but simultaneously it could also be interpreted as a parody of these very same images and roles. The song, after all, is performed in a gay, humorous, carnivalistic style. In the complex dynamics of transition in China today, however, these two interpretations should not be seen as mutually exclusive. On the mainland today, tradition is often simultaneously embraced and negated, even by the same people. Contradiction and ambivalence are at the core of China's post-revolutionary culture.

Though in the last decade popular Chinese music has received an increasing amount of scholarly attention, it has not been studied yet from a gendered perspective. The purpose of this chapter is to fill this gap. It will examine how popular music is used today in China to construct and articulate different gender images, and how general gender practices and discourse inform the popular music scene and vice versa. It also explores the relationship between musical style and gender, as well as the agencies, meanings, voices, and politics involved in the representation of manhood and womanhood. Finally, I will examine the relationship between these issues and domains such as state politics, nationalism, and commercialization.

The chapter is divided into two parts: the first focuses on (re)constructions of manhood and the second on (re)constructions of womanhood. The two parts, nonetheless, are interwoven into each other, so there is much of each in the other. In the first part I explore the much talked about post-revolutionary crisis of masculinity and the search for the "real man[hood]." This search has received a significant amount of scholarly attention, but the attention has been limited to the domains of literature and film (Wang Yuejin 1989; Zhang Yingjin 1990; Louie 1991, 1992; Louie and Edwards 1994; Zhu 1993; Zhong 1994, 2000). The first part of this chapter expands the scope of inquiry and discusses the crisis of masculinity in conjunction with rock and *xibeifeng*. The rich but clear identity of rock in China (at least until the mid-1990s) in particular, that is, its association with men on the one hand, and with intellectuals, rebellion, boldness, resistance to the state, modernity, Westernization, creativity and individualism, freedom, northern China, wildness, and dance, on the other hand, enables me to link all of these themes to the discussion of gender and to offer a new perspective on both the masculinity crisis in post-Mao China and the negotiation of gender in general.

From the discussion of rock with its Western macho type of manhood I move on to discuss mainstream pop and point to the fact that this style, contrary to rock, has always been dominated by images of delicate men, which many today, both in China and the West, see as extremely effeminate. The decline of rock and the increased popularity enjoyed since the mid-1990s by soft songs that celebrate a more effeminate image of men lead me to propose, contrary to what is often suggested in the pertinent literature, that the Western image of the macho man has not really replaced more traditional models of manhood in China. In my discussion of the traditional male image, I explore the origins and implications of its extreme popularity in the 1990s. My main arguments suggest the influence of the trauma of the Tiananmen incident of 1989, nationalism and cultural continuity, the disempowering effects of the radical commercialization of the 1990s, and the new power of female consumerism, an important factor that so far has received little or no attention. The last two factors provide the basis for my insistence throughout this chapter that the influence of the market on gender roles in post-Mao China is much more complex than what is generally thought and that it has also empowered women in significant ways.

The second part of the chapter, on the (re)constructions of womanhood, begins with a discussion of the agencies, meanings, and politics involved in the construction and representation of the most dominant female image of the 1990s, that of a domesticated, gentle, sweet, restrained woman, which exists in either sexualized or chaste form and which I call the neotraditional feminine image. After acknowledging and providing important evidence from the popular music scene to the "liberating" possibilities for women that are embedded in this image (Rofel 1994a; Notar 1994), I move on nevertheless to show in concrete terms how this image in the popular music scene is male-dominated, and then to analyze other unfavorable implications that this image carries for women.

Together with the part on manhood, my discussion of the most prevalent female image of the 1990s lends much support to the widely held view that the post-Mao era, with its liberalization and free-market economy, have led to a comprehensive deterioration in women's sociopolitical and cultural status and role compared with the revolutionary era (Hooper 1984; Dalsimer and Nisnoff 1984; Robinson 1985; Honig and Hershatter 1988; Woo 1994; Notar 1994; Li Xiaojiang 1994; Dai 1995). However, the final sections of this chapter suggest that the last decade also saw some significant positive new trends in the status and position of women in the sociocultural sphere. In these sections I propose that a new feminine public voice, independent of the state, of men, and to a large extent also of the male-centric market, emerged in the early and mid-1990s in the popular music scene.

The emergence of independent women's voices in the post-revolutionary public sphere is not completely new, but it was mentioned so far only in connection with serious intellectual (and academic) literature (Duke 1989; Lu

1993; Barlow 1993; Gilmartin et al. 1994).[3] By contrast, when popular culture and electronic mass media such as television and film are studied, it is generally implied that women in these domains are either powerless, voiceless, and at times even nonexistent, or alternatively that they are unable to produce an independent feminine perspective.[4] Thus, the main contribution of chapter 3, taken as a whole, is in proposing that women's position and role in popular Chinese culture today is much more complex than what has usually been thought, and that autonomous feminist voices are not limited anymore to writings by intellectual women. As in the previous chapter, I argue that the emergence of these new independent women's voices in the popular music scene is intimately connected to the distinctive mass media involved in this domain, in this case cassettes and CDs.

NEGOTIATING GENDER IN POPULAR MUSIC CULTURE I: RECONSTRUCTING MANHOOD

Rock and Roll and the Post-Revolutionary Search for Masculinity

The masculine ethos of the revolutionary period did not mean that men were necessarily empowered during those three decades. Male artistic expressions since the mid-1980s, in fact, suggest that many men felt emasculated as a result of the oppressive political order brought about by the Communists. One of the earliest public artistic engagements with the issue of masculinity in post-revolutionary China is found in Zhang Xianliang's 1985 novel *Half of Man Is Woman (Nanren de yi ban shi nüren)*, in which the male writer not only reintroduced explicit sexuality into Chinese literature but also critically addressed issues of sexual repression, impotence, castration (mental and physical), and manhood. One of the most memorable statements in the book is delivered by a castrated horse, who says to the narrator: "I even wonder if your entire intellectual community isn't emasculated. If even 10 percent among you were virile men, our country would never have come to this sorry state" (Zhang Xianliang 1989, 129).

The masculinity crisis among Chinese male writers was reflected in many literary works since the mid-1980s in the fact that these works featured male protagonists full of virility and sexual power, who were obviously created to compensate for the sense of mental and physical impotence shared by those writers; as Dai Jinhua suggested with regard to *The Abandoned Capital (Fei du)*, a novel by the male writer Jia Pingwa: "It's a daydream, the psychological compensation of a man who is repressed both socially and sexually" (quoted in Zha 1995, 156). Another well-known literary work that exemplifies the post-revolutionary search for masculinity is Mo Yan's novel *Red Sorghum*, on which Zhang Yimou's famous 1987 film of the same title was based. I shall return to *Red Sorghum* later in this chapter.[5]

The voice of the repressed male trying to recover his masculinity is heard loud and clear in Chinese rock. Chinese rock has been studied by numerous scholars since the late 1980s, but little if anything has been written on its gender-related aspects. Two lines from the rap song "Say Say" *(Shuo shuo)* by the male rocker Zang Tianshuo provide a good starting point for the discussion of these aspects: "I want to read once more the *Three Kingdoms* and the *Water Margin*, to get a little bit of the feeling of the forefathers' manhood."[6] Zang's 1995 album *My Last Ten Years (Wo zhe shi nian)*, which I discuss in more detail in the next chapter, is a manifesto of masculinity. The manifesto opens with these statements, which appear in the first song in the album ("This Is What I Am"): "You cannot change my direction. . . . I have blood and I also have flesh, I have a knife and I also have a rifle. . . . [I am] very healthy . . . [and] no one should play the fool with me." These statements, together with Zang's many photos in the album, in which he is shown with an old-fashioned porter's shirt that leaves much of his healthy upper body exposed (see figure 4), constitute an explicit display of physical power and masculinity. Read against the lines from "Say Say" cited above, where the musician articulates his wish to "get a little bit of the feeling of the forefathers' manhood," this display of masculine power cannot escape being interpreted as the male musician's attempt to reconstruct or compensate for his repressed masculinity. The reconstruction uses not only the lyrics and photographs, but above all the music: the aggressive rock style (and rap in "Say Say") and the rough, uninhibited vocal delivery.

Zang's desire to achieve masculinity is closely tied, as is the case with many other rockers, to his rebellious attitude and the many expressions of dissent and resistance to the state that are found in his music. An example of this link is found again in "Say Say," where in addition to expressing his wish to "get a little bit of the forefathers' manhood," the rocker also attacks state officials for banning rock from television, and boldly states that "after all, it is we the people who should decide what is wrong and what is right." The juxtaposition of these two agendas is not incidental. It is obvious that Zang hopes to regain his sense of masculinity also through confronting and challenging the state, as if to break the psychological authority of the entity that has denied his masculinity.

In his book on Cui Jian and Chinese rock, Zhao Jianwei devotes lengthy

Figure 4.   Zang Tianshuo, *My Last Ten Years,* cassette cover. Courtesy of Zang Tianshuo.

sections to a discussion of sexuality and masculinity in China, and draws a direct link between the state and what he sees as the longstanding loss of masculinity affecting Chinese men and Chinese civilization in general. After accusing the "cannibalistic," "feudal" Confucian ideologies and practices of suppressing human desire and causing Chinese culture to turn into a "castrated culture" *(yan'ge wenhua)* (1992, 277–78), Zhao goes on to address in more concrete terms the issue of castration in the context of state politics:

> Beginning in the Zhou Dynasty, castration was listed as one of the ancient five forms of punishment. . . . The great historian and literati Sima Qian [Han Dynasty] was castrated because of his straightforward writing. The emperors of later successive dynasties followed this example and extended the use of castration to the punishment of all those who were found guilty in rebellion *(pan'ni)* or conspiracy. (278)[7]

It is in this context that Zang Tianshuo's bold criticism of the state in "Say Say," and his rebellious attitude in general, become so intimately linked to his attempt to gain and assert masculinity. It is also within this context that rock in China in general, whose essence according to many is "rebellion" *(pan'ni)*, gains its masculinity as a musical style and as a subculture. In other words, the fact that men in Chinese history have been castrated by the state because of their rebellious attitude implies that rockers in their resistance to the state are "real men," which is what Zhao Jianwei asserts. It is not surprising, therefore, that Zang Tianshuo chooses *Water Margin* as a model for masculinity, as this novel is about a group of outlaws and rebels, most of whom are men who fight the government.

The relationship between political resistance and masculinity is articulated in Cui Jian's "Opportunists" *(Toujifenzi)*, the song that the rocker dedicated to the hunger strikers in Tiananmen Square during the 1989 democracy movement and in which he called on them to carry on the struggle, to bring about change, and to demonstrate courage ("Oh . . . we have an opportunity, let's demonstrate our desires / oh . . . we have an opportunity, let's demonstrate our power"). Though this call is not gender-specific in its address, other lines in the song nevertheless reveal a clear male-centric attitude and suggest that Cui Jian is addressing only male demonstrators, as if the whole movement was a celebration of masculinity or a test of masculinity. The implication is that it is only men who are expected to demonstrate their desire and power, and that desire and power are the criteria for masculinity, as if women did not share these qualities. Three times in the song women are mentioned, but they are always the female other, referred to by the male-centric, objectifying word *guniang*, which means "girl." The "us" and the "you" in the song are both male. The female other is transformed into yet another challenge or test for manhood, very much like the state, and the struggle against the state is even compared at the end of the song to conquering a girl. It is by confronting both, Cui Jian's song implies, that masculinity can be gained:

> The truth is always in a distant place, girls are always beside you
> But when you face them you always compete with them for power . . .
> Friend, you are given an opportunity, have a try in handling affairs for
>   the first time
> Like when you are eighteen years old and you are given a girl

"Opportunists" supports Lee Feigon's suggestion that "the men in the student movement, though enlightened about many of the inequalities of Chinese society, were not particularly enlightened about the role of women in society," and that "in both the official and subversive acts of political theater performed in 1989, women were relegated for the most part to traditional kinds of supporting roles" (1994, 128). Feigon further notes that

> at a time when Chinese men have questioned their own virility as a
> result of their subordination to an oppressive authoritarian model . . .

the flaunting of masculine sexuality by Wu'er Kaixi and the other male student leaders may be interpreted as a political act, demonstrating their strength and independence from the restrictive values of the government. (129)

This argument, of course, could also be reversed to suggest that the whole political act was an attempt to reconstruct damaged masculinity.

Attempts to define and assert masculinity are abundant in Chinese rock. In the cover notes for the all-male heavy-metal band Tang Dynasty one finds the following statements:

If you can hear courage and power, this is because of their [the band members'] fearless character as northern men [*beifang hanzi*]. If you feel that you are watching the ancient gallant men and sword men, this is because they have a broad mind from growing up in the midst of a gigantic land.

To further construct the masculine image of the band members, the designers of the cover of the band's album specify under the photograph of each how tall he is. As all the band members happen to be relatively tall (over 1.80 meters), height becomes yet another means of constructing and asserting their masculinity. The cover of the album also features two red flags on which the band's name is printed, immediately invoking the flags used in wars in ancient times. The use of this militant, masculine icon further enhances the masculine image that the band tries to construct for itself, an image that makes use of the same motives that construct masculinity in Zang Tianshuo's album—namely, militarism, healthy physique, power, and courage, the last two of which are also used in Cui Jian's album. The attempt made by Chinese rockers to construct and assert their masculinity is also illustrated in the account given by Xue Ji, the author of another book on Chinese rock, on how the members of the rock band Black Panther chose their name. Xue writes: "The buddies thought that this kind of silent, bold and powerful, brave, fierce, and very masculine (*nanxinghua*) animal tallied very much with their own disposition" (1993, 42–43).

The fascination with the macho, Rambo-like, tough, masculine image among Chinese rockers seems to have been inspired, like their music, by Western culture. Although full of brave, great warriors, it is the refined, gentle, and restrained male scholar-official that Chinese culture traditionally, at least in the last millennium, identified as the ideal man. Rey Chow has suggested that "Chinese literary history has been a history of men who want to become women" (1993, 34), and in his essay on the construction of masculinity and femininity in Zhang Yimou's *Red Sorghum*, Wang Yuejin writes:

> Narratives of overblown masculine warriors outdone by feminine wits are worn-out subjects for historical/fictional cautionary tales. Historical and poetic narratives about Xiang Yu, the masculine warlord and the loser of the Chu-Han war, all seem to contain an implicit critique of his masculinity by celebrating his final rare moment of tenderness (a touch of femininity so rare in him) shown to his mistress when they are hemmed in by the surrounding enemy troops. (1989, 35)

Wang Yuejin further suggests, however, that this traditional preference for more delicate male heroes has changed more recently:

> In the early 1980s, the speculation on the past, on our cultural history and on the structure of Chinese mentality led to a radical change in taste. The intelligentsia awakened to the ideological implications of feminization, while the average theater-goer became fascinated by the charisma of the icon of "tough guys" in Japanese and Western movies. Suddenly there was the excruciating realization of a fundamental "lack." There was a "masculinity" anxiety, which culminated in a stage play: *In Search for Man.*[8] The once popular, delicate and "creamy" male stars lost the audience's favor: they even became despicable. (36–37)

The "lack" that Wang mentions is identified in concrete terms by Zhao Jianwei as mental and physical impotence or castration. After reviewing the history of castration in China in the last two thousand years, Zhao suggests that the solution lies in rock, that it is through rock that Chinese men and Chinese culture as a whole can regain their lost masculinity. For Zhao, rockers are the yearned-for "real men":

> The "hooligans" [*pizi*] who are engaged in rock music do not generally suffer from "character impotence" [*yangwei*]. They would rather "put the telescope on their own blind eyes, and will truthfully declare that they see nothing," and will not make an empty show of strength after masturbating, telling other people in groaning and moaning that they just slept with a girl. (1992, 37)

Zhao's promotion of rock is closely tied to his own and rockers' negation of traditional values like self-restraint, obedience, suppression of the individual self and his(/her) sexual desires, values that were celebrated under the Confucian order and are still celebrated today in communist China. The association of rock, on the one hand, with rebellion, power, freedom, individuality, boldness, straightforwardness, and truthfulness, and its equation, on the other hand, with masculinity, implies that all the former qualities are characteristics of masculinity. It equally implies that the negative past is feminine. Discussing Cui Jian's performance in Chengdu (Sichuan Province), Zhao refers to the reputation of the people of this city as refined *(wenya)* and civilized *(wenming)*, and as people who do not like intense and stirring things and prefer the sweet lyrical pop songs from Hong Kong and Taiwan. This reputation conforms, of course, to traditional Confucian ideals and, not surprisingly, is mocked by Zhao, who then suggests that Cui Jian will be able to liberate the men in Chengdu from their psychological impotence and by implication will also liberate China from its inferior femininity:

> Although a certain environment can often cause mental impotence in people, it cannot strangle their sexual ability, just like a bumpkin male, you just need to give him a woman and he will know what to do without any help. Of course, arriving here, Cui Jian is absolutely not going to give anyone a woman, but rather a real man. Because in China, the flourishing of *yin* [femininity] and the waning of *yang* [masculinity] [*yin sheng yang shuai*] have already brought Chinese men to a position where they have no place to hide their shame. (1992, 65)

Despite attempting at several points in his book to argue that rock equally liberates both men and women from both the traditional and the communist oppressive orders, Zhao nevertheless objectifies women, turning them often into sex objects, and often seems to compensate for his own sense of loss of masculinity through chauvinistic and misogynistic discourse. In Zhao's book, women and femininity represent all the negative qualities and values from which he, like many rockers and male writers today in China, is trying to liberate himself. Lu Tonglin has offered the following explanation for the phenomenon:

> The Chinese people's resentment of the communist regime is very often rearticulated by men as their resentment of women's equal rights, as if Chinese men had been disempowered by women's empowerment. (1993, 8)

An example of Lu's explanation is found in Cui Jian's "Opportunists," from which I quoted earlier, in which the struggle against the party-state is compared to a power struggle against women. The two equally become rivals for the male self, who desires to overcome and conquer both.

There are many examples of an objectification of women in Chinese rock. In many rock songs, women are an abstract entity, devoid of subjectivity, the *guniang* other. One such example is found in a song entitled "Pretty Girl" *(Guniang piaoliang)* by the famous male rocker He Yong:

PRETTY GIRL
(lyrics, music, and performance by He Yong)

Girl girl, you are pretty pretty . . .
You say you want a car, you say you want a Western-style house . . .
I only have a squeaking bed
I can take you on my bicycle to see the sunset
My tongue is like tasty delicacies for you to taste
I have a new story that I want to tell you . . .
You say this story is not a sausage
I know that this sunset cannot wrap your body . . .
You already have a car, you already live in a Western-style home
You hold a baby in your arms and I still think about you
Should I have a girlfriend or should I raise a dog?

In this song He Yong criticizes his ex-girlfriend—whom he depicts as one who cares only about having a car and a house, and about being beautiful—for being materialist and disloyal, lacking in feeling, demanding, and greedy, as well as for her inability to appreciate his spirituality and sincere love. When I asked one young woman associated with a circle of rockers how she felt about the song, and specifically about its last line, she replied that she agrees completely with He Yong's criticism: "There really is this kind of women today who think only about money and being beautiful, and they deserve to be cursed," she suggested to me. The post-revolutionary popular female image that stresses outer appearance and sexuality has been widely acknowledged in recent literature about China and has often been interpreted by feminist scholars as the manifestation of yet another form of subjugation or subordination of women, who are now expected to be beauties, but still lack control over their bodies (see, for example, Honig and Hershatter 1988, 51, 67, 335).[9] It could be argued that He Yong's song is another feminist critique that attacks what can be seen as the new post-revolutionary enslavement of women, in which they are forced to assume the traditional role of the beauty. Yet despite the reaction of this particular young woman, I interpret it rather as an extreme misogynist expression, in which He Yong is trying to construct his individuality and masculinity by way of structural opposition through the undoing of women. Even though most of the lyrics in "Pretty Girl" talk about one particular girl, He Yong leaves the listener with the impression that all girls are bad after stating that it is perhaps better to raise a dog than to establish relationships with any of them. The criticism is not of women who are forced to become something other than themselves, but rather of a set of intrinsic qualities, such as materialism, greediness, disloyalty, and the inability to feel true love, that, He Yong suggests, characterize women in general.

Materialism is one of the main targets for attack in rock, a style that celebrates, in addition to power and courage, lofty ideals, true feelings, and spirituality. These cannot be separated from the masculine image that rockers celebrate. My reading of He Yong's song also draws upon the fact that "Pretty Girl" is not the only song in contemporary Chinese rock that essentializes women as materialistic in order to articulate the spirituality and masculinity of the male self, as if "femininity and masculinity exist in an opposition-structural relationship" (Zhu 1993, 126). A more famous early example of an attempt to assert masculinity through the negation or undoing of women is found in Cui Jian's most famous song, "Having Nothing" *(Yiwusuoyou)*, in which the male self is repeatedly turned down by the female other, who keeps laughing at him for having nothing despite his true love and his willingness to give her everything he has:

> I have endlessly asked when you will go with me
> But you always laugh at me having nothing
> I want to give you my aspirations and also my freedom
> But you always laugh at me having nothing . . .

Like Cui Jian, He Yong is ultimately engaged in constructing his own self-image rather than in discussing women, or even his relationship with them. In both cases, the female other is mentioned only to be negated, in order to articulate the masculinity of the male self and to assert his superiority. "Having Nothing" has a happy masculine ending when the idealism of the male self defeats the materialism of the female other, a victory that further enhances the superior power of masculinity: "This time your hand is shaking, this time your tears flow / Can it be that you are telling me you love me having nothing?"

Women are not, however, always negated in rock songs. There are times when they are also featured as desired objects that help to construct and articulate male desire. After all, desire is in itself, as Cui Jian's "Opportunists" suggests, masculine. An example of such a treatment of women is found in "The Beautiful Mountain of Girls" *(Meili de guniang shan)* by Zang Tianshuo:

THE BEAUTIFUL MOUNTAIN OF GIRLS
(lyrics, music, and performance by Zang Tianshuo)

> A long, long time ago
> There were three hundred very honest big men
> They heard that in the very distant south

There was a beautiful mountain of women . . .
The three hundred big men bid farewell to their fellow townsmen
They will surely find the beautiful mountain of women . . .
We still have to walk . . .
Time cannot change the aspiration for happiness
No matter how difficult is the way . . .
The three hundred big men kneeled down on the ground
Raising their heads toward the blue sky
We only wish to find beauty
Why do we need to face so many difficulties . . .
The blue sky . . . said: the mountain of girls is not far at all
They should be right next to you . . .

This song may appear at first glance to carry a universal message—namely, that good can be found right next to us and that people should not look for it far away. But again, although in the legend-like story there are male heroes and female heroes, the story and its message turn out to be yet another androcentric expression. The musician's subjective self becomes identified with the male heroes in the story (referred to as "big men"), whereas the female heroes serve as purely physical objects—denied any subjectivity, any nonphysical quality and voice—which are used simply to enhance the masculinity of the big men—and Zang Tianshuo—by articulating their/his desire.

Lu Tonglin has suggested that the "searchers for masculinity [today in China] use women as objects—onto which to project a 'self' largely predicated on Western humanism and individualism. On the other hand, they show nostalgia for a premodern time when Chinese women were still kept in 'their places'" (1993, 9). This point helps to explain why Zang Tianshuo chooses to position his ideal men and women and construct his masculinity in the past. The past offers a clear-cut differentiation, which is looked for today in China by both men and women. As is the case in "The Love of the Boat Tower," which is also positioned in a traditional setting and whose title at least suggests that it is also told from an androcentric point of view, the essential distinguishing factor between the male subject/self and the female object/other in Zang's story is that the former is active while the latter is passive. One finds a similar positioning of men and women in the past also in Tang Dynasty's best-known hit, "Returning in Dream to the Tang Dynasty" *(Meng hui Tang chao)*, in which the traditional image of men plowing and women weaving *(nan geng nü zhi)* is invoked by the group as part of their poetic journey to the desired past. A closer look at the song reveals that this desired past is male-dominated, as it is associated with a masculine, militant heroism. The dream of returning to the Tang Dynasty thus is not only a dream about a time when China was strong and rich (see the next chapter), but equally a dream about a desired, lost masculinity. This aspect of the song is enhanced by the repeated references in the song to wine and drinking, which, as Wang Yuejin notes (1989, 38), are closely associated in Chinese texts with the attainment of masculinity.

The female images that are constructed in Chinese rock are not limited to weavers, materialist creatures, or passive beauties, the object of male desire. In the following song by Cui Jian, entitled "Flower-House Girl" *(Huafang guniang)*, which was hailed as the song that introduced sexuality into the post-revolutionary Chinese pop scene, the musician constructs a female image that is more powerful than himself:

FLOWER-HOUSE GIRL
(lyrics, music, and performance by Cui Jian)

> . . . You asked me where do I want to go, I pointed in the direction of
>   the ocean . . .
> You brought me inside your flower-house
> I couldn't escape the enchanting fragrance of the flowers
> Without noticing I lost, *ao* . . . direction . . .
> Without noticing I have turned out to be, *ao* . . . like a flower . . .
> You want me to stay in this place, you want me to be like the others . . .
> I want to return to the old place, I want to walk on the old road
> But I'm fully aware that I'm already unable to leave you, *ao* . . . girl

The reference to sexuality in "Flower-House Girl" in the lines "You brought me inside your flower-house / I couldn't escape the enchanting fragrance of the flowers / Without noticing I lost, *ao* . . . direction," may seem subtle to the average Westerner. But in the context of the puritanical discourse that prevailed in China in the mid- and late 1980s these lines were a breakthrough. Though Cui Jian uses the traditional metaphor of flowers to invoke sexuality, he nevertheless uses it in a straightforward manner that alludes explicitly to sexual intercourse. Thus, on the one hand, "Flower-House Girl" celebrates an intoxicating physical union between a man and a woman that is initiated by the latter, and in the context of which the male self is depicted as completely passive and literally silent, whereas the female other is depicted as active and powerful. But simultaneously, despite the affirmation of sexuality and its intoxicating pleasures, Cui Jian suggests that the power that the female other exerts on him has turned him into a victim. The female other is a static creature who uses her sexuality to domesticate the dynamic male self. The male self becomes a captive who loses his individuality and freedom. He loses his direction, unable to escape and reach the ocean, and is forced to stay and become "like the others."

"Flower-House Girl" cannot escape invoking another song by Cui Jian, called "A Piece of Red Cloth," which I discuss in detail in the next chapter, in which the rocker articulates a powerful criticism of the subjugation of the individual self by the Communist Party. In both songs the self is depicted as a powerless captive who loses his individuality and freedom. In both he is intoxicated and paralyzed by a powerful force that makes him completely passive. The relationship between the songs is also suggested through the use in both of the line "you asked me where do I want to go," which in both cases appears in the context of a state of captivity and disempowerment. Thus, like "Opportunists," the relationship between "Flower-House Girl" and "A Piece of Red Cloth" establishes a parallel between the state and the female other, where the two equally oppress the individuality and freedom of the male self.

Cui Jian's masculinity is articulated in "Flower-House Girl" through his pursuit of nonconformist individuality, which is manifested in being and wanting to be different "from the others" and in his pursuit of freedom, which includes among other things his unwillingness to be committed to any woman and to stay in one place. Similar to the way He Yong asserts his masculinity in "Pretty Girl," Cui Jian articulates his masculinity through the construction of a structural opposition between himself and the female other who wishes to domesticate him and make him like the others. Like He Yong, Cui Jian also articulates his masculinity through a bold, straightforward reference to sexuality. Despite his passivity in the song, it is he, after all, who speaks boldly about sexuality, not the female other, a fact that makes him a man.

The search for the "real man" *(nanzihan)* in Chinese rock is revealed also in sound and performance. Chinese rock follows Western rock in both sound and performance style, yet it is associated almost exclusively with men, and its unique sonic and performance-related stylistic features are perceived almost as synonymous with masculinity. In a recent encyclopedia on Chinese and Western pop, after noting that Cui Jian's "Having Nothing" introduced into Chinese music "straightforwardness" *(haoshuang)* and the possibility of "shouting oneself hoarse" *(shengsi lijie),* the author adds:

> In "Having Nothing" . . . the yearning of the "search for the real man" in Chinese artistic circles has finally found something to depend upon. The firmness, powerfulness, and forcefulness of straightforwardness were let out thoroughly. (Yang Xiaolu and Zhang Zhentao 1990, 369)

The characteristic features of rock—a fast tempo, an accentuated, forceful, stirring beat and danceable rhythms, loudness and an aggressive, noisy

quality—as well as its general aesthetics of roughness, force, straightforwardness, and unrestraint, are accepted by many Chinese as symbols of
masculinity even when found in other styles. For example, one mainstream song called "Boys" (Nanhai; lyrics by Wang Xiaoling, music by
Gu Jianfen), which was performed in 1988 in CCTV's annual Spring Festival Party[10] (Yang Xiaolu and Zhang Zhentao 1990, 388), used many of
the musical characteristics of rock to construct a masculine sonic image. In the short discussion of the song in the 1990 pop encyclopedia from
which the citation above is taken, the author writes that the use of syn-
copation in the song provides a feel of rock, that the song creates a sense
of wildness, roughness, and unrestraint, and uses large leaps and fast
tempo, and that all of these characteristics are masculine. The second line
in "Boys"—"boys speak in a husky, loud voice"—further illustrates the
association of sonic roughness and high volume, and by extension also uninhibitedness, with masculinity. It is in this context that the obvious trend
among rockers during the late 1980s and early 1990s to subscribe, within
the wide spectrum of musical expressions offered by Western rock, to a
rather limited range that highlights extreme loudness, forcefulness, and
roughness of sound can be interpreted as linked to their attempt to assert
and project masculinity. Since uninhibitedness, wildness, and roughness
are associated with masculinity, rockers' hippie-like appearance and carefree behavior on stage, which manifests itself in dancing, shouting, and
getting out of control, could similarly be seen as yet another means to articulate masculinity. Masculinity is also articulated among rockers through
similar everyday behavior, which can generally be described as more
coarse, straightforward, and even vulgar compared with the common
behavior of people in China. Such behavior, which constitutes an important characteristic of the rock subculture, also reflects the general disgust
among rockers with traditional modes of behavior, which stress self-
control and refinement.

Although I did not conduct comprehensive, systematic surveys, it was
obvious to me that males were more generally favorable toward rock than
females were.[11] When asked about the music they liked the most, men often pointed specifically to rock as their favorite style and often mentioned
names of particular domestic and foreign rock bands. Women, by contrast,
rarely mentioned either rock in general or a rocker or rock band in particular when asked about their favorite musical style, songs, and musicians.
Thus it became clear to me that young men establish their sense of masculinity through the patronization of rock.

With such a close association between rock and masculinity, it is not surprising that there were very few female rockers in China in the mid-1990s. With few exceptions—the most important of which is the all-female rock band Cobra, which as noted earlier is also referred to as the Female Rock Band, a name that acknowledges the uniqueness of the phenomenon—rock musicians in China in the mid-1990s were almost all male. The same is also true for the rock subculture in general. In gatherings of the "rock circle" *(yaogunquan)* that I attended, the few women who were present were associated with men who attended the gathering and were conspicuously silent and detached, as if not in their own territory. When I asked the music critic Huang Liaoyuan why women do not participate in Chinese rock, he replied that "rock is very crazy and unbridled *(fengkuang)*, and because women in China are more reserved *(hanxu)*, it is only natural that they do not participate" (Huang Liaoyuan, interview with the author, Beijing, 22 June 1996). These details suggest once more that rock in China is about masculinity at least as much as it is about making music.

The absence of women from rock could be seen as a result of their own rejection of their previous masculinization. But this is only part of the story. Rock bands on the mainland today in fact celebrate a brotherhood that consciously excludes women, not unlike male-exclusive clubs or fraternities.[12] One young woman with whom I spoke, who used to spend time with rockers, referred to them as "chauvinists," while the members of Cobra are quoted as saying: "Chinese people traditionally don't think women can achieve anything . . . [and] a lot of men who play rock-and-roll despise us and say there's no way we'll play well" (Tyson 1991).

This is not to say, however, that male rockers do not have their female fans who, like male fans, consider Chinese rockers to be the "ideal men." The young woman mentioned earlier, who enthusiastically supported He Yong's misogynistic criticism of women in his "Pretty Girl," is one good example.

Rock, Xibeifeng, *Masculinity, Northern Chauvinism, and Chinese Nationalism*

The search for masculinity among Chinese male artists, which started in the early and mid-1980s, was closely related to the collective Root-Seeking cultural movement *(xungen)* that took place around that time. Similar to the statements by Zhao Jianwei that I quoted earlier, the prevalent notion among Root-Seeking artists, who were predominantly male, was that China as a whole had lost its virility due to longstanding political and cultural oppression, and that there was an urgent need to revitalize it and revive its masculinity. The personal search for masculinity among Chinese artists, therefore, was from its very inception inseparable from a collective nationalistic agenda. Thus the masculine, vulgar male protagonist in Mo Yan's novel *Red Sorghum*, one of the most representative works of the movement, not only represented Mo Yan's personal desired image of his own masculinity, but also that of China as a whole.

The Root-Seeking cultural movement was closely tied to China's opening to the world, especially to the West, and the disappointing realization that China was not the strong, rich nation that people had been made to believe it was during the revolutionary period. The new search for personal and collective masculinity was thus also closely tied to the recognition of China's economic, technological, and cultural backwardness and the strong sense of inferiority that was shared by many who perceived China's position vis-à-vis the West as metaphorically feminine. The cultural colonization of China by the West in the early and mid-1980s, initially through Taiwan and Hong Kong but later more directly, further contributed to this sense of emasculation. This is, of course, not the first time in which the encounter with the West caused Chinese to see their country as feminine. Such a view had its roots at least a century earlier during the first and most traumatic encounter with the modern West (and Japan). This paragraph, taken from the preface to a popular knight-errant bestseller from the 1930s, provides an early example of this notion of China as feminine:

> It's a pity indeed that this hundred-times refined steel has become soft enough to twist around your little finger. An effeminacy has obscured the martial spirit of our ancestors and a gloomy darkness has descended upon us until, today, we bow and scrape before foreign cavalries. Foreign insult is pervasive. (Quoted in Link 1981, 14)

Against this background, it was not surprising that the earliest musical attempt to assert mainland cultural independence and hegemony following the renewed encounter with the West subscribed to a masculine sonic image. The *xibeifeng* fever (Northwest Wind), which swept China between 1986 and 1989 and was the musical manifestation of the Root-Seeking movement, was another manifestation of the movement's search for masculinity. In terms of China versus the West, the style was quite ambivalent. Through its adoption of the strong beat of Western disco/rock music, because of which it was also referred to as *xibei* rock *(xibei yaogun)*, it articulated the yearning in China for modernity, and in a sense its aspiration to become like the West. But at the same time, through its adoption of the vocal style and melodic characteristics associated with the rural area of northern Shaanxi

Province, one of the most backward but historically significant geographical areas in China, the style simultaneously articulated its Chineseness, or in other words, its independence from the West. There is much less ambivalence in this style, however, if we examine its hybrid character in the context of gender. This is because the common feature of the otherwise different musical materials combined in the style is their association with masculinity.

Two of the most important *xibeifeng* songs articulate male experience. One of these songs, Cui Jian's "Having Nothing," was credited with initiating the style and embodied its link to rock, being seen by many as both China's first *xibeifeng* song and its first rock song. The other song is "Young Sister Go Boldly Forward," which was introduced in Zhang Yimou's 1987 cinematic adaptation of Mo Yan's *Red Sorghum*. The androcentric nature of this latter song is inseparable from the masculine image of the protagonist in the film, the half-naked, well-built, rough, wild, and uninhibited porter, who shouts the song while running, after wildly making love to the female protagonist in the film, to whom he addresses the song. Although most other *xibeifeng* songs are not gender-specific in their lyrics or associated with a particular male performer, they are nonetheless still considered masculine, mainly because of their music. Like rock, *xibeifeng* songs celebrated loud, yelling, unconstrained deep vocal delivery, rough sound (both vocal and instrumental), a forceful, fast rhythm, and an aggressive and agitated bass line. These elements clearly identified the style as masculine despite the fact that many of the songs in this style were sung by female singers. As for these female singers, they in a sense assumed once again the masculine image that their elder sisters, the Iron Girls of the Cultural Revolution, had assumed two decades earlier.

The history of popular music on the mainland is often described by Chinese musicologists and music critics in terms of *yin* and *yang*, two abstract categories that may mean various things but which in this discourse of popular music often imply femininity and masculinity, respectively. Earlier I cited Jin Zhaojun's characterization of the music of the Cultural Revolution as "lacking in *yin* and abundant in *yang*." By contrast, the music scene on the mainland in the first few years following the reforms, when China was flooded by soft, sentimental songs from Hong Kong and Taiwan, has been characterized by Jin as "abundant in *yin* and lacking in *yang*" (1988). Consistent with his use of gendered terminology to describe the stylistic changes in the popular music scene, Jin implies in his 1988 article on the *xibeifeng* fad, from which the last quotation is taken, that this style is a revival of masculine forces. A more concrete link between the abstract forces of *yin* and *yang* on the one hand and femininity and masculinity on the other is suggested by Ling Ruilan, the editor of a 1994 compilation of popular songs. Ling writes:

> Around 1985 . . . female pop stars outnumbered male singers. The leap in number of male pop stars took place after the appearance of *xibei* rock, because male singers are qualified with the masculine *(yang gang)* temperament and dynamics required by the "strength songs." So after 1986 the number of male singers increased day by day, everywhere there was their husky, yelling singing. (1994, 13)

For many on the mainland, *xibeifeng* signified the return of mainland creativity and cultural independence after almost a decade in which it was flooded by "feminine" songs from Hong Kong and Taiwan. Hong Kong and Taiwan thus became the feminine other, whereas the new *xibeifeng* songs came to represent the masculinity of the mainland self. The creativity and cultural independence of the mainland, which *xibeifeng* came to represent, were associated with masculinity. Similarly, the roots, or Chinese essence, which these folksy songs symbolized were perceived by implication as synonymous with masculinity. All this suggests that in the context of the Root-Seeking movement and the *xibeifeng* fad women and femininity were once again relegated to the margins of Chinese history and culture.[13]

Like the Root-Seeking movement, the search for masculinity in Chinese rock has often gone beyond the personal. Concentrated mainly in Beijing, rockers often view southern China as more feminine and northern China as more masculine. It is not surprising, therefore, that the cover notes in Tang Dynasty's album asserting the masculinity of the band members specify that they are "northern men" *(beifang hanzi)*, and that the "big men" in Zang Tianshuo's "The Beautiful Mountain of Girls" need to go southward to find their desired girls. The association of masculinity with northern China was also implied in the *xibeifeng* style, which drew upon northern musical style rather than southern style, and whose lyrics, too, referred to the yellow earth of the north. The fact that rock music is found mainly in the north (Beijing) is viewed by many as yet another affirmation of its masculinity vis-à-vis the south. The emphasis on the close association between rock music, *xibeifeng*, and northern China could certainly be seen as one manifestation of the revival of different regional cultures in China after decades in which a single, homogenous national mass culture suppressed much of the country's regional diversity.

However, it is nationalism that still predominates in rock and in *xibeifeng*. I suggested earlier that rockers articulate their masculinity, among other ways, through challenging the state. Somewhat paradoxically, however, they simultaneously promote and assert their masculinity through linking themselves with the same state. *Gangtai* music is often mocked by rockers and others in ways that imply its femininity. Jin Zhaojun, for example, refers to *gangtai* music as "yin rou," or feminine and soft (1991), and contrasts it with Chinese rock. The music critic Song Wei, writing about the visit of the Chinese Mongolian musician Teng Ge'er to Taiwan, referred to the latter's music as "yang gang," or masculine and firm, and contrasted his songs with the "cotton candy" *(mianhuatang)* and "sentimental/soft" *(ruan mianmian)* love songs of Taiwan (1992, 4). The specific words used by Song to describe Taiwanese music and the general context — that is, contrasting it with Teng Ge'er's masculinity — implies the negative femininity of Taiwanese pop music, and by extension of Taiwan as a whole. Another example of mainland chauvinism and the association of *gangtai* music with inferior femininity was mentioned earlier in the quotation from Zhao Jianwei's report on Cui Jian's concert in Chengdu. Zhao contrasts the masculinity of Cui Jian, to whom he refers as "real man" *(zhenzheng de nanren),* with the traditional aesthetics of the people of Chengdu. The argument suggests that their aesthetics of "abundant *yin* and lacking *yang*" "caused Chinese men to have no place to hide" and is equal to "impotence." The inferiority, impotence, and femininity of music from Taiwan and Hong Kong is implied in Zhao's preceding statement that the people of Chengdu like *gangtai* music and not rock (1992, 65).

As in the case of the *xibeifeng* fever, the assertions of masculinity in Chinese rock are closely linked to expressions of patriotism and nationalism. The cover notes in Tang Dynasty's album, for example, end with several lines in bold print: "If you hear a kind of Chinese self-confidence, that is because they [the band members] are doing something that you originally thought only Westerners can do." These lines cannot be separated from the opening lines of the same notes: "If you can hear courage and power, that is because of their fearless character as northern men." The close link between Tang Dynasty's assertion of masculinity and their articulation of nationalistic sentiments (their "Chinese self-confidence" and challenge to Western superiority) illustrates the impact that world politics have on concepts of manhood in China. The paragraph suggests that doing something that people heretofore thought "only Westerners can do," which is to perform heavy-metal rock, is yet another justification for the band's claim to masculinity. Somewhat paradoxically, however, the implication is that if to be like Westerners means to be men, then to be Chinese means to be feminine. The cover notes on Tang Dynasty's album provide a vivid illustration of the point that the widespread sense of the loss of masculinity among Chinese male artists in the post-revolutionary period cannot be separated from the (re)discovery of Chinese inferiority/femininity vis-à-vis the West. It is against this background that the relationship between masculinity and rock becomes even clearer. Rock is masculine because it is Western and modern. Chinese rockers, however, did not invent the association between rock and masculinity, because, after all, rock has often been associated with men and masculinity also in the West. This point implies that rock was not only an important vehicle used to assert masculinity but also an inspiring force that provided Chinese rockers with a particular model of masculinity.

Mainstream Pop and the Neotraditional Mode of Manhood

Wang Yuejin's suggestions that "the once-popular, delicate and 'creamy' male stars lost the [Chinese] audience's favor . . . [and] became despicable" and that the new Western-inspired macho male role model is taking over Chinese culture (1989, 36–37) are either explicitly stated or implied in most of the literature on masculinity in post-Mao China (Zhang Yingjin 1990; Louie 1991, 1992; Louie and Edwards 1994; Zhu 1993; Zhong 1994, 2000). These suggestions, however, were made in the late 1980s, and much of the literature published subsequently deals primarily with the 1980s too. I propose here that preferences in the domain of gender shifted more recently, and since at least the mid-1990s the macho type of manhood has lost much of its past appeal and there has been a return to the more traditional type of soft and delicate manhood, which, as stated earlier, many in both the West and China today see as a "feminized" type of manhood. I do not mean to imply that the search for the contemporary Western "macho man" is dead. Zang Tianshuo's 1995 album offers a vivid illustration of the continuation of this search. Rather, I propose that, as in many other domains, the cultural landscape in China has become more complex and pluralistic in the 1990s also where images of manhood are concerned. As the masculine *xibeifeng* fad and the emerging popularity of rock in the late 1980s certainly lent support to Wang Yuejin's observations, the loss of appeal of the macho image, which has also been noted by several film scholars in relation to film (Larson 1997; Dai 1999, 200–2),[14] has revealed itself in the popular music scene most forcefully in the decline of these two styles. In positive terms, the decline of the macho image is evident in the fact that much of mainstream music today celebrates the same traditional male image that Wang characterized in 1989 as "delicate and 'creamy.'"

The idea of the traditional male image being feminized needs some qualification here. As already noted, the delicate male image has a long history in China, and during much of Chinese history this ideal of manhood dominated Chinese culture. This ideal often embodied all the qualities associated with *wen* in the context of the *wen-wu* divide—namely, civility, mildness, literacy, and intellectual and fine art capabilities, as opposed to the physical strength and military prowess that constitute *wu*. In a 1994 article entitled "Chinese Masculinity: Theorizing *Wen* and *Wu*," Kam Louie and Louise Edwards propose that "Western paradigms of masculinity are . . . inappropriate to the Chinese case and their application could only serve to prove that Chinese men are 'not quite real men' because they fail the Western test of masculinity" (1994, 138). Louie and Edwards, in other words, warn against naturalizing Western perceptions and practices of masculinity and against the tendency to perceive Chinese men as feminized or neutered. They argue that the categories of *wen* and *wu* are applicable traditionally only to men, that these categories constitute two different types of masculinity, and that they are equally masculine: "Chinese masculinity . . . can comprise both *wen* and *wu*, with the result that a scholar is considered to be no less masculine than a soldier" (1994, 139–40). Louie and Edwards conclude, among other things, that men in China actually have available to them "a broader range of notions of self than would be available to a Western male" (140).

Indeed, the traditional delicate, *wen* type of masculinity, which experienced a resurgence during the 1990s, does not necessarily, either today or in the past, imply femininity. Nevertheless this mode of manhood cannot be entirely divorced from femininity either. This is especially so in the modern context, since after all China was greatly influenced by Western paradigms of masculinity. The quotation from the preface to the knight-errant story from the 1930s cited earlier, the Maoist body culture, and the writings of Zhang Xianliang, Sun Longji, and Zhao Jianwei all attest to the fact that Chinese perceptions of masculinity in contemporary Chinese culture cannot be separated from Western ones. Zhang, Sun, Zhao, and the many others who think like them certainly are not less Chinese than their predecessors, and we should not ignore their voices. Moreover, the *wen* type of manhood could not be completely divorced from femininity in the traditional context either. It is true that this type, personified by the scholar-artist-official, had a broad range of meanings that did not necessarily include femininity, but conscious references to femininity nevertheless often did constitute part of the *wen* male experience, and no less importantly, femininity, at least as an abstract idea, was not necessarily considered to be inferior. So strong was the desire among educated male writers and artists to articulate qualities traditionally associated with femininity that they often assumed the role of a woman in their art. As Wang Yuejin observes, "The 'beautiful woman and fragrant plant' is a clichéd classical poetic figure that ancient poets, mostly male, identified with to embody their yearning for spiritual purity and loyalty" (1989, 35). Wang further points to "the persistence of the Chinese poetic convention of a male poet, figured in his poems as a dramatic persona [of a] sentimental woman, who waits and longs for her lover's arrival after an overdue time, or the return from a long journey" (35). With this background in mind, let us now return to our discussion of the neotraditional model of manhood in the popular music scene today, and the reasons for its enhanced revival since the early and mid-1990s.

"I Don't Dare to Face This Love That Gradually Goes Away" *(Bu gan miandui zhe jianjian yuan qu de ai)* is representative of the large body of mainstream songs that celebrate the neotraditional model of manhood. The song is performed by the male singer Mao Ning:

I DON'T DARE TO FACE THIS LOVE THAT GRADUALLY GOES AWAY
(no attribution of lyrics and music; performance by the male singer Mao Ning)

Oh Helen, don't cry . . .
I don't understand what you once said
That we do not have a future
I don't dare to face this love that gradually goes away
Although at night my heart yearns for you in sorrow . . .
But I will be still waiting for you to return

Mao Ning's song constructs the image of a male who obviously assumes qualities that are traditionally regarded in both the West and China as essentially feminine: he is so sentimental, fragile, passive, and gentle that he does not even dare to face his lost love. The parallel between this image and the traditional practices and conceptions of male writers who want to become women is also obvious. The feminization of the male persona in the song is enhanced by the fact that he is the one who is being deserted, the one who waits, and the one with the broken heart who yearns at night for the beloved who left. The reversal of the traditional gender roles in this song applies to some extent also to the female other. Though she is the one who cries, she is nevertheless the one who had control over the relationship and who ended it and left, whereas the male self is left waiting for her to return. This inversion is at the core of many mainstream *gangtai* and mainland songs sung by male singers. Similarly, in "Let's Wait Awhile Before Saying Goodbye" *(Wan xie fenshou;* no attribution), Mao Ning sings: "Oh! You are not going to stay here for long, I have a kind of feeling that . . . you will . . . leave soon . . . could you wait a little?"[15] Again, it is the female other who comes and goes, leaving the static and powerless male self to beg and yearn with a broken heart.

The feminization of the male character in these mainstream songs is reinforced through the music. Male singers perform such songs with a sweet voice, in a restrained, soft singing style, which often includes a whisperlike delivery, and sometimes a falsetto voice. This style of singing started to reappear on the mainland pop scene in the 1980s, but at the time most disliked it, largely because of the persistence of the masculine, militant Maoist ethos. An example of this distaste can be found in an essay on the history of popular music in China by the musicologist Liang Maochun, who came of age in the late 1950s. After referring to Yan Hua, a male pop star from the "old Shanghai" period, whose voice he describes as "feminine" *(nü li nü qi)*, Liang Maochun writes: "Several male singers and performers today in China also often use this 'sissyish singing *(niangniang qiang)'* which causes one to feel very uncomfortable. This is an old illness that was inherited from the 1930s" (1988, 33).

Like the singing, the style of the music in these songs is soft, the beat is gentle, and the tempo ranges from very slow to moderate. The songs have sweet melodies, and the lines are sung in legato. Words are pronounced with the clarity *(xini)* that has been traditionally associated with women. This feminine, coquettish, sweet flavor is further enhanced by use of soft vibratos, slides, yodeling ornamentation, and the doubling of words in the lyrics. The instrumental accompaniment, too, is sweet and gentle, usually featuring a restrained, subdued synthesizer, a soft electric bass, and light percussion accompaniment, to which acoustic guitars and violins are often added. In addition, many of the songs are sung in duet with a female singer who, despite the reversal that I just mentioned, sings in a style similar to that used by the male singer, thus enforcing the song's overall feminine flavor.

The popularity of Mao Ning's songs derives, in part at least, from the traditional conceptions of *wen* and *ya* (refinement). These help to explain why rock-and-roll has always been considered by many, especially in Shanghai and Guangzhou, where it enjoyed considerably less popularity than in Beijing, as *"su"* or *"tu,"* meaning "vulgar," and "unrefined" or "countrified," respectively. In other words, the rejection of rock and the new model of manhood it celebrated was inspired by the same traditional aesthetics and values that rockers have been trying with limited success to turn upside down: that is, to turn the traditionally idealized refinement *(wen* and *ya)* into an inferior femininity.

As with the different opinions about rock, while for some the macho protagonist in Zhang Yimou's *Red Sorghum* represented the embodiment of a desired lost masculinity, there were others who accused the film of being "uncivilized," "savage," and "crude." Wang Yuejin explains:

> Bluntly addressing issues of desire (not tender love) and sexuality (not marital bliss), the film transgresses a lot of boundaries and codes: the deep-rooted Confucian ethical and moral codes of sobriety and decorum, the ingrained artistic codes of representation favoring strategies of concealment and restraint and an aesthetic taste which exalts emotional delicacy and refinement. (1989, 33)

Indeed, mainstream pop stars, like Mao Ning, who assume the refined male image seldom express physical desire and seldom make explicit reference to sexuality. The body, in fact, becomes in their songs almost irrelevant. This treatment of the body manifests itself, among other ways, in the fact that the male singers who sing such songs rarely move on stage. The love in these songs is most often spiritual, with spiritual yearnings being the main theme. The fact that these yearnings are never fulfilled also helps to establish the powerlessness and effeminacy of the male persona in these songs.

The deep-rooted Confucian codes of refinement, restraint, and concealment, and the delicate type of manhood that is intimately linked with them, extend in popular music culture well beyond professional male singers who assume an effeminate male persona in their songs. These codes, together with this type of manhood, are probably enacted by millions every day in karaoke singing in work units, in karaoke bars, in private homes, in the streets, and elsewhere. And if earlier I suggested that the popularity of karaoke cannot be separated from the popularity of mainstream pop music, with its sweet melodies, soft rhythms, moderate and restrained aesthetics, then I also suggest now that it cannot be separated either from the traditional mode of manhood. Love songs sung in duet were one of the most popular genres in karaoke singing on the mainland in the 1990s and one of the most popular modes of interaction between the sexes. There are different kinds of karaoke contexts, and men can also sing masculine male parts in karaoke, like the one in "The Love of the Boat Tower." But the most common style in karaoke love songs since the early 1990s, at least in urban areas, has been the soft, feminine style described above. In fact, the soft, gentle, refined style that has been celebrated in karaoke and in much of mainstream pop since the early 1990s has become synonymous for many with a new desired urban identity.

In karaoke singing of songs in this style, young men and young women, holding a microphone, sing to each other the male and female parts of popular love songs to a prerecorded accompaniment. Both usually face the video screen, where the lyrics appear against the background of a romantic clip, and rarely face each other. Usually surrounded by others, they normally do not touch each other, nor do they dance. Singing is usually done while sitting or standing still. The performance of mainstream love songs in this context is a celebration of restraint, concealment, and chastity, in which tender words replace physical contact, and even the exchange of words is indirect.

The ideal man in this common karaoke context is not new. He has his origins in a long tradition that reveals itself most vividly in many Qing novels where young delicate men become "excited by reading a poem written by a girl they have never seen" (Gulik 1961, 296; see also McMahon 1994). The expression of physical power, physical desire, and carnal sexuality that is so essential in the construction of the Western macho type of manhood that is celebrated in rock simply becomes irrelevant here. The following point by Susan Brownell concerning the different relationship in China and in the West between sports and manhood is most instructive to the present discussion:

> In the West, sports have played an important role in defining the essential male identity. . . . In China . . . sports were a lower-class activity and . . . gender was grounded more in preordained social roles and less in an innate biology. (1995, 28)

It is not surprising, then, that rockers, who construct their masculinity as a reaction not only to the puritanical, oppressive order of the Maoist era but also to traditional ethics articulate it also through straightforward and bold or vulgar (according to the point of view) references to sexuality. Indeed, the mere emphasis on the male body, which is so important in rock, reverses in itself deep-rooted traditional codes and as such constitutes a central component in rock's attack on tradition. Conversely, soft and refined manhood is an important element that makes mainstream pop music, where this type of manhood prevails, more traditional and more Chinese.

The negotiation of manhood in China, today as in the past, is closely tied to the negotiation of other cultural values and power in various realms. For rockers, their search for masculinity has been linked with their sense of personal disempowerment and marginality vis-à-vis the state, their sense of collective or national disempowerment and inferiority vis-à-vis the West, their aspiration to achieve Westernization and modernity, and their negation of traditional values like restraint and obedience. Similarly, the refined, tender male image that is celebrated in much of mainstream Chinese pop today reflects cultural continuity and the resurgence of the traditional preference for more implicit expression, refinement, delicacy, and restraint after a comprehensive, imposed divergence from these traditional preferences during the revolutionary era, with its "militaristic and proletarian Maoist body culture" (Brownell 1995, 56–60). It could also be argued that if the popularity of rock, with its macho image, during the late 1980s and early 1990s reflected Western hegemony and a break from tradition, then the unprecedented popularity of mainstream music, with its refined and gentle male role models, during the 1990s reflected the limits of Western hegemony and the power of resistance of traditional Chinese culture in the global cultural struggle.

A question that still needs to be asked, however, is why the challenge posed by rock (and other styles) to the traditional male image in the post-Mao era failed and why the traditional image became so popular in the 1990s. The resurgence of the traditional male actually started in the 1980s, but until the early and mid-1990s it was much less pronounced, in part because it was overshadowed by the masculine voice of *xibeifeng*, rock, and to some extent the Mao craze of the early 1990s, which also perpetuated some of the revolutionary masculine fervor. It was at the point when all these fads declined that the traditional male image became conspicuous to an unprecedented degree. The decline of rock was no doubt one factor that contributed to the unprecedented prominence of the soft style of mainstream music with its delicate male. But could it also be that rock declined because of its own masculine image and because this image clashed with new circumstances that favored the traditional mode of manhood offered by the mainstream?

In chapter 1, I linked the decline of rock to several domains, among which were the position of China's intellectuals, the main patrons of rock, vis-à-vis the West and Westernization, the majority of Chinese society, Chinese tradition, and the government. Other factors that I mentioned were the increase in commercialization, the commercial inroads made by record companies from Hong Kong and Taiwan, and the related rise of *gangtai* music on the mainland. This web of links could be expanded now to include the practices and discourse relating to gender, to offer a gendered perspective on the decline of rock. Such a perspective will in turn help to explain the unprecedented popularity of soft songs on the mainland in the 1990s. Since China's male intellectuals were always the main patrons of rock, in what follows I am interested particularly in why many of them gave up rock and embraced the type of manhood they had so strongly rejected not long before.[16]

As the previous section suggests, since its emergence in 1986 rock, with its masculinity, signified in China a desired Westernization and modernity. Adopting it offered a solution to the sense of inferiority and marginality experienced by China's intellectuals and many others in the context of the renewed encounter with the powerful, modern West. Through rock, rockers and their audience were hoping to become masculine (modern and powerful) like the West. The desire to become masculine like the West was also one of the main driving forces behind the demonstrations of 1989. But this desire was suppressed. The failure of the 1989 movement indicated that becoming like the West was not a viable option, at least not for the near future. While some kept on struggling to imitate or compete with the West (Erwin 1999; Mayfair Yang 1997), many others gave up. The embrace of soft songs by many intellectuals is reflective of their coming to terms with or acceptance of their femininity vis-à-vis the West. Singing masculine "power songs" was simply incompatible with their persistent experience of femininity, which many now realized could not be challenged. This sense of femininity became even more difficult to avoid after the early 1990s in the context of the Western-dominated post–Cold War global order and the aggressive economic encroachment of the West into China. The sensitivity of Chinese rockers and intellectuals to their depressed economic condition was already evident in the late 1980s and very early 1990s. Two examples that demonstrate such sensitivity are Cui Jian's "Having Nothing" and He Yong's "Pretty Girl." In both songs material lack cannot be separated from a strong sense of damaged masculinity. With the growing commercialization of the 1990s the situation for most intellectuals became even more problematic.

At the same time, however, the ability of the Chinese regime to maintain political and social stability as well as economic growth, while the USSR and most other communist polities were disintegrating, caused many hitherto skeptics to adopt the official notion that China should and could pursue a modernity with a "distinctive national character" *(minzu tese)* as an alternative to imitating the West. Simultaneously, in the context of the rise of Chinese nationalism, and as the blind fetishization of the West during the 1980s gave way during the 1990s to a more complex attitude, of which disillusionment, criticism, and suspicion became an inseparable part, the once-popular traditional male image came to symbolize once again for many who had rejected it not long before desired Chinese qualities of refinement, restraint, civility, harmony, humanism, and spiritualism. These qualities, which many Chinese identify as the essence of the notion of China being a proud "spiritual civilization" *(jingshen wenming)*, offered an alternative to the ethos of the capitalist West, which was now often seen as aggressive, cruel, vulgar, and materialist. This was certainly not the first time in Chinese history that men were feminized, then idealized in their effeminate role, and then became associated with Chineseness as a result of a traumatic encounter with a powerful non-Chinese nation. As Robert van Gulik has noted:

> Under the Manchu occupation the martial arts were monopolized by the conquerors, and as a reaction the Chinese, and more especially the members of the literary class, began to consider physical exercise as vulgar and athletic prowess as suited only to the "Ch'ing [Qing] barbarians," and Chinese professional boxers and acrobats. This change in the Chinese attitude supplies doubtless one of the reasons for the increasing tendency to eschew the physical aspects of love and to stress sentimental, "literary" affection. The novels of that time mention young men becoming sexually excited by reading a poem written by a girl they have never seen. . . . The ideal lover is described as a delicate, hyper-sensitive youngster with pale face and narrow shoulders, passing the great part of his time dreaming among his books and flowers, and falls ill at the slightest disappointment. (1961, 296)

The interaction between the diverse agencies within China in the context of the 1980s and 1990s is no less important in understanding why the Western macho type of manhood became less appealing in China in the 1990s. Much of the preceding discussion has shown how the search for masculinity that was essential to the identity of rock was closely linked to another essential characteristic of the style, which is political resistance to the government. I suggested that this was the result of a popular belief that the totalitarian state was the main cause for the long history of effeminate or castrated manhood in China, which implies that masculinity could be gained through resistance to the state. The link between political dissent and masculinity was also manifested in the demonstrations of spring 1989, during which demonstrators held a poster depicting Deng Xiaoping as Empress Dowager Ci Xi. For a century Ci Xi has been a symbol of corruption, despotism, and conservatism, and was held responsible for China's decline vis-à-vis the West. But there has always been, including in 1989, also the gendered perspective. The derogatory feminization of Deng was one means used by the demonstrators to gain and assert their own desired masculine identity.

The relationship between the Chinese government and China's intellectuals in the 1980s and 1990s has been repeatedly compared to a father-son relationship (Zha 1995, 12–19; Dai 1999). During the 1980s, it has been suggested, China's intellectuals were like rebellious sons, whereas the regime and Chinese traditional culture were like a hated father. But in the 1990s, after the Tiananmen incident of 1989, the traditional order was restored. The rebellious spirit decayed and the son came to recognize once again the authority of his father. The following comments on the Tiananmen incident and its aftermath, made by a Chinese media reporter who participated in the 1989 protests, nicely illustrate how the two realms (father-son/government-intellectuals) are perceived as parallels in many people's minds today in China:

> It's like getting a hard punch in the face from your father. Very hard to get over. Only by and by do you realize he's your father after all. And there is nothing you can do but slowly chip away at that hard socialist wall. (Quoted in Zha 1995, 12)

This parallel has, of course, a long history in China. But it is also important to note that the sociopolitical paradigm that generated the father-son metaphor also generated a gendered parallel, which is that of husband and wife.[17] Viewed from a gendered perspective, the relationship between the government and China's intellectual dissidents during the 1980s and 1990s could be described thus: the challenge of the 1980s was like a wife challenging her husband or, more generally, like an attempt of the effeminate subject to claim ownership over or challenge the masculinity or authority of his(/her) ruler. The June 4 brutal and total suppression of the democracy movement, however, crushed these claims for masculinity, which many demonstrators articulated through mere participation in the movement. Through this total suppression, the government restored traditional order and power relations, reasserting its own power and masculinity, and denying it to those who challenged it.

June 4 was, in other words, an act of castration whose purpose was to place China's intellectuals back in their traditional position of woman-like state subjects. And, according to the traditional paradigm, the most important feminine qualities to which these subjects had to re-conform were loyalty, submissiveness, and obedience.[18] Viewed in this way, we could conclude that the unprecedented popularity of the traditional male image among significant portions of China's intellectuals since the early and mid-1990s and the concomitant decline of rock also tell the story of how China's intellectuals reverted to their traditional, effeminate identities as a result of the masculine suppression of 1989. This new position was not necessarily negative, but rather part of the new wave of nationalism and the idea of China being a "spiritual civilization." China's political stability and

economic progress in the 1990s caused many intellectuals to believe that
Chinese sociopolitical Confucianist tradition, with its emphasis on hierarchy, obedience, and strong authoritarian government, was the right path
for China to take. In the context of resuming their traditional identities and
roles, giving up rock and connecting with mainstream pop and its traditional mode of manhood offered intellectuals a much-needed way out not
only from their political alienation vis-à-vis the government but also from
their social alienation vis-à-vis the rest of society.

For many, however, the crying over a tragic ending of a love affair and
the endless yearning in songs that celebrate the traditional male image constituted a safe and expressive surrogate that facilitated the articulation of
a general state of disempowerment in the context of continuing political
oppression. This surrogate, moreover, simultaneously helped them to forget and escape the actual source of the traumatic experience.

The decline of rock (and *xibeifeng*) and the unprecedented popularity of
soft songs in the 1990s not only reflected a shift in perceptions of manhood
but have also played a significant role in shaping this shift. In her recently
edited volume, Mayfair Mei-hui Yang mentions a male Shanghainese
playwright who predicted that the "American 'cowboy-type individualist'
in China would sooner or later run afoul of the state and be put into prison"
(1999, 51–52). This prediction, I believe, has already come true, at least
partially, since the late 1980s. The June 4 crackdown was a successful blow
to the cowboy image with which many Chinese started to identify in the
1980s. This one-time military act, however, was only part of a more comprehensive effort. The long-term pressures exerted on rock by the government, which reached their apex in 1993 and 1994 with strict restrictions on
rock performances, was another important aspect in the suppression of the
challenging masculinity of China's rockers. Because rock music has always
been a culture, of which the acquisition and acting out of masculinity constitutes an essential component, by suppressing rock the government in
fact not only suppressed a musical style but also diminished significantly
the possibility of practicing and developing alternative undesirable notions
and practices of manhood. Similarly, the official acceptance of *tongsu* music in 1986 and its full incorporation and extensive appropriation by official
media since then has played a vital role in fostering nonrebellious, obedient, docile male state-subjects.

Despite everything said above about cultural continuity, the extreme
popularity in the 1990s of soft songs, with their delicate male images, is not
simply a return to tradition. There is at least one factor that is crucial today
to the maintenance and perpetuation of these traditional images that was

not crucial in the past, and this is women's patronage.[19] If traditionally both male and female public images were constructed and maintained in China almost exclusively by men, the situation is quite different today, when women are active participants in public life. Whereas rock, with its new masculine male image, has been patronized mainly by men and is male-centered and a male creation, it became obvious to me during my fieldwork that women patronize male singers who conform to the traditional refined male image at least as much as men (through attendance of concerts and purchase of cassettes, CDs, posters, and other star-worshiping paraphernalia), and therefore are at least equally responsible for the maintenance of this image.[20] Thus, in contrast to its traditional origins, the neotraditional male image that is found today in Chinese pop is also a product of female agency.

This projection of a female self in popular male images was made possible in the post-Mao era, especially in the 1990s, more than ever before because of the introduction of a market economy in which women have a significantly greater influence over cultural construction through their buying power and their share in market demand. In other words, capitalism empowered women with an unprecedented ability to exert direct influence not only over culture but also over the construction of manhood. For the first time in Chinese history, men became a commodity for female consumption. The influence of women is not limited to the construction of abstract images, since these images, because of their commercial success, become role models that are imitated by men. Chinese women became active participants in the public sphere almost half a century ago, after the communist revolution, and some even earlier. Nevertheless, during the revolutionary period, cultural construction was normally prescribed unilaterally from above by the party-state, which was and still is male-dominated. Women's new buying power does not necessarily imply that the status of women as a whole improved as a result of the reforms, but it is nevertheless an important factor, which certainly has not received enough scholarly attention. The new power that women in China acquired in the 1990s is doubtless another cause for the decline of rock and the unprecedented ascendance of soft songs that celebrate softer males.

The change in the patronage of music and the old image of manhood has also introduced new, female-specific meanings. Women are perhaps influenced as much as men by traditional aesthetics and values when they patronize this image, but they also bestow on it a whole new set of meanings, which derive from their unique experience as women. If traditionally the main force that maintained and perpetuated the image of the delicate man was an androcentric aspiration to achieve abstract feminine purity, refinement, and other related qualities, then today this image is maintained at least as much by a similar gynecentric preference for such qualities but also, and no less importantly, by romantic or sexual desires and fantasies, an attempt to compensate for actual experience, and a sense of empowerment. Having a man begging in a soft voice for love and asking the woman in the song to stay, implying that she is in control and free to come and go as she wishes (even to another man in some cases), is something that obviously gives many women today in China considerable pleasure, which is not unlike the pleasure that such statements sung by female singers in a soft voice have always given to men, especially when the actual position of women vis-à-vis men is still reversed, as the following section will demonstrate.

NEGOTIATING GENDER IN POPULAR MUSIC CULTURE II: RECONSTRUCTING WOMANHOOD

The Neotraditional Model of Womanhood

> What women in China want today is to have the freedom to express their femininity, including the freedom to wear skirts, put on makeup, and stay at home to take care of their child.
>
> WANG ANYI (a famous Chinese female writer; quoted in Feigon 1994, 130)

The dominant female image in Chinese popular culture between the mid- to late 1980s and the mid-1990s has been that of a domesticated, soft, gentle, sweet, restrained woman, the antithesis of the superwoman-like Iron Girl, which the state under Mao propagated during the Cultural Revolution. Though sometimes described by Chinese women as "an explicit attack on 'feudal' notions of behavior that required women to make themselves as inconspicuous as possible" (Honig and Hershatter 1988, 47), the most prevalent female image in post-Mao China nevertheless draws heavily upon traditional images of womanhood and tends to emphasize traditional feminine features and qualities (Croll 1995, 155). This link to tradition manifests itself in an emphasis on outer appearance and beauty, in the revival of traditional symbols of femininity, such as long hair, makeup, jewelry, and dresses, and in the adoption of Western symbols of femininity, such as high-heeled shoes (Honig and Hershatter 1988, 41–80). Womanhood, especially in urban popular culture, is often defined today on the mainland as fragility and softness.

The post-Maoist, neotraditional model of womanhood has been most conspicuous in the popular music scene. In fact, the most famous female pop singers of the late 1970s and early 1980s have probably played the most significant role in introducing this model and disseminating it throughout the mainland. Beginning with young female singers who imitated the Taiwanese female superstar Deng Lijun in the early 1980s, many mainland female singers have adopted a traditional feminine outlook after the beginning of reforms and began to sing slow songs in a soft, sweet voice about waiting for men and wanting to be loved. As if to conform to traditional images of feminine restraint and passivity, these women singers hardly moved on stage, a performance practice that is still prevalent today. While this style of performance characterizes much of mainstream Chinese pop, including both male and female performers, female singers stand at the very end of the no-motion/dance continuum and seldom break away from this norm, as male performers sometimes do.

Chinese critics and audiences are so used to this neotraditional image that one critic who reported on Björk's 1996 concert in Beijing seems to have been most fascinated by the fact that the famous female musician from Iceland took off her shoes and ran on stage, adding that she "did not change her clothes" and most of her songs were "fast songs" (A Se 1996, 17).[21] Although these characteristics contrast with much of mainstream Chinese pop, including both male and female singers, the critic's emphasis on these points seems to have been fueled by the fact that Björk is a woman, which makes her departure from the norm even more sensational and thus worthy of mention. So prevalent is women's static posture on stage in the Chinese pop scene that another critic suggested that a young female musician named Fang Fang, who bounced modestly while singing one of her songs, could have become "the first young female pop star in the country . . . who leaps and bounces in a lively way" if she had released her album three years earlier ("Fang Fang" 1996, 22).

Although the neotraditional feminine image was already introduced into the Chinese pop scene in the late 1970s, during the 1980s it was much less conspicuous than during the 1990s. This was in part because the *tongsu* style with which it was connected was officially banned until 1986. Another reason was the *xibeifeng* fad of the mid- and late 1980s, with its masculinist ethos. Many famous female singers of that time, such as Mao Amin, Na Ying, and Wei Wei, became famous rather because of their powerful and uninhibited *(benfang)* voices. With their powerful voices, these female singers conformed to the orthodox communist, masculine female image, which the state still propagated in the 1980s, and it is not surprising that they were also closely linked with the state. The link revealed itself in the fact that in the late 1980s they often sang officially sanctioned songs on television variety shows and in officially organized live events.

The Neotraditional Image of Womanhood as Women's Resistance

The situation changed, however, in the 1990s. The transformation that Mao Amin underwent in the 1990s is representative. By the mid-1990s Mao was one of China's most famous and senior female pop stars. For several years already, she had been referred to in popular music discourse as "*dajieda*," an honorific title that means "big sister," implying power and connecting with her image of the 1980s. In 1994, however, Mao released a new album that presented a whole new image, one that has been generally referred to on the mainland as the "urban female" image. With its soft songs and a hit entitled "Real Woman" *(Zhenshi de nüren)*, Mao's new album, which was entitled after the singer's own name, was a celebration of what one music critic named a "return to femininity" (Song Xiaoming 1995b, 40). So drastic was the change that this critic commented critically that Mao had lost the power that characterized her singing in the past and noted cynically that in her new album it seems as if "her voice unceasingly reiterates 'woman, woman, I am a woman . . .'" (Song Xiaoming 1995b, 40). Similar criticism was articulated under a pen name by Wu Xiaoying, the female editor of the important music magazine *Audio and Video World (Yinxiang shijie)*, who wrote:

> Mao Amin's performance lacks the kind of spirit that the "big sister" of
> the pop scene should have. . . . The feeling that [she] gave people in the
> past was natural. . . . Back then she set up her own separate flag among
> the large group of bold and unconstrained women. Perhaps it is the
> long period of boldness and unconstraint of the past that caused them
> (the large group of female singers who started their careers together
> with Mao Amin) to become tired, so they all shifted to the image of the
> "little woman" [*xiao nüzi*]. ("Mao Amin" 1995, 18)[22]

The new "return to femininity" trend among female singers has also been acknowledged by Jin Zhaojun and Wang Xiaofeng, the famous Beijing-based male music critics, in conversations I had with them. Both blamed companies from Hong Kong and Taiwan for this new image, suggesting that these companies "are used to packaging women in this way."

In the 1990s, parallel to the increase in free-market activity, women's return to the domestic sphere on the one hand and their change to a sexualized commodity in a market dominated by male desire on the other hand became clearer than ever before (Notar 1994; Mayfair Yang 1999). The state feminism that supported images of strong, masculine women was now obviously in decline. Nevertheless, simultaneous with the acknowledgment of the intensification of these trends, there was now among students of gender in China also more recognition and a deeper grasp of the complex and unique position and sensibilities of Chinese women in the new, post-revolutionary context. It became clearer among a growing number of Chinese and Western scholars that the Western notions of gender equality and progress or regression in women's status were not necessarily applicable or instructive in the Chinese context. More and more attention was paid to the important liberating functions that the emphasis on women's sexuality and bodily difference fulfilled for women after decades of gender erasure (Rofel 1994a; Notar 1994; Mayfair Yang 1999) in which "women were invited to enter . . . male spaces . . . [but] with very few concessions to female-specific qualities" (Croll 1995, 7). Meng Yue and Dai Jinhua have summarized the unique position of Chinese women in the 1980s and 1990s in the following way:

> The road of Chinese woman's liberation is different from that of Western woman's liberation because the [Chinese woman] has a different reality and past. For her, "equality of men and women" was once a mythical trap, and "equal pay for equal work" was all but forced upon her. Gender difference is not a concept to be discarded or abandoned, but a necessary path through which she must pass. (Quoted in Mayfair Yang 1999, 35)

Viewed in this way, the post-revolutionary, neotraditional female image could be understood as telling the story of women's reaction against their masculinization during the revolutionary period and their struggle to revive femininity and regain their distinctive and what many of them see as their "natural" gender identity. Proceeding along similar lines, the emphasis on adornment and sexuality, in particular, could be interpreted as a form of resistance to government policies in the post-Mao era and as women's struggle to gain "some measure of control over the definition of their bodies" in the context of continuing official pressures exerted on them to participate in production (Rofel 1994a, 245). It is important to add that this struggle of women to gain control over their bodies becomes even more meaningful amid the new, unprecedented aggressive encroachment of the state (and society) into their bodies in the context of the one-child policy.[23]

It is against such a background that Mao Amin's shift to her new feminine image becomes understandable. In one article, Mao described this shift: "For too many years I sang too many songs that a lot of people liked very much and that were good songs. But [among these songs] there were very few that were really songs that I wanted to sing" (quoted in Jin 1995b). In this statement Mao asserts her agency and control, implying that the new image was her own choice. For her, as for the several other famous "bold and unconstrained" female singers of the 1980s who made a similar shift in the 1990s, gender erasure persisted through the 1980s. These women have already made it in the public sphere. They achieved respect and fame, probably even more than most of their male colleagues, but like their elder revolutionary sisters of yore, they were still denied a distinct gender identity.

Mao's new "urban female" image certainly did not run counter to market demand, and it is quite likely that profit was a consideration in assuming this image. Such a consideration does not, however, necessarily exclude her identification with her new image and does not necessarily contradict the possibility that her sensibilities and taste changed, similar to the change in the sensibilities of many Chinese women since the 1980s.

This discussion suggests that no clear-cut dichotomy of men as agents and women as victims could be applied in the case of the post-Maoist neotraditional female image that is so popular today in China. Certainly we should be cautious not to equate this neotraditional image with real traditional images of womanhood and everything they stood for. In the post-revolutionary context, female singers who assume a feminine image can use it not only to gain a lost gender identity and make themselves more visible but also as a means to achieve economic success and public status. No less important is the fact that whereas in the past women were impersonated on stage by male performers (as in opera, for example), today women are representing themselves.[24]

Neotraditional Femininity and Male Subjectivity

The agency of women in the construction and representation of the neotraditional female image also has clear limits, however. In most previous studies, such limits were often suggested but seldom explored and substantiated by concrete ethnographic data. In what follows I draw the limits of women's agency in concrete terms. I will show how men literally control the production of the neotraditional image of womanhood and the definition and representations of womanhood in general in the popular music scene, how those women who assume this image actually speak in voices produced by men, how pressure is exerted on women to conform to this image, how women are offered a significantly narrower range of artistic expression than men, and finally, how they are objectified and marginalized by a dominant masculine discourse. This discussion will also provide the necessary context for the last sections of this chapter on new women's voices in the Chinese pop scene.

My discussion begins with the song "Night Rose," the opening song on the 1994 album of the female singer Chen Ming, who gained the honorific title of "the most popular female singer" of that year in Guangzhou.

NIGHT ROSE
(lyrics by Chen Jieming; music by Wang Gang; performance by Chen Ming)

Waiting for you to love me sincerely
When I am beautiful
If you are not there, who will appreciate me? . . .
Why don't you come to see me? . . .
I am a rose in the moonlight
The waiting heart is fragrant like water
The charm of my dreaming about you is left in my world
Do not let me wait until my heart is broken

"Night Rose" is sung in a moderate tempo to a subdued jazzy accompaniment in a soft, restrained, often whisper-like voice, which according to one critic has "the unique sexy tone of a woman" (Qiu 1996). This song, like the rest of the songs in Chen Ming's album, is about a romantic relationship between a man and a woman in the context of which the female persona assumes the role of a passive, waiting woman who depends completely on her male lover: his love, appreciation, and sheer presence. The main characteristics of the female persona in the song are beauty, fragility, static position, and resemblance to a flower.

Like most of the songs in Chen Ming's album, "Night Rose," both in its music—especially Chen Ming's voice—and in its lyrics, is full of sexual overtones. Conforming to the traditional aesthetics of refinement and concealment, however, the sexuality in the song, at least in the text, is always implied through references to the moon and a flower, two objects that have always been used in Chinese literary tradition to suggest romance and eroticism.

In one article about Chen Ming, the reporter states, after praising her, that "girls who move men ought to be gentle and soft [*wenrou*]" (Fang 1995). In this short statement, the reporter articulates two widespread beliefs among both women and men today in China: first that the essence of womanhood is softness, and second, that women exist for men. In this short statement, the reporter also provides a context within which Chen Ming's album can be fully understood. The album is about femininity, and like femininity it is for men. This conceptual framework is encapsulated in the female singer's seductive voice, which obviously aims not only to identify her as a woman, but also to attract men. The cover notes of Chen Ming's album further articulate these points about womanhood:

> Chen Ming is a name you already know, but this time there is a little bit of difference. Different because the songs she brings are for your heart to listen to, the pale appearance she brings makes you feel "woman," this word, is so beautiful and nice, so moving, so mysterious. Mysterious, as if she was always waiting for you to come near, waiting for you to really come near and discover that she is also quietly moving away a little. This distance in between is beautiful, it beautifies your memories and your sorrow, so beautiful that you can see her clearly, taste her and not be lost. Getting lost, perhaps there is a little bit of that, because her voice tells you she is one hundred percent a singer, because her romantic feelings tell you she is one hundred percent a woman, one hundred percent a singer, one hundred percent a woman.

The notes above objectify Chen Ming, objectify womanhood, and turn both into the other. Chen Ming is referred to as "she," written with the radical for female, whereas the "you" to whom the text is addressed is obviously a male listener. The text not only objectifies the female singer and women in general, but also exoticizes them to the point of mystification. The woman other is turned into a mysterious object whose essence is beauty, a pale appearance, evasiveness, and the ability to move the male self and intoxicate him, and yet she allows him to be in control. Unlike Cui Jian's "Flower-House Girl," the text guarantees the male listener that he can maintain control when it states that he "can see her clearly, taste her, and [yet] not be lost." Chen Ming is offered to the male listener as a sex object, who is "waiting" for him to "come near," "really come near[!]." The text is full of sexual implications, suggesting that the female singer can provide the male listener not only with aural pleasures but also with more bodily ones.

Chen Ming's sexual appeal is also constructed visually on the cover of her cassette, which features two seductive photographs of her with her mouth slightly open, her lips covered with heavy rosy lipstick, and her face powdered white, as if to fit the description that appears in the cover notes (see figure 5). Like the music on the album, specifically the submissive, soft, seductive voice and the corresponding image that the lyrics construct, the photographs suggest tamed and domesticated sexuality that does not challenge male control. The black background framing her face invokes the intimacy and romantic atmosphere of night. The title of the first song,

Figure 5. Chen Ming, *Loneliness Makes Me So Beautiful,* cassette cover.
Courtesy of Zhongguo changpian Guangzhou gongsi.

"Night Rose," is printed on a background of purple roses. Purple, pink, and blue and flowers are often featured on albums by women singers, and are used to differentiate between male and female singers. Above the image of the roses, beside Chen's pale inviting face, printed in bright white, is the title of the album, "Loneliness Makes Me So Beautiful" *(Jimo rang wo ruci meili)*, which is also the title of the second song. This song articulates a wish to stay alone, which is referred to in the cover notes as her "quietly moving away a little." This wish to be left alone, the only one in the album, might suggest in isolation a kind of resistance to men. Nevertheless, when placed in the context of the rest of the album, it appears as yet another seductive gesture, not to mention the fact that the image of a lonely, beautiful woman at night is also full of sexual overtones. It is, after all, the title of this song that the designers of the album decided to place in big characters on the cover of the album to attract and fuel the imagination and desire of potential male consumers. Not surprisingly, I first heard Chen Ming's album in a cassette shop when a male client in his late twenties asked the shop attendants to play the cassette for him before making his final decision.

Chen Ming's album is representative of a whole new trend of women becoming sex objects for men, a trend that became increasingly visible in the 1990s. This trend, whose most extreme manifestation is the revived practice of prostitution (increasingly visible in urban areas in the last decade), reveals itself in popular music culture in various ways. Earlier I described a common karaoke context that is quite chaste, in which women are positioned in a rather favorable position vis-à-vis men. But this proper context is one of several possible karaoke contexts. Karaoke bars in particular are actually designed to serve and entertain men. They employ young women dressed in sexy clothes who not only serve drinks and dishes but also offer other services, such as joining the men for a chat, dancing with them, and singing solo songs for them or duet songs with them. In addition, as several male informants indicated to me, in many of the karaoke bars it is also possible for male clients to have sex with the hostesses at a private room that is located within the bar.

Women's role as sex objects in this karaoke context manifests itself also in the videos that accompany many of the songs that are sung in this context. These videos often feature young women in swimsuits posing in seductive ways. In 1995 and 1996 such videos were also common in big malls, where they were often played nonstop in departments that sell televisions, video machines, and karaoke and other music equipment.

Going back to Chen Ming, the emphasis on womanhood in the cover notes and the repeated assertion that the female singer is "one hundred percent a woman," to which the whole text seems to lead, reflect post-revolutionary sensibilities with regard to gender. The implication of this line is, of course, that there is a problem with womanhood, that many women are not real women or one hundred percent women. As with the cover notes in Tang Dynasty's rock album, which assert the masculinity of the band members and the heavy-metal music of the band, which in this context almost ought to be understood as masculine, the claim that Chen Ming is "one hundred percent a woman" and her soft style, against which such a claim cannot be understood as anything else but feminine, reflect an attempt to reestablish gender distinctions after decades during which these distinctions were blurred. The emphasis on "real womanhood" in Chen Ming's album, like the emphasis on "real manhood" in many rock cassettes, reflects the sense of loss shared by many women in China with regard to their gender identity. But the parallel between the search for masculinity and the search for femininity does not imply symmetry between the role and position of women and those of men in popular culture today in China. Women, as Chen Ming's album nicely illustrates, tend to be more objectified than men and have less subjectivity. It is not only that women are almost completely excluded from the masculine territory of rock, in which male subjectivity is overt, but men also dominate most of what is supposedly the domain of women. Both rock and soft mainstream music by female singers like Chen Ming exist for men. Although, as I suggested earlier, women do participate in and perhaps even dominate the patronage of soft mainstream music by male singers, the latter are seldom objectified in the way Chen Ming and other female singers are objectified. Women often assume the role of the other in music discourse, while men rarely do. As Chen Ming's album illustrates, it is the male self that dominates popular music, even when it is women who sing and supposedly speak.

The objectification of women manifests itself also in the way women are referred to and described in music discourse, which often suggests not only male subjectivity but also male superiority, and often exhibits a patronizing attitude, even misogyny. The female singer Cheng Lin, for example, has been referred to for years as "Little [*xiao*] Cheng Lin." In the personal notes attached to a 1994 album by the male musician Gao Feng, one finds under the category "girls that I like the most" the following description: "Beautiful, knowledgeable about cooking, and ones who speak little." The revival of traditional femininity clearly implies the revival of traditional power relationships and hierarchy. Another example of objectification is the exoticization of women in the cover notes of Chen Ming's album, in which women are referred to as "mysterious." A similar adjective was used to describe women in the title of a 1995 officially organized, large-scale women's pop concert that took place in Beijing in June 1995, and which I discuss at some length in the next chapter. The concert was entitled "Wonderful Women" (*Shenqi de nüren*, which could also mean "magical women") and demonstrated that women are also objectified in official culture. It is hard to believe that women would refer to themselves as "wonderful" or "magical," and not surprisingly the concert program (figure 6) revealed that this "women's concert" was organized exclusively by men, who were probably also responsible for this title. Thus, in this concert women assumed the role of exotic other, invited to participate in a festival that was not their own.

The word *guniang*, which is often featured in rock and pop songs today, is another manifestation of the objectification of women. One rarely hears, if at all, in pop songs the word *xiaohuozi*, which is the male equivalent of *guniang*. When I asked one young woman why one rarely hears *xiaohuozi* (or *nanhai*) in Chinese pop songs, she replied: "Isn't it that most songs are by men and about women?" This rhetorical question describes very well the position of women in Chinese pop, namely, their otherness, marginality, and lack of subjectivity.

Figure 6.   Program of "Wonderful Women."

Objectification is applied not only to individual female singers, but also to womanhood in general. Whereas the negotiation of manhood is usually done exclusively by men, the negotiation and definition of womanhood is open to all and is very much dominated by men too. Furthermore, womanhood is objectified and negotiated in the pop scene much more than manhood. The most obvious manifestation of the negotiation of womanhood in popular music culture is the proliferation of songs about women and womanhood. Almost every famous female singer in the mid-1990s had a song that discussed womanhood and attempted to define it. Such songs, whose titles usually featured and emphasized the word "woman" *(nüren),* were yet another manifestation of an intense engagement with gender issues, but they also reflected the objectification of women. There were very few songs about *nanren*, or men, a fact that reveals more than anything else the male-dominated nature of Chinese popular culture, because after all, individuals and groups tend to objectify the other rather than the self. Chinese women are like the ethnic minorities in China I discussed in the previous chapter, who have been sung about in popular songs for decades, whereas men, like the Han majority—the self—are seldom objectified and sung about as such.[25]

Although men today seldom impersonate women in poetry and opera, as they did in the past, they nevertheless often speak as women. Many of the songs in mainstream pop that speak about womanhood or about being a woman are sung by women singers but written by male lyricists. Mao Amin's "Real Woman," for instance, which was mentioned earlier, was written by the famous male lyricist Luo Bing. Luo Bing also wrote the lyrics for the mandatory song about being a woman on Na Ying's 1994 album *I Yearn For You Day and Night (Wei ni zhaosi muxiang)*, a song entitled "This Is the Way Women Become Mature" *(Nüren jiushi zheyang chengshou de)*, which celebrated Na Ying's return to femininity. These two examples illustrate most vividly the active role played by men in the definition of womanhood in post-revolutionary China in general, and their dominant role in constructing the neotraditional model of femininity in particular. This active role is not confined to lyrics, but manifests itself also in the music. Like the lyrics, most of the music performed by female singers today in China is composed by male composers, and thus it is mainly they who are responsible for the soft, gentle, sweet, restrained (often sexy) sonic image that is associated with most female singers. Wang Yuejin's observation with regard to the traditional practice of male poets in female persona thus is obviously still applicable for much of the Chinese pop scene in the 1990s:

> [These] men not so much speak for women as stand in their place to speak, thereby replacing women's linguistic space, usurping their world of consciousness and depriving women of the right to speak. . . . These speechless women have no way of articulating "I." Worse still, they live in a limbo: they could not even inhabit the place of "thou," as the "thou" addressed in the poems is male when the speaker is a textual female. (1989, 35–36)

The near-absolute absence of Chinese women from Chinese rock is another example of the inferior position of women in the Chinese pop scene. This absence is significant not only because it makes rock a male territory but also because it implies that women possess a narrower range of musical expression. Whereas men can express themselves in all the major styles—the feminine mainstream sentimental, sweet style, the folksy or rustic style, and the masculine rock style—women are associated only with the first two, and unlike men, they have no exclusive female musical territory. Women's absence from rock has far-reaching implications because the style is associated with a wide and important range of artistic, social, and political ethos to which women, because of their lack of participation, have with few exceptions little or no access. In chapter 1, I suggested that it was through rock that new values, like individualism and nonconformism, authenticity and originality, personal freedom, protest, and nonrestraint were (re)introduced into China. This is not to say that expressions of rebellion and protest, individuality, and so on cannot be found in other styles, but it is in rock that they constitute an inseparable part of the style and are articulated most forcefully. Thus, women's absence (with few exceptions) from Chinese rock is closely related to the fact that the predominant female image today in China is characterized by restraint, that one rarely finds expressions of protest of any kind in women's songs, and that women tend more than men to sing songs by (male) others and thus to have less subjectivity.

Pressures on Women to Conform to the Neotraditional Image of Womanhood

Certainly there are women singers today in China who choose to conform to the neotraditional female image, as in the case of Mao Amin. Nevertheless, there is also evidence that the dominance of this image is not the result of women's choice alone, but often involves external pressures to conform to this image. Though different from the pressures exerted on women by the state during the revolutionary period to conform to its official image of the ideal woman, such pressures are nevertheless significant. One example of such pressure can be found in a 1995 critique of a rap album in which the critic implies that women cannot and should not sing in rap style. The critic is critical of Chinese rap in general, writing sarcastically that "listening to rap in Mandarin is really a tiring matter" ("Daoban" 1995, 18). However, he/she also makes a clear distinction between several male rappers on the album and the one woman who participates in it. The sex of the singer seems important to the critic, as he/she places next to the name of the female rapper (placed last in the list) a note in parentheses that she is a female. There is no such specification next to the names of the other three participants, which in itself suggests that the female rapper is an unusual phenomenon. Whereas the criticism of the songs by the male rappers, who are discussed as a group, stresses the unintelligibility of the words, the lack of any central idea in the rap, and the failure of the singers to communicate with the audience, when it comes to the female rapper, He Jing, who is discussed separately, considerations of gender suddenly take over. The critic ends with the following paragraph: "He Jing's 'Women's Street' [*Nüren jie*] is the only rap song in Mandarin sung by a woman that I have ever heard, and it feels like a witch chanting incantations" (*"Dao-ban"* 1995, 18). In this statement, the critic not only confirms the scarcity of female rappers, but seems to suggest that He Jing's song does not even deserve a serious discussion, as do the songs by male rappers, and that it is a rare and abnormal phenomenon that should not exist at all. The argument seems to be that women should not even try to sing rap; otherwise they are risking their proper femininity. Reading this paragraph together with the cover notes of Chen Ming's album, one is led to conclude that a woman can be a woman (and not a witch) only if she sings sweet, soft, sexy songs about waiting for her male lover.

Another example of pressures exerted on women to conform to the neo-traditional image of womanhood concerns the female singer Sun Yue. In an interview that was broadcast 23 June 1995 on BCTV2 (Beijing Cable Television), Sun revealed her admiration for Sinead O'Connor, the famous Irish female rocker, referring to her shaved head and suggesting that it takes courage for a woman to shave her head, a courage she herself does not have. In expressing admiration for something she herself cannot or does not dare to do, Sun implicitly acknowledged the pressures put on her to conform to the neotraditional image of femininity, of which long hair is an essential component.

In the same interview, Sun Yue also explicitly acknowledged her inferiority vis-à-vis male musicians in terms of agency when she expressed admiration for two *gangtai* male musicians, Tong An'ge and Zhou Huajian, because they not only sing but also write lyrics and compose. Those who not only sing but also write lyrics and compose tunes are referred to in Chinese as *quanneng*, meaning artists with "complete ability," or sometimes, as Sun Yue herself referred to them, as *shili pai*, meaning that they belong to the "strength school," as opposed to the *ouxiang pai*, or "idols school." [26] In contrast to the latter label, which often has negative implications, suggesting that one's fame was achieved due to commercial packaging and outer appearance, *quanneng* and *shili pai* always have positive connotations, being associated with creativity, originality, and individual character (*gexing*), values that were introduced into the Chinese pop scene mainly by rockers and became increasingly important in mainstream pop in the mid-1990s. The fact that Sun Yue chose to mention two male musicians as her models for *quanneng* musicianship is not incidental, as there were few female musicians in China performing *gangtai* music in the mid-1990s who sang their own songs. Although this situation started to change around that time, as even women whose musical activity had been confined to singing songs by others started to write and compose their own songs (e.g., Tian Zhen in her 1996 album and Cheng Lin in her 1995 album), "complete ability" has historically been associated almost exclusively with men.

In expressing her hope to become a member of the "strength school," Sun Yue was in fact affirming her inferior position as an artist and musician vis-à-vis Tong An'ge and Zhou Huajian, and women's inferior position vis-à-vis men in Chinese pop in general. Sun's implied hope to sing her own songs may be also interpreted as a hope to gain more subjectivity and perhaps a more autonomous and authentic voice. Her entire interview, first with its reference to Sinead O'Connor and then to Tong An'ge and Zhou Huajian, was about wanting to be something that she is not, or more accurately something that she is not in her sweet, slow, soft hit "Wishing You Well" *(Zhu ni ping'an)*, which made her famous but which she is obviously not so excited about. The popularity of Sun's serene song not only reflected aesthetic preferences on the mainland in the mid-1990s but also the kind of female image that many Chinese, male and female alike, prefer.

A famous male musician with whom I spoke who knew Sun Yue personally suggested to me that unlike her sweet and restrained image in "Wishing You Well," "she is in fact very wild." The implication is that Sun Yue had to give up her natural personality and conform to the dominant feminine image in order to succeed as a singer. Similarly, one critic, when discussing Chen Ming's album, wrote cynically that "actually in life, Chen Ming . . . is one hundred percent 'a woman of good home,'" and then expressed the "hope that next time we will be able to hear the other sides of the character of this 'one hundred percent woman'" ("Chen Ming" 1995, 18). What this critic was suggesting is that there is a significant gap between the real Chen Ming and the image that she assumes on her album, and that the image assumed on the album restricts Chen Ming to a limited range of artistic expression, of which the critic is obviously critical. As if to summarize the point, the male critic Wang Xiaofeng has observed:

> In some of the popular music that we hear today, the relationship
> between the song and the singer is as follows: A song is for a singer like
> a kind of commercial disguise which can only express an illusory per-

sonality of the singer. . . . This is especially obvious in the case of female singers. (1996, 5)

Wang suggests, in other words, that women have less control than men do over their image, and that they are less able than men to maintain their real selves and speak in their own voices. Although male musicians today in China often fall victim to similar pressures—for example, if they want to gain access to the state-run television channel, they have to give up whatever wildness they have—they nevertheless can still choose to celebrate wildness in rock. Women, however, do not have a musical space, venue, or sanctioned territory in which they can celebrate their wildness or anything else other than sweetness, softness, and restraint. Chinese rockers did succeed in introducing wildness and craziness into Chinese culture, but with very few exceptions this behavior and artistic expression is reserved for men only and is legitimate (in nonofficial culture) only when they celebrate it.

Women, Restraint, and Tradition

The post-revolutionary reconstruction of manhood and womanhood also includes the assumption that women do not even have the need to act wildly. The use of the words *faxie* or *xuanxie*, which according to one dictionary mean to "get something off one's chest" but which often also imply to "let off steam" or to "give vent" in a rather intense, carnivalistic, unrestrained fashion, provides one example of this assumption. These words are often used today in popular music discourse, illustrating the post-revolutionary allowance for expressing personal emotions and for unrestrained behavior in order to compensate for various kinds of repression. But they are nevertheless often associated exclusively with men and manhood. Thus, for example, discussing the duo Yu Wenhua and Yin Xiangjie, who were mentioned at the very beginning of the chapter, and their 1995 new hit "There Is No Rain and Wind and the Sun Is Shining" (*Tian bu xiayu tian bu guafeng tian shang you taiyang*; lyrics by Zhao Xiaoyuan, music by Li Fan), which was modeled after their successful hit from 1993, "The Love of the Boat Tower," one critic wrote:

> The interweaving of the rough, bold, and unconstrained [*cuguang*] male voice with the coquettish sweet and charming [*jiaomei*] female voice both conforms to the division of male-female roles in traditional society, and even more so it satisfies men's need in the tense modern life to let off steam [*xuanxie*] in karaoke. ("Yu Wenhua, Yin Xiangjie" 1995, 18)

This paragraph implies that men are the only ones who have the need to let off steam and thus the need and justification to sing in a bold and unconstrained manner, like Yin Xiangjie. The extreme popularity of the duets by Yu Wenhua and Yin Xiangjie, which offer one of the most vivid manifestations of the post-revolutionary popular effort to establish a clear-cut gender distinction, suggests that this assumption is shared by many.[27]

The rustic love songs by Yu and Yin, though hated by many intellectuals, who label them "vulgar" *(su)* or "peasants' songs" that "lack character and innovation," are nevertheless hailed by many others (including many intellectuals too) for having a "distinct national character" *(minzu tese)*. It was because of this "distinct national character" that the songs were enthusiastically promoted by the state-run media, and thus could not escape becoming important models of manhood and womanhood. However, a closer look at "The Love of the Boat Tower," "There Is No Rain," and similar songs by Yu and Yin that, because of their "traditional" folksy character, have been labeled "new folksongs" *(xin min'ge)*, reveals that it is mainly the female singer who is responsible for the heavy traditional flavor in these songs, whereas the male singer is quite modern in his overall performance.

This point is also implied in the paragraph that I quoted above, in which the critic suggests that men are the only ones who are influenced by modernity and as a result also have new needs, as if women stood outside of time or were stuck in the past. It is only Yu Wenhua who uses a traditional singing style in her "new folksongs" with Yin Xiangjie. The latter, by contrast, sings in the most ordinary contemporary, nonorthodox pop/rock style. In an article written by Li Fan, the composer of "There Is No Rain" and Yu's husband, in which he describes the creative process involved in the production of Yu and Yin's folk hits, the composer suggests that originally "The Love of the Boat Tower," the earliest hit of the duo, was sung entirely in a traditional folk singing style and that he decided to limit the use of this "old" singing style because he was "afraid that the song [would] not provide the listeners with a sense of freshness" (1996, 4). The fact that the attempt to create "freshness" was applied only to Yin Xiangjie's part implies that it is fine and acceptable when women sing in "old" style.

The association of the male performer with modernity and the female performer with tradition is extended to the duo's costumes and other performance-related aspects. When performing the songs on television, Yin Xiangjie was usually dressed in modern clothes (when not half naked), whereas Yu Wenhua wore typical traditional feminine costumes. In one television performance, the relationship between the female performer and tradition was further enhanced when she was carried to the stage in a sedan chair, like a traditional bride being carried to her wedding. This pattern of modern image for men singers and traditional image for women singers is quite common in the state-run Chinese Music Television, as I describe later in the chapter.

Finally, as Dru Gladney (1994a) has suggested in relation to the representation of ethnic minorities in China, the fact that Yu Wenhua and other female pop singers are dressed in traditional costumes and sing in traditional style much more often than male singers is an important factor that makes them exoticized objects and ultimately the other in contemporary Chinese pop. By contrast, in his normal clothes and singing, Yin Xiangjie represents the normality and subjectivity of men. It could also be argued that the tendency to position female singers in tradition and to emphasize their softness, weakness, passivity, and restraint helps to highlight, by way of a structural opposition, the modernity of men and their boldness, power, and uninhibitedness—that is, their masculinity.

New Voices of Women in the Popular Music Scene and Alternative Models of Womanhood

Although, since the early to mid-1990s, more and more female singers on the mainland conformed to the soft, passive, static, and restrained image of womanhood, be it that which celebrates chastity, like the image assumed by Sun Yue, or that which celebrates controlled sexuality and existence for men, like the image assumed by Chen Ming, the pop scene of the mid-1990s nevertheless simultaneously saw the emergence of new women's voices who started to challenge this dominant image and to present alternative models of womanhood. These new voices emphasize difference but at the same time also power, dynamism, boldness, freedom, creativity, and independence. Although in terms of content they do not differ in any essential way from the voices that started to be heard at least a decade earlier in the PRC, they were nevertheless novel and significant in that they were articulated by women who were not necessarily intellectuals, and no less importantly, in that they were communicated in the domain of popular music, thus reaching the most general public sphere through the electronic mass media associated with this domain.

In this section I discuss three female musicians who have attempted to gain a larger degree of subjectivity and to extend the range of expression allowed to women in Chinese pop, and who thereby challenge the near-monopoly of men over creativity and the representation of women. With their new voices these three female musicians also challenge the state by contesting both its orthodox representation of women, which always suppressed gender distinction, and the popular neotraditional female image of a domesticated, self-sacrificing, "virtuous wife–good mother" (Rofel 1994b, 710–12; Notar 1994; Croll 1995, 157), the propagation of which the state has supported with enhanced vigor since the early 1990s. Through this double challenge, the new voices discussed here constitute a significant shift in women's representation in popular culture and mass media in the PRC and in women's role in this representation. My discussion opens with the musician Ai Jing and her 1993 hit "My 1997" *(Wo de 1997):*

MY 1997 (ORIGINAL VERSION)[28]
(lyrics by Ai Jing; music by Ai Jing and Aidi; performance by Ai Jing)

My music teacher was my father
He spent the last twenty years in a state factory . . .
When I was seventeen I left my home in Shenyang
Because I felt my dream was not to be found there
I arrived alone in Beijing, which I didn't know . . .
From Beijing I moved to sing in Shanghai's beach
And from Shanghai I moved to sing in the south, which I once used to
    yearn for
I stayed quite a while in Guangzhou
Because my boyfriend stayed in Hong Kong
When will I be able to go to Hong Kong, what are the people in Hong
    Kong like?
He can come to Shenyang, but I can't go to Hong Kong . . .
I never thought I would certainly become Mei Yanfang[29]
I am like the cat in the street
Because I feel I lead a vagrant life like it does
When will it be possible to go to Hong Kong without a visa and
    a stamp?
Let me go to this dazzling world, give me this big red stamp . . .[30]
I heard it's old Cui [Jian]'s important market . . .
1997, please come quickly! So I can go to Hong Kong
1997, please come quickly! So I can stand in Hung Hom Coliseum[31]
1997, please come quickly! So I can see what the clothes in Yaohan are
    actually like . . .

Although in "My 1997" Ai Jing does not overtly engage gender issues, the song is nevertheless a significant statement about womanhood and women's representation.[32] "My 1997" is one of the earliest songs both written and performed by a female musician in post-revolutionary China.[33] Unlike most of the songs that I described earlier, which are only sung by female singers, "My 1997" is in that respect the voice of a woman who is struggling to gain subjectivity and control over her own representation. In her song Ai Jing challenges the near-monopoly of men in the pop scene over not only creativity and subjectivity, but also authenticity and individualism. "My 1997" is a bold personal statement in which the female musician assumes that her short personal autobiography is of value. The boldness of Ai Jing's expression can be fully appreciated only once the song is contextualized in the still dominant collective ethos of the early 1990s. In her individualistic celebration of the self, Ai Jing also challenges the state, which has always promoted collectivism and suppressed individualism; and in this she also challenges men's near monopoly over political protest in the pop scene and in popular culture in general.

Ai Jing's relationship with the state and official discourse in "My 1997" and in her overall musical activity is a complex one. The line "When will it be possible to go to Hong Kong without a visa and a stamp," in particular, invokes the official agenda of reunification and may explain why Ai Jing was embraced by the state and why the song became so popular on the mainland. After all, most people on the mainland share the official aspiration for reunification. The implied official agenda of reunification in "My 1997" also dominated the reception of the song in Taiwan. A Taiwanese friend told me that, in contrast to the mainland, most people in Taiwan did not like Ai Jing's "My 1997," and consequently all of her later songs, because they interpreted it as a manifestation of mainland chauvinism.

Nevertheless, Ai Jing's song subverts the state and officialdom in very important ways. Even though the subject of the song is the 1997 return of Hong Kong to the mainland, the song belittles the collective nationalistic significance of the historic event, implying that it is of little relevance to Ai Jing and that she has her own personal agenda, which has little relationship with that of the state. In one interview, Ai Jing told the reporter that originally she entitled her song "1997," but after people commented that it was very "political," she decided to add the word "my" to stress that it was her own private 1997 (Cheng 1993, 4). Ironically, it is this statement and the additional "my" that make the song even more politically potent, as Ai Jing suggests that she stands apart from the collective or state, as a separate, autonomous entity.

A challenge to the party-state is also articulated quite explicitly when Ai Jing complains that her boyfriend can come to visit her but she cannot go to visit him. This and the articulation of her strong desire to get out from China establish a strong sense of imprisonment that is certainly not flattering to the government. The fact that Hong Kong, and not China, is glorified in the song further adds to the challenge. Another related challenge to the state, albeit more subtle, is articulated through the implied contrast between Ai Jing herself, whom the song presents as a free, dynamic person who is not associated with any governmental unit, and her father, whom the song suggests is imprisoned in the state factory. Ai Jing also articulates her independence from the state in the above-mentioned interview, where she emphasizes that she is a self-employed *(geti)* musician—that is, a musician who does not work for the state (Cheng 1993, 4).

Ai Jing discloses some of her politically problematic artistic and ideological inclinations also when she mentions Cui Jian and Hong Kong female superstar Anita Mui (Mei Yanfang in Mandarin). The sheer mention of these two musicians invokes subversive sentiments, especially since Cui Jian is referred to as "old Cui," which implies respect and familiarity in Chinese. The reference to Anita Mui is at least as important. The line "I never thought I would certainly become Mei Yanfang" is the only point in the song where Ai Jing identifies herself explicitly as a woman. Anita Mui revolutionized *gangtai* pop in the 1980s when she assumed a provocative, Madonna-like image, dancing wildly and celebrating an overt and provocative sexuality on stage. Several of her hits, the most famous of which is "Bad Girl" *(Huai nühai),* were banned on the mainland because they were considered pornographic. It is against this problematic nature of Mui's wild, overtly sexual, unrestrained image of femininity that Ai Jing's reference invokes subversive sentiments.[34] Nevertheless, the reference to Anita Mui is not unequivocal. Though on first hearing it communicates the message that Ai Jing never had much hope of becoming as great as Anita Mui, it could also suggest a challenge to Anita Mui and the kind of womanhood she represents. After all, Ai Jing constructs for herself a very different image of womanhood from that associated with Mui.

In contrast to Anita Mui and many female singers like Chen Ming, who appear on the cover of their albums with fancy hairdo, dresses, and makeup, Ai Jing appears in the photographs that are attached to her 1993 and 1995 albums, as well as in her television and live performances, in casual clothing, usually consisting of pants and a plain shirt, with no makeup at all and without ornaments or fancy hairdo. In the above interview the musician states that she does not like to adorn herself, and then adds that she "hates writers who write about romantic love as if it were humans' only pursuit" (Cheng 1993, 4). Thus, in her statement and her overall image Ai Jing offers an alternative to the dominant image of womanhood today in popular culture on the mainland, in which women seem to exist only for men, adorned, "feminine," and waiting. "My 1997," the only song on Ai Jing's 1993 album that she wrote herself, constructs an image that is almost the opposite of the "little sister" in "The Love of the Boat Tower," who sits on the boat, towed by her male lover and waiting for him to kiss her. Instead, Ai Jing depicts herself as an independent, free, active, dynamic, perhaps even rebellious woman, who left home at the age of seventeen and became a vagrant, roaming all over China looking for her dreams.

Although Ai Jing acknowledges in her song the existence of a boyfriend, she nevertheless refers to him in the most ordinary manner, using the unromanticized term *neige,* which literally means "that one." The implication is that she is not available and by extension that she does not exist for men, as opposed, for example, to the beautiful, lonely, nocturnal female persona in Chen Ming's album, who exists only to attract the male listener and provide him with erotic fantasies. Quite in contrast to most pop songs during the mid-1990s in China, which were androcentric, and in which women were objectified even in their own songs, in Ai Jing's song it is rather the male who becomes the other, not "you" but rather "that one." It is also clear that Ai Jing's boyfriend is only a part of her life and that her existence is not dependent on him or dedicated to him.

The times I saw Ai Jing in 1995 and 1996 (on television and in concert), she always accompanied herself with a guitar. Singing and accompanying oneself with a guitar in China is a musical practice that is found, with few exceptions, only in rock, and it is thus associated almost exclusively with men. "Boys," one of the few songs written about men, which I mentioned earlier, lists playing a guitar as one of the things that characterize men. Ai Jing's guitar-playing is significant not only for its challenge to the monopoly of men over the practice but also for what this practice signifies. Writing and performing her own songs, and furthermore accompanying herself with a guitar, Ai Jing became one of China's first female *quanneng* musicians, that is, a female musician with "complete ability." She ceased being just a singer who sings songs written by others (mostly male) and, like rockers, she gained an independent, authentic voice and more control over her musical expression and performance, not being restricted in performance anymore, as most singers in China up to the mid-1990s were, by a prerecorded soundtrack.

Ai Jing also articulates her alternative image of womanhood in "My 1997" through sound. Generally speaking, her song constructs a sonic image of casualness and simplicity, employing the Western aesthetics of folk rock. She sings in an unadorned voice, which corresponds to her visual image as well as to the image constructed through the lyrics. The delivery is sometimes halfway between singing and talking, as if to fit the narrative quality of the lyrics, and the accompaniment throughout most of the song is simple, featuring an acoustic guitar. The guitar is percussive, providing a rock-like rhythmic drive, which enforces the dynamic, vagrant image that the lyrics construct. This sonic image prevails throughout most of the song, except for two times when a group of women, accompanied by a *sanxian* (a traditional three-string Chinese lute), join in to sing in Chinese folksy style the lines "When will I be able to go to Hong Kong, what are the people in Hong Kong like?" and later, "When will it be possible . . . without a visa and a stamp?" In the last stanza of the song (starting just before "1997, please come quickly! So I can go to Hong Kong"), drums are introduced and the tempo speeds up. The sentence "1997, please come quickly," accompanied by the same rhythmic line, is repeated over and over again, altogether eight times. This energetic repetitiveness constructs a carefree, unrestrained, hippie-like atmosphere of merry-making. The mild, trance-like repetitiveness suggests a carnivalistic defiance of structure and artistic orthodox discipline and a celebration of spontaneity, which is normally found only in rock, and because of which, in part at least, rockers were often not allowed to perform in public and were banned from the state-run television for many years. This free, joyous, nutty image is enforced when, toward the end of her song, Ai Jing bursts into free laughter while singing. In the last repetitions the words are replaced by nonsense vocables, yet another expression of a free, unconstrained spirit rarely found in songs by female singers.

Despite the obvious subscription to Western rock and folk values and an aesthetics of freedom, naturalness, protest, individualism, authenticity, and directness of expression, Ai Jing nevertheless chooses not to express herself in the conventional, aggressive, masculine style that male rockers on the mainland have celebrated, at least until recently, in order to assert their defiance, modernity, nonconformism, and masculinity. Ai Jing thus acquires the language of rock but resists assimilation. She maintains her independence not only vis-à-vis the state and vis-à-vis the mainstream but also vis-à-vis male rockers.

"My 1997" introduced a whole new style into China, which was labeled "urban folk ballads" *(chengshi minyao)* and was identified with Ai Jing and the male musician Li Chunbo. The pathbreaking, independent, free image of Ai Jing in "My 1997" reveals itself most clearly in the fact that she seems to obey no stylistic rules of any kind. The song proper combines pop and folk. Following the singing of the nonsense vocables mentioned earlier, the musician suddenly starts to sing a preexistent folk tune. The original version of "My 1997," which appears at the end of Ai Jing's album, lasts seven minutes and thirty-three seconds, thus defying the conventional time limits to which most pop songs today conform. The song also cele-

brates irregularity in terms of form and structure: lines have a varying number of words, and after the three opening stanzas, stanzas are of
different lengths. Lu Tonglin has suggested that "the search for female
voices can only take a highly individualized form" (1993, 12), and later,
when discussing the female writer Can Xue, she writes that because of the
latter's "double marginality" as a woman vis-à-vis the party and vis-à-vis
male experimental writers, she "does not need to acknowledge or follow
any particular masters, be they Western or Chinese" (1993, 178). Despite
the significant differences between Can Xue and Ai Jing, Lu's observation
can also be applied to the latter. In other words, Ai Jing's unique style may
be interpreted as a result of her "double marginality" as a woman vis-à-vis
the party-state and vis-à-vis the male-dominated mainstream and male-
exclusive rock. The new style was not only a choice but also something inevitable. As a woman who wishes to speak in an autonomous voice, she had
to invent her own style, as all other styles were male-dominated, thus
denying female subjectivity.

Ai Jing's personal unique image is developed further in her 1995 album
The Story of Yanfen Street (Yanfen jie de gushi), in which for the first time
she directly addresses the issue of gender. Whereas on her 1993 album only
one song was written by her ("My 1997"), on the new album she is responsible for most of the songs. The new album, like the earlier one, does
include love songs, but its main focus is again not on romantic love or
men. *The Story of Yanfen Street* is a very personal, nostalgic engagement
with the musician's past, her childhood, and her beloved grandparents. The
musician once again demonstrates her nonconventional artistic tendencies when she ends the album with a lengthy spoken monologue about
her beloved late grandfather, which she delivers to the accompaniment of
the somber sounds of a cello. Preceding this monologue is Ai Jing's most
famous song from this album, "Grandmother, This Kind of a Woman"
(Waipo zheyang de nüren), in which she speaks about her grandmother,
but also about womanhood in general:

GRANDMOTHER, THIS KIND OF A WOMAN
(lyrics, music, and performance by Ai Jing)

Woman, woman's life, ah
Living for whom . . .
For her man
For her and his children
In her first awakening of love she is drawn by love
In her maturity she suffers for love . . .
Grandmother, this kind of a woman . . .

Who opened the door of the house in wind and rain . . .
It is you who made for me a colorful cotton-padded jacket . . .

"Grandmother, This Kind of a Woman" is a sigh of agony. It is sung in a slow tempo, in somber fashion, to the accompaniment of an acoustic guitar, a keyboard, and a cello. The point of the song is straightforward— namely, that women do not live for themselves, and that their lives are dedicated to others, their men and their children. This lyrical content, however, does not automatically have a negative connotation, since women's dedication and self-sacrifice have always been praised. However, the overall tragic sonic image that Ai Jing constructs in her song turns the song into an elegy. And yet, in this tragic, dark image of women's destiny, Ai Jing nevertheless carves some lines of light, expressing her love and gratitude to her grandmother for her love and care, as if trying to compensate through her expression of appreciation and gratitude for the suffering of the old woman. After singing parts of the song in intense, loud, powerful, crying fashion, Ai Jing once again breaks away, as in the original version of "My 1997," from this masculine sonic image to return toward the end of the song to a more lyrical "feminine ending" (McClary 1991). The song ends with a soft, unaccompanied lullaby from northeast China, Ai Jing's birthplace, which immediately invokes images of cherished motherhood. Following this lullaby, Ai Jing recites in traditional style a children's rhyme, during which she bursts into tears, for her own lost childhood, for women's fate. One magazine article reported that when Ai Jing performed this song in Japan she became so emotional after exchanging a few words with a Chinese woman who attended the concert and burst into tears that she did not even complete the song ("Ai Jing Dongjing Gechanghui" 1995, 13).

It is not incidental that the short exchange of words mentioned above was with another women and adjunct to this particular song; as "Grandmother, This Kind of a Woman" is about constructing an exclusive territory for women. It is a song created by a woman, performed by a woman, about womanhood, and it is very much for women. The use of the lullaby at the end of the song plays a crucial role in this construction of an autonomous territory, as lullabies are associated exclusively with women. Ai Jing's use of the lullaby articulates her identity as a woman, but it also poses a challenge to men. Traditionally, lullabies have been sung in private, at home, where women have been, and still are, believed by many to belong. In public, when women were allowed to sing, they were almost always supposed to sing for men, as most Chinese and non-Chinese female singers still do today. Against this background, Ai Jing's challenge is embodied in the fact that she articulates in public an exclusive feminine voice which with few exceptions has always been kept at home, and, no less importantly, also in the fact that not only does she not sing for men, but she in fact marginalizes them and even warns women that the initial romantic relationship with men may end for women in suffering.

It is only after conducting an in-depth analysis of this song that I started to understand some of the antagonism of many men toward Ai Jing. Ai Jing became one of the most famous female singers on the mainland after she released her 1993 album, probably because in "My 1997" the collective agenda of the anticipation to Hong Kong's return to the mainland overshadowed her subtle, subversive femininity and her strong individualism. This reception of "My 1997" provides a recent example of the century-long practice in China of interpreting, appropriating, and subjugating women's voices to serve masculinist, nationalistic discourse.[35] In 1995 and 1996, however, after the release of her second album, Ai Jing's popularity decreased significantly, and on several occasions men with whom I spoke expressed a strong antagonism that I did not initially comprehend, especially amid the enormous popularity that "My 1997" had enjoyed just three years earlier. One young male intellectual, for instance, labeled Ai Jing "luosuo," meaning long-winded, over-elaborate, and troublesome. There is no doubt that the general decrease in the popularity of Ai Jing's songs can be attributed to their increasingly personal and nonconformist flavor, which defies the traditional preference in Chinese culture for more collective and standardized forms of expression, a preference that still prevails, despite the new post-revolutionary sensibilities and the change in aesthetics and values. However, I strongly believe that at least some of the male antagonism I came across may also be related to Ai Jing's alternative model of femininity, which although not explicitly anti-men, nevertheless poses a challenge to them. In addition to deflating the importance of her relationship with them, Ai Jing's song challenges men also by the fact that it talks about an old grandmother who cannot be sexually objectified and thus cannot appeal to male desire, the main driving force in the pop market.[36]

Ai Jing's invention of her own musical style is probably the most serious challenge to men, because it challenges their control over musical language. This is perhaps the reason why, despite the general acknowledgment of her innovative role in introducing a new style into the Chinese pop scene, her womanhood is seldom acknowledged in the male-dominated music media. While this may be partly because Ai Jing herself avoids turning her gender into an issue, it may also be understood as an attempt to soften her challenge to the control of men over musical language in the pop scene. The 1993 article from which I quoted earlier (Cheng 1993), for example, which was written by a male author, assumes an obviously patronizing attitude toward the musician, as indicated by its title, "The Soar of the Little Swallow: Reporting on the Young Singer Ai Jing." In another article, published two and a half years later, after the release of her second album, Ai Jing is repeatedly praised for her musicianship, and yet, despite her straightforward engagement with the issue of womanhood on this album, the article simply ignores it. All the author has to say about "Grandmother, This Kind of a Woman" is that it is about Ai Jing's "affectionate grandmother" (Zhan 1995b, 2). This simplistic reading may be understood as lack of comprehension, but also as an attempt to silence Ai Jing's alternative feminine voice, one of the few in popular music culture on the mainland of the early and mid-1990s that problematized the position of women in contemporary Chinese society.

Yet Ai Jing's statement about womanhood in "Grandmother, This Kind of a Woman," like her "My 1997," is not unambiguous. The tragic tone is obvious, but motherhood or grandmotherhood seems to be highly cherished, even if it implies that women still live for someone else, a point that rests at the basis of Ai Jing's critique. It is after all the grandmother's "living for someone else" that causes Ai Jing as a particular "someone else" (a granddaughter) to cherish her. I believe that it is this kind of reading that led to the official embrace of Ai Jing's song. Officials at CCTV and the Ministry of Culture seem to have read the song or hoped that it would be read by others as a praise song for motherhood and by extension as an affirmation of the traditional values of women's dedication and self-sacrifice. These Confucian values have been more explicitly endorsed in official discourse since the early 1990s as part of the post-Tiananmen official pursuit of sociopolitical stability and order, as well as distinctive national identity and modernity. It was also at this point that orthodox state feminism, with its images of masculinized women, started to give way in official media to the neotraditional image of the loyal, family-oriented, dedicated woman. This neotraditional image, which has often been referred to as the "oriental woman" (dongfang nüren), is celebrated today both in and outside official media, and it is this image that the state ironically seemed to have hoped to advance through the promotion of Ai Jing's song. Another, related factor that probably contributed to the embrace of the song by the state is Ai Jing's asexual feminine image.[37] Such an image obviously conformed to the desexualized womanhood that the Chinese state has always propagated.

The criticism in "Grandmother, This Kind of a Woman," becomes much clearer once it is examined in the context of Ai Jing's album, in which she clearly reacts against the traditional image of womanhood that is invoked in this song. Ai Jing distances herself from this image even in the reference to her grandmother as "this kind of a woman," which implies otherness vis-à-vis Ai Jing herself. Ai Jing articulated her wish to distance herself from "this kind of woman" explicitly and publicly in a 1995 article, in which she was quoted as saying: "I love my grandmother, but I do not want to live like her" ("Ai Jing" 1995, 31). Seen against the increasing official efforts to propagate the new image of the "oriental woman," the negation of women's dedication and self-sacrifice in Ai Jing's song is yet another challenge to the state.

The Story of Yanfen Street constructs an image that is similar in many ways to that constructed in "My 1997," namely, of a dynamic, active, free, vagrant *(liulang)* woman who has "a desire to fly" (from "Desire to Fly," *Xiang fei de yuwang;* see below) and is "used to leading a vagrant life" (from "You Are My Wings," *Ni shi wo de chibang;* see below). Though several of Ai Jing's songs are about love and men, she speaks about a different kind of love and a different kind of relationship between herself and her man. The album talks about a relationship that will not force her to be domesticated like her grandmother or like the feminine role models represented by female singers like Chen Ming, a relationship that will allow her the freedom to roam and still be loved, the kind of freedom that has always been monopolized by men. This kind of freedom, which revealed itself musically in the carefree, improvisatory ending of the original version of "My 1997," is articulated musically also in "Grandmother, This Kind of a Woman." The latter goes on and on to include the lullaby and then the children's rhyme, and then the lullaby once again, all of which are performed in an overtly improvisational style.

Another song included on Ai Jing's 1995 album, entitled "You Are My Wings," is a paraphrase of Cui Jian's "Flower-House Girl," where the male rocker asserts his masculinity through the image of a dynamic male who wishes to be free. The female other in Cui Jian's song, by contrast, is a static entity, a force that denies the male self his freedom and turns him into a captive. Ai Jing uses a similar narrative in her song, speaking of a desire to go to the sea, which suggests freedom, a loss of direction because of love, and the intoxicating warmth of love. She even borrows a line from Cui Jian's song: "I am fully aware that I'm already unable to leave you" *(wo mingzhi wo yi li bu kai ni).* This rearticulation of Cui Jian's line, however, reverses the order of things, turning the male other into the static element that threatens to domesticate the female self. Although she wishes to love and to be loved, Ai Jing is nevertheless unwilling to give up her freedom and her vagrant life.

As if to identify herself as a woman while assuming what many regard as a masculine quality, Ai Jing constructs a relationship between herself and the moon, the ultimate manifestation in nature of the feminine *yin* force. This association immediately stands out against the repeated mention in many rock songs of the sun, the greatest masculine, *yang* force in nature, which is used by rockers almost as a totem of masculinity.[38] Again, Ai Jing refuses to be assimilated in the masculinist ethos and symbolism of rock. She struggles to maintain and articulate her femininity, while challenging men's monopoly over certain qualities and possibilities. Moreover, in contrast to Cui Jian's song, which constructs a fixed structural opposition between the male self and the female other that cannot be solved and in a sense is doomed to be contradictory, Ai Jing suggests that she and the male other in her song can perhaps fly together, and that he is her wings, a statement I understand as meaning that his love gives her the power to be free and to roam.

YOU ARE MY WINGS
(lyrics by Ai Jing; music by Xiao Zhe; performance by Ai Jing)

I got used to leading a vagrant life . . .
I have fallen in love with flying . . .
I tell you my direction
It is there, where the sea is . . .
But a strange sadness has been added
I have fallen in love with the moon
When this moonlight illuminates your face and mine
I lose direction . . .
When you hold me in your arms . . .
I am fully aware that I'm already unable to leave you . . .
You are my wings
Flying together over cities and through villages . . .

The reconciliatory approach to love and personal freedom found in "You Are My Wings" is, nonetheless, reversed in another song from Ai Jing's 1995 album, entitled "Desire to Fly." Here Ai Jing contrasts the attempts of the male other to domesticate her with her wish to "have true life" and to "experience real existence." The contradiction between love and personal freedom remains unresolved in the song, which ends with Ai Jing's insistence on not giving up her personal freedom.

DESIRE TO FLY
(lyrics by Ai Jing; music by Chen Jing; performance by Ai Jing)

I have a desire to fly
To fly to a distant place
Where my dream is . . .
You said I'm like a child
A child who doesn't understand a thing . . .
You said I must find a serious job
So when I get old I'll have security
You'll make me stop roaming about
Give me a place
Give me a sweet dream
But I want to live a true life
Experience real existence . . .

Cheng Lin: "None of Your Business"   Cheng Lin was one of the most famous female singers in China during the 1980s. Referred to at the time as "little Cheng Lin" and at other times as "little Deng Lijun" after the Taiwanese female superstar whom she imitated for a while, Cheng has been hailed in several Chinese publications on popular music as a "brave" singer, who, together with other female singers like Li Guyi and Su Xiaoming, introduced into China in the early 1980s the sweet, slow, "feminine" *tongsu* singing style as well as many foreign pop songs (see Ling Ruilan 1994, 2). Yet today Cheng Lin has a different view of these years, for which she is referred to as "brave" because she sang officially disapproved songs in what was an officially disapproved musical style. After five years abroad, during which she stayed in Australia, France, and the United States, Cheng Lin returned in the mid-1990s to the mainland and started to speak in a new voice. In a 1995 article, in which the author states that she is "not the naive and vivacious 'little Cheng Lin' of the past anymore" (Wu Xiaoying 1995a, 2), Cheng Lin made the following comments with regard to her past:

> The five years abroad were a very happy period in my life. Because since I was thirteen I did not have my own life. Everything was arranged for me by other people: "little Cheng Lin, sing this song," "little Cheng Lin, it's your turn to go up to the stage." . . . In the past my songs were mostly things by other people, now I start to bring my individual character into play. (Quoted in Wu Xiaoying 1995a, 3)

Cheng Lin clearly does not view her past as heroic or brave in any sense, but rather as a period during which she was manipulated by others and could not articulate her own voice or bring her own character into play. The musician does not hide the link between her lengthy stay in the West and her new attitude toward her past, her future, music in general, and Chinese music in particular. The article above suggests that the West turned Cheng Lin into an independent, mature, assertive, creative individual, who believes in herself and her music. It is filled with many statements by Cheng Lin, one of which, quoted below, is about Chinese traditional music. Cheng Lin's reference in the article to the *erhu*, the Chinese two-string fiddle, has to do with the fact that she herself plays the instrument:

> The *erhu* is an ancient, traditional musical instrument. Many of the compositions that are played on it have been circulating for several hundred years. Each tuning and each fingering is immutable and frozen. I, however, like to display my individual character very much. Since I was small I wanted to be different from other people. This time, I added to the *erhu* the rhythm of black music, to turn "River Water" [*Jianghe shui*, a famous traditional instrumental piece] with its hidden bitterness into a joyous "River Water."[39] I didn't change only the tuning and fingering of the *erhu* but also the character of the instrument. In the past I always felt that the Chinese pentatonic scale was the most beautiful thing, but now I don't think so anymore. The *erhu* is a musical instrument with a lot of potential, but if it is to go through any new development, new concepts must be added to it. (Quoted in Wu Xiao-ying 1995a, 3)

This paragraph is significant in several respects. First, it vividly illustrates that women are far from silent in the pop scene. Cheng Lin presents a bold critique of Chinese musical tradition and asserts her individuality—that is, her wish to be different from others, her critical, innovative, and creative capabilities, and her unwillingness to conform to traditional musical standards, qualities that are usually associated in the pop scene almost exclusively with men. The second significant thing about this paragraph is Cheng Lin's discussion of the transformation of "River Water." Although she does not make any direct reference to issues of gender in this paragraph (or in any other statements in this article), her discussion of the musical transformation of "River Water," for which she credits herself and therefore can be held responsible, suggests a new concept of womanhood. This concept is implied in the rest of the article as well as in Cheng Lin's new 1995 album, *Returning Home (Hui jia)*, which was released upon her return to the mainland. "River Water" is a traditional composition that invokes extreme sorrow and that has been traditionally associated with the deep sorrow or crying of a woman whose husband died. On Cheng Lin's album, this instrumental piece is turned into a song with lyrics (by the Hong Kong male lyricist Huang Zhan). The song nevertheless retains the original melody and the *erhu* playing, which Cheng Lin herself provides, in addition to the singing. In her transformation of the elegiac piece into a "joyous" *(huanle)* song through the introduction of rhythms taken from black music, which she learned abroad, Cheng Lin challenges the representation and image of woman and womanhood in much of traditional Chinese culture and throughout history, where women are doomed to wait in agony for their men who do not return, or to cry forever over their dead husbands or lovers. This image was more than just an artistic convention. Confucian ethics idealized widows who did not remarry, and arches were often built to commemorate those women who maintained their chastity and loyalty.

Through her new musical treatment of this traditional piece that perpetuates the tragic destiny of women, Cheng Lin offers a symbolic liberation for the female persona who inhabits the piece and much of Chinese history. She suggests that women are not doomed to wait in agony forever for their departed men and that they can start anew and leave the past behind them. Leaving the past behind is also the main point of the lyrics of the song, which talk about the river taking away the past and the tears forever. The new musical narrative created by Cheng Lin tells her own story: her marriage, her divorce (Wu Xiaoying 1995a), and her new independent comeback, which resulted in her new album, where most of the songs—both lyrics and music, as Cheng Lin herself emphasizes—were created by her.

Cheng Lin's assertion of her individuality and independence is articulated most vividly in a song entitled "None of Your Business" (*Bie guan wo*, literally meaning "don't bother about me"; "None of Your Business" is the musician's translation). Most of the song is sung in a stirring, rhythmic hip-hop style, whereas the fourth stanza, which has longer sentences, is delivered in rap style. The use of hip-hop and rap in this song are closely related to Cheng Lin's articulation of her independence and resistance to male domination and are almost a natural choice. Resistance and protest are almost inherent in the Western musical styles that Cheng Lin uses, and her use of these styles in itself implies resistance to the androcentric attempt to restrict female musical expressions to sweet, soft songs. Another, related challenge in "None of Your Business" has to do with the fact that both the music and the lyrical content in the song are Western-inspired, reflecting Cheng Lin's stay in the United States and other Western countries. In explicitly articulating this influence, the song challenges the attempts made by men in China today to monopolize Westernization and modernization, both of which are intimately tied, of course, with power:

NONE OF YOUR BUSINESS
(lyrics, music, and performance by Cheng Lin)

What I say is none of your business
What I do is none of your business
There are people who tell me
That I can't speak as I please
There are people who lecture me
That I can't behave like that . . .
Do you mind singing your own song?
Do not mind other people's business, saying that I'm right or wrong . . .
I have my own way
And I alone will explore it
You are you, I am me
I live for myself

Wayhwa: "I Only Wanna Make Love to You"   Wayhwa is the only female musician of the three discussed here who could be considered an intellectual in the strict sense of the word, being the only one with any formal higher education. She attended the Beijing Broadcasting College and in the late 1980s became known nationwide when she served as the anchor of the English news program on CCTV. Her bright career at CCTV, however, ended after a problematic interview she gave to Ted Koppel during the 1989 democracy movement (Wayhwa, interview with the author, 25 June 1996). Following a forced official distancing from the screen, Wayhwa decided to leave her work unit altogether and became the lead singer of Breathing *(Huxi)*, one of China's earliest rock bands. In the early 1990s the band disbanded and Wayhwa disappeared from the music scene only to return a few years later with her own solo album, *Modernization (Xiandaihua)*, which was released in 1995.

Like Cheng Lin and many other female musicians who have recently complained that in the past they could not speak out in their own voice, Wayhwa suggested to me that with Breathing, despite being a rocker, she did not have her own real voice. Although she was the lead singer in the band and wrote the lyrics for some of the band's songs, the female musician has been quoted as saying:

> During the period with Breathing I was confused and anxious music-wise and mood-wise. I only wanted to express, but I did not know how to express. Although I did try hard at that time, I did not find a more suitable music. I also never considered creating music. Moreover, back then I simply did not think of myself as a woman. . . . During the period with Breathing . . . I was unable to decide for myself, and I was not sure of

myself because the creation of music was all done by them [the rest of the band's members, who were all male]. I simply did not realize that I could write songs myself. (Quoted in Wang Xiaofeng 1996, 5)

Wayhwa's account is revealing because it provides an important insider affirmation of the male-dominated nature of the rock subculture on the mainland and sheds a whole new light on her assertive, powerful image during the period with Breathing. In her 1995 solo album, as opposed to her role in Breathing, Wayhwa celebrates creativity and individuality, as the lyricist, composer, and performer of all the songs included on it. On the cover of the mainland version of her cassette album (unlike a CD version that was released in Hong Kong), the musician is shown holding a guitar, a rare sight in the Chinese pop scene, which suggests that she is more than just a singer who sings songs written by others (figure 7).

In this album Wayhwa breaks away from the extremely rough and tough masculinist ethos and aesthetics that characterized Chinese rock during the late 1980s and early 1990s. This break manifests itself in the overall sound of her album, which tends to be much less aggressive and seems to reflect her discovery of her own femininity. It is also revealed in the more feminine and less aggressive look of her photographs on the covers of the two versions of her album, in which she is shown wearing makeup, longer hair, what seems to be a skirt, a necklace (on the Hong Kong CD), and no sunglasses. Despite this departure from her previous image, however, the musician nevertheless retains much of the rock spirit and still sees herself as a rocker (Wayhwa, interview with the author, 25 June 1996). Imbued with the rock spirit, Wayhwa's 1995 album constitutes another important challenge to the positioning of women in Chinese mainstream pop in a little box in which they are expected to "beg for love in a soft, sweet voice" (Jin Zhaojun, interview with the author, 16 August 1995).

The most obvious challenge in the album is in the form of sociopolitical and cultural critique. In this criticism Wayhwa not only challenges the state, society at large, and mainstream culture, but also men in particular and their near-absolute monopoly in popular Chinese music over expression of political dissent and sociocultural commentary. In "Fresh" *(Xian)*, the opening song in the album, the female rocker articulates a powerful criticism of life in China and Chinese people, whom she depicts as numb, emotionless, and lifeless, and urges them in a high-pitched, yelling voice, delivered on a single pitch, to come out of their state of stagnation and death, get out into the sun and light, breath the fresh air, and come back to life (Wayhwa, interview with the author, 25 June 1996):

Figure 7, above and right.   Wayhwa, *Modernization,* images from cassette cover. Courtesy of Beijing Jingwen Record Company Ltd. and Wayhwa.

FRESH
(lyrics, music, and performance by Wayhwa)

. . . Come out, come out, and get some sun . . .
Sing, dance, talk, and laugh
Brush the dust off your body
Stamp your numb feet
The light irritates the eyes
The crowds of people are not used to it anymore
The air is very fresh . . .
Desires grow under the sun . . .
I am, ya, quivering and frightened, gasping for breath . . .[40]
Exhale the pain that you cannot speak about . . .
Inhale and absorb oxygen and vitamins. . . .

Similar sociopolitical and cultural commentary and criticism are also found in another song, entitled "The Forbidden City," in which the musician articulates her desire, but lack of power, to be liberated from this officially celebrated site, which she views as a symbol of the oppressiveness of China and Chinese culture. In "Visa," to give yet another example, she deconstructs the Great Wall, another cherished national symbol, using it as a metaphor

for the long line of people waiting to get visas to leave the mainland. These two songs will be analyzed in more detail in the next chapter, in my discussion of expressions of political dissent in popular Chinese music.

Though full of sociopolitical commentary, Wayhwa's album also contains personal songs, and it is in these songs that her statements become gendered. In "Honey," written and performed in English, Wayhwa constructs an image of womanhood that is the antithesis of the restrained, submissive, soft woman who was celebrated in the mid-1990s in much of mainstream pop. The most serious challenge in this song to the dominant model of womanhood has to do with female sexuality, a subject that on the one hand has always been denied in official culture, and on the other hand has been objectified and controlled by men in much of nonofficial culture.

HONEY
(lyrics, music, and performance by Wayhwa)

After drinking all the wine
I only wanna make love to you . . .
After climbing all the mountaintops . . .
After givin' up all my hope
I still have one more goal . . . that's love
Honey, please hold my hand
Honey, I do need rest . . .
Honey, you'd better tell me right here that you can liberate me now . . .

Rockers are the only Chinese pop musicians who have consistently and comprehensively challenged the traditional aesthetics of refinement, subtlety, and concealment. However, since most of them are men, statements like "I want to touch you" (from "Moon Dream" [*Yue meng*] by Tang Dynasty) and "My tongue is like tasty delicacies for you to taste" (from "Pretty Girl" by He Yong) are almost always sung by male singers. Even in "The Love of the Boat Tower," in which the female character suggests in the last line of the song that she is waiting to be kissed, not to kiss ("I only wait for the sunset to let you kiss me until you have enough"), a line that caused some to consider the song vulgar, the song as a whole still follows the traditional strategies of subtlety.

In the mid-1990s overt public expressions of sexuality were still banned by the state, and songs about romantic love that were broadcast on the state-run television channel almost always conformed to these traditional strategies. "The Love of the Boat Tower" was promoted by the state despite its overtly sexual ending because it is considered a folksong, in the context of which this overtly sexual line was transformed in the eyes of officials into part of the traditional, "healthy" life of the peasants, the "pure folk." The critic Jin Zhaojun suggested to me that such a line, the directness of which is very rare in Chinese pop, would never have been permitted on television if it was not within the framework of a "folksong" *(min'ge)* (Jin, interview with the author, 16 August 1995). There is no doubt that the enormous popularity that this commercial pseudo-folksong enjoyed in the mid-1990s was related, at least in part, to its subversive expression of overt sexuality.

Interestingly, it was after several young female intellectuals directed my attention to this line with conspicuous delight that I became aware of its existence and started to explore its implications. The song, which was written by urban, intellectual, professional (male) musicians, obviously provided many, both men and women, with a carnivalistic pleasure amid the longstanding suppression of overt sexuality in China. The fact, however, that it was women in particular who pointed out to me on several unrelated occasions the last line of the song, a line sung by a woman, indicated a female-specific pleasure, as if Yu Wenhua, the female singer in the song, was providing those women with a rare voice. For men, such an overt expression of sexuality was not so rare because of their familiarity with and ability to identify with rock, in which such expressions are found in abundance and with few exceptions are always androcentric.

It is within such a context that Wayhwa's "Honey" gets much of its meaning. The song challenges not only sociocultural taboos and political restrictions on expressions of explicit sexuality in China, but more importantly, the situation in which women are almost always expected to be sex objects rather than sexual subjects. Wayhwa does not wait for a man to appreciate her for her beauty (like the female persona in Chen Ming's "Night Rose") but rather "want[s] to make love," plain and simple. She does not beg for love but demands it, almost threatening: "Honey, you'd better tell me right here that you can liberate me now."

In her song, Wayhwa not only challenges the sexual objectification of women in the general culture, where they are usually denied any control over their sexuality and its representation, but also the male monopoly over sexual desire and its artistic articulation. The opening line of "Honey," "After drinking all the wine," also challenges men's monopoly over drinking, getting out of control, and behaving in an uninhibited manner, and by extension also the widespread assumption that woman are or should be more restrained. The challenge in the song is further enhanced by Wayhwa's deep, masculine voice. A forceful danceable beat contributes to the challenge by bolstering the physicality communicated by the lyrics. Wayhwa articulates every syllable to the beat in a way that invokes a powerful, even aggressive, sexuality.

In the second stanza, Wayhwa temporarily explores another kind of womanhood and another kind of sexuality. Here she almost whispers to create a softer, more feminine sonic image. Rhythmic hand-clapping toward the end of the song, however, revives once again the stirring, danceable drive with which the song opened. The singing, too, once again becomes forceful, rough, and rhythmic, and again a strong sense of body movement is established. In the line "Honey, you'd better tell me right here that you can liberate me now," several words are sung at the same pitch in staccato, syllable by syllable, as if to emphasize the anxiousness and the demand, the challenge to the male other.

The fact that "Honey" is written in English is closely related to its content, as there are certain things that people in China are not used to saying or even cannot say in Chinese. Several individuals have suggested to me that even saying "I love you" in Chinese is problematic and "does not sound right," and therefore they and others say "I love you" in English instead. As I have argued throughout this study, the introduction into China of English and modern Western popular musical styles, like rock-and-roll, cannot be separated from the emergence on the mainland of a whole new ethos and practice. Although this is not necessarily always the case, there is a high correlation in Chinese popular music culture today between musical style and linguistic and semantic content. Like Cheng Lin's choice to articulate individuality and independence from the male other in hip-hop and rap style, Wayhwa's choice to sing about her sexual desires in English and in rock style seems almost natural and inevitable, as mainstream Chinese popular music (like Chinese language) simply does not have the vocabulary to articulate such feelings and ideas.

But there is also a more pragmatic aspect to Wayhwa's choice of English, and that is censorship. Attached to the English lyrics of "Honey" in Wayhwa's album is her translation of the song into Chinese, which omits all the references to sexuality found in the original text. Wayhwa told me that she "couldn't write something like that in Chinese" (Wayhwa, interview with the author, 25 June 1996). Her hope that the use of English would save her song from censorship was justified, as the original text of "Honey" did indeed pass the censors. Nevertheless, whereas in the Hong Kong version of her album the English lyrics appear in the attached pamphlet as sung, in the cassette version that was released on the mainland, by contrast, "I only wanna make love to you" has been replaced by "I only wanna talk to you," a vivid reminder that overt sexuality is still taboo in China. Wayhwa comments on this continuing suppression of sexuality in another song on her 1995 album, called "Modernization" *(Xiandaihua)*, in which she sings: "Men and women are in love but cannot look at each other because the director does not allow them to."

The choice to use the word "liberate" in "Honey" (in the line "Honey, you'd better tell me right here that you can liberate me now") is meaningful. It may certainly be interpreted as one more example of how official discourse infiltrates and influences the most personal discourse in China, even that used by dissidents. But on the other hand, the context in which Wayhwa uses this word may also suggest a conscious parody of official discourse and officialdom in general, not unlike the similar recontextualization of the language of the state in Wang Shuo's novels.[41] Viewed in this way, the use of the word "liberate" may actually be even more meaningful than it first appears. It may be interpreted as trivializing and even negating the party's claim to the liberation of women by suggesting that there is a need for a whole different kind of liberation. In other words, Wayhwa's song may suggest that, for her, real liberation means sexual freedom and sexual equality. The implication of such an interpretation is that not only that the state is not a liberator, but that it is actually the oppressor. This implication is enhanced by the line from "Modernization" cited earlier.[42]

The fact that Wayhwa sings two songs on the album in English ("Honey" and "Visa"), very much like her use of rock, has far-reaching implications with regard to gender and specifically with regard to the positioning of women in Chinese pop today vis-à-vis modernization. English is widely used in Chinese rock and is closely associated with the ethos of cosmopolitanism and modernity that is embraced by rockers. Titling the all-rock concert of 1990 "Modern Music Concert" (see chapter 1) was a vivid indication that rock, in fact, is seen by many as synonymous with modernity, even if the word "rock" was replaced by the word "modern" at that particular event because of political reasons. The use of English by rockers in many of their songs articulates their desire to reach out, to "go to the world" *(zou xiang shijie)*, and aims to construct and assert their image of modernity. Yet, since most rockers are men, the implication has always been that modernity is essentially men's work. The critique from which I quoted earlier, which implies that men are the only ones who are influenced by modernity and, as a result, the only ones who have the need to let off steam because of the pressures of modernity, is an example of the widespread assumption that modernity has a closer relationship with men than it has with women. The way Yu Wenhua and Yin Xiangjie perform their male-female duet songs—that is, the fact that she sings in traditional style dressed in traditional-style costumes while he sings in a modern singing style dressed (when not half nude) in modern clothes—provides another example of the tendency to position men in modernity and, in contrast, to position women in tradition. This gender differentiation through the different positioning of men and women in time is obvious in Chinese Music Television, where men are also often represented as dynamic and outward-oriented, in contrast to women, who are often represented as static, inward, and home-oriented. A common image in songs broadcast in 1996 was of a young woman dressed in traditional clothes waiting in the village for her male lover or elder brother, who had gone to the big city to explore the world and is now returning, dressed in modern clothes. This is not to say that there are no songs about modern women, but in general, men tend to sing in traditional singing style *(minzu changfa)* and to be dressed in traditional-style costumes when performing their songs significantly less frequently than women.

The neotraditional image of Chinese women has become an important element in China's recent attempt to revive its traditional culture and construct an alternative, non-Western model of modernity. There is no male equivalent for the new notion of the "oriental woman," which is celebrated today in official and unofficial culture alike and stresses traditional values, like motherhood and other family-oriented roles, as well as softness *(wenrou)*. Although the typical male image in much of mainstream music in the 1990s, as noted earlier, assumes important traditional qualities, no one but its critics talks about this image in terms of tradition. China is clearly much more enthusiastic about celebrating its tradition through the bodies of its women than through the bodies of its men. In other words, tradition is perceived much more positively when it is linked with women, a linkage that, as in the case of China's minorities, also affirms their status as the other.

It is against such a background that Wayhwa's use of rock and English can be read as a challenge to men's attempt to monopolize modernity. Naming her album *Xiandaihua/Modernization* is another challenge. Although in the last song of her album, which bears the same title, she criticizes and parodies Chinese modernity, she nonetheless resists the attempt to marginalize women in the course of the collective search for modernity and claims her right to be an active and vocal participant in the shaping of modern China. As for her explicit criticism and parody of modernity, this criticism may be her way of resisting the state and male domination, since modernity is so intimately tied with men and the masculinist state.

Wayhwa's challenge is so powerful because, unlike her position in the past with Breathing, she now stands by herself and identifies herself as a woman, using the male-dominated musical language and yet resisting the kind of assimilation that she experienced in the past when she "simply did not think of [herself] as a woman." In her album, Wayhwa suggests that she can do what men can do, perhaps even better, and still be a woman.

Nevertheless, Wayhwa's position and message are not without ambivalence and ambiguities. In stark contrast to the general straightforward, rebellious, challenging attitude of her album, the song "Women" *(Nüren)* presents a rather ambivalent view of womanhood, one that stresses the woman's love for the male other and their sense of unity, and that suggests that she will follow him wherever he goes, but at the same time problematizes this very same experience. The problem is encapsulated in the sentence "Thinking about you, I lose myself" *(xiang ni wo meiyou ziji)*. This key line is stressed musically through a sudden break to a higher register and the move from a monotonous, subdued delivery, which may suggest acceptance, to a cry-like vocal burst. Moreover, Wayhwa's song is far from being a happy one. She seems to suggest that she simply cannot help losing herself, and to imply that this is perhaps what makes her a woman. When I interviewed her, Wayhwa suggested that she is well aware of American and Western feminist thinking "that stresses independence and sameness [with man]," and that she is "beyond" that. She also noted that she accepts reality and acknowledges the fact that men and women are different physically and psychologically; "I love, and yes, I will follow my lover. This is woman's nature. [After all,] women are different, they are weaker . . . more emotional and less rational . . . they need the warmth of a man" (Wayhwa, interview with the author, 25 June 1996).

In the last four lines of Wayhwa's song, which is a general statement about womanhood, Wayhwa incorporates, as if to make it sound as a more collective feminine statement, a female group who provides vocal accompaniment. Despite the affirmation of the androcentric stereotype of women as beautiful, the musician nevertheless acknowledges in these lines the suffering of women and the fact that they work hard but their contribution is seldom acknowledged. Thus, the song affirms some aspects of the traditional image of womanhood and acknowledges, perhaps even accepts, in what seems to be a disillusioned tone, the fact that the world is male-dominated. But at the same time, it problematizes this domination, at least to some degree.

The acceptance of male domination and the appeased tone of Wayhwa's song, however, may also be viewed as an attempt to cater to, or at least avoid alienating, the male audience and female audience who take for granted the existing power relationship between men and women.[43] It is, after all, a more useful strategy to maintain an ambivalent tone rather than to attack bluntly, if one wishes to reach to a larger audience, a wish which I believe is also shared by Wayhwa, despite significant statements like "I don't care what other people like" and "I write for myself," which she made when I interviewed her.

WOMEN
(lyrics, music, and performance by Wayhwa)

. . . Thinking about you, I lose myself
No matter where you go, I'll follow
Women are beautiful like that
It is only because of them that the world has sorrow

Women are difficult like that
It is only because of them that men are capable of great achievements

When I asked Wayhwa about her audience, she suggested that most Chinese men do not like women like herself and that it is mainly intellectuals and intellectual women in particular who like her songs, probably because they offer these women a sense of empowerment and liberation. Wayhwa and her alternative model of femininity are not very popular in China, to say the least, a fact that was reflected in the poor sales figures of her album on the mainland.[44] The musician, however, was praised by several intellectual male music critics, who through their positive reviews demonstrated that not all men in China prefer the neotraditional image of womanhood and that alternative models of femininity are more than tolerated today in the country. Below are excerpts from two extremely positive reviews by the male critic Wang Xiaofeng, in which he articulates a criticism of the dominant image of womanhood in Chinese pop and urges women to learn from Wayhwa. Though praising Wayhwa's alternative model of womanhood, however, these reviews provide yet another illustration of how the discourse on ideal womanhood in China is still controlled by men:

> We package female singers either as pure girls or mature women. . . .
> [Both] are men's psychological demands to satisfy themselves. . . .
> [Wayhwa is the first woman] who sings out in a voice that belongs to
> her. . . . [She] has found herself and, as a result, she also achieved a
> musical personality, and this is precisely what Chinese female singers
> in the last decade or two have been lacking the most. (1995b, 49)

> In her album, Wayhwa establishes an independent feminine musical
> personality. . . . [She] ended a long period in which men have been
> exploiting commercial means to sacrifice female musical personality for
> profit. . . . [She] causes men to feel awkward, and she also causes
> women to feel awkward. But this album deserves to be listened to with
> respect, especially by women. (1996, 5)

Implications for Women

It has often been argued that since the reforms of 1978 the position and status of women in China have deteriorated as a result of the resurgence of traditional patriarchal attitudes in society and the fact that they are less protected by the state (or "too protected"; see Woo 1994) in the context of the general liberalization and the emergence of a free-market economy. In the conclusion to their book about Chinese women in the 1980s, Emily Honig and Gail Hershatter make a statement that articulates some of the somber tone that is often evident in writings about Chinese women in the post-revolutionary era:

> Adornment and sexuality, topics that had been off-limits to the genera-
> tion of the Cultural Revolution, dominated publications for young
> women in the 1980s. Attention to beauty and fashion was part of grow-
> ing concern with the quality of personal life, and clearly captured the
> public fancy. But the bejeweled, high-heeled, tastefully made-up young
> woman was no more free to create her own image than the Iron Girl of
> yore, and the image of the Iron Girls may have presented women with
> more possibilities for participation in the public realm. (1988, 335)

Based upon the kind of data that I present in the last sections of this chapter, I would like to conclude in a more optimistic tone, by suggesting that despite their continuing subordination to men and the obvious discrimination against them in different realms of life, including the popular music scene, increasing numbers of Chinese women nevertheless achieved in the music scene of the 1990s a new, independent voice vis-à-vis Chinese men, the state, and the male-dominated market. The emergence of these new, independent women's voices in popular culture constitutes a significant improvement in the status of women in China because this is probably the first time in Chinese history when Chinese women have succeeded in gaining an independent voice in the widest public sphere.

Although they face difficulties, limitations, and pressures, the new ability of some Chinese women today, not only to have independent conceptions of womanhood that challenge orthodox conceptions, but also to communicate them through the most widely distributed mass media (via cassettes and, at least in Ai Jing's case, also via national television), opens the possibility of introducing such alternative conceptions to an unprecedentedly wide and diversified audience. It remains to be seen how successful these women and others like them will be in disseminating their alternative models among the large populace, and in inspiring change. For the time being, however, the mere activity of these women artists, and the scale of this activity, certainly defy broad generalizations about Chinese culture in the reform era (and especially in the 1990s), which too often imply that women are powerless and voiceless.

The emergence of the new, independent female voices in the popular music scene provides vivid support to Mayfair Mei-hui Yang's observation that "the market is at once an enabling and constraining device for women" (1999, 60). The radical commercialization of the 1990s no doubt turned women and their bodies into an objectified commodity and in many respects had the effect of marginalizing them (Evans 1997, 167–81). However, it also offered them unprecedented opportunity to (re)develop a distinct gender identity after decades of gender erasure, of which they were the prime victims. Although many women developed their gender consciousness along lines drawn and images produced and controlled by men, others, albeit significantly fewer, were able to develop a more independent consciousness, and more significantly, to communicate this to an unprecedented, wide and diverse audience. This is true especially where Ai Jing is concerned. After the great success of *My 1997*, she started to sing her songs on television, thereby reaching millions of listeners even with the less popular songs from her later album.

It is not incidental that the new female voices described in the last part of this chapter emerged in the domain of pop music rather than television or film. Television and film were less favorable to these alternative feminine voices for two main reasons. First, since these voices challenged both orthodox state feminism, which always de-emphasized gender differences, and the new, Confucian-style femininity that, since the 1990s, had replaced the orthodox state feminism in much of official discourse, it was only natural that these media, on which the masculinist state still exerted a significant amount of control, would be the least accessible to them. The second important factor has been the male-dominated market, with its obvious preference for the neotraditional, sexualized female image. This nature of the market had the strongest impact on television and film productions because of the great expense involved in these media. Thus, as with the new minority voices described in the previous chapter, it was again the simple and cheap media associated with popular music culture that made possible the emergence of the new, alternative feminine voices examined here in the widest public sphere. Because of the technological simplicity and low cost involved in the production and dissemination of cassettes (and CDs) these media were much less controllable by the state. The fact that a considerably lower investment was required for their production and dissemination, which is closely related to their relative independence from the state, also made these media relatively free of the limits posed by mainstream market demand. Yet, though the market certainly posed limits, it was nevertheless the same free-market economy, with its foreign influence and its persisting drive for innovation and independence from government control, that also made possible the production and unprecedentedly wide dissemination of these new, nonofficial, alternative voices.

Another positive trend suggested by the data presented in this chapter is a new plurality of legitimate female images. This plurality has been pointed out previously by several scholars (Croll 1995, 9, 109; Mayfair Yang 1999), yet so far little attention has been paid to its implications for women or to the role that women play in informing it. I propose that the most important significance of this new plurality of female images is that women today have more choices (albeit also increased experience of "tension and confusion"; see Croll 1995, 172) with regard to one of the most essential aspects in their lives, that is, what kind of women they could be. Although, as I argue in this chapter, women are still generally offered a narrower range of choices than men, they nevertheless have more choices than ever before in Chinese history.

Of course, the plurality of female images in itself, even if all are legitimate, does not automatically imply more choices for women, since there has always been a gap between the cultural and artistic spheres in which such images circulate and actual reality. The last sections of this chapter, however, support my argument concerning the increase in choices for Chinese women by showing, first, that women played a most active and independent role in expanding the repertory of female images in the public sphere by constructing their own alternative images, and second, that these female-constructed images are embedded in the actual experience and lives of the women artists who construct them.

4 Popular Music and State Politics: Hegemony, Resistance, Symbiosis, and Unity

This chapter examines how popular music on the mainland in the period between the late 1970s and the mid-1990s was informed by and used in the negotiation of state politics. Previous studies of popular music in China, which have usually taken the theme of state politics as their main focus, have offered some brief descriptions of how the state uses popular music to advance its political agenda. The more significant contribution of many of these studies to our understanding of state politics was in studying important dissident voices that emerged in the context of Chinese popular music culture in the late 1980s and early 1990s (Chow 1990–91; Jones 1992a, 1992b, 1994; Brace 1991, 1992; Brace and Friedlander 1992; Friedlander 1991; Schell 1994, 311–20; Micic 1995).

The great majority of these studies, however, tended to examine the data in terms of rigid dichotomies, which often led to simplistic depictions of reality that ignored important complexities. Hegemony versus resistance, state versus society, government versus market, and official versus popular are some of the dichotomies explicitly employed or implied in many of these studies, as in many related studies of other domains of popular culture in China. These dichotomies may have had some validity where the 1980s and early 1990s are concerned—the main period covered by most of the studies of pop music—but they are surely outmoded in the context of the mid- and late 1990s.

The main purpose of this chapter is to go beyond these binary oppositions and categories to explore the complex relations and subtle practices of ambivalence that cross the above-mentioned divides. In the course of doing so, the chapter also introduces the reader to new developments in the popular music scene during the 1990s, such as the new Chinese MTV, new figures, new albums, new concerts, and new practices and discourse.[1]

The first part of the chapter is dedicated to the state. The chapter opens by examining in detail the methods that the state uses today in its attempt to control the popular music scene and how it uses popular music culture to disseminate its ideology and consolidate its hegemony and control. In my discussion of state control and use of popular music, which focuses on the 1990s, I put special emphasis on the use of television, and particularly on the state-run Chinese MTV, which was established in 1993, and has never been studied before. The opening section of the part on the state also introduces the reader to officially organized concerts and song competitions and to one of the most important genres of popular songs in China today, that is, state-sponsored propaganda songs.

Whereas in the first section of the part that focuses on the state, the latter appears as extremely monologic and repressive of voices that conflict with its own, the subsequent section nevertheless proposes that state control and ideology should not be seen in oversimplified terms. In this second section I highlight the responsive and adaptive capabilities of the state and its different organs and its ability to compromise. The main argument here is that hegemony and resistance in popular music culture do not simply occupy opposite ends of the political spectrum, as most previous studies on the subject imply, but are constantly in dialogue with each other and interact in a dialectical fashion.

After suggesting that even the most authoritative official expressions in the popular music scene today bear in them traces of past and current resistance, and thus are not totally monologic, I proceed to examine other complex relations and interactions. One such relationship is a symbiosis that often exists today between the state and self-employed musicians, in which the latter produce politicized songs that conform to official ideology not because of harsh political pressures but in return for promotion in the market by official media. These musicians depend on the state for promotion because the Chinese state tightly controls all television stations, and television is the most effective promotional tool in China's new capitalist market economy.

Examples of such a symbiotic relationship challenge not only the widely held assumption that the state and self-employed artists in China are necessarily in conflict with each other, but also the assumption implicit in many studies that the state and the market are in opposition to each other. Another central argument in this chapter is that the capitalist system introduced into China in the last two decades not only resulted in the termination of the official monopoly over cultural production, and thus in increased diversity, a point emphasized in previous chapters, but simultaneously has been appropriated by the state to advance its hegemony and control. The official appropriation of the new economic system in China today offers another important reminder that capitalism and authoritarian political systems are not necessarily mutually exclusive.

My discussion of the symbiosis between the state and self-employed artists also includes examples of Chinese musicians from outside the mainland, who are often invited to participate in highly politicized official events. Such examples highlight a possible new relationship between two other categories that are often positioned in a dichotomous framework in studies that deal with Chinese culture in the 1990s, namely, mainland nationalism versus Chinese transnationalism. In this chapter I contend that although transnational flows indeed pose a threat to the Chinese government and mainland nationalism and identity, the Chinese government nonetheless constantly appropriates Chinese transnationalism to advance the notion of a unified Greater China, of which the mainland is the core.

The last part of this chapter returns to the subject of rock. It opens with a discussion of expressions of resistance to the state and the dominant culture, in which I elaborate on the discussion of the rock subculture found in chapter 1. The second section of the part on rock, however, explores the limits of this resistance among rockers, pointing to important points of unity with the state and the dominant culture, a unity that has too often been overlooked in literature that deals with popular culture in China in general and particularly in studies that focus on rock.[2] Another major argument in this chapter is thus that the relationship between the state and even the most dissident voices in China today is not necessarily always antagonistic or in total opposition and that these forces may share important concepts, aspirations, practices, and discourse.

THE VOICE OF THE STATE

State control and music have been linked to each other in China since antiquity. In the *Book of Music (Yueji)*, an important Chinese classic that was compiled more than two thousand years ago,[3] we find the following statement, which offers a powerful testimony to this link:

> Music is . . . the production of the modulations of the voice, and its source is in the affections of the mind as it is influenced by (external) things. . . . [The] six peculiarities of sound are not natural; they indicate the impressions produced by (external) things. On this account the

ancient kings were watchful in regard to the things by which the mind was affected. And so (they instituted) ceremonies to direct men's aims aright; music to give harmony to their voices; laws to unify their conduct; and punishments to guard against their tendencies to evil. The end to which ceremonies, music, punishments, and laws conduct is one: they are the instruments by which the minds of the people are assimilated, and good order in government is made to appear. (Chai and Chai 1967, 92–93)

The political use of music is also one of the major themes in Zhou Xiaowen's 1996 film *Qin song* (literally meaning *Ode to Qin*), a highly fictionalized film that tells the story of the First Emperor of Qin, who unified China in the third century B.C.[4] While engaging in bloody wars to fulfill his plan to unify China, the emperor is simultaneously engaged in a personal war with a talented musician whom he kidnaps from a rival state so the former could compose a powerful hymn for the new unified state. In one of the climaxes of the movie, the emperor states his belief that through music he can "control the minds and the hearts of the people." Music is perceived by the emperor as being as important as the sword with which he defeats his rivals; whereas the latter may be used to exert physical control, the former is necessary in order to exert spiritual and ideological control.

The powerful reference in *Qin song* to the close association between music and state control, though embedded in a story about ancient China, reflects the actual experience of contemporary mainland artists. It was, after all, in the modern era under the Communists, that the association between music and politics became closer than ever before in Chinese history. In his Yan'an Talks of 1942, in the midst of the war against Japan and the struggle against the Nationalists, Mao Zedong stated:

Victory over the enemy depends primarily on armies with guns in their hands, but this kind of army alone is not enough. We still need a cultural army, since this kind of army is indispensable in achieving unity among ourselves and winning victory over the enemy. . . . Literature and art [should] become a component part of the whole revolutionary machinery, so they can act as a powerful weapon in uniting and educating the people while attacking and annihilating the enemy, and help the people achieve solidarity in their struggle against the enemy. (McDougall 1980, 57, 58)

The Yan'an Talks have been the basis of official cultural policy in China ever since 1942 and, as will be shown, they didn't lose their relevance in the 1990s. The link between the cinematic past and the real present was made explicit by Zhou Xiaowen himself. At the premiere of his movie on 7 June

1996 in Beijing, while answering questions by the audience, the director noted: "Chinese rulers have always wanted to control our spirit. But they cannot succeed in doing so." Later in this chapter I will take issue with the second half of Zhou's statement, a statement that provides another example of the kind of dichotomous discourse that I criticize in this chapter. I open, however, by showing first how the Chinese state indeed still aims at exerting tight control over the minds and spirits of the people, as well as over their bodies, and how it utilizes popular music for this purpose.

Chinese MTV

By the mid-1990s China's television audience had grown to 900 million people, approximately 75 percent of the country's population. In the cities, more than 90 percent of the households had at least one television set (Erwin 1999, 234).[5] Television is the most important mass medium today in China, and all television stations in the country are run by the state. The hegemony and control of the party-state today depend to a large extent on television broadcasts, and it is in connection with this medium that the political use of popular music by the state reveals itself most vividly.

The relationship between popular music and television in China became closer than ever in 1993 when the CCTV's Chinese Music Television was established. As a body within the CCTV, Chinese MTV was put in charge of the production and presentation of video clips for popular songs to be broadcast on television. In a 1995 production planning meeting of the new body, Yang Weiguang, the head of CCTV and the vice minister of the Radio, Film, and Television Ministry, stated that "the Music Television has to carry on and develop China's traditional culture, and reflect the deep love of the people toward the homeland and life" (quoted in Wang Pingping 1995). Yang's statements point explicitly to the political purpose and agenda of China's Music Television.

Except for its emphasis on traditional culture, the official agenda of Music Television, as stated by Yang, closely follows the basic principles that underlie the cultural policy of the revolutionary period, allowing for a limited range of expression that basically includes only expressions of patriotism and nationalism, and positive, idealized sentiments toward life in general. Nevertheless, the creation of Chinese MTV is an excellent example of the adaptive capabilities of the Chinese Communist Party in the reform era. Officials at the Radio, Film, and Television Ministry are well aware of the important role that popular music plays in modern life and its power to influence people's thought, sentiments, and behavior. They are also aware of the power of television and the fact that if they do not provide people with music they enjoy, people will look for it elsewhere. Through Chinese Music Television, the state attempts to satisfy people's musical needs and limit their exposure to nonofficial channels of communication and nonofficial music, through which they could be exposed to alternative ideologies and practices. The political and nationalistic agenda of Music Television was manifested in the mid-1990s, for instance, in the fact that it excluded China's rock as well as all extra-mainland popular music, including *gangtai* songs, which enjoy an enormous popularity in the Chinese market.[6]

Until late 1995 videos of the state-run Music Television were featured sporadically on various television stations between programs, as part of programs, and in a few programs specializing in music. In late 1995, however, after CCTV decided to establish specialized television channels to cover different cultural domains (apparently in order to maximize advertising revenues as part of its search for commercial profit), a new art channel was born. The new channel, CCTV-3, broadcasted music (and commercials) all day long with few breaks, and based upon my observations in the mid-1990s it was one of the most popular channels in Beijing. The channel featured different kinds of music, including Western art music, Chinese instrumental art music, Chinese opera, and Chinese pop. The CCTV's acknowledgment of the usefulness of popular music in particular for both political and commercial purposes manifested itself in the assignment of time slots. While programs on Chinese traditional opera, for example, were usually broadcast in the morning and early afternoon, obviously to cater to retired people who are the main patrons of this genre, Chinese pop was featured during prime time. This includes the noon hour, when even working people have a break, and early evening, when most people are back home with their families. Even before the birth of the specialized art channel, pop songs were inserted during these same hours. The pattern then was that one or two songs are broadcast repeatedly at prescribed hours for a whole week as a short musical interlude. On the new art channel, however, one could now watch pop music programs that lasted half an hour or even a whole hour, programs that were broadcast several times a day and on a regular, daily basis.

The structuring and content of pop music programs on CCTV-3 were as revealing as the number of slots they were assigned and their timing. Both showed, again, the ability, or at least the attempt, of the Communist Party to adapt itself to the post-revolutionary dynamics and the new sensibilities of the people. Both also revealed the state's utilitarian view of popular music and the different strategies that it employs in the utilization of popular music for political purposes. The thirty-minute and one-hour programs had a similar structure, namely a succession of clips presented by a young, lively, casual, smiling anchor, who from time to time also conducted short interviews with singers and musicians before, after, or between songs. These programs were mixtures of songs in very different styles and with very different content. The styles included standard modern/urban Westernized pop, folk-style songs, art songs sung in Western operatic style, and contemporary politicized songs that are usually sung either in the orthodox Western bel canto style or the orthodox Chinese artistic folk style. CCTV leaders seem to be aware of the fact that straightforward and blunt official propaganda is not as easily accepted today as before and that it may even be rejected if presented too explicitly and too aggressively. An extreme example of such rejection was provided to me by several intellectuals with whom I spoke, who told me that they completely avoid watching Chinese television because of its propagandistic nature. As if to avoid such a reaction, Chinese MTV programs featured different songs that alternated with one another, some very politicized, some with subtle propaganda, others with no political message at all. The result, taken as a whole, was a hybrid of popularized, sugarcoated political propaganda. The people's post-revolutionary demand for fashion, entertainment, sexuality, and romance was satisfied in a controlled manner, with very strict limitations on the last two, and simultaneously they got a dose of official propaganda and education.

Through Music Television (and other television programs that include popular songs), CCTV, and by extension the state, propagates a variety of themes, the most important of which include nationalism and patriotism, good citizenship, collectivism, productivity, education, the centrality of Beijing, Chinese sovereignty, especially over Hong Kong (before 1997) and Tibet, and in a more subtle way, the Communist Party. Another major purpose that Music Television obviously aims to achieve through its mixed repertory is an increase in unity and integration within China—that is, bridging the gaps between social groups such as peasants and urbanites, minorities and the Han majority, and different regions in the country. Finally, through the use of mixed repertoire that combines modern, urban, Westernized pop with folk-style songs, and sometimes also through individual songs that combine traditional and modern elements, the state is obviously also aiming to mediate one of the most serious conflicts in the process of modernization, that between tradition and modernity.

The state speaks today in China in different voices, and in a sense all the songs broadcast on Music Television may be considered the voice of the state. At the same time, in each program of songs there are always several songs that can be placed at the most official end of a spectrum of varying degrees of officialdom. It is in these most official and politicized songs that the state really speaks, whereas other songs can be seen as part of the sugarcoating the state is willing to tolerate in order to succeed in reaching the people.

Below are excerpts from the lyrics of seven representative songs that illustrate the propagandistic and didactic use of popular music in China by the party-state:

TODAY IS YOUR BIRTHDAY, CHINA
("Jintian shi ni de shengri Zhongguo"; lyrics by Han Jingting; music by Gu Jianfen; performed previously by Mao Amin and Wei Wei and more recently by Dong Wenhua)

Today is your birthday, my China
In the early morning I set a flock of white doves free to fly
To bring you an olive branch
The doves have flown to the high mountain ridges
We bless you on your birthday, my China
Wishing that you will never suffer and will always be peaceful . . .
Today is your birthday, my China
In the early morning I set a flock of white doves free to fly
To carry back for you the longing of the children who are far away
The doves have flown to the boundless sea and sky . . .
We bless you on your birthday, my China
These are the words of love of the children who are far away . . .

THE GREAT WALL IS LONG
("Changcheng chang"; lyrics by Yan Su; music by Meng Qingyun; performance by Dong Wenhua)

Everyone says that the two sides of the Great Wall are the homeland
Do you know how long the Great Wall is? . . .
Do you know how much wind, snow, and frost
Condensed the flesh and blood of millions upon millions of heroic
    idealists
Which gave rise to the red sun on top of the ten thousand *li* of
    mountains and rivers?
The sun illuminates the long Great Wall
The awe-inspiring air of the Great Wall will be displayed forever
If you ask where the Great Wall is
Look at these many suits of green army uniforms

HONEST WORDS
("Shuo ju xin li hua"; lyrics by Shi Shunyi; music by Zang Yunfei;
performance by Yu Junjian)

To be honest
I also miss home
Old mom,
Her hair has already turned completely white . . .
I also have love
I often miss her in my dreams . . .
Come, come, come
Now that I have become a soldier . . .
I know that responsibility is grave
If you do not shoulder a gun and I do not shoulder a gun
Who is going to defend our mother? . . .
There is home only if there is a country
If you do not stand sentry and I do not stand sentry
Who is going to defend our homeland?
Who will defend home? . . .

SPRING STORY
("Chuntian de gushi"; lyrics by Ye Xuquan and Jiang Kairu; music
by Wang Yougui; performance by Dong Wenhua)

In the spring of 1979
There was an old man
On the coast of China's South Sea
Who drew a circle
As if in a myth, many cities suddenly appeared on the horizon
And many golden mountains appeared as if in a miracle
Spring thunders, ah! Awakened both sides of the Great Wall
Spring sunlight, ah! Warmed up both banks of the Yangtze River
Ah! China! Ah! China!
You stride in new steps that are full of power and grandeur
You walk into a spring in which everything looks fresh and gay . . .

GOOD PERSON, GOOD HEART
("Hao ren hao xin"; lyrics by Shi Shunyi; music by Tie Yuan;
performance by Hu Mingdong)

You are a good person . . .
Living a busy life
Busy and serious . . .
You have never had too high and extravagant hopes
You only believe that sweat is gold . . .
Good people are the lofty spirit of this world
I hope that good people in the world will get their reward . . .
Always believe that the world will become better

Quietly fulfilling the duties of being a human being . . .
Good people are the root of this world . . .
Good people will have good luck

RETURN HOME SAFELY
("Ping'an hui jia"; lyrics and music by Wang Xinyu; performance by
the male singer Zheng Dongsheng and an anonymous female singer)

Female: You said you'd be back home today . . .

Male: I said I'll be back home today
But the alarm lamp is glimmering and calling me to set out
The wind outside is strong and the rain is heavy
But the difficulties of other people are more serious . . .
Of course it's not that I don't think about home
But how can there only be a small home and no big home?

Female: I don't blame you at all for not being back home . . .

I BELONG TO CHINA
("Wo shuyu Zhongguo"; lyrics by Tian Di and Yan Su; music by Wang
Yougui; performance by Peng Liyuan)

You said I am your distant star
The sky in the past also had my twinkle . . .
You said you all along listened attentively to my wandering footsteps
You said you all along watched attentively the lights of my fishing
    boats on the seashore . . .
Only after one hundred years of vicissitudes
There is my indomitable body
You said my drift is the memory of humiliation . . .
You use a thousand years of history that never gets old to tell me
You use the flag that is raised every day to tell me
I belong to you, ah! My China . . .

The songs above focus on different issues, but there is nevertheless one
underlying theme that runs through all of them, which is an emphasis on
the state. This emphasis is one manifestation of the oft-mentioned powerful wave of nationalism that took over China after the Tiananmen incident
of 1989; nationalism that the state enthusiastically promoted in order to
maintain stability, unity, and its own legitimacy in an era of liberalization,
pluralism, and diversity. "Today Is Your Birthday, China" is a typical,
straightforwardly patriotic song. This song was first broadcast on October 1, 1989, China's National Day (Wang Xiaofeng, personal communication), and since then it has been performed not only on every National Day
but also quite frequently throughout the year. The song treats the state as

a person for whom a birthday party is held. At one point in the video that accompanies the song, a huge birthday cake is offered to the state, shown on the stairs leading to the Temple of Heaven in Beijing, one of a stock of national symbols celebrated in official popular culture and used repeatedly to represent the state. The personification of the state in "Today Is Your Birthday, China," which is clear from the fact that China is referred to in the song as "you," is developed further in "Honest Words," in which the distinction between the speaker's mother and the state is deliberately blurred.

"The Great Wall Is Long" illustrates the state's use of concrete national symbols to create unity and a concrete focal point for patriotic sentiments. The Great Wall is one of China's most important and celebrated national symbols and its unifying function is pointed out explicitly in the line "It links the hearts of the sons and daughters of China." Other national symbols that are celebrated and praised in officially sponsored patriotic songs include the Yellow River and various sites in Beijing, especially Tiananmen Square. The video of "Today Is Your Birthday, China" includes a whole array of national symbols. Besides the Temple of Heaven, it also features the national flag, which is shown again and again, People's Liberation Army troops on parade, Mao Zedong's huge portrait on the north side of Tiananmen Square, and the square itself.

While often the visual representation in a song video overlaps or enhances what is already articulated clearly in its lyrics, there are many songs for which the video is essential to the understanding of the message conveyed in the lyrics and which otherwise may remain obscure. "I Belong to China," for example, is about the 1997 return of Hong Kong to the mainland. Despite the straightforward statement "I belong to you, my China," which is repeated several times in the song, most of the lyrics are nevertheless rather subtle, and Hong Kong itself is never mentioned in the lyrics. The video that accompanies the song, however, constantly juxtaposes shots of Hong Kong's famous skyscrapers with the Great Wall, the national flag, the Temple of Heaven, and Tiananmen Square, thus suggesting first of all that the song is about Hong Kong, and, more importantly, visually enhancing the message articulated through its lyrics, that Hong Kong is part of China.

Visual images of national symbols are also utilized on Chinese MTV to create unity within the ethnic diversity that is represented in the programs on a regular basis, as well as to assert state control over ethnic minorities. The most obvious use of this technique is found in songs about Tibet, whose relationship with the Chinese state has always been problematic. As noted in chapter 2, the videos of many songs about Tibet juxtapose shots of local Tibetan scenes, especially Potala Palace, Tibet's national symbol, with China's national symbols, a juxtaposition that asserts a link between the two entities and the control of the latter over the former. The Potala is even shown in the video of "I Belong to China," suggesting that not only does Hong Kong belong to China, but also Tibet. National symbols, many of which are associated specifically with Beijing, whose central political status the videos help to establish and perpetuate, are also inserted in videos that accompany songs about various Han regions. In the video for "Spring Story," for instance, a song that praises the miraculous growth of Shenzhen, in addition to repeated shots of the southern city's skyscrapers— which aim to show how modern this city has become thanks to the government's economic reforms—there are also shots of the Great Wall and Tiananmen Square. Through visually linking Shenzhen with the center, Beijing, the video makes sure that the viewer does not perceive Shenzhen as an independent entity. Part of the message of the song, in other words, is that Shenzhen's miraculous development is not its own alone, but rather the manifestation of China's overall development under the control of the center. Shenzhen's prosperity, the video suggests, is the prosperity of the entire mainland, and sooner or later, as party leaders often stress, it will be shared by the entire country. The video is so careful not to overemphasize Shenzhen that it would have been impossible for someone who has never visited the city to know that this is Shenzhen if the Chinese characters for Shenzhen had not been briefly displayed on the screen.

By avoiding emphasizing locales other than Beijing, the state obviously aims to maintain China's political unity. During several months of Music Television watching, I saw only songs that praised Beijing and not a single one that praised Shanghai, Guangzhou, or any other major city. Similar to monotheistic religions that celebrate the notion that there is only one god, China's state-sponsored MTV discourages the existence of any other object of worship, and it ensures that worship focuses on Beijing. Beijing's centrality is suggested in many songs in an implicit manner, but its privileged status is often articulated explicitly in praise songs for the capital. One such praise song, which was broadcast in early 1996, was sung by a teenager from Guangzhou, who described in the song his tour of the capital. This song asserted the dominance of Beijing vis-à-vis another major city, as if to dispel the challenge of the latter to the capital's authority and superiority, and by extension to the general unity of the state.

The function of Music Television as a national unifier can be seen from the fact that, with the exception of minority songs, all the songs in the various popular music programs are sung in the official language, Mandarin. By excluding, for example, pop songs in Cantonese, which enjoy an enormous popularity, not only in southern China but also in Beijing, the state not only asserts the dominance of the north, with which Mandarin is associated, but also propagates a sense of unity and nationalism, and resists regionalism, which has always been a major threat to China's political unity.

Always presenting together Han folk-style songs, modern urban songs, minority folk-style songs, and patriotic songs is apparently another technique used by Chinese MTV to advance national unity and integration. By catering to different audiences, Music Television also maintains a channel of communication between the state and different segments of society and demonstrates the commitment of the center to each of these different social segments. At the same time it also ensures that each of these segments always sees itself as a part of a whole, linked to other segments, and most important to the state. Chinese MTV acknowledges and affirms diversity, but at the same time resists exclusiveness and real autonomy. People today can enjoy nonpoliticized (e.g., romantic) songs on CCTV, but often only in the framework of programs that include at least one or two overtly politicized songs. Thus, even when they watch pop songs on television, viewers in China are intimately linked with the state. Patriotic and other politicized songs are indeed part and parcel of contemporary Chinese pop.[7]

The state's attempts to maintain its control over, presence in, and relevance to all domains of life, and thus to politicize them all, is also apparent in its utilization of videos for songs whose lyrics have nothing to do with the state. Here the icons of national symbols turn into a completely autonomous language of signs directed at the audience's subconscious. China's national flag, for example, is featured in many songs that are otherwise completely nonpoliticized. To give another example, a video for one romantic song that was broadcast in early 1995 featured shots of the Great Wall, even though the latter had no relationship whatsoever with the lyrical content of the song. The message of the clip is that even love between two individuals is ultimately linked to the state, and that the private cannot and should not be separated from the collective/national/public. This message is articulated explicitly in "Return Home Safely" and "Honest Words," which are sung by singers dressed in police and army uniforms, respectively, and which, in addition to depicting the love between two individuals, simultaneously promote official values like social responsibility, self-sacrifice, and love for the state and society.

Somewhat different from these two songs is "Good Person, Good Heart," which propagates more universal values and attitudes, such as optimism and "fulfilling the duties of being a human being." But even in this song there are also more politicized values, the most important of which is hard work: "You are a good person . . . / Living a busy life / Busy and serious . . . / You are a good person . . . / You have never had too high and extravagant hopes / You only believe that sweat is gold." Though the lyrics of the song do not have any direct relationship with the state, its didactic tone nevertheless suggests an official voice; as the state in China has always insisted on playing an active and dominant role in defining what is moral and what is not. A concrete and explicit link to the state, however, is established through the video for the song. The video offers the listener/viewer several concrete images of goodness. While some of them, like an old man helping a lost young foreigner to find his way (an example that may also be understood as an official instruction to support foreign tourism) and a young man running with his umbrella to protect a girl in a heavy rain, can serve as examples of a universal, nonpoliticized goodness, the majority of the images in the video nevertheless imply a link to the state because the characters wear uniforms of state organizations (a railway worker, two different soldiers, a traffic policeman in action, and a postman). The video thus makes explicit that working for the government and serving the people are important qualifications for goodness.

Like the majority of the good people shown in the video of "Good Person, Good Heart," the majority of the people who contribute to the production of didactic or propaganda songs are also employed by the state. These people, who work for official cultural and artistic organizations, usually specialize either in writing lyrics or in composing tunes. Shi Shunyi, who wrote the lyrics for both "Good Person, Good Heart" and "Honest Words," for instance, works for the Song and Dance Troupe of the Air Force Political Department *(Kongzheng gewutuan).*

Other images featured in the video of "Good Person, Good Heart" are factory workers, workers cleaning railways and sweeping streets, and a peasant sorting corn. The video thus transforms the song, whose lyrics are not politicized, into a politicized praise song for soldiers (and policemen), workers, and peasants, suggesting that they are the "lofty spirit" and the "root of this world." By praising soldiers, workers, and peasants, the hardworking common people, and by excluding intellectuals, businesspeople, and *getihu* (private entrepreneurs), the video perpetuates the old revolutionary social hierarchy but, more importantly, reestablishes the old association between the party and the masses of the people. By producing and broadcasting this video and similar ones about soldiers, peasants, and workers, the party reasserts its traditional role as the representative of the common people and signals to those people its continuous commitment. "Good Person, Good Heart" is also an attempt to reassure these social segments amid growing frustration among large portions of them who see the economic gap widening between themselves and other segments of society. It is against such a background that some of the lyrics of the song become more telling. The party not only appeases soldiers, workers, and peasants by praising them and telling them that they are good, but it also suggests that "good people in the world will get their reward" and "will have good luck." At the same time, however, the video also suggests that the reward depends upon goodness, that hard work for the state is especially good, and no less importantly, that goodness also means "never [to have] too high and extravagant hopes."

In addition to its utilization of pop to promote nationalism, unity, and other official values and attitudes, Chinese MTV is also engaged in legitimizing the government and its policies, and it is against this background that Yang Weiguang's prescription that "the Music Television has to . . . reflect the deep love of the people toward the homeland and life" gains its full meaning. In accordance with Yang's statement of purpose, China's Music Television creates a reality that not only seldom excludes the state, but is also almost always bright, positive, and optimistic. If earlier I emphasized the important role that national symbols play in the videos, then blooming flowers, children, sunrises, doves, and the like are at least as important. Shots of a rising sun are featured, for example, in "The Great Wall Is Long," "Spring Story," "I Belong to China," and "Today Is Your Birthday, China," while "Good Person, Good Heart" features a variant of this motif—shots of sun rays penetrating green leaves. Children, the symbol of renewal, life, naiveté, the future, and hope, are featured in all these songs, and "The Great Wall Is Long" even starts with a line recited by children. By presenting an idealized reality that excludes evil, darkness, doubts, criticism, protest, discontent, sorrow, and a whole range of other human expressions that the state regards as negative and unhealthy, the latter attempts not only to educate the masses, as it often asserts is the case, but also to convince people that everything is fine, thus legitimizing itself. The exclusion of criticism, pessimism, protest, and the like from the daily discursive universe of Music Television and official media in general also implies that such sentiments and expressions are abnormal.

While more often than not today the relationship between the idealized reality and the party-state and its leaders is only implied, there are times when it is still drawn rather explicitly. In "Spring Story," for example, which is only one of many songs that praise China's development and economic boom, after shots of flowers opening in slow motion and pictures of Shenzhen's skyscrapers, the video shows the female singer Dong Wenhua twice in front of a huge placard of Deng Xiaoping, suggesting rather explicitly that it is he who is responsible for the miracle that is described in the lyrics of the song. This song was also sung in the 1997 CCTV's Spring Festival Party, and prior to its performance the anchor explained that the song was indeed written about Deng Xiaoping, the "old man" in the song, who envisioned and directed the creation of Shenzhen and China's economic boom. As in the video, the performance of this song in the 1997 television New Year's program was accompanied by photographs of Deng, China's paramount leader, who died several days later.

The distinctive character of official pop songs extends also to their musical and performance style. These songs are usually sung either in Chinese artistic folk singing style *(minzu/min'ge changfa)* or in Western bel canto style *(meisheng changfa)*, as opposed to the loosely defined heterodox pop singing style *(tongsu changfa)*. These two orthodox styles of singing require formal training and immediately invoke the official communist aesthetics of professionalism, as well as the seriousness and the sense of formality and authority that are inseparable from much of official culture on the mainland. The tempo of the songs is usually very slow, and it seems to reflect the official post-revolutionary attempts to promote stability and calmness, just as the fast and stirring songs of the revolutionary period reflected the militant revolutionary spirit of that time and the official attempt to stir the people and mobilize them for revolutionary action. The accompaniment of many official songs combines strings, brass, electric bass, a keyboard, moderate percussion, and often a choir singing in bel canto style. The choir, strings, and brass further enhance the sense of officialdom, seriousness, and high art that these songs aim to communicate. The choir in particular enhances the collectivist patriotic ethos that these songs aim to invoke and maintain.

Official songs are sung by a handful of professional singers, male and female, who work for the state and specialize in performing such songs in the two orthodox styles of singing. One of the most famous state singers is the female singer Dong Wenhua, who works for the Song and Dance Troupe of the General Political Department of the Chinese People's Liberation Army *(Zhongguo renmin jiefangjun zongzhengbu gewutuan)*. Dong sings three of the songs above: "The Great Wall Is Long," "Today Is

Your Birthday, China," and "Spring Story." In contrast to the majority of contemporary female singers in China, she sports a short haircut, which seems to suggest an attempt to desexualize her, an attempt that may be related to her affiliation with the army.

Many state singers, including Dong Wenhua and the male singer Yu Junjian, who sings "Honest Words," perform in army uniform. The uniforms immediately identify them with the state and transform them into priests of the state ritual that they perform. As is the case with many official rituals, official popular songs are usually performed in a highly polished, tame, choreographed, disciplined fashion. Like their musical style and their videos that depict larger-than-life national symbols, so the performance of these songs is highly representational, more like a display of power and authority. During the performance of official songs, the singers stand almost still and move their arms from their chest outward to the side of their bodies in standard, well-disciplined, broad, slow movements. They are denied individuality and transformed into the voice of a force bigger than themselves or the viewer/listener, a force that represents thousands of years of history and millions upon millions of people, a force that gives many people a sense of power, pride, solidarity, belonging, and purpose, but is simultaneously something with which no one is really supposed to argue.

Fulfilling its prescribed official purpose—to "reflect the deep love of the people toward the homeland and life"—China's Music Television privileges the collective, the public, the national, and the state, and denies individualism. Although MTV programs do feature individuals in the videos, which often focus on the individual singer, as well as in short interviews with singers and other musicians, these individuals are nevertheless more often than not instrumental in fulfilling the official purpose of the programs, representing something other than themselves. The denial of individuality applies not only to the official songs discussed above, which constitute only part of the repertory of the Music Television, but even to songs in the heterodox singing style that talk about romantic love, which, if analyzed apart from the Music Television context, may be justly viewed as a celebration of individuality. The individualism celebrated in such songs is almost trivialized, or at least loses much of its force, as it is contextualized in a medley of songs by other singers and in other styles within an official framework that stresses nationalism and patriotism. During several months of television watching, I did not see a single pop music program on CCTV that was dedicated to a single musician. Neither have I seen pop musicians given an opportunity to present themselves and talk seriously about their music and thoughts in terms other than the officially pre-scribed ones.[8]

The official utilitarian view of art and artists is nicely illustrated in the interviews that are often featured on Music Television, events that other-wise might have been an excellent opportunity for musicians to celebrate their individuality. These interviews are always short, extremely superfi-cial, and completely controlled by the anchor, who subordinates them to the official agenda of the program. The few singers and musicians who are chosen to speak almost always use the same official hegemonic discourse and talk about the same prescribed themes, the most important of which is the notion of "distinctive national character" *(minzu tese)*; thus they often describe, for example, how their music conforms to the official principle that by definition underlies the activity of the Music Television. The inter-views often end with a clichéd address of the interviewees to the audience, in which they affirm their official status as subordinate civil servants, and which runs as follows: "I hope to keep on producing more and better works of art and to offer them as a tribute to all of you."

State-Sponsored Pop Concerts

Pop concerts are one of the few types of activity left today in China that can still draw a large crowd of people together for several hours. As such, they are viewed as a potential threat to the state,[9] but they simultaneously pro-vide the latter with an excellent opportunity to exert a direct and powerful influence upon a large number of people. If rock is included, which is often the case, then such concerts are also a rare opportunity for the state to com-municate with and exert influence over many people who consciously avoid watching state-run television or connecting themselves with other official sources of influence. Live large-scale pop concerts today in China are al-most always controlled by the state and are utilized to promote official ide-ologies, such as the centrality of the state, unity, and integration. In this section, I also propose that such concerts serve as rituals through which the state reestablishes its authority and, both symbolically and practically, defines and recreates public order and discipline.

During my fieldwork, I attended several large-scale officially organized concerts, all of which repeated a similar pattern. One concert was per-formed, as is usually the case with large-scale pop concerts, twice in a row on 1 and 2 May in the Capital Gymnasium, which, as noted earlier, is one of Beijing's largest halls, accommodating close to 20,000 people. The con-cert was advertised several days before the assigned date, and an advertise-ment board placed in downtown Beijing read as follows:

LARGE-SCALE CONCERT

"Love the Homeland, Love Beijing" cultural activities series and commemoration of the 3040th year of the founding of Beijing

Domestic and *gangtai* performers take the stage side by side

Anchors: Wang Ji, Zhang Shurong, Zhao Ning

Performers: Zang Tianshuo, Xie Dong, Wu Qixian, Chen Shaohua, Wang Jingwen, Huang Gexuan, Lin Yilun, Luo Qi, Cheng Lin, Gan Ping, Teng Ge'er, Sun Guoqing

Organizers: Beijing TV Station, Beijing Music Radio, Beijing Performance Company

The above advertisement is symbolic of the official view of popular music. Like television variety shows, television music programs, and most large-scale concerts, the advertisement minimizes the importance of the individual musicians, who almost always share the stage with many other musicians and perform in medley one after another, and it positions them within an official, state-centered framework. The musicians are denied all individuality and importance, and are enlisted in groups in the service of something other than themselves and their music. It is not the musicians or their music that the concert celebrates, at least not from the official point of view, but rather a collective official national event. This subordinate and enlisted position and role of pop musicians was reflected symbolically in the above advertisement not only in the fact that their names appear at the bottom, but also in the size of the characters for their names, which were significantly smaller than everything that was written above.

The official attempt to own and control large-scale pop concerts manifests itself more directly in what musicians are allowed and not allowed to do during their performance. The rocker Zang Tianshuo, who was invited to participate in this concert, told me that the choice concerning which songs to sing in the concert was not his own but rather was made by the organizers of the event, and added that he was instructed by officials prior to the concert "to avoid talking to the audience, not to try to stir them, just to sing and get off stage" (Zang, interview with the author, 16 August 1995). All talking in the concert was left to the anchors, and they delivered a prewritten text in the typical formal, representational, highly choreographed, authoritative official anchoring style. The memorized lines read by the anchors placed the event in the prescribed official political framework of nationalism, patriotism, pan-Chineseness, and praise for the capital, which was suggested in the advertisement above. Most of the official messages read at the concert had very little to do with the songs that were performed that evening, but they nevertheless provided a context and established an overall meaning for the event.

The official, politicized, state-centered context within which the official organizations that organized the event placed it was indicated to begin with by its timing on May 1, International Labor Day, which is celebrated in China as a public holiday. Inside the concert hall, on opposite sides, there were two huge red banners which read: "Celebrating the May 1 International Labor Holiday," and "Long Live the Unity and Friendship of the World's Peoples," the latter of which was written in both Chinese and English. These banners contextualized the concert within an official framework and reminded the audience that art in China is still seen by the state as means to promote official ideologies and educate the masses rather than as an end in itself.

Like the Music Television, the program of the concert was a celebration of diversity in both style and content, combining soft, sweet mainstream urban pop, rock, and old and new folk-style songs. Among the latter there were orthodox minority songs, which are almost mandatory today in such large-scale events. These songs were sung by the famous Yi female singer Qubi Awu, who as usual performed in traditional Yi costume. She apparently replaced Teng Ge'er, who did not show up. The diversified program illustrated once again how the state uses popular music to attempt to increase integration and unity, something that Timothy Brace has already noted in connection with pop concerts that he observed during the late 1980s (1992, 178–83). It was also obvious that presenting China as a diversified, pluralistic, liberal state was among the main aims of the event. This aim was articulated explicitly by one of the anchors who, when inviting the female rocker Luo Qi to sing a hard-rock song about freedom, entitled "Follow Your Desires" (*Suixinsuoyu;* lyrics by Luo Bing, music by Zhou Di), stated that "there are plenty of different musicians today in Beijing who work and create freely." But there was also the central issue of control. To assert state control over the rebellious-looking singer, who performed her song in punk-style tight black leather pants and casual T-shirt with the number 10 printed on it, the anchor added that she is "very lovely" (*feichang ke'ai),* the kind of remark that, in the patronizing tone that the anchor used, invoked the way adults speak about young children. The fact that the anchor was a male made his statement even more degrading.

By incorporating rock and contextualizing it in this way, the organizers were hoping to disempower and tame the style, which has become synonymous to rebellion, and simultaneously to empower themselves and assert their control over the disobedient child. Indeed, Luo Qi's nonconformist, punkish, provocative, challenging appearance and her hard-rock song about freedom lost much of their force and air of resistance and were almost trivialized when performed to the accompaniment of a prerecorded soundtrack, between sweet, soft pop songs, in an official event that celebrated the May 1 public holiday and "love for the homeland and for Beijing." Denied the ability to introduce and present herself and to contextualize herself and her performance, and thus denied her subjectivity and individuality, Luo Qi, like the other rock musicians who participated in this concert, was forced to become an object in the hands of officialdom.

The concert communicated and symbolically reaffirmed state control in other ways as well. Like the majority of large-scale pop concerts today in China, it was held in a hall, as if an open space without walls, assigned seats, roof, and solid structure would pose a challenge to state control and a threat to general order. People who came to the concert did not stand up at any point, nor did they try to approach the stage, as such behavior is not permissible. The stage was placed in the middle of a basketball court, well away from the nearest seats, which were separated from the stage by metal bars. The space between the stage and the nearest seats remained empty during the entire concert.

The physical arrangement of the concert distanced the performers from the audience and turned the concert into a highly disciplined, nonparticipatory, representational activity. Policemen in uniform, who were scattered along the main aisles, further tamed the space. The concert was not supposed to be interactive, but rather was a well-choreographed presentation, running according to a strict, pre-existing, officially prescribed plan to ensure maximum control. At no point did the audience have a share in the ownership over the concert. This was most obvious in the second evening, during which the loudspeakers instructed people to keep silent because the event was going to be recorded. In short, there were many elements in the May 1 concert that made it not only a drama of state control and authority but also an actual act of disciplining and practicing social order.

The May 1 concert ended with Gao Feng's famous song, "Great China" *(Da Zhongguo)*, which served almost as an official seal, asserting once again state control over the entire event and its meaning:

GREAT CHINA
(lyrics, music, and performance by Gao Feng)

We all have one home, which is called China
Plenty of brothers and sisters and a nice landscape
There are two winding dragons at home, these are the Yangtze River
    and the Yellow River . . .

Look at that Great Wall of ten thousand *li* shuttle back and forth in the
  clouds
Look at that Qinghai Xizang [Tibet] Plateau, vaster than the sky
Our great China, yah! What a big home . . .
I want to accompany her forever and ever . . .

"Great China" is another example of a politicized popular song that celebrates the state. The song's lyrics depict the country, praise its beauty and
vastness, and articulate sentiments of unity and patriotism, and a collective
optimistic ethos. They also mention many of the important national symbols: the dragon, the Yellow River, and the Great Wall, and even assert the
sovereignty of China over the problematic territory of Tibet. Musically,
"Great China" combines folk melodies from different parts of China,
which enhance the image of the rich, diverse, vast China depicted in the
lyrics and propagated today in official discourse. The melody of the song is
based on two well-known folk tunes: one is the famous southern melody
"Liang Zhu" (Liang Shanbo and Zhu Yingtai), and the other is a famous
northeast *yangge* (Gao Feng, interview with the author, 8 June 1996). The
use of folk melodies makes "Great China" a song with a "distinctive national character." The fact that the song nevertheless does not include any
folk instruments, like the rustic *suona*, for example, which is often used to
accompany folk-style songs, makes it sound modern (interview, ibid.) and,
in that sense, even more politically correct. The collectivist ethos articulated in the lyrics is enhanced musically through the use of group singing
in part of the song. More overt political musical statement is found at the
very beginning of the song, where "The East Is Red" *(Dongfang hong)*, one
of the Communist Party's most celebrated anthems, is played as a prelude.
This musical tribute to the party is played, at least in one video, on the famous Marquis Yi's Bells, a 2,400-year-old set of chime bells that were
excavated in 1977 and have become one of China's national symbols.[10]

As politicized as the songs I mentioned earlier, but still lively, danceable,
and lighter in its overall tone, "Great China" was the most appropriate song
to conclude the May 1 concert. Gao performed the song wearing a red shirt,
which he always wears when singing this song to symbolize the Chinese national flag (interview, ibid.). As noted in chapter 2, the song was also accompanied by several dozen dancers who were dressed in the typical costumes of
China's different nationalities and who, in the song's middle part, unfolded a
huge Chinese flag that covered all of them like a roof to represent China's
unity. Following the performance of "Great China," all the participants in
the concert lined up on stage to receive a certificate of acknowledgment that
was given to them by officials. Officials and high-ranking officers in uniform

occupied the front seats in all the large-scale officially organized concerts that I attended. This short ceremony was one last reminder that the concert was owned by the state, rather than by the individual musicians who participated in it or the audience who came that evening.

Official celebrations like the one described above are also performed, of course, in the West, but in China individual musicians are offered very few opportunities to perform in front of a mass audience (as opposed to small-scale concerts in bars, clubs, and so on) in contexts independent of the state. A month and a half after the May 1 concert, another large-scale pop concert, held two nights in a row, on June 18 and 19, in the same hall, repeated exactly the same pattern. Again, the event was a celebration of something other than the individual musicians who participated in it or their music. This time the musicians were enlisted to mark the upcoming International Women's Conference with the event mentioned in the previous chapter, entitled "Wonderful Women," which featured only female performers. The titles given to pop concerts are another important means used by the state to assert its control over these events and to bestow official meanings upon them. Official titles often provide a vivid illustration of the official view of popular music as a means to promote official messages and ideologies. As in the May 1 concert, on June 18 and 19 the hall was again decorated with official slogans printed on two red banners hung on opposite sides of the hall: one read "Advance along the Road of Socialism with Distinctive Chinese Character," and the other "Solemnly Commemorating the 50th Anniversary of the World War Against Fascism and the Victory of the Chinese People in the War of Resistance Against Japan."

The women's event opened with a lengthy prewritten official address that praised women and discussed the problems faced by them all over the world. This address was followed by a song written especially for the event, which was entitled, like the event, "Wonderful Women." Following this song, several of China's and Beijing's most famous female singers, including Mao Amin, Na Ying, Ai Jing, and Luo Qi, mounted the stage one after another in medley fashion, each singing a song or two to a prerecorded soundtrack (with the exception of Ai Jing, who accompanied herself with her own guitar and brought her own band). The female singers were introduced by a group of anchors who again read prewritten texts between the songs and denied the singers any chance to directly address the audience.

Many of the songs at the June event, as in the May 1 concert, were accompanied by group dances. In June, in fact, the concert was referred to as a "culture and art party" *(wenyi wanhui)*, and it included, in addition to songs, independent dances and acrobatics. Such a combination of arts is typical of official celebrations in China, both live ones and ones that are broadcast on television, and it has the effect of further reducing the importance of the music and the individual musicians who participate in these events, who are thereby transformed into small components in a huge variety show. Large-scale pop concerts today in China are more often than not like state rituals, and as is the case with many rituals, the music in such events is subordinate to the ritual itself, at least from the point of view of the state.

State-Sponsored Music Competitions

From time to time one sees in newspapers and magazines on the mainland announcements of singing competitions organized by governmental units. Song competitions have been one of the methods used by the Communist Party to increase musical production and encourage the involvement and participation of people in musical creative activity, at least since the early 1960s (Isabel Wong 1984, 129–30). Isabel Wong suggests that one practical reason for organizing such competitions has been the fact that the government simply could not supply its propaganda needs alone (130). By organizing song competitions, however, the government not only increases production, but also incorporates. new talents into the official production mechanism and the official sphere; no less importantly, it encourages people to conform to official ideology and official artistic standards. The competition in turn presents the state as democratic, in the sense that it encourages the common people to create their own music and speak out in their own voices. Songs from such competitions are later often presented as *vox populi*, similar to the labeling of many revolutionary songs "folksongs." Below are portions of one competition announcement that appeared in *The Drama and Film Newspaper (Xiju dianying bao)* in April 1996:

> THE FIRST NATIONWIDE LARGE PRIZE COMPETITION TO PROMOTE NEW SINGERS IS ABOUT TO BE HELD
>
> [Organizers] 1. The Capital Association of Old Artists
>
> 2. *The Drama and Film Newspaper*
>
> The competition will be divided into three styles of singing: bel canto, *tongsu*, and national style. Contestants in the competition have to sing songs that have a healthy and positive [*xiangshang*] content and are rich in the flavor of the period. . . . After the conclusion of the competition a cassette will be released and promoted in the audiovisual market. The CCTV will broadcast nationwide the evening of the final competition.

Conditions for participating in the competition:

1. [Songs and musicians need to] adhere to the Reforms and Openness [*gaige kaifang*], adhere to the Four Basic Principles of the party, [express] warm love for the homeland, and observe discipline and abide by the law. (*Xiju dianying bao*, no. 795)

This announcement provides another example of how the state attempts to appropriate the popular music scene. By constantly organizing such competitions and monopolizing the right to organize and publicize them, the state attempts to define standards for creativity and performance, and a whole discourse of what is good or bad and legitimate or illegitimate in popular music. The attempt to control starts with limiting the competitions to particular styles of singing. These styles imply a particular lyrical content and ideology, and thus limiting the competition to particular styles in fact implies limiting the universe of general discourse in the competition. One needs to remember that one of the three styles mentioned above, namely *tongsu* singing, was officially recognized only in 1986. The exclusion of *tongsu* style from officially organized competitions until that year meant that up to 1986 one could not find in such competitions songs about personal romantic feelings, a theme that is inseparable from this style. The above announcement, however, suggests that the state nevertheless still attempts to separate this particular singing style from its natural content and to utilize it for the popularization of hegemonic politicized ideologies. *Tongsu* music, which as noted earlier is often understood as melody-oriented music (as opposed to rhythm-oriented) that is relatively moderate in tempo, soft, relaxed, and sweet, is the most popular style today on the mainland, at least in urban areas, and by incorporating it since the mid-1980s the state has obviously been attempting to reach a larger audience. By excluding rock-and-roll from the program, on the other hand, the state makes a clear statement that the style is illegitimate and by extension abnormal. In banning rock from television programs and organized competitions, the state attempts to create a reality in which the wild and rebellious style simply does not exist.

A major part of the above announcement deals with content, illustrating once again what the state regards as good and bad and how it tries to utilize musical activity for propaganda and didactic purposes. Similar to the declared purpose and actual practice of the Music Television, the guidelines for this competition define a limited range for artistic expression, which centers around the state and official policies. But perhaps the most interesting and revealing item in the advertisement is the section about the reward. The state is well aware of the fact that its hegemony is constantly contested nowadays and that, in the context of the new market economy, the increase in individualism, and the depoliticization of art and life, it has to offer a substantial reward to individuals (or units) to encourage them to conform to its political agenda and strict, politicized standards. It is here that part of the power of monopolizing television broadcasts in a semi-communist, semi-capitalist state becomes clear. By maintaining its monopoly over television (and radio) stations, the state maintains its control not only over information but also over the best promotional tool for artists in a capitalist market economy. In other words, by offering participants in the competition an opportunity to perform on nationwide television, the state is in fact offering them a chance to gain both fame and a lot of money, as this medium is the most efficient medium of nationwide promotion. Thus, it is principally by maintaining its control over television and large-scale concerts, rather than through harsh political pressure, like that practiced during the revolutionary period, that the state today is able to make many artists conform to its ideology and discursive practices and help it maintain and perpetuate its control and hegemony. The section in the announcement concerning the reward, which includes, in addition to a nationwide television broadcast, an officially sponsored release of a cassette album and its promotion in the market, provides a vivid illustration of the symbiotic relationship that often exists today between the state and self-employed artists. It also demonstrates that the state and the market are not necessarily in opposition to each other.

THE STATE'S TREATMENT OF VOICES
THAT CONFLICT WITH ITS OWN

Although harsh political pressure upon artists to conform to official standards is practiced today significantly less than during the revolutionary period, in its attempts to maintain its hegemony and control the state nevertheless often actively suppresses voices that do not conform to its own. In the popular music scene, the state uses various methods to silence other voices, the most important of which are censorship of lyrics, restrictions on live concerts, and exclusion from television.

Censorship

During my stay in Beijing in 1995 and 1996, I was told by several musicians and individuals engaged in the music industry that song lyrics have to pass official inspection before an album can be released and before a song can be performed in an officially approved large-scale concert. Even though most musicians are aware of official limits and write their lyrics so as to avoid censorship, some songs are still censored, at least from time to time. Like many aspects of life today in China, there are no clear standards for censorship and whether or not a song will be censored depends to a large extent upon local and temporal conditions, such as the relationship between a particular musician and officialdom, and the general political atmosphere. There are nevertheless clear indications that the state is most likely to practice censorship when the lyrics may be interpreted as directly opposing the government and its policies, or are too critical of reality and thus challenge the party's legitimacy.

The most severe example of censorship that I came across during my research, and which actually resulted in a temporary ban on the release of an album, concerned the first album of the rock band Breathing *(Huxi)*. As noted in chapter 1, Breathing was established during the carnivalistic-turned-tragic spring of 1989, and both its name and many of its songs reflected the anxiety, frustration, anger, and sadness that the members of the band felt just before and after the June 4 incident. Wayhwa, who became the lead singer of Breathing after she was forced to give up her job as the anchor of the CCTV English news program because of a controversial interview during the democracy movement, recalled when I interviewed her that in 1990 officials prevented the release of the band's album after claiming that its theme song, "The Sun Is Rising" *(Taiyang sheng)* contained subversive messages. The album, Wayhwa noted, was ready to be released in 1990 and could have become an enormous success, as it was China's second rock album after Cui Jian's 1989 *Rock and Roll of the New Long March*. However, it was not released until 1992, and Wayhwa still believes that officials picked on the band mainly because of her post-Tiananmen stigma as a politically problematic figure (Wayhwa, interview with the author, 25 June 1996).

Another example of official censorship was mentioned to me by the members of the rock band *Lunhui*/Again. The musicians told me that one of their songs, called "Mountain Song" *(Shan'ge)*,[11] which was released in a 1994 rock collection,[12] was originally entitled "The Celebration of the Poor" *(Qiongren jie)*. This song starts with an excerpt of a male peasant from northern China singing a folksong, which Wu Tong, the leader of the band, helped to collect as a graduate student in the national/traditional music division at the Central Music Conservatory in Beijing. The point of the song, according to the band members, was to suggest that one does not need to be rich in order to be happy, free, and truthful. However, despite the song's romanticization of peasants' life and its "distinctive national character,"—elements that make it more politically correct than most other rock songs—the band was nevertheless instructed to find a new title for the song after officials who reviewed the lyrics commented that "there are no poor people in China" (*Lunhui*/Again, interview with the author, Beijing, 25 July 1995). In celebrating material poverty the band intended primarily to criticize Western capitalism. Their celebration, however, ironically ended up challenging not only orthodox socialist realism, which is still practiced in China today, as we have already seen, but also the new post-revolutionary Dengist motto that "to get rich is glorious."

Restrictions on Performance

Zang Tianshuo's story of being instructed by officials not to speak to the audience during his performance in the 1995 May 1 concert and to just sing his songs and get off stage is not uncommon. In my interview with Wayhwa (interview with the author, 25 June 1996) she, too, recalled how she was similarly warned not to speak to the audience or try to stir them up during one of the few public performances that she was allowed to give in the mid-1990s.[13] But what happens if musicians do not conform to the strict official regulations? The following case provides an answer. On 1 May 1990 (May Day again), a huge concert was held in the Workers Stadium in Beijing to help raise money for the Asian Games, which China hosted that year. Among the participants in the concert was Tang Dynasty, one of China's most famous rock bands. In his book on Cui Jian and Chinese rock, Zhao Jianwei reports that during the band's performance in front of 80,000 people, Ding Wu, the band's leader, directly addressed the audience: "Isn't it that you haven't felt comfortable for a long time now? Good, tonight we will make everyone feel very comfortable" (1992, 294). The author then reports that because of this remark the band was not allowed to perform the following day in the second round of the same concert and adds cynically, parodying official discourse: "Why? No why, life is already sweet as honey. How can anyone still be uncomfortable?" (294)

Cui Jian was forced to give up performances for similar reasons. The famous rocker offered the state in early 1990 to raise one million *yuan* for the upcoming Asian Games, apparently so that he might be allowed to conduct a nationwide concert tour. The state did grant official permission to launch the tour, but its tolerance did not last for long. The tour was cut off halfway through by officials after Cui Jian was blamed for not abiding by official instructions not to speak between songs about anything that was not related to the performance, not to get off the stage, and not to stir up the audience or encourage them to stand up (Zhao 1992, 83). By the mid-1990s the government adopted a stricter policy toward rock performances. Several well-known rockers with whom I spoke remarked that since 1993–1994 the government does not even allow large-scale all-rock concerts to take place, especially in Beijing, because the latter serves as China's political center and is therefore more sensitive politically (*Lunhui*/Again, interview with the author, 25 July 1995; Zang Tianshuo, interview with the author, 16 August 1995; Qin Qi, personal communication, 11 July 1995; Black Panther, personal communication, 9 July 1995). They added that the ban is not formal and that nobody has ever really told them that rock is officially banned, but that in order to organize a concert one needs to get an official permission or license, and since 1993–1994 such permission is not granted to rockers who wish to perform in the capital. Many rockers felt strangled and blamed the state for trying to suppress the style. The significance of giving live performances was explained to me in concrete terms by Wayhwa, who noted that most musicians today in China earn their living through performances, and so if a musician is prevented from giving live performances he or she will "die musically" (Wayhwa, interview with the author, 25 June 1996).

During my stay in Beijing I witnessed one case of active official intervention concerning a live performance, which vividly illustrated the close relationship between pop concerts and politics in China. The case involved "China's First Unplugged Pop Concert," mentioned in chapter 2, which took place in Beijing in mid-1995. This concert was organized by several nonofficial bodies and was enthusiastically promoted for several weeks before the assigned date in *Guide to Shopping Best-Quality Goods (Jingpin gouwu zhinan)*, then one of Beijing's new nonofficial newspapers and one of the bodies responsible for the event. The large-scale nonofficial concert, which was originally to be held in Beijing Exhibition Hall on May 27, received official approval, I believe, because among the sponsoring bodies was the Company for the Development of Han and Tang Culture *(Han Tang wenhua fazhan gongsi)*, a privately owned recording company whose declared purpose is to promote popular music with distinctive Chinese characteristics. However, a few days before the assigned date, and after weeks of intensive advertisement, when I arrived at the box office outside the Exhibition Hall to purchase tickets for the event, I was told by the attendant that the concert was canceled by the PSB (the Public Security Bureau). Huang Liaoyuan, a music critic, one of the managers of the record company and the main organizer of the event, explained to me several weeks later that the PSB canceled the "Unplugged" concert because its original assigned date was too close to June 4. Apparently the security body did not want to risk another eruption of disorder and dissent from students and others who might have used the event as an opportunity to commemorate the 1989 incident.

One individual who is active in organizing large-scale concerts all over China suggested to me that officials today are mainly concerned about basic security rather than politics. He noted that "Chinese [audiences] are so oppressed that one word can cause them to explode" and that this is the major reason why musicians are not allowed to talk to the audience and why the audience is not allowed to stand during performances. He then added that before every concert he is required to deposit significant sums of money to cover potential damage that might be caused by the audience. This idea that the recent ban on rock concerts has less to do with politics or ideology than with security was also suggested to me by Jin Zhaojun, who explained: "Around 1993 rock became too hot *(huo)* and the audience became too enthusiastic. . . . [In rock concerts] people act wildly, burn things etc., and those in charge are simply afraid that things will get out of control and that an accident will happen. No one wants to take responsibility" (Jin, interview with the author, 16 August 1995).

Despite this view, I believe that even if the disorderly behavior of the audience in rock and other nonofficial concerts is indeed the immediate cause for the restrictions on such concerts, nevertheless such restrictions cannot be separated from state politics. The relationship between the attitudes and policy of the state and the behavior of rock musicians and the audience is dialectical rather than simply a response of the former to the behavior of the latter. In other words, the "wild" behavior of rock audiences derives from state attitudes and politics at least as much as the ban on rock concerts derives from audiences' alleged violation of public order, and therefore it is essentially also political in nature. What the above discussion reveals more than anything else is how narrow the state's definition of proper audience behavior is, and that the state is unwilling to tolerate deviation from its standards of absolute control and discipline in live concerts. The importance that the state attributes to discipline in connection with popular music performances is also apparent in the competition announcement that I discussed earlier, in which one of the conditions for participating in this competition is to "observe discipline and abide by the law."

CCTV Bans

The 1995 May 1 concert was broadcast several times on different television channels in the days that followed the holiday. The broadcasts, however, excluded all the rockers who participated in the actual event, with the exception of the Hong Kong female rocker Faye Wong (Wang Jingwen or Wang Fei in Mandarin). The exclusion of rock songs sung in the concert from the broadcast was yet another manifestation of the continuous, systematic ban on rock at China's Central Television. The general exclusion of rock from CCTV is another form of censorship, which illustrates once again how the state attempts to silence voices that conflict with its own. From the point of view of the state, rock is the antithesis of almost everything that it attempts to promote in general and via the CCTV in particular. Rock conflicts with the official purpose of the Music Television because it is considered purely Western. The problem with the Western origin of rock was implied to me by Li Tong, the leader of Black Panther *(Hei bao)*, who suggested that rock declined after late 1993 and early 1994 because of an official campaign to promote music with distinctive Chinese characteristics (personal communication, 19 July 1995). Obviously, however, it is not the Western origin of rock as such that the state resisted or aimed to suppress, but rather the ethos embodied in rock, which does not conform to state ideology and practices.

The challenge of rock starts with the sheer physicality of rock musicians, which challenges official notions of normality. The following case provides an example of the negative official view of rockers' outward appearance. In July 1995, thanks to some personal connections, the members of *Lunhui*/Again were filmed performing several of their songs for a prospective CCTV film whose subject was the life of contemporary urban youth in China. However, when I returned to Beijing in the spring of 1996 I found out that the band's filmed performance had not been approved for broadcasting by CCTV leaders because of the long hair of two of the band's members.

By celebrating individuality, nonconformism, alienation, and exclusiveness, rock also challenges the national unity, the collectivism, and the conformism that the state promotes. The style also challenges the official idealized and self-legitimizing discourse with its general critical attitude. In addition, with its wild, uninhibited, aggressive, stirring sound and behavior, and its aesthetics of rebellion and of being out of control, rock also contests the official aesthetics and ethos of discipline, control, moderation, and by extension, the overall notion of stability and order, and of China being a "spiritual civilization." Rock aesthetics symbolize defiance of state control as much as the aesthetics of the officially approved musical styles today symbolize and reflect decades, perhaps centuries, of oppressive state control.

Banning songs from CCTV, however, is not only practiced in relation to rock. It may also be used as a temporary punitive measure against any individual musician who does not cooperate with CCTV. The following case illustrates this point. The CCTV today often invites self-employed musicians to participate in television variety shows, and in late 1994, Li Chunbo, one such musician who became famous because of his hit "Little Fang" *(Xiao Fang)*, was invited to participate in the upcoming CCTV Spring Festival Party. For most artists, participation in the grand event is a significant privilege, and it often serves as a springboard to future success, as many songs become hits after being performed in this event. Li Chunbo did not feel privileged, however, and after he found out exactly what CCTV expected of him—namely, to sing just a small portion of one of his new songs—he decided to quit the rehearsals for the event (Wu Xiaoying 1995b, 5). A person who knew Li explained in the article that Li decided to quit the show "because [his] song was placed in the 'New Generation' 'song combination,' and [he] felt that he did not belong there, [and because] 'Little Peach Red' [*Xiao tao hong* (the song that Li was supposed to sing)] was a new artistic work, and singing only half of it simply made no sense." This person was further quoted as saying that CCTV's treatment of Li was "not too respectful" (quoted in Wu Xiaoying 1995b, 5). These statements suggest that Li was required to sing a section of his new song as part of a *lianchang*, that is, a medley of songs sung in succession. The practice of *lianchang* is very common in television parties, as well as in commercial recordings, and is welcomed by many in China because it packs more songs and more singers in a short time. This practice, in the state-run television parties in particular, may be added to the list of official practices mentioned earlier that deny musicians subjectivity and individuality. In his refusal to sing a small portion of his song and to be lumped together in a *lianchang* with a bunch of singers with whom he felt he had no relationship, Li Chunbo was resisting official control over his contextualization and representation, as well as the contextualization and representation of his music. He was also resisting official control over the meaning and value of his performance, and was struggling to gain subjectivity and individuality and to speak in his own voice rather than to serve as the voice or mouthpiece of the state. Li's resistance, which in light of CCTV's new commercial function could also be viewed as an attempt to maximize the marketing value of his performance, did not go unnoticed. CCTV retaliated to his challenging declaration of independence by "sealing" him "to death" *(fengsha)*, that is, by banning him from CCTV for half a year (Wu Xiaoying 1995b, 5). Li's case reflects the emergence of a whole new artistic and overall ethos in contemporary China, and the tensions between this ethos and the official view of art and the intolerance of the state and its different bodies toward voices that are in dissonance with its own.

THE PLURALITY AND AMBIGUITY OF RELATIONS IN CHINESE POP

The opening part of this chapter suggests that the Chinese state is still quite authoritative and oppressive toward voices and practices that do not conform to official ones. These characteristics, however, should not be over-emphasized. In this book I have provided many examples from the popular music scene indicating that state power and control have limits and that the state is in fact often rather flexible, compromising, and responsive to criticism and other forms of opposition, albeit in its own peculiar, nontransparent way. In what follows I focus on the complex relationship between the state and other forces. I begin with a critique of the simplistic popular dichotomy that for quite a while has dominated the literature on popular culture in general and Chinese popular culture (including music) in particular—namely, that of hegemony and resistance.

The Dynamics of Hegemony and Resistance

Contrary to Stuart Hall's 1980 view of hegemony and resistance as fixed, structural positions or modes of communication, and of negotiation as a kind of a middle position between hegemony and resistance, I prefer to view hegemony and resistance as two forces that are in a constant process of negotiation.[14] In other words, I am interested not only in studying "hegemonic codes" or "oppositional [resisting] codes" and their manifestations in music as such, but also in seeing how they influence each other and how the interaction between them brings about change in the reality of which both are part. Numerous studies of popular culture in general and popular music in particular imply that the hegemonic or dominant is almost, if not completely, static (see, for example, Fiske's 1989 general study of popular culture, and Jones's 1992 book on popular Chinese music). I prefer, however, to view every hegemonic utterance as containing within it some signs of previous or current resistance. To use Raymond Williams's words: "A lived hegemony is always a process. It is not, except analytically, a system or structure. It is a realized complex of experiences and limits. . . . It has continually to be renewed, recreated, defended and modified. It is also continually resisted, limited, altered, challenged by pressures not at all its own" (1977, 112).

The idea that resistance (even in the form of negative reception) may influence and shape hegemony implies that the distinction and hierarchical power relations between the two may not always be clear or fixed. Moreover, it also implies that resistance may even be transformed into hegemony. It is because of this dynamic nature of hegemony and resistance that it is often impossible to know who or which is hegemonic, and by implication more powerful or dominant.

To fully understand the dialectical relationships between the state and resisting forces in society today in China we need to view them in historical perspective. The above account on the official view and use of popular music today suggests significant continuity with the revolutionary period. As in the past, the state still uses music today for educational and propaganda purposes: to assert its control, to establish its hegemony, and to unify and discipline the people. However, at the same time there are also significant differences between current and past official views and practices that have to do with popular music. As hegemony also implies the "maintenance of the status quo" (Pratt 1990, 9), these differences from the past, or changes, therefore reflect the limits of hegemony and the power of resistance. The discussion below aims to illustrate this power, showing how current hegemonic utterances often contain within them signs of previous or current resistance or, in other words, how resistance may actually shape hegemony.

The most obvious difference between revolutionary and post-revolutionary official popular music (especially since the mid- to late 1980s) is the overall tone of many of the songs. Post-revolutionary official songs are often subtle in their messages (relatively speaking, of course), and the sphere of official popular culture today also allows for nonpoliticized expressions. The state has practically acknowledged the legitimacy of art for entertainment's sake, a change that reveals itself most vividly in the viability and dominance of *tongsu / liuxing* music today on the mainland, a category that I suggest, contrary to Andrew Jones (1992a), often implies nonpoliticized pop. Moreover, official popular music today acknowledges in a sense the limits of its own power and influence, and by extension of officialdom in general. It is often sugarcoated in an attempt to cater to people's new sensibilities, which suggests that the audience's positive reception cannot be taken for granted, and that songs and messages cannot simply be imposed upon society, but rather have to compete for popularity.

In contrast to the resolute, prescriptive, ordering tone of songs from the revolutionary period, many post-revolutionary official songs, even the most politicized ones, show signs of some kind of a dialogue and negotiation. In "Return Home Safely," one of the official songs that I translated earlier, there is an obvious attempt to mediate between loyalty to the state and loyalty to the family. The song asserts the centrality of the state and society but, in contrast to revolutionary songs, allows for a multiplicity of loyalties and a multiplicity of voices. It accepts loyalty to both home/family and the state/society. The song enacts the conflict in the way it is performed. It opens with several recited lines by a frustrated young girl, who is waiting for her policeman father who has not returned home from his shift. Then her mother voices concern, too. These problematizing voices are answered by the policeman father, who sings: "It's not that I don't think about home, but how can there be only a small home and no big home." This line, which encapsulates the official message of the song, is answered by the wife, who now sings: "I don't blame you at all for not being back home, it's just that I'm worried about you." The wife's answer legitimizes both loyalties and suggests that they can coexist without a conflict.

"Return Home Safely" reflects past and current resistance and the adaptation of official ideology to the new circumstances also in its music. Its melody is slow, soft, and sweet, and it is performed almost like a love duet. The male singer, although dressed in police uniform, sings in a casual, non-heroic, and nonprofessional style. I believe the song owes much of its popularity to this musical style and to its polyphonic and negotiative nature.

Another trace of negotiation is found in "The Great Wall Is Long." As if to counter the century-old criticism of the Wall, in which it has been attacked more than once for symbolizing China's enclosure and isolation,[15] the video that accompanies the song includes shots of foreigners visiting the Wall. Thus despite its obvious nationalistic, sinocentric overall message, the video nevertheless suggests that the Great Wall is in fact a bridge to the world, as an attraction for non-Chinese. The song attempts to mediate not only the traditional conflict between China and the West but also the traditional conflict between old and new. The video's emphasis on children suggests that the Wall is not only the embodiment of the past and the old (represented in the video by an old man who carries a flag with the words "Chinese man" printed on it) but also of renewal and the future. In short, the video reflects the problematic nature of the Great Wall and projects much of the criticism of it that has been voiced in the past. The video also offers a brief symbolic escape from the state, as Dong Wenhua, the famous female state singer who sings most of the song in army uniform, appears several times in civilian dress.

This hybrid image, which dominated Dong Wenhua's television appearances during the mid-1990s, is an example of the polyphonic quality to be found even in the most extreme variety of official culture, and the responsive, compromising nature even of the most hegemonic of expressions. A high-ranking CCTV editor who was interviewed in 1996 on Music Television and discussed the song noted that it was created four years earlier but became popular only two years after its release, when a video was produced to accompany it.[16] The successful popularization of "The Great Wall Is Long" seems to be related not only to the fact that it was adapted for Music Television by having a video created for it, but also to the negotiative qualities that are embodied in this video.

The same negotiative and polyphonic quality is found in "Honest Words." In contrast to songs from the revolutionary period, and especially from the Cultural Revolution, which prescribed absolute loyalty to Mao and the party often without even trying to justify it, this song, very much like "Return Home Safely," problematizes patriotism and thus reflects the existing resistance to the hegemonic agenda: "To be honest / I also miss home / Old mom / her hair has already turned completely white / Honestly speaking, I also have love / I often miss her in my dreams. . . . / To be honest, I am also not naive / I understand what is involved in joining the army, blowing wind and beating rain / honestly speaking, I also have feelings. . . ." Again, the song allows for multiple loyalties and attempts to mediate the conflict between loyalty to one's family and loyalty to the state. Like Dong Wenhua's symbolic change of costume, this song acknowledges the limits of patriotism and collectivism, and reflects the fact that they are being challenged.

However, the most obvious traces of resistance in many hegemonic expressions are musical. Despite the attempt to assert authority through the use of the orthodox professional bel canto and artistic folk singing styles, highly polished and choreographed performances, and semiclassical instrumental accompaniment, many official songs today are sugarcoated in the sense that they are easy listening, that is, slow in tempo and melodically sweet. The *shuqing* lyrical style, which was banned in China during much of the revolutionary period, today dominates even the most official and politicized songs. Unlike their revolutionary forebears, which privileged content and direct expression, many official songs today pay equal attention to form, and often conform musically to traditional aesthetics of subtlety and restraint.[17] Whereas Dong Wenhua's short hair and uniform still invoke the masculine, militant, desexualized, puritanical revolutionary ethos, the appearance and performance of another famous female singer, Peng Liyuan are charged with sexuality and emphasize feminine beauty despite the fact that she is employed by the same military unit for which

Dong Wenhua works. In the video of "I Belong to China," Peng appears several times in fancy traditional feminine costumes, her long hair often loose, and one cannot avoid noticing the fact that she even changes her earrings several times during the video. Peng Liyuan's appearance offers an escape from the highly politicized message in the song, about the 1997 return of Hong Kong to the mainland. If we did not pay attention to the more direct lines in the lyrics and images in the video that juxtapose Hong Kong with the Great Wall, we would have never guessed what this song is all about. Today this kind of hybridity dominates much of Chinese popular culture, including its most official branch. If hybridity "contests, challenges, weakens and ultimately invalidates the authority and legitimacy of dominant monolithic . . . cultures," as Gregory Lee suggests (1995, 105), then the hybrid nature of much of contemporary official popular culture today on the mainland is a vivid testimony to the influence that resistance has already exerted and continues to exert on the monolithic culture of the revolutionary past.

The dialogic character of official popular music manifests itself also in the extra-official music that is frequently featured in officially sponsored or sanctioned events. Music Television is a good example. The highly politicized official songs by state singers like Dong Wenhua constitute only a small percentage of the program. The majority of songs in these programs are, in fact, "normal" *tongsu/liuxing* pop songs. Though these nonpoliticized songs can be seen as yet another sugarcoating, they nevertheless acknowledge the legitimacy of art for entertainment's sake. The invitation of so many rockers to participate in the official May 1 concert of 1995 reflects both the limits of the party's orthodox hegemony and tight control, as well as its ability to compromise.

The status quo is constantly challenged even in single events. One Music Television program that was broadcast around the 1996 Chinese New Year, which included an interview with Lin Yilun, a mainstream pop singer who now lives in Guangzhou, provided a nice illustration of this dynamic. After being asked to tell about how the New Year is celebrated in his home, the singer started to recite the traditional congratulatory lines for the Chinese New Year in Cantonese and did not stop until the anchor reminded him that he was on CCTV. By his use of Cantonese, a southern local dialect, instead of Mandarin, the official standard language, the singer challenged the unity and uniformity imposed by CCTV and the centrality of Beijing and rearticulated one of the most ancient tensions in China: between unity and centralism on the one hand and diversity and localism on the other. Lin Yilun's challenge was perhaps inspired by the fact that the 1996 CCTV

Spring Festival Party was broadcast for the first time simultaneously from three locations: Beijing, Xi'an, and Shanghai, and thus celebrated localism in addition to the regular celebration of unity. This rare celebration of localism, too, was a clear trace of resistance, in this case specifically to the hegemony and centrality of Beijing, which are celebrated constantly in official culture.[18]

The "state" (and its hegemony), of course, has never been absolutely uniform or monolithic, and the status quo has always been challenged also from within, that is, by the different forces, individuals, and institutions (e.g., CCTV, the Ministry of Culture, official newspapers, and the like) that make up the state. One example of this dynamic was reported to me by the members of *Lunhui*/Again. The band members recalled how, despite the ban on rock on state-run television, a local television station in the city of Hangzhou did broadcast one of their songs.[19] This case recalls how the same band was filmed for a prospective CCTV program about the life of contemporary urban youth in China despite the official ban on rock. Although eventually their filmed performance was censored because two of the band members had long hair, the fact that the band was filmed by CCTV photographers in the first place reflects the complex dynamic between hegemony and resistance in present-day China.

Symbiosis

Previous studies of popular culture and music in China have tended to focus on tensions and conflicts between the state and other forces. Popular culture in these studies was more often than not perceived as oppositional to the state and to officialdom. The interaction between the state and other forces, however, is much more complex than simple antagonism, and it takes various forms, one of which is symbiosis. One good example of this symbiotic relationship is Cui Jian's 1990 concert tour. The state allowed the rocker to launch the tour, which originally was to cover ten major cities—despite his notorious rebellious attitude and the problematic nature of his music—because the rocker offered to donate one million *yuan* to the state to help it in hosting the Asian Games that year. Cui Jian, of course, would not have had the chance to launch such a large concert tour if he had not presented it as a fund-raising project for a nationalistic cause. The state accepted the offer, presumably because it needed the money and in the early 1990s Cui Jian was probably the only mainland musician who was capable of raising such a substantial amount of money. Officials may also have thought that turning down the musician's offer could damage official efforts to ease tension and to boost public morale, especially in the cities after the June 4 incident. Although the concert tour was terminated half-way through after officials realized that the one million *yuan* might not be worth the political damage that Cui's concerts were causing, the case nevertheless illustrates how the state and one of its most articulate dissidents could cooperate at least temporarily because of mutual need.

The invitation of so many rockers and other self-employed musicians to the large-scale May 1 concert that was held in Beijing in 1995 is another example of the symbiotic relationship between the state and extra-official and even oppositional forces. The official organizations that sponsored the event needed Zang Tianshuo, Dou Wei, and Luo Qi, the three mainland rockers, and Faye Wong (Wang Jingwen) and Wu Qixian, the two *gangtai* singers, to attract more people to the concert. One has to keep in mind that, after all, one of the main driving forces behind the May 1 concert was profit, and it is questionable whether the organizing bodies could have made a profit without these musicians. The state can afford to ban rock and ignore music from Taiwan and Hong Kong in its television music programs, but when it comes to public live concerts in large cities it has to compromise because people can simply choose not to attend. Seen from another perspective, these nonofficial elements are also useful for the propagation of official messages among a wide spectrum of urbanites. At least where part of the audience is concerned, they are the sugarcoating that makes people swallow Qubi Awu's minority folk-style songs (see chapter 2), the slogans on the walls, and the politicized messages delivered by the anchors between songs. This technique is not new. Bell Yung notes that in the 1950s and 1960s the state organized opera performances that included both traditional operas and revolutionary ones, the former to draw the crowd and the latter to propagate revolutionary messages (1984, 146). In addition, the invitation of the above-mentioned rockers may be seen, of course, as a kind of safety valve.

But the participation of rockers and *gangtai* singers in official events, as I have briefly suggested, is also a political statement in its own right. Rockers' participation in such events helps the government to propagate a tolerant and democratic self-image. This image helps to legitimize the government in urban China, where these hybrid concerts take place and where people tend to be much more critical as a result of intense exposure to alternative ideologies from the West and elsewhere. CCTV omitted the rock performers when the 1995 May 1 concert was broadcast nationwide several weeks later because such an image is not crucial to the legitimacy of the government when China's peasants, who cannot relate to rock music anyway, are concerned. The official justification of this particular omission, like that of the banning of rock on CCTV, is that nationwide television caters to the entire population of China, close to eighty percent of which are peasants, and therefore it should not privilege the urban minority. This rationale, however, is apparently applied selectively, and only when rock is concerned. It does not apply to cultural products that serve the hegemonic interests of the state and which the latter considers "healthy." A good example of such a "healthy" product is Western and Chinese art music.

Chinese rock helps to present a democratic and modern image of the Chinese state, not only within China but also outside the country. With few exceptions, rock albums by mainland rockers, many of which are produced by companies from Hong Kong and Taiwan, are the only albums of mainland popular music that are sold today outside of China, in Hong Kong, Taiwan, Japan, and the West.[20] This is partly because mainstream pop from the mainland has always been considered inferior to *gangtai* music both in China and elsewhere. The export of Chinese rock is not limited to recordings; Cui Jian has visited and performed in the United States several times,[21] and he and several other rockers performed in the early 1990s in Europe in the Chinese Vanguard Culture and Art Festival. In late 1994 a group of mainland rockers, which included He Yong, Dou Wei, Tang Dynasty, and a musician named Zhang Chu, performed in a large-scale concert of mainland rock held in Hong Kong. It is reasonable to assume that if the state thought the rockers' foreign tours could cause political damage it would not have allowed any of them to travel abroad to perform.

Let us now consider in what ways the Chinese state benefits Chinese rock. The most important benefit, of course, is economic. Since most large-scale concerts are controlled by the state, Chinese rockers are dependent on the state if they wish to earn significant profits. There is no doubt that such profits are the main incentive for Chinese rockers to agree to participate in officially organized events despite their oppositional stance. This dependency is enhanced because of the widespread practice of cassette pirating in China, which significantly reduces the profits they earn from the sales of their cassette albums. In addition to profit, there is also the wide exposure that comes from officially organized concerts, and which is difficult to achieve in nonofficial events, at least since the mid-1990s.

The state, however, also benefits Chinese rock in more abstract ways. Paradoxically, it helps Chinese rockers through its oppressive image. It is questionable if Chinese rock could have received the international attention that it receives since the early 1990s without the package of dictatorship that accompanies it. In other words, Chinese rock has gained much of its value, both in and especially outside of China, because of the context of

China's oppressive political reality and the unique meaning that rock gains in such a context. An example of this view is found in the following statement made by the musician and music critic Zhang Guangtian. Despite his recent distaste for rock, Zhang commented when I interviewed him: "What do Westerners know about rock, did any of them ever experience the kind of pressures that Cui Jian and other Chinese rockers have experienced?" (Zhang Guangtian, interview with the author, 24 June 1996). Similar comments were also made by rockers and other individuals with whom I spoke. The most famous Chinese rockers are understandably less inclined today to draw any connection between the value of their music and Chinese politics, because in addition to political risk such a connection implies that their music would have less value if considered in itself. Cui Jian's recent insistence that he wants to be accepted in the West for his music rather than his politics provides a vivid acknowledgment of the fact that his music is accepted abroad because of its politics.[22]

Chinese Transnationalism Becomes Greater Mainland Nationalism

Like the incorporation of rock in the 1995 May 1 concert, the participation in the event of the two *gangtai* singers, Wu Qixian and Faye Wong, not only helped to maximize profit. The state excludes *gangtai* songs from Music Television to assert mainland cultural independence and to resist Westernized music from the Chinese "periphery." But it nevertheless uses *gangtai* singers quite often in order to promote its agenda of pan-Chineseness, a reunified China, and to assert the mainland's position as the core of the pan-Chinese community. In addition to giving live concerts, singers from Hong Kong and Taiwan are invited every year to participate in the CCTV Spring Festival Party. Pan-Chineseness is always celebrated in this popular, lengthy annual program through a ritualistic exchange of greetings for the New Year between representatives of the Chinese state and Chinese from all over the world. The program always opens with greetings read by the anchors to Chinese all over the world, with a special emphasis on those who live in Taiwan (and Hong Kong before 1997), all of whom are referred to as "compatriots" *(tongbao)*. These greetings are answered toward the end of the program with greetings by groups of Chinese abroad, mostly students, which are often directed to the state itself.

The participation of *gangtai* singers in officially organized live or televised concerts provides another example of the symbiotic relationship between the state and its others. As with the rockers, the benefit that official events offer to nonmainland Chinese singers is mainly economical. By performing in the May 1 concert, which was later broadcast on national and local television stations, Wu Qixian, for instance, was promoting his music and introducing himself to one of the largest markets on earth for Chinese pop. Singers from Hong Kong, who normally sing in Cantonese, have started since the early 1990s to produce enormous numbers of albums in Mandarin Chinese for the same reason.

But the nonmainland Chinese singers who participate in officially organized events on the mainland are well aware of the political meaning of their participation, and some of them consciously help to articulate the hegemonic messages that their participation aims to communicate. Thus, even though Wu Qixian did not sing any patriotic or pan-Chinese song in the 1995 May 1 concert, as the Hong Kong singer Zhang Mingmin, for example, did ten years earlier when he sang a song entitled "My Chinese Heart" *(Wo de Zhongguo xin)* at the 1985 CCTV Spring Festival Party, he nevertheless made a statement on the issue. After introducing the singer and describing his migration from Malaysia to Singapore and his recent popularity in Hong Kong, Taiwan, and all over the Chinese diaspora, the anchor asked Wu how he defined himself in the final analysis. The musician's reply, "I am Chinese" *(wo shi Zhongguo ren)*, which stirred a most enthusiastic and warm response from the audience, encapsulated everything Wu's participation in the official event stood for, at least from the point of view of the state. Wu's response may very well come from a wish to advance his economic interests. But we should not necessarily exclude the possibility that he may also identify with the official purpose that his participation aimed to fulfill. Not all ethnic Chinese who live outside of China, after all, would identify themselves as "Zhongguo ren."[23]

In addition to illustrating the symbiotic relationship that often exists between the state and self-employed musicians, who in this case are not even from China, the participation of *gangtai* singers in officially organized events also offers an alternative perspective to the theme of Chinese transnationalism. Parallel to the trend throughout the humanities, an increasing amount of scholarly attention has been paid in recent years to the nature and effects of transnational cultural flows and globalization on popular culture in China. As with the general study of transnationalism worldwide, the assumption in studies of Chinese transnationalism, sometimes explicit and sometimes implicit, has been that in the context of transnational capital flows, the globalized cultural market, the significant increase in transnational population flow, and new media technology, concepts and practices that relate to the Chinese nation-state weaken.

In the introduction to their 1997 edited volume on Chinese transnationalism, *Ungrounded Empire*, Donald Nonini and Aiwha Ong, for example, propose that we should cease to treat mainland China as the core of Chinese identity. They write:

> We decenter the Middle Kingdom as the ultimate analytical reference for an understanding of diaspora Chinese. . . . We do not . . . accord China a privileged ontological or epistemological position; it is one among many sites within and across which Chinese transnational practices are played out. (Nonini and Ong 1997, 12)

> Transnational publics provide alternatives to state ideologies for remaking identity, thus eroding not only the nation-state but also "the national identities which are associated with it." (25)

> Transnational publics are forming new Chinese subjectivities that are increasingly independent of place . . . and subversive of national regimes. (26)

In the same volume, Mayfair Mei-hui Yang explores challenges to the Chinese nation-state in various domains of popular culture. One of the examples that she discusses in her article is Ai Jing's song "My 1997." She suggests that the main theme in this song is as follows:

> The longing to be reunited with or merged with the Chinese Other outside the borders of the Chinese state. . . . In contrast to mainland official discourse about 1997, which stresses Hong Kong's "return to the embrace of the motherland" *(huidao zuguo de huaibao),* the song expresses a yearning to break out of the motherland and to cross the state borders that forbid another way of being Chinese. (1997, 302–3)

Ai Jing's song was read in a similar way by Zha Jianying, who in a concise analysis noted: "For the first time, suddenly, political walls melt down, regimes and territories become irrelevant." (1994, 405).

Indeed, much of Chinese pop since the late 1970s—and especially in the 1990s when pop from Hong Kong and Taiwan became important to an unprecedented extent in the mainland's pop scene—could be interpreted along similar lines. No doubt, much of Chinese pop today constructs (and depends on) a transnational Chinese identity and discourse that challenge a separate mainland identity and culture and, by implication, also mainland nationalism. The exclusion of *gangtai* music from Chinese Music Television is a powerful affirmation of the threat posed by this music to mainland nationalism.

However, at the same time, the new globalized, transnational conditions may also lead to the opposite result. Chapter 2, on the negotiation of ethnicity in popular Chinese music, provided several examples of how the increased presence of *gangtai* music on the mainland's pop scene in the 1990s caused both music makers and critics to appropriate minority music extensively and assert mainland identity more forcefully as a kind of reaction. Similarly, the discussions of *xibeifeng* in chapters 1 and 3 illustrate how intensification in transnational flows between China and other Chinese cultures (as well as the West) resulted in a popular surge of nationalism or nativism in an effort to strengthen mainland identity, as opposed to Taiwanese and Hong Kong identities.[24]

In this section, however, I contend that the official invitations of *gangtai* singers to participate in the most official of events implies that the relationship between transnationalism and nationalism in the Chinese context is even more complex than previously realized. By inviting Wu Qixian, Zhang Mingmin, Tong An'ge, and other *gangtai* singers to participate in concerts and television programs, the Chinese state is not engaged so much in competing with other Chinese polities and identities (as *xibeifeng* and more recent appropriations of minority music do) but rather in contesting their independence and in co-opting them into a greater Chinese nationalism, of which China is the core. In other words, the Chinese state is engaged in appropriating the concept of Greater China *(da Zhonghua),* "a term coined by overseas economists to describe the increasing integration among China, Hong Kong, and Taiwan produced by globalization" (Ong 1997, 175). Ong insists that this concept "challenges the modernist project of the Chinese state" (1997, 176) and adds: "On the mainland, patriotic scholars are quick to reject Greater China as a bankers' fantasy, and illusion of outsiders greedy to cash in on China's booming economy. They fear that any ideological recognition of a Chinese transnational capitalist zone will undermine China as a territorially based political entity" (176). Contrary to Ong's emphasis on the conflict between Chinese nationalism and the concept of Greater China, I suggest that the two are in fact often combined by the Chinese state to serve its own hegemonic nationalistic discourse.

The context and discourse with which nonmainland Chinese singers are contextualized and represented emphasize unity under mainland hegemony. In this official discourse and contextualization, neither Hong Kong (before 1997) nor Taiwan challenges the Chinese nation-state, but rather they become an integral part of it. As for those Chinese who are far away, they are viewed as intimately tied with the motherland, as an extension of greater Chinese nationalism, not as an alternative kind of Chineseness. An excerpt of the video of "The Great Wall Is Long," in which an old overseas

Chinese man is shown on the Wall with a banner that says "Chinese man" (*Zhongguo ren*), provides another example of this official attempt to domesticate Chinese transnationalism. The same message is communicated even more explicitly in "Today Is Your Birthday, China" in the following lines: "Today is your birthday, my China / In the early morning I set a flock of white doves free to fly / To carry back for you the longing of the children who are far away / the doves have flown to the boundless sea and sky. . . . / We bless you on your birthday, my China / These are the words of love of the children who are far away. . . ."

Illustrating once again, however, how every event may turn into an arena for negotiation, Wu Qixian sang part of his songs in the 1995 May 1 concert in Cantonese. By challenging the hegemony of Mandarin and the centralized, uniform Chineseness that the state promotes today in many official events and in the media despite its simultaneous emphasis on diversity, Wu was asserting his otherness and his autonomous position and power vis-à-vis the Chinese state and Beijing.

Hand in Hand: The State and the Market

Much of this book so far has implied a dichotomy between the state and the market, suggesting time and again that the emergence of a free-market economy had a democratizing and decentralizing effect that resulted in the weakening of state control. The relationship between the state and the market, however, is not necessarily dichotomous.

In chapter 1, I noted how Gao Feng got involved with rock in the early 1990s but then decided to change direction because of his realization that the style had reached a dead end, in the sense that if one was a rocker, one could not survive and would never become a star. Gao Feng ended up writing "Great China," which, not surprisingly, was immediately adopted by the state and, eventually, after it was broadcast nonstop on national and local television and radio stations, became one of the most popular songs on the mainland in 1995. "Great China" was the result of a calculated effort to cater to official taste by an individual who wanted to gain success. Ironically, Gao wanted so much to please the official establishment that he ended up with a song title with which even officials felt uncomfortable. The officials decided to omit the word "great" (*da*) from the title and to simply name the song "China" (*Zhongguo*) because they felt that otherwise the song would appear too nationalistic and chauvinistic. Apparently, as Gao himself suggested to me, officials were concerned that the original title could invoke negative sentiments when the song was performed abroad (Gao Feng, interview with the author, 8 June 1996).[25]

Gao is ambivalent about his song. He does not consider it "art" *(yishu)* (interview, ibid.) but is nevertheless understandably very proud of his meteoric success, which he attributes to his innovative combination of many preexisting elements into a new song. The musician, who has been labeled by several rockers with whom I spoke an "opportunist" who caters "to the taste of both the government and the common people," did end up being a star. He appears regularly on television, is recognized on the street by many people, who often approach him and ask him for his autograph, and tours China on a regular basis to participate in officially organized concerts that earn him significant sums of money.[26] As catering to official taste proves useful and profitable, Gao continues to produce politicized songs while saying that creating "real art" can wait (interview, ibid.). In early 1996, Gao wrote another folksy song with "distinctive national character" that, like "Great China," was also based on existing folk tunes, one of which is a work song. Gao's song, which talks about hard work, was accordingly labeled "Work Song" *(Laodong haozi).*[27] "Work Song" was ready just in time for the 1996 May 1 International Labor Day and was performed by Gao on the annual television variety show that celebrated the holiday. Later that year Gao produced another politicized song, this time about the upcoming return of Hong Kong to the mainland.

Gao's case is representative of the new symbiotic dynamics and relationships between the state and independent artists today in China. Many official politicized songs today on the mainland are produced, like Gao's songs, not because of the political conviction of their creators or any direct political pressure from the state, but because the state needs new official songs and rewards those who fill this need by promoting them and their music and making them rich and famous. The state's monopoly over television, the most effective channel of communication and dissemination, means that if musicians wish to become known nationwide and achieve commercial success, they have to maintain a good relationship with the state and conform at least partially to official political artistic standards. The capitalist system that has been introduced into China in the last two decades has resulted not only in increased diversity and the termination of the official monopoly over cultural production, on which I elaborated earlier, but simultaneously has been appropriated by the state to advance its hegemony and control. The official appropriation of the new economic system today in China is, as already noted, another important reminder that capitalism and authoritarianism are not necessarily mutually exclusive.

Gao's submission to the state, however, is not absolute, and he has not given up his artistic ideals and autonomy altogether. Most of the songs in the musician's 1994 album *Love Over There in the Sky (Tian na bian de ai),* on which "Great China" first appeared, are quite different from the highly politicized and nationalistic tone of the latter song, and they seem to articulate Gao's more authentic voice. Thus, in a sense the musician exploits the state at least as much as the state exploits him. "Great China" was like a tribute to the state, perhaps providing lip service (but not necessarily, as I argue below), which helped Gao not only to become famous and rich but also to promote his independent, authentic voice. Gao is not the only musician who uses this strategy of producing one or more politically correct songs in order to promote an album that speaks in an entirely different voice. This strategy was mentioned to me on separate occasions by several individuals in the music industry.

Popularization-Legitimization Cycle

The cases mentioned above are only a few examples that illustrate an important development in post-revolutionary China, especially during the 1990s, which is the blurring of old lines and clear-cut distinctions. This development, which Geremie Barmé (1992a) has labeled "the greying of Chinese culture,"[28] manifests itself in myriad forms of hybridity, many of which are the result of what I call a popularization-legitimization cycle between the state and nonofficial forces.

Like vernacular literature from the Ming Dynasty (1386–1644), in which blunt pornography is placed in the framework of a very detailed, serious, orthodox historical narrative and combined with didactic, hegemonic messages, in many cases it is not at all clear today whether a particular popular cultural product is official or nonofficial, or whether it originated from "below" or from "above." In other words, it is not clear whether a hybrid is an attempt to popularize an official message or to legitimize the nonofficial or nonorthodox. Earlier I suggested that many of the popular songs that appear on Chinese MTV and are performed in officially organized concerts serve as a kind of sugarcoating for political propaganda. This characterization, however, privileges the state, envisaging the phenomenon from the standpoint of officialdom. After discussing some of the different agencies that negotiate in the pop scene in addition to the state and after suggesting that the state itself is in fact far from monolithic, it could be argued that these hybrids are perhaps sugar coated with politics. In other words, like Gao Feng and his album *Love Over There in the Sky,* it is obvious that many of the hybrids are not necessarily the result of officialdom attempting to popularize political propaganda but rather of nonofficialdom trying to gain legitimacy and thus access into official media.

RESISTANCE TO THE STATE IN ROCK MUSIC

Resistance to the state appears in popular music culture in a multiplicity of forms. It may be articulated in active, direct protest and challenge through verbal attacks on the party-state, its leaders, and its policy, or in the less direct form of parodying and satirizing official culture and policies. It may also be articulated in the celebration of extra- or nonofficial ideologies, values, and behavior in musical practice and discourse, or in what Craig Calhoun has labeled (after Charles Taylor) the "affirmation of ordinary life," which is "an assertion of the value of everyday personal and family life, of simply being happy" (1994, 105–8). Resistance may also be found in the negative reception of official culture and in conscious and subconscious attempts to escape state control. In what follows I discuss several expressions of resistance, focusing specifically on Chinese rock, where resistance is most common. Some of the expressions that I discuss are explicit, whereas others are more subtle, but all of them take the form of "public transcripts," to use James Scott's terminology (1990).

In chapter 1, I discussed Cui Jian's "Opportunists," a song written during the 1989 democracy movement and performed for the hunger strikers in Tiananmen Square. This song is doubtless one of the most direct and powerful expressions of resistance in contemporary Chinese popular music, encouraging the participants in the midst of one of the most significant political movements in recent Chinese history to carry on their active struggle against the government. Below is the translation of another famous song by Cui Jian, "A Piece of Red Cloth" *(Yi kuai hong bu)*, which like "Opportunists" is also widely interpreted as an attack on the Communist Party:

A PIECE OF RED CLOTH
(lyrics, music, and performance by Cui Jian)

On that day you used a piece of red cloth
To blindfold my two eyes and also the sky
You asked me what do I see
I said that I see happiness
This feeling really made me feel comfortable
It made me forget that I had no place to live . . .
My hands are also clasped by you
You asked me what do I think
I said I want you to decide . . .
I feel that I want to drink some water
But your mouth blocks my mouth
I can't go and I can't cry . . .

I want to accompany you like this forever
Because I know best your pain . . .

"A Piece of Red Cloth" addresses a theme that many individuals with whom I spoke in China in 1995 and 1996 kept referring to, namely, how Chinese society was blindfolded by the Communist Party during the revolutionary period, especially during the Cultural Revolution. "We were made to believe that we are the richest and strongest nation on earth," one restaurant owner told me, "but after the Cultural Revolution was over and China opened itself to the outside world, we discovered that we were actually far behind the West, so backward. . . . We were deceived all these years."

In his book on Cui Jian, Zhao Jianwei refers to "A Piece of Red Cloth" as "a true historical elegy" and describes the blindfolding somewhat cynically in more concrete terms, writing that during the Cultural Revolution people were

> immersed in an "ocean of red" [a color "that symbolized belief . . . ideals . . . aspirations . . . hope . . . revolution and happiness"] that went wild. This made people feel comfortable, the hand holds the red treasured book, the heart faces the sun, long live Chairman Mao, the tears flow, saliva splashes out, the soul is flying, it made people forget that they didn't have a place to live. (1992, 261–62)

"A Piece of Red Cloth" describes a violent experience of someone who is not only blindfolded, but whose hands are clasped and whose mouth is blocked by someone else so he cannot see, speak, drink, escape, or even cry. The speaker in the song turns into a subjugated creature who cannot think and make decisions, distinguish between right and wrong, true and false, and eventually loses even the ability to cry, thus the ability to feel and, by implication, his humanity. This frightening, violent, sensual nightmare, which becomes so concrete because of the mention of warm blood elsewhere in the song, was enacted several times on stage by Cui Jian, when he blindfolded himself during the performance of the song with a piece of red cloth. Zhao Jianwei, who accompanied Cui in his 1990 concert tour, during which the song was performed, writes:

> Whenever Cui Jian blindfolded himself with the red cloth it was impossible to escape this kind of feeling of wanting to cry. . . . You would feel a kind of desire to weep yet having no tears, a desire to cry out yet having no voice, a desire to jump yet having no force. Thereupon you would stand in silence and carry out a bathing ritual for the soul. (1992, 41–42)

A fan who attended one of Cui Jian's concerts during his 1990 tour describes a similar emotional experience during the performance of this song:

> The scene of restless moving clamor suddenly became motionless,
> became silent. At this moment it was impossible to see anything inside
> the hall besides two eyes covered by a piece of red cloth. I couldn't
> dance any more, and already couldn't shout, unable to distinguish
> between the tears on the face and the sweat on the body, I only felt that
> I couldn't bear that "piece of red cloth." (Quoted in Zhao 1992, 74)

After performing "A Piece of Red Cloth" in one of his concerts during the 1990 tour, Cui Jian addressed the audience with the following words: "If you feel that some things in life are not reliable, I hope you will exclude one thing, which is music. Music will never deceive you" (Zhao 1992, 74). With this statement, the rocker was obviously contrasting his rock music with the piece of red cloth with which he blindfolded himself while performing his song to symbolize the deceptive effect of the revolution and party politics.

Deconstructing National Symbols

In "A Piece of Red Cloth," Cui Jian deconstructs one of the most precious symbols of the Chinese state and the Communist Party and bestows on it a whole new set of negative meanings. He turns the color that is celebrated in Gao Feng's performance of "Great China" and in numerous official videos that are shown daily on Music Television into a nightmare, a rapist, a symbol of violent deception and subjugation. Cui is not the only person in China today for whom red symbolizes a nightmare. One ex-*zhiqing* (a rusticated youth) is quoted in Zhao's book as saying:

> When I first heard Cui Jian's "A Piece of Red Cloth" it deeply affected
> me. . . . The impact that red color has on us *zhiqing* . . . is extremely
> deep. It symbolizes our belief and ideals during those years. I remem-
> ber in the midst of the Cultural Revolution there was once a violent
> debate. In order to protect the red flag of his own Red Guard organiza-
> tion, one of my best schoolmates cut someone with a knife more than
> ten times, and the ground was filled with blood, red too. Now when I
> see red I feel uncomfortable from head to toe and I lose my appetite. I
> repainted all the doors and the windows in my home white, wishing to
> escape red, red is like a nightmare. . . . (1992, 263)[29]

Cui Jian's performance of "A Piece of Red Cloth" is like a catharsis through which the musician attempts to achieve liberation from the red nightmare. In the song, the rocker comments about the present as much as he comments about the past. The song's criticism of the Communist Party, however, is

Figure 8.   Cui Jian, *The Egg under the Red Flag,* cassette cover. Design by Wang Wangwang. Courtesy of Cui Jian and Wang Wangwang.

understandably articulated in a subtle way. If taken at face value, the song suggests little if anything of the meaning described above and could have a wide range of interpretations. One Chinese graduate student in his mid-twenties with whom I spoke in late 1996 in the United States, and who considers himself a fan of Cui Jian, was completely unaware of the above interpretation. He himself interpreted the song as a description of a wedding.[30] Obviously it is this ambiguity that allows Cui Jian to keep exercising his critical and rebellious voice.

Cui Jian's cathartic engagement with red continues in his 1994 album *The Egg under the Red Flag (Hong qi xia de dan),* where the connection between this color and the party-state is drawn explicitly (see figure 8). The cover of the album features a picture of an embryo blindfolded with a strip of red cloth, which immediately invokes "A Piece of Red Cloth." The blindfolded embryo is placed under another piece of red cloth on which the album's title is printed and which obviously symbolizes China's national flag, as the title of the album suggests. The cover makes a clear reference to the national flag also through the placement of yellow stars and yellow characters on different kinds of red backgrounds. The red flag is thus directly linked to the piece of red cloth with which the embryo on the cover is blindfolded, as well as to the red cloth with which Cui Jian blindfolded himself while performing "A Piece of Red Cloth."

One also finds an articulation of resistance to the party-state through deconstruction of cherished national symbols in other rock songs. Below are excerpts from the lyrics of three such songs, two by Wayhwa and one by He Yong, which deconstruct the Forbidden City and the Great Wall:

FORBIDDEN CITY
("Lao Gugong"; lyrics by Wayhwa; music by Wayhwa and
Zou Shidong; performance by Wayhwa)[31]

The city walls of the Forbidden City are both old and long
Firmly tying me to this place
The sun that comes out in winter is warm
My thoughts are empty
Ai, I want to have a little bit of distress
I want to have a little bit of loss
Wu, but I have no power
Wu, to get out from these old city walls . . .

VISA[32]
(lyrics, music, and performance by Wayhwa)

I had to be up really early for my visa interview
I got there on time
Thought I was the only one appointed by then
But I was wrong
The waiting line had been as long as the Great Wall
Everybody here wants to travel abroad . . .
Everybody here wants to visit the USA
To see Disneyland . . .
What's wrong with my born status?
Why was I so nervous waiting in the line? . . .
Just wanna get on the plane, grab some money I have, fly away . . .

GARBAGE DUMP
("Lajichang"; lyrics, music, and performance by He Yong)

The place we live in
Is like a garbage dump . . .
You can see the Forbidden City shines with golden light
And there is also a very long wall . . .
The place we live in
Is like a slaughterhouse . . .
The footbinding bandage of Ci Xi was both stinking and long
Is this a game? No! Blow it up! . . .

Rockers and intellectuals often talk about 5,000 years of feudalism, which has only gotten worse after 1949 (Jones 1992a, 123–24, 153–54). This message is articulated in two of the songs above. Despite the references in "Forbidden City" and "Garbage Dump" to historical sites (and in the latter also directly to history), Wayhwa and He Yong make it clear that the problem does not lie in the past alone. Part of the criticism in the songs is that nothing has really changed and that the despotism and enclosure of the past are still alive. In their songs, the two rockers articulate their wish to achieve personal liberation in the present from a state of imprisonment and oppression. This is a common theme in many rock songs on the mainland since the late 1980s. Wayhwa and He Yong, however, differ from each other in one significant respect. Whereas in "Forbidden City" Wayhwa describes, like Cui Jian in "A Piece of Red Cloth," a state of disempowerment and an inability to achieve release, He Yong offers a solution, ending his song by shouting wildly, "Blow it up! Blow it up!"

Both Wayhwa and He Yong refer in their songs to the Great Wall. As we have seen, the Wall is one of the most celebrated objects in official popular culture today on the mainland, and it is used by the state almost as an emblem of kingship, a symbol of legitimacy, authority, power, and control. By associating itself with the Great Wall through repeated representation and constant praise, as in, for instance, "The Great Wall Is Long," the current government is in fact engaged in self-praise and self-legitimization, presenting itself as the legitimate and natural successor of China's legacy of "5,000 years." Like previous rulers in Chinese history, the agents of the state today hope that with such a long history (and a long, mighty wall) no one will dare to argue. The solemn, bright, idealized Great Wall in "The Great Wall Is Long," however, is trivialized by He Yong, who refers to it in his song as "a very long wall." Whereas the official song juxtaposes the Great Wall with "millions upon millions of heroic idealists," "green army uniforms," and the "red sun," He Yong, by contrast, places it on the top of a garbage dump, which he also calls "a slaughterhouse," and which he juxtaposes with the "stinking" and "long" (*chang,* like the wall) footbinding bandage of the hated dowager Ci Xi.[33] The cry "blow it up" at the end of "Garbage Dump" applies to everything mentioned in the song, including the "very long wall."

Wayhwa's recontextualization of the Great Wall in "Visa," in which she uses it as a metaphor for the line of people waiting to get their visa, may seem trivial at first glance. However, a closer look at the lyrics suggests that the Great Wall mentioned in this song is not different from the oppressive walls in "Forbidden City," which not only imprison the musician but also deny her the ability to feel. The line of people that looks like the Great Wall in "Visa" is wishing, in fact, like Wayhwa herself in "Forbidden City," to get off the very same wall to which they are compared and which imprisons them. In a message disguised by light humor, Wayhwa suggests that everybody wants to leave China. When I interviewed her, the musician noted that people in fact wish to immigrate, not to travel, but that to say this in a song would have been too much (Wayhwa, interview with the author, 25 June 1996). "Visa," like Ai Jing's "My 1997," is about transnational subjectivity, one that desires liberation from the state. But at the same time, the song also implies criticism of the United States, which denies entrance to so many Chinese and humiliates them. Thus it also communicates a sense of nationalism. This sense is made explicit in the line "What's wrong with my born status?"

The struggle over the meaning and value of the Great Wall is symbolic. Through the desecration of this emblem of kingship, Wayhwa and He Yong challenge not only the official, idealized view of the Great Wall, but also the state itself and its idealized view of itself and of Chineseness in general. He Yong's "Garbage Dump" is one of the most direct and bold attacks on the state in Chinese popular music. In 1994, however, when the musician released his first album, which is named after the above song, the song's lyrics underwent considerable modification. All the elements in the original version that identify the garbage dump as China were omitted, and the new version talks instead about the "world."[34] The new version also omits the loaded reference to the slaughterhouse and the radical call to "blow it up." The modification of the lyrics may be related to several factors. First, it is possible that the lyrics of the album underwent censorship. Another possible explanation is that it was a marketing strategy. The producers perhaps thought that with such radical lyrics the album would not appeal to a wide audience, and therefore decided to temper some of the more extreme expressions. A third possibility, however, is that He Yong himself underwent an ideological transformation in the few years between the original version of the song and the one released in the 1994 album. Indeed, there is evidence (which I will present later in this chapter) to suggest that around the mid-1990s He Yong became less antagonistic toward the state.

The facts that "Garbage Dump" was performed in its original form in public[35] and that its original lyrics were printed in a book sold in China (Zhao Jianwei's book) testify to the significant liberalization that has taken place on the post-revolutionary mainland, as well as to continuation of resistance after Tiananmen 1989. Another example of this liberalization and the continuity of resistance can be found on Zang Tianshuo's 1995 album,

My Last Ten Years (Wo zhe shi nian), where in his lengthy rap song "Say Say" *(Shuo shuo)* the rocker criticizes in the most straightforward manner the ban on rock by state-run television and demands more democratization in this official organization. Below are three verses from the song, the first two containing the criticism, and the third, which ends the song, qualifying the criticism, probably in order to temper a possible negative reception by officialdom. This attempt, however, which calls for a dialogue, is filled with cynicism:

SAY SAY
(lyrics and music by Zang Tianshuo; performance by Dai Bing and Zang Tianshuo)

. . . I see too many television variety shows
It feels as if the homeland only has these few new stars
Over and over again always these few gestures
And *gangtai* songs that fill the streets

The people want to hear their own songs
I heard that in Beijing there is a lot of rock
Why not put some on television?[36]
After all, it is we the people who should decide what is good and what
    is bad . . .

I only say what can be said[37]
I certainly don't want to offend any great immortal
If there is any problem, let's discuss it calmly
Don't make my mother worry

Thanks and goodbye

The explicit challenge to the state articulated in these lines is enhanced by the rap style that is used in their performance. In addition to the typical recitation-like, aggressive, challenging accentuated rhythmic rap delivery, emphasized slides and nasality turn the first verse into a mockery. Powerful accents on the words "after all," "bad," and "good" in the fourth line of the second stanza above, which are created through a shouted delivery, accentuated drumbeats, and a sharp deviation from the fast flow of words—where a whole beat is suddenly given to each of the first two words ("after all," *daodi*) and half a beat to each of the next two ("bad" and "good," *hao, huai*)—transform this line into an angry demand. The use of the colloquial/vulgar idiom *ganma* in the third line of the second stanza enhances the rhetorical power of the attack by challenging the civilized official language. This idiom also identifies the speaker with "the people" *(laobaixing)* whom he claims to represent.

Challenging Official Values and Aesthetics and the Official Discursive Universe

When asked in 1990 about his opinion with regard to the possible influence of rock on Chinese culture, Cui Jian replied:

> The Chinese people have a submissive mentality, as if we only had one muscle that is relatively developed whereas the rest are diseased. I hope that through rock we can discover the other muscles in our body and their function. A person cannot have only one developed muscle. As a human being I have a lot of desires and demands, and I hope that the abnormal cells in our bodies which . . . suffer from necrosis will recover. We should not always feel that we are tiny and insignificant. In fact every individual has his/her great parts. I remember that the Beatles have a song in which they sing: "When I was fourteen, I was [already] a great person." I think that in Chinese culture there ought to be a new concept, namely, that each one of us is great. This kind of greatness will make people understand that they are individuals who have independent meanings and functions of existence, and that they should not just know how to obey. Obedience can only make people destroy themselves and make themselves become more and more tiny and insignificant. In this way they will virtually strangle their ability to create. The reason for the progress of a society lies in the ability of every person to use his/her creativity. . . . I hope that my rock music can help other people to discover themselves. . . . (Quoted in Zhao 1992, 272)

Like most of the rockers with whom I spoke in 1995 and 1996, Cui Jian has repeatedly stated that the target of the criticism that he articulates in his music is traditional Chinese culture, that the purpose of his music is to promote personal liberation, and that he is not concerned with politics *(zhengzhi)* (Jones 1992a, 124, 132). However, Cui's statements, which derive in part from political caution and in part from the musician's genuine attempt to place his music in a broader, universal context and to be acknowledged as a musician, do not change the fact that his music, its ethos and aesthetics, and his statements (like the one quoted above) challenge official values, state control, and the hegemony of the state, and are therefore essentially political.

Cui Jian's celebrated individualism contrasts sharply with the collectivist ethos that the state still promotes today, which manifests itself vividly in the official songs that I quoted earlier. The way the state in China today views individuals was nicely illustrated by a new official song called "The Workers' Song" *(Laodongzhe zhi ge)* that was broadcast on television around 1 May 1996. Like songs from the revolutionary period, "The Workers'

Song" compared the individual to "a drop of water," suggesting that separately they are insignificant but when they are combined together they may turn into a mighty river. Songs like "The Workers' Song" are broadcast today on Chinese television on a regular basis. The entries in one mainland dictionary published following the end of the revolutionary era[38] under the words *miaoxiao* (tiny and insignificant) and *fucong* (to obey or to be subordinated to), the two central words in Cui Jian's statement, offer an example of the orthodox official view of the individual to which the rocker is reacting: under *miaoxiao* we find the following example: "The strength of an individual is insignificant *(miaoxiao)*." Under *fucong,* the dictionary offers the following sentence: "One's personal interests must be subordinated *(fucong)* to the interests of the revolution." The only major difference between the current official view of the individual and the official view of the individual during the revolutionary period is that in the latter the individual was seen as insignificant in relation to the communist revolution, whereas today he or she is viewed as insignificant vis-à-vis the state.

In "A Piece of Red Cloth," Cui Jian describes a nightmarish experience of absolute submission, but he offers no escape or release. Release is achieved, however, four years later in his 1994 album *The Egg under the Red Flag.* In contrast to the "highly constricted" (Jones 1992a, 141–42) voice employed in the earlier song to express suffering and repression, this time, in a song also entitled "The Egg under the Red Flag," the musician sings in an assertive, confident, self-controlled, and somewhat cynical style:

> We are not going to follow blindly other people anymore . . .
> We have already eaten our fill and our brain is already open
> Do not say that this is kindness that can never be repaid to the end
> We are no longer chessmen who follow the marks that other people
>   draw
> We want to try and stand up, go everywhere and take a look. . . .

In these lines Cui Jian destroys the "masochistic" (Jones 1992a, 140) bond found in "A Piece of Red Cloth" between the subjugated self and the party-state and offers release from the mental and physical grip of the latter. The release is achieved through the negation of the moral and rational justification for the obligation or subjugation of the people to the party, which the latter has always propagated through the slogan that the kindness of the party, the savior, can never be repaid. The Communist Party's longstanding commitment to provide everyone in China with enough food to eat has always been its major source of legitimization and has also justified the party's authoritarianism. Cui Jian boldly counters this notion, suggesting that having enough to eat is not enough and asserting his independence and release from any obligation to the party.

The challenge to the party's psychological and moral authority is also articulated musically through the vocal delivery, which is assertive and simultaneously cynical. Unrelated interludes played on *suona* and saxophone, which are interwoven into the song and create a feeling of parody, further enhance the challenge. These humorous and cynical improvisational interludes, which include a short passage from a well-known *yangge*, and which are often played in a highly distorted manner, have the effect of trivializing the subject matter of the song—that is, the red flag and, by extension, the party-state. In "The Egg under the Red Flag," Cui Jian is transformed from the oppressed and powerless creature who inhabits "A Piece of Red Cloth" and who is emotional almost to the point of hysteria, into a detached, calm, cynical satirist, who is distant from and independent of the subjugating forces of the party-state.

Another challenging celebration of individualism is found in Zang Tianshuo's 1995 album, whose title *(My Last Ten Years)* already asserts the musician's "greatness," to use Cui Jian's words. In his album, Zang struggles to gain subjectivity, independence, legitimization, and control over his representation amid the official ban on his rock music,[39] and his trivialization and reduction to a "chessman" (à la Cui Jian again) in official events, such as the 1 May 1995 concert that I discussed earlier. When I asked Zang several months after this concert how it felt to perform in that event, his reply was short but forceful: "meaningless" *(mei yisi)* (Zang, interview with the author, 16 August 1995). So strong was the musician's desire to speak in his own voice after ten years of silence, that in order to have full control over his first album he produced it himself with his own money, without the sponsorship of any company (interview, ibid.). Zang's album thus provides another example of how the combination of a free-market economy and the cheap cost and simple technology involved in cassette production have enabled alternative voices to gain access to the widest public sphere.

On the cover of his album, Zang Tianshuo wears a unique haircut and directs a stern look at the viewer, thus articulating not only subjectivity and significance but also general defiance. These are enhanced by the traditional porter's shirt that he wears, which I mentioned in the previous chapter, and which exposes much of his healthy body. Through the cover of his album, which, besides his photograph, has nothing but a light blue background with his name and the album's title in big characters, Zang Tianshuo asserts his centrality and communicates something like the following message: This cassette is mine, and is about me, simple, true, and plain, my life and my music, take it or leave it. The pamphlet attached to the cassette features eight more photographs of the musician, two of which are printed once again on the cassette itself. In one photograph, which occupies a whole page, Zang is shown standing in front of his synthesizer in a casual posture, rubbing his eyes. This photograph is decorated with the musician's signature written in large red characters. Another page features an old photo of Zang as a young boy, with his young sister, in revolutionary uniform and holding a rifle. Five other small photographs feature the musician in casual poses, while only one shows Zang with his band. In marginalizing his band ("1989") Zang Tianshuo, like Cui Jian, deviates from the norm in Chinese rock of celebrating band brotherhood, a norm that illustrates that despite the rhetorical celebration of individualism in Chinese rock, many rockers nevertheless still perpetuate a collectivist ethos. I return to this paradox later in this chapter, where I also point to the limits of Zang's individualism.

The cover of Zang Tianshuo's album and its pamphlet contrast sharply with covers of official productions of popular songs. For instance, a 1996 album released by the China Record Company and entitled *Original Edition of Original Renditions of Songs by China's Giant Stars (Zhongguo ju xing shouchang yuanban)* is, as the title suggests, a collection of songs by different singers in various styles. The front cover of the cassette features the title, which opens in Chinese with the word "China," and a red square on top of which are shown the faces of seven of the singers on the cassette, two of them in army uniform. The seven faces cover about the same amount of space covered by Zang Tianshuo's face alone on the cover of his album. The names of the singers shown in the photograph do not appear on the front side of the cover, but rather are listed on the back, next to the title of their song, along with the names of nine other singers whose photograph does not even appear on the cover. This collection reminds one of the officially organized May 1 concert. It is a medley that lumps together many singers and reduces them to small photographs without names, a medley in which the individual singers whose songs are included in it have no control whatsoever over their representation and contextualization, both of which highlight the state. The centrality of the state in the album is reflected in the word "China" in the title, the red square that binds all the small faces together and suggests the red flag, the army uniforms of two of the singers, and finally the fact that many of the songs in this collection are classical official songs, for instance, "Party Ah, Dear Mother" *(Dang Ah, qin'ai de mama)*, a famous song that compares the Communist Party to a mother.

In the mid-1990s, state singers like Dong Wenhua, who normally appear on such albums, did not have their own individual albums. Official collections praise the state; they do not celebrate one individual singer or his/her music. The state has been practicing its collectivist musical practices for so long now that for most people on the mainland medleys of songs by various musicians, which include at least some praise songs for the state, seem as normal as eating rice in a meal. Because of these collectivist ethos and practices, few singers or musicians in China today have had the opportunity to give solo concerts. So rare is the practice of solo concerts on the mainland that Ai Jing, who did give solo concerts in Japan, was praised for having "a lot of guts" (Zhan 1995b). The extreme popularity of song medleys that de-emphasize individual musicians, even when nonofficial music is concerned, is another manifestation of decades of state-sponsored collectivist ethos. So deep-rooted are some of the collectivist concepts and practices in relation to art that paradoxically often even rock cassettes follow this format and are organized as collections with titles like *Chinese Rock (Zhongguo yaogun 1, 2)* and *The Fire of China (Zhongguo huo)*.

In contrast to official songs—which usually praise the state and are more often than not produced and performed by professionals employed by the state, with their lyrics written by one or two individuals, music by another, and their performance done by yet another individual (or group)—Zang Tianshuo's music is a personal statement and an exhibition and exploration of the self, his creativity, and his individuality. With the exception of two older songs, whose lyrics were written by others, and "Say Say," whose rap portions are sung by another musician who specializes in rap singing, all the songs in *My Last Ten Years* are written by Zang and performed by him. Unlike state singers, who serve as a mouthpiece for the voice of the state, Zang attempts in his album to speak in his own voice. In the context of the state's unwillingness to concede (in its rhetoric, at least) its absolute control over and superiority vis-à-vis the "insignificant" individual, Zang's celebration of individuality is subversive in itself. Moreover, the rocker also goes beyond asserting his individuality to negate and attack the forces that have denied it to him. Zang opens his album with a song entitled "This Is What I Am" *(Wo jiushi zhe ge moyang)*, which serves as a prelude to the demonstration of power, independence, and individualism in his album:

THIS IS WHAT I AM
(lyrics, music, and performance by Zang Tianshuo)

. . . You can reject my goodness and honesty
But you cannot stop my firmness . . .

You can open your aging wings
To use them to beat my broad chest
I can endure your dying excitement
But you cannot change my direction . . .
I have blood and I also have flesh
I have a knife and I also have a rifle . . .

Very healthy
I understand perfectly
No one should play the fool with me

When I asked Zang Tianshuo to whom he directed this song, he replied that the song addresses "everyone around me, society, the government," and added that "it is not directed to a woman" (Zang, interview with the author, 16 August 1995). In "This Is What I Am" Zang is thus engaged in a physical and mental duel with Chinese society and the state, asserting his power, confidence, determination, and most importantly his independence. In claiming that he is "healthy" *(jiankang)*, Zang challenges the official stigma that is attached to rock and to rockers, which, like other cultural expressions, practices, and people that are disapproved by the state, are often referred to as "unhealthy" *(bu jiankang)*. Zang challenges state control in the most straightforward manner when he sings: "You cannot stop my firmness . . . you cannot change my direction." The oppressive power that society and the state still exert over the rocker reveals itself in the fact that his independence is articulated as a kind of reaction. Like a shaman performing an exorcism, Zang attacks his opponents with words intended to disempower them and dispel their mental and physical influence: "Your aging wings . . . your dying excitement."

This exorcism is also done musically. Like the lyrics, the song's music articulates power, freedom, and defiance. The song is like a powerful stream of energy. It is fast and loud, and it has a strong beat. Zang shouts the lyrics in his characteristic coarse voice, as if to show off his physical strength and scare his opponents. A distorted electric guitar and synthesized rhythmic brass turn the song almost into "noise" (cf. Attali 1985), a noise that challenges the sweet, tame, but simultaneously oppressive sounds of official music. A wild improvisational solo on the distorted guitar toward the end of the song communicates freedom, defiance, and individualism. One never hears improvisation in official songs. The last three lines in the song are shouted halfway between singing and talking, without any accompaniment—again, to show off physical strength and courage, but also to express their seriousness and the fact that this song is not intended to be nice. Following this section, Zang starts to improvise vocally in blues style with nonsense vocables, once again to articulate his independence and freedom. The song ends with a short, challenging instrumental section that several times halts abruptly and irregularly and then resumes, as if to demonstrate the musician's control and power. Zang's musical challenge to the listener, who is completely manipulated by the music at this point, is symbolic of his challenge to the "you" in the song, that is, to society and the state.

In another song, entitled "Di Ba Di Ba," a title that semantically means nothing, Zang celebrates a narcissist, sardonic self-alienation:

DI BA DI BA
(lyrics, music, and performance by Zang Tianshuo)

I'm di ba di ba
I'm saying a sentence that no one can understand . . .
I'm di ba di ba
I'm singing a song that no one can understand

In this light, silly, and semantically meaningless song, which was written by Zang to celebrate his birthday (Zang, interview with the author, 16 August 1995), the musician challenges the orthodox communist view of art and the artist. Zang suggests in his song that art can be a personal, individual thing that centers around the artist and fulfills his/her personal needs, and that he as an individual artist is not obliged to serve anyone other than himself, be it the people or the state. The meaning of Zang's song lies precisely in its "meaninglessness." Through its unintelligibility, the song challenges the orthodox official notion that songs (and art in general) must always carry clear didactic messages, and that art should always be serious. Ironically, however, even this celebration of autonomous art cannot escape being as politicized as official art. In the context of the orthodox official prescription that art should always serve political and social goals, art for art's sake, or for sheer pleasure (entertainment, fun, and the like) inevitably becomes subversive. "Di Ba Di Ba" is subversive also in its anti-social, self-centered, cynical stance. In publicly celebrating his own birthday in song, rather than praising the state or celebrating its birthday, as "Today Is Your Birthday, China" does, for instance, Zang asserts his "greatness" and suggests that he is as worthy as the state.

• • •

"A Piece of Red Cloth" and "Having Nothing" are similar. What they have in common is a kind of tragic beauty. I think that this tragic beauty has a lot of power. After getting used to hearing those things that deceive us, as well as others of the type of "Our Life Is Sweeter Than Honey," Cui Jian's "A Piece of Red Cloth" and "Having Nothing" immediately shake us because of their truthfulness and tragic power. (A university student, quoted in Zhao 1992, 263)

"Our Life Is Sweeter Than Honey" *(Women de shenghuo bi mi tian)* is a typical orthodox official praise song, which, like the more recent official songs mentioned earlier, idealizes reality, albeit much more bluntly, and constructs a universe that lacks defects, negative feelings, and doubts. Through the constant production of "healthy," "positive," and idealized praise songs, the party-state has always tried to legitimize itself by constructing a discourse that excludes antagonism, criticism, and challenge. But this official practice has been challenged most vehemently by rock. One rocker, in fact, went so far as to suggest to me that the whole aim of rock is to tell the truth and expose the lies of the party. It is in the realistic, critical, de-idealized discourse of rock in itself, even when the song does not make direct reference to the party-state, that we find yet another powerful form of resistance to the state. An example of a challenge to the idealized hegemonic discourse is found in "Advanced Animal" *(Gaoji dongwu)* by the rocker Dou Wei, which gains much of its critical power because it parodies a famous official song entitled "Where Is Happiness?" *(Xingfu zai nali).* Here are the lyrics of the official song on which Dou Wei comments, followed by Dou Wei's song:[40]

WHERE IS HAPPINESS?
(lyrics by Dai Furong; music by Jiang Chunyang; performance by Yin Xiumei)

Where is happiness?
Friend, ah, let me tell you . . .
It is in industrious work . . .
Ah! Happiness is in the sparkling and crystal-clear sweat . . .
It is not under the moonlight
It is not in one's sleep dreams
It is in meticulous plowing and weeding . . .
Ah! It is in the glitter of your intelligence . . .

ADVANCED ANIMAL
(lyrics, music, and performance by Dou Wei)

Contradiction, hypocrisy, greed, deception
Fantasy, uncertainty, simplicity, fickleness . . .
Hell, Paradise, they all exist in the world . . .
Joyfulness, suffering, war, peace . . .
Resentment, revenge, imperious, censure

Where is happiness? Where is happiness?
Where is happiness? Where is happiness?
Where is happiness? Where is happiness?

"Where Is Happiness?" became popular all over China in 1984, after it was performed at the CCTV Spring Festival Party of that year (Yang Xiaolu and Zhang Zhentao 1990, 269–70). Like "Good Person, Good Heart," it promotes official values and has a strong didactic tone. The song opens with a question, reflecting the uncertainty that took over China after the beginning of reforms. But it is this uncertainty and confusion that the song aims to dispel. The song is engaged not in asking questions but in providing answers. The question is followed by a crystal-clear answer, another hegemonic prescription. Like the official definition of goodness in "Good Person, Good Heart," this song's definition of happiness is simplistic and narrow, and it leaves little room for doubt. The song rejects fun, romance, and fantasy, and identifies happiness with hard work, sweat, and hard study only. The prescription to work and study hard cannot be separated from the contemporary national agenda on the mainland, that is, the modernization of China and increased productivity. "Where Is Happiness?" provides another example of how universal values and aspirations are subjugated in official songs in China to the interests of the state. Official discourse leaves little room for doubt, hesitation, and complexity, always providing an answer, which is more often than not plain and simple. The song aims to boost popular morale, and as usual involves a universe that consists of positive, optimistic, idealized rhetoric.

Optimism, determination, and resolution are also articulated musically in the song. Like many revolutionary songs that call for action, it is sung in a fast tempo, in a high-pitched, loud voice, in polished bel canto style, in an elevated, excited, and authoritarian manner that leaves no room for introspection, contemplation, or argument. As with the "happiness" mentioned in Cui Jian's "A Piece of Red Cloth," so in this song happiness is imposed through the resolute rhetoric and delivery, and blindfolds with its simplicity. Resolution is articulated in the song also through its clear tonality. The question "Where is happiness?" is sung once at the beginning of each of the song's two verses, and ends on the fifth degree of the scale. The lengthy answer that follows in each of the two verses ends with a lengthy melodic line, which repeats itself twice at the end of the first verse and three times at the end of the song, ending heroically after a long note on the tonic one octave higher.

The relationship between Dou Wei's song and "Where Is Happiness?" is established only at the end of his song, in which he quotes the question from the earlier song and uses the same well-known melody to sing it, although in a very different style. It is this ending and the relationship it establishes with the official song that provide the new song with much of its meaning. Viewed separately, "Advanced Animal" may be interpreted as a general ironic comment on human nature. However, the relationship with "Where Is Happiness?" turns the song into a powerful, politicized statement. Dou Wei's song presents a long list of single words (a couple of characters for each), through which the musician attempts to describe the complexity of human existence. "Advanced Animal" suggests that reality is not so simple as "Where Is Happiness?" (and official discourse in general) would have the listener believe, and that it includes a much wider range of experiences and feelings, some good, some bad, and others that are not necessarily good or bad. However, the placement of the words "contradiction," "hypocrisy," "greed," "deception," "imperious," and "censure" at the beginning and end of the long list of otherwise undifferentiated words gives these words more weight and thus emphasizes the musician's antagonism.

By titling his song "Advanced Animal," Dou Wei may have indeed intended to articulate an ironic view of human nature. But viewed in the context of political satire, he may also have intended to say, like Cui Jian in "The Egg under the Red Flag," that he is an intelligent creature who can use his brain and cannot be fooled or blindfolded by simplistic propaganda. The musician struggles in his song to expand the limits of official discourse and to depict reality as it is, but he also suggests at the end that he has not found happiness, thus articulating and legitimizing despair and doubts and directly discrediting the answer given in the official song and by implication also official discourse in general.

Whereas "Where Is Happiness?" opens with a brief question and then moves to provide us with a lengthy answer, "Advanced Animal," by contrast, ends with the very same question that is asked rhetorically at the beginning in the former. Dou Wei repeats this question six times, thereby transforming it into a cry of despair and frustration. The relationship that Dou Wei establishes between his song and "Where Is Happiness?" creates a relationship between his failure to achieve happiness and the voice in the official song. In other words, the question "Where is happiness?" is transformed into an attack directed at the voice that always promises happiness and denies individuals anything other than happiness by perpetuating a discourse that lacks the words to name other experiences.

The official voice in "Where Is Happiness?" is also negated musically in "Advanced Animal." Since the borrowed melodic fragment from "Where Is Happiness?" that ends "Advanced Animal" ends on the fifth degree, the latter song ends away from the tonal center that this fragment establishes and is thus tonally unresolved, thereby enhancing the strong sense of uncertainty that it articulates. Moreover, with the exception of these ending lines, which borrow the melody from "Where Is Happiness?," "Advanced Animal" almost lacks a melody, as if to deliberately contrast with the enthusiastic, warm, optimistic, lively, positive, bright, promising tone of the former. Dou Wei's song is delivered in a cold, dark, alienated, low, speech-like singing, and is accompanied by the psychedelic sounds of a synthesizer, creating the sonic image of a nightmare. This nightmare quality is enhanced by much of the album's content; the album is entitled *Black Dream (Hei meng)*, it includes songs with titles such as "Sad Dream" *(Beishang de meng)* and "In a Black Dream" *(Hei se meng zhong)*, and it is dedicated to the exploration of the dark sides of human existence, dealing with themes such as loneliness, alienation, helplessness, despair, and uncertainty.

Alternative Concerts

Zang Tianshuo is not the only musician in China who wishes that large-scale concerts in the country were different. Ai Jing was quoted in a recent article describing the kind of concerts that she would have liked to participate in, suggesting her discontent with official control over live performances:

> All the audience will come [to the concert] only because they like to hear me. . . . Everyone will sit a little bit closer. The best will be a large open playground, with lights on, our band is all around, the audience can sit on the ground, if they are hungry or thirsty they shouldn't be prevented from fetching beer or the like, it will be great. In fact, abroad . . . the audience is part of the performance, everyone participates together. (Quoted in Zhan 1995b, 2–3)

What Ai Jing describes above is the antithesis of the kind of pop concerts that one usually sees today on the mainland, especially in Beijing. The musician provides us with another important insight into the way many of the musicians participating in officially organized large-scale concerts feel about them. Ai Jing constructs an alternative model for a Chinese pop concert, one that is free, casual, interactive, and intimate, one that will be her own. In this paragraph the musician challenges the way concerts are held today in China, and since this way is officially prescribed, she also indirectly challenges officialdom itself.

While so far Ai Jing has been unable to fulfill her dream in China, some musicians, all of them rockers, have been able to do so, at least to some extent. Cui Jian is, ironically, one of the few mainland musicians who has had his own solo concerts, and his large-scale concerts, although officially approved, provide a vivid example of resistance to the state. The most direct, overt resistance to the state in Cui's concerts was, of course, embodied in the lyrics of his songs. But the content of some songs was only part of the challenge; no less important was the way Cui performed his songs. Earlier I mentioned how, when performing "A Piece of Red Cloth," Cui enacted the song by blindfolding himself with a piece of red cloth, an enactment that significantly increased the song's impact. Another performance-related expression of resistance is found in the fact that, since his first large-scale public appearance in 1986, Cui habitually performed in the 1980s and 1990s in an old army uniform, an appropriation of an official symbol that is widely understood as a parody of the party-state.[41] Another important means of articulating resistance in Cui's concerts was the occasional speeches made before and after songs. For instance, the famous drummer Liu Xiaosong, who joined Cui Jian in his 1990 concert tour, addressed the audience at the end of Cui Jian's concert in Chengdu with the following remarks: "We wish that everyone will return home safely, attend to work happily, manage household hygiene well, and manage birth control well, good evening!" *(Zhu dajia pingping an'an hui jia, gaogao xingxing shangban, gao hao jiating weisheng, gao hao jihua shengyu, wan'an)* (quoted in Zhao 1992, 75). Liu's remarks were a straightforward parody of standard official propaganda slogans that one can still see today in many streets and entrances to state-run factories and other governmental units.

Resistance to state control and hegemony was articulated in Cui Jian's large-scale rock concerts also through his general behavior on stage and the behavior of the audience. As mentioned earlier, officials decided to cut off Cui's 1990 concert tour after the rocker stirred up the audience and encouraged them to stand up during his concerts (Zhao 1992, 83). Cui's concerts contained the usual ingredients that one finds in rock concerts in the West: loud music, noise, shouting, hand-clapping, dancing to the beat, interaction between the performers and the audience, and individuals getting out of control, some climbing on the stage, others taking their cloths off, and so on (Zhao 1992, 13, 26–27, 31, 33, 66, 73, 78). Nevertheless, in China, where people are not even supposed to stand up in pop concerts, these Western-inspired practices have been transformed into a symbolic celebration of defiance to state control as much as official concerts are symbolic of state control and public order. The meanings of resistance to officialdom are suggested in the following passage from an article that was published in the *Beijing Evening Post* in March 19, 1990, which reported on Cui Jian's concert in Zhengzhou:

Everyone sang along, clapped their hands, and even danced. There were continuous thunder-like cheers. One local official could not refrain from exclaiming: "What happened to the people of Zhengzhou today?" This is the first time that he has seen a scene like that. He really couldn't understand why the children of the Central Plains with whom he is so familiar, who are famous for being gentle, polite, and peaceful, are like this. (Quoted in Zhao 1992, 27)

After quoting this passage in his book, Zhao Jianwei adds the following cynical remarks: "Yes, this official didn't understand. There is no way he could understand, because he probably didn't wish that such a scene would have appeared in the first place" (1992, 27). Zhao then parodies the official, assuming his voice: "What is everyone doing? Running wild, don't they have any discipline? Don't they know what spiritual civilization is? Where did the traditional moral excellence of the Chinese nation go?" (27). In the same spirit of self-empowerment and defiance of officialdom that many experienced during Cui's performances, Zhao concludes:

Go ahead and say whatever you like, go ahead and condemn, we don't care anymore. When people all of a sudden discover a new life stretching its arms toward them they will rush to catch it bravely, even if it is the worst offense, even if it means broken heads and bleeding. They wouldn't care about anything anymore. (27)

Cui Jian's large-scale all-rock solo concerts, however, are exceptional, and as for 1997, very few such concerts have been held in China since rock was introduced to the country in the mid-1980s. The more typical rock concerts have been in the form of the small-scale "underground" "parties" mentioned in chapter 1. These events usually have been held in small settings, like pubs, nightclubs, and small halls, hidden from the eyes of the general public and often also from the eyes of the local police. The early 1990s are regarded today by many senior rockers as the golden age of rock in China, partly because during that period rock parties took place on a regular basis. Despite increased official pressure to limit rock activity in the capital since late 1993 and early 1994, rock concerts and parties are nevertheless still held in the city from time to time. Information about the rock parties that I attended in 1995 and 1996 was passed orally, and the events closely followed Ai Jing's description. One such event, for example, took place in a disco-bar of a moderate-size Chinese hotel (that is, one that does not accommodates foreigners). As is usually the case in rock parties, the evening featured several local bands, which performed in succession. The bands performed on a low stage that was placed on one side of the hall, and the audience occupied the space just in front of the stage. The majority of the audience literally besieged the stage, almost touching the performers, and cheered, shouted, and sang along with the different bands, while others danced or just stood at the bar drinking beer, smoking, and chatting. In contrast to official concerts, the event was a celebration of casualness, informality, interactiveness, and participation. Before and after performing, band members mingled with the audience, who consisted mainly of their friends, and while performing they introduced themselves and addressed the audience directly as they wished. There were no anchors and no speeches, and the songs that were performed that night did not pass any official inspection or approval. The event was controlled and owned by the bands that performed that night and the audience who came to see them. On one of the walls a placard with the words "rock party" (*yaogun* party) was hung, featuring the forbidden word that rockers had to replace with the word "modern" in the large-scale all-rock concert held in the capital in 1990.

Despite the use of the forbidden word and the obvious differences between this event and officially organized concerts, however, this small placard also recalled by its mere existence just how much even rockers share with the state and official practices. In having this placard with its written words and providing a title for the event, rockers were following the well-established official practice of naming events and using written words to communicate with the audience and bestow meaning upon such events. Another manifestation of shared practices between rockers and their audience on the one hand and the state on the other was the dancing. As in many other rock parties and discos, there was little partner dancing. Instead, most people who danced (and not many did, which is typical and also very telling) engaged in group dancing that reminded one of mass calisthenics. Indeed, even the bodies of the rockers and their audience, though situated in a nonofficial context, revealed the collectivist ethos and restraint inscribed on them for years by the state and society.

Nonetheless, despite these similarities, in contrast to the mass official concerts that cater to an audience that is as diversified as possible, rock parties celebrate exclusivity and are usually patronized by a few hundred urban youngsters, mainly university students, workers, and bohemians, whose ages range from twenty to thirty, and who are connected to one another mainly by their patronization of rock and their shared access to the nonofficial, oral network of communication through which these events are advertised. The exclusivity of these events manifests itself immediately in the nonconformist appearance of many of the participants: the jeans and long hair for men, features that became the symbols of the rock subculture in the capital. Through their unique outer appearance, these core participants in the rock subculture identify themselves as a unified but, more importantly, also a separate and autonomous group vis-à-vis mainstream culture.

Rock concerts are a celebration of nonofficialdom. They are structured almost as the exact opposite of officially organized concerts, thus as "rituals of reversal" (*cf.* Victor Turner 1969), and thus—even in their structure and much of the related behavior, not to mention the song lyrics—turn the official order upside down and articulate resistance to the hegemony and control of the state. If state-organized concerts celebrate the state and symbolize through their structure state control and authority, as well as order and discipline, then rock parties celebrate in their "anti-structure" (*cf.* Turner 1969) release from this control and the undoing of all these official values.

THE LIMITS OF RESISTANCE: ROCKERS' UNITY WITH THE STATE AND THE MAINSTREAM

There is no doubt that part of the popularity of "Great China" was related to the fact that it was broadcast time and again on television and radio, but this is only part of the reason why the song became so popular. After all, there are many patriotic and nationalistic songs that are broadcast on television but never become popular. "Great China" became so popular because it articulated pride in and love for the country in a way many people could relate to. We should not assume that the state necessarily imposes nationalism and patriotism upon the people in China. Patriotism and nationalism are the most powerful unifying forces today in this country, and they constitute a theme that runs through many post-revolutionary popular songs, both official and nonofficial.

After Cui Jian describes in "A Piece of Red Cloth" the nightmarish experience of his absolute and violent subjugation to the party-state, which results in his physical, mental, and emotional withering, he nonetheless paradoxically ends his tragic song with the following lines: "I want to accompany you like this forever, because I know best your pain." One can hardly fail to notice the similarity between the first part of this statement and one of the last lines in Gao Feng's "Great China": "I want to accompany her forever and ever." This similarity offers one example of the important points of convergence that exist today in Chinese culture between subcultures that are otherwise very different. Zhao Jianwei suggests that the last two lines in "A Piece of Red Cloth" are the embodiment of what he calls the "bitter love complex" *(ku lian qingjie)*, and explains that this complex is "the tragic nature of the Chinese people and especially [China's] intellectuals in the last several millennia. No matter how many times history destroys them and juggles with them, they always endure silently" (1992, 262). In articulating a powerful criticism but at the same time asserting loyalty and patriotism, Cui Jian's "A Piece of Red Cloth" embodies the paradoxical and contradictory nature of much of the criticism and resistance that is voiced today in Chinese popular culture, especially in rock, where resistance is most intense and conscious. Through the articulation of nationalistic and patriotic sentiments Chinese rockers no doubt seek legitimization, but they also assume the role of generation upon generation of Chinese intellectuals, who with very few exceptions have always been linked with the state and have always seen themselves as its loyal servants.

In her analysis of the failure of the 1989 democracy movement, Elizabeth Perry suggested that "the very people who launched the Tiananmen protest—urban intellectuals—were perhaps the greatest fetter on its further development" (1992, 148). Whether or not this is the reason or part of the reason for the failure of the movement will remain an open question, and answering it is beyond the scope of this study. The relevant point in relation to the present discussion, however, is that "contemporary intellectuals remain bound to traditional styles of protest" (149). This traditional style of protest, according to Perry, revealed itself during the movement in "the longing for heroes," in the fact that "state strengthening was the sine qua non of democracy," in "the students' deference to state authority [which] was seen in their demand for dialogue" (151), and in the fact that "even in the act of protest [they entertained] state-centric tendencies . . . [and were unable] to liberate themselves from the hegemonic claims of the state" (159). Cui Jian's ending to "A Piece of Red Cloth" nicely illustrates this strong bond between China's intellectuals and the Chinese state.

Similar to Perry, Jing Wang suggests in her analysis of the 1988 controversial television series *River Elegy (He shang)* that despite its iconoclastic and anti-history agenda, radical attack on Chinese tradition and its "imperial nationalism," and attempt to bring about "cultural enlightenment," the series, paradoxically, shared many of the traditional concepts it attacked. "The enlightened elite," Wang notes, "are ironically no less nostalgic for power symbolism than their historical [and contemporary] Confucian [and communist] counterparts whom they roundly condemn" (1996, 120–21):

Even at those moments when Su Xiaokang [one of the writers of the script of the series] preaches most eloquently the elimination of such nostalgia, his vision for the future is helplessly and unconsciously embedded in the same rhetoric of imperialistic nationalism. At its heart, *He shang* often betrays the cause of enlightenment and lapses into the nationalist discourse it is struggling so hard to free itself from. . . . The modern elite are, after all, dreaming the same dream as their forebears of the dynastic past: wealth, power, and hegemony. The obsession of the old Confucian official-gentry with the domination of the Chinese empire is merely replaced by the same overriding interest in the power of the modern nation-state. It is a power that is presented as an abstracted monolithic structure external to its relationship with society and the individuals that make up the nation. What *He shang* forcefully calls for—the agenda of enlightenment by means of cultural introspection—is time and again eclipsed by a stronger, perhaps unconscious drive for what it rejects—the revival of the glorious past in the future. (122–23)

The "paradoxes of the Chinese enlightenment," to use Jing Wang's words (1996, 118), also manifest themselves in Cui Jian's inability or unwillingness to liberate himself from the collectivist ethos, even at times when he preaches extreme individualism. In his individualistic credo, in which he calls to demolish the obedient mentality of the Chinese people and proposes the "greatness" of every individual, Cui Jian nevertheless still places this pursuit in a collective, nationalistic framework, suggesting at the end of his lengthy credo that the realization of his individualistic aspirations will lead to the progress of society: "I think that in Chinese culture there ought to be a new concept, namely, that each one of us is great. . . . The reason for the progress of a society lies in the ability of every person to use his/her creativity."

Chinese rockers, who at least until recently have been associated with China's young "enlightened" intellectuals, and who have been celebrating since the late 1980s the negation of Chinese history, which many of them see as a "burden" that prevents them from moving forward, have simultaneously indulged in nostalgia for the glorious, remote imperial past, as well as the more recent revolutionary past. Like *River Elegy*, they have been calling for wholesale Westernization (at least until the early 1990s) and modernization, but at the same time they often remain strongly connected to traditional attitudes and modes of expression. They have been celebrating individualism and calling for the liberation of the individual from the party-state and the social collective, but simultaneously have often been immersed in a collective, patriotic mental framework. They have been suggesting the negation of the state in their deconstruction of its most precious symbols, like the Great Wall, but at the same time they often celebrate nationalism in their own way. They have often expressed spite for authority, but at the same time look consistently for official legitimization and for dialogue with officialdom.

In chapter 1, I cited the notes to the 1995 album of the rock band *Lunhui*/Again, which highlight the new Westernized, modern, cosmopolitan outlook embraced by the band, as well as their "spite for authority." Paradoxically, however, their most famous song is a hard-rock rendition of a twelfth-century nationalistic poem. The poem *(ci)*, called "Thinking of the Past at Beigu Pavilion in Jingkou" *(Jingkou Beigu ting huaigu)*, was written by Xin Qiji (1140–1202), a Song Dynasty poet who was born in north China after it was occupied by the Jurchens. The official-poet urged the Chinese government, which had moved to the south, to fight the invaders and liberate the north, but was ignored. In "Thinking of the Past," one of many patriotic poems Xin Qiji wrote, the poet bitterly recalls the glory of the past when China was unified, and thus articulates a subtle criticism of the contemporary leaders who did nothing to reunify the country:

THINKING OF THE PAST AT BEIGU PAVILION IN JINGKOU [42]

In this ancient land
What trace remains of Wu's brave king Sun Quan? [43]
Towers and pavilions where girls danced and sang,
Your glory is swept away by wind and rain:
The slanting sunlight falls on grass and trees,
Small lanes, the quarters of the humble folk:
Yet here, they say, Lin Yu [44] lived.
I think of the days gone by
When with gilded spear and iron-clad steed he charged
Like a tiger to swallow up vast territories.
In the days of Yuan Jia [45]
Hasty preparations were made
To march to the Langjuxu Mountains, [46]
But the men of Song were routed from the north.
Now forty-three years have passed,
And looking north I remember
The beacon fires that blazed the way to Yangzhou [47]
Bitter memories these
Of sacred crows among the holy drums
In the Tartar emperor's temple, [48]
Who will ask old Lin Po [49]
If he still enjoys his food?

By appropriating Xin's poem, which they studied in school (*Lunhui/* Again, interview with the author, 25 July 1995), the members of *Lunhui*/Again place themselves in the poet's position and join the long line of scholar-poets who dedicated their lives to the well-being of society and the nation, and who remained loyal and patriotic even when criticizing the government. Their rendition of "Thinking of the Past," which they retitled "The Beacon Fires that Blazed the Way to Yangzhou" *(Fenghuo Yangzhou lu)* after one of the famous lines in the poem, provides another illustration of how much Chinese rockers share with the state, history, and tradition that they challenge through their Westernized music and their rebellious, individualistic behavior and attitude.

The complex and contradictory nature of the revolutionary voice of *Lunhui*/Again reveals itself not only in the use of nationalistic lyrics, which long for lost hero-kings and emperors, the unification of China, and the revival of the glorious past, but also in the adoption of a classical poem. Despite their subscription to the modern Western ethos of inventive creativity and the enthusiastic statements in the album notes about breaking away from tradition, the band nevertheless perpetuates the well-established artistic practice of reorganizing old material.

The bonds to tradition can also be heard in the music of the song. Although most of the song is performed in a typical Western heavy-metal style, it nevertheless opens with a short instrumental prelude performed on the *pipa* (a Chinese four-string lute) in traditional performance style. The particular style that the band chose for this prelude—the martial, bold, unconstrained *haofang* style—seems to be related in part to Xin Qiji's poetic style, which is also characterized as *haofang.* But more importantly, it constructs a powerful sonic image of China, which not only compensates for the sense of disempowerment that is articulated in the lyrics, but also symbolizes the powerful entity that the band members, like many others today on the mainland, would like China to become.

Another example of how rockers today in China are often "dreaming the same dream as their forebears of the dynastic past [about] wealth, power, and hegemony" (Jing Wang 1996, 123) is provided by Tang Dynasty *(Tang chao)*, one of China's most senior and famous rock bands. In their most famous song, "Returning in Dream to the Tang Dynasty" *(Meng hui Tang chao)*, the band articulates its dissatisfaction with China's present situation through the expression of a passionate nostalgia for one of the most glorious periods in Chinese history. In expressing their longing for the glorious past, the members of Tang Dynasty criticize the present and thus challenge the party-state. At the same time, however, the song also reveals that the band is immersed in a traditional, collective, patriotic, almost militant nationalistic mental framework that paradoxically links them closely to the current official hegemonic agenda. In one article about the band, Zhao Nian, the band's drummer, was quoted as saying: "The Tang Dynasty . . . is a source of pride for the Chinese people. Its military affairs, culture, art, and poetry are the height of power and splendor. We hope very much to have this kind of splendor again" (quoted in You Wei 1996, 6). Like "The Beacon Fires that Blazed the Way to Yangzhou," "Returning in Dream to the Tang Dynasty" is inspired by the style of classical poetry, and it even cites a line from a poem by the famous Tang Dynasty poet Du Fu, who like Xin Qiji wrote many nationalistic poems. Like *Lunhui*/Again, Tang Dynasty articulates its ties to tradition also through music when, toward the end of "Returning in Dream to the Tang Dynasty," they temporarily deviate from the Western heavy-metal style that dominates the song to recite two lines in the traditional recitative style of Beijing opera. Music is used to express Chineseness also at the very beginning of "Returning in Dream to the Tang Dynasty"; the prelude to the song, which opens the album, includes effects that remind one of the sound of harmonics played on the ancient Chinese seven-string zither *(guqin)*. The band's use of gongs enhances the national flavor (Huot 2000, 172), as does the powerful playing of barrel drums. More national flavor is added in the band's videos, which are typically set at Chinese historical sites. "Returning in Dream to the Tang Dynasty," for example, which was voted Best Video in Asia at the 1993 MTV Music Video Awards, is set in the Ming tombs (ibid.).

Despite his iconoclastic comparison of China to a "garbage dump" and a "slaughterhouse," his juxtaposition of China's "long wall" with dowager Ci Xi's "long" and "stinking" footbinding cloth, and his call to "blow up" everything, He Yong is also strongly connected to patriotism, nationalism, and tradition. A series of statements made by the rocker before his 1994 Hong Kong rock concert with Dou Wei, Tang Dynasty, and Zhang Chu reveals how much he shares with the official China that he has criticized so enthusiastically. Contributing his share to the struggle over cultural hegemony between the mainland and Hong Kong, just before he left for Hong Kong He Yong launched an unprecedented public attack on Hong Kong's pop music, stating that: "Hong Kong only has entertainment [*yule*], [it] has no music. Out of the 'Four Great Heavenly Kings' only Zhang Xueyou can be considered a singer, the rest are all clowns" (quoted in Yi 1995, 1).[50] In his provocative public comments, He Yong articulated sentiments that are shared by many rockers and intellectuals in northern China, who see themselves as culturally superior to musicians and others from Hong

Kong, Taiwan, and southern China. It was often suggested to me by young intellectuals and rockers in Beijing that, as a "colony," Hong Kong has the "meaningless" culture of a colony and actually has no culture at all; that being a "small island," Taiwan can only produce insignificant "little tunes" or ditties *(xiaodiao)*, and that southern Chinese, like people from Hong Kong, care only about money and lack culture *(wenhua)*. It is within this politically loaded discursive context that He Yong's attacks on Hong Kong music and culture gain their full meaning. His comments reveal the widespread mainland chauvinism toward Hong Kong and Taiwan, as well as the northern chauvinism toward the south in China.[51]

Nationalistic overtones can be seen in the title of the mainland rockers' 1994 Hong Kong concert, "The Power of Chinese Rock Music" *(Zhongguo yaogunyue shili)*. This title is another variant on the collectivist nationalistic framework within which many rock song collection albums released in Beijing between 1992 and 1994 placed themselves, carrying titles like *Chinese Fire (Zhongguo huo)* and *Chinese Rock (Zhongguo yaogun)*.

The nationalistic meaning of the 1994 Hong Kong rock concert appeared clearly also in articles published on the mainland following the event. After a brief introduction to the factual aspects of the event, the critic Wang Xiaofeng, for instance, an iconoclast in his own right and one of the most articulate advocates of rock on the mainland, talks about "us" and "them," writing that "they think we learned everything we do from them," and later adding in an overt collectivist patriotic tone that "He Yong and the other rockers provided a live testimony to the development and progress of China's popular music and . . . defended the dignity of every [mainland] Chinese musician" (1995a, 3). In another article about the concert, after suggesting that in commercialized Hong Kong "the superficial has replaced the profound, the simple has replaced the rich and thick, and the false has replaced the true," the music critic and producer Zhang Peiren, who was involved in producing the Hong Kong concert, proudly asserted mainland cultural hegemony:

> The cultural nutrient that came from the abundant mainland mother can cause people [in Hong Kong] to have a new field of vision and imaginative power. . . . In Hong Kong Chinese rockers publicly told the [local] media that it is Beijing that constitutes the source of their life, that it is China that constitutes the root of their creativity. (1995, 4)

The 1994 rock concert revealed a less obvious side of Chinese rock that with few exceptions has been ignored in the past.[52] During the event, rock was transformed from an expression of resistance to the Chinese state into a nationalistic display of power representing the same entity He Yong ironically labeled "garbage dump" and "slaughterhouse."

Like his complex relationship with the state, He Yong's relationship with tradition is full of contradiction and ambivalence. Despite his radical, straightforward anti-traditionalist attitude, which is clear in the lyrics of "Garbage Dump" and in its Westernized punk/hard-rock wild celebration of out-of-control aesthetics, aesthetics that according to Zhao Jianwei "will never be tolerated by Chinese traditional forces" (1992, 292), He Yong nevertheless maintains and consciously asserts his links to tradition in several of his songs. Even though in "Garbage Dump" he makes a call to "blow up" everything, "The Bell and Drum Towers" *(Zhonggulou)* reveals that, after all, the iconoclastic radical musician is attached to China's past and traditional culture in his own way:

> . . . The bell and drum towers inhale the dust and smoke
> and allow you to draw their face
> I can't hear your voice
> It's too noisy and too chaotic now . . .

In these few lines, He Yong articulates his sense of nostalgia for the past, when life was simpler and less confused, when Beijing was cleaner and quieter, and when he could still hear the drums and the bells of the old city. The link to the past is also articulated in the music of the song. Whereas in "Garbage Dump" He Yong uses the psychedelic sounds of an electric guitar, aggressive drumbeats, no melody, an irregular tempo, wild screams, and a redundant, annoying bass line to articulate modernism, Westernization, and the violent negation of history and tradition, "The Bell and Drum Towers" embraces tradition through the use of traditional Chinese instruments, such as the *sanxian* (three-string lute), the *dizi* (bamboo flute), and traditional percussion instruments. The embrace of tradition is also communicated through the song's slow and restrained storytelling delivery, which is interrupted only once, when He Yong sings the lines quoted above in a more forceful way to express his criticism of modernization, and by implication also of the West.

He Yong's traditionalist side revealed itself also in the way "The Bell and Drum Towers" was performed in his 1994 concert in Hong Kong. In complete contrast to the wild and crazy performance of "Garbage Dump," which involved running on stage, jumping, playing the guitar while kneeling, and other conventional punk/hard-rock gestures, "The Bell and Drum Towers" celebrated restraint and classicism. He Yong performed it with his father (who also participated in the recording of his album), a professional *sanxian* player who accompanied the song on this traditional lute while seated in a classical posture, dressed in a traditional long robe. After performing the song, He Yong identified him proudly as his father and then, in a powerful gesture, bowed to him.[53] In publicly expressing his respect to his father, but even more so in the fact that this respect was expressed in the most traditional and now obsolete way, He Yong was obviously asserting his link to tradition. In the context of the general discourse that accompanied the 1994 concert, this assertion also signaled to his Hong Kong audience that the mainland is the authentic China, the core and root of all Chinese.

Despite Zang Tianshuo's powerful assertions of individuality and independence from the state, tradition, and society on his 1995 album, *My Last Ten Years*, a new song that he released a few months after the release of this album revealed that he, too, is strongly connected to the state and its collectivist ethos. The song, entitled "Waiting for That Day" *(Dengdai na yi tian)*, was released as part of a song collection by some of China's most famous pop singers that was named after Zang's song and was presented as a tribute to China's soccer teams during the 1996 series of international soccer games. In this patriotic album, whose title is printed on the cover in bright red on top of a photograph of a large football floating above crowds of Chinese soccer fans, and which includes among other cheering songs a heroic song by Gao Feng that draws both musically and textually upon China's national anthem, Zang joined the collective that he had tried so hard to liberate himself from in his first album:

WAITING FOR THAT DAY
(lyrics, music, and performance by Zang Tianshuo)

Flowers fall, flowers open, but eventually there will come a time when
    we will raise our heads
So many years of pain and sorrow will disappear in the twinkling of
    an eye . . .
A huge crowd of people singing together, the national anthem shakes
    the sky . . .
When this time comes the five-star flag will flutter in all directions
We are waiting for that day . . .
The day of victory

"Waiting for That Day" is a nationalistic, patriotic song that celebrates the state, its flag, its anthem, and collectivism in general. Collectivism manifests itself in the lyrics in the emphasis on the words "together" and "we," and is articulated musically in recurring passages sung by a choir in a style reminiscent of old revolutionary songs. Despite the fact that a rock style predominates, an opening instrumental prelude that invokes the sounds of the traditional *suona* and traditional drums identifies the song as Chinese and thus adds to the patriotic sentiments articulated in its lyrics.

"Waiting for That Day" is the antithesis of the celebration by Zang and other rockers of individualism, nonconformism, alienation, and rebellion. The contrast is emphasized because Zang's song uses phrases that are often used in famous nonofficial songs, while bestowing on them opposite meanings. The line that I translated as "a huge crowd of people singing together" is written in the original text as "a tide of people, a sea of people together" *(renchao renhai qi)*. The four words Zang uses to depict the crowds were almost a cliché in popular songs of the 1990s. In these songs, however, the metaphor was often used to stress individuality and the alienation of the self from the crowds of people. This line is used, for example, three times in one of Black Panther's earliest and most famous hits, "No Place to Hide" *(Wu di zi rong)*, which opens with the phrase: "In the midst of a tide of people, a sea of people, there is you and me" *(renchao renhai zhong you ni you wo)*. Zang's use of the same words to emphasize the collective and its togetherness and solidarity *(qi)* instead of the individual almost has the effect of satirizing the alienation and individuality that he himself celebrates in *My Last Ten Years*.

THE MULTIPLE AND CHANGING RELATIONS BETWEEN STATE, SOCIETY, AND CULTURE: CONCLUDING REMARKS

In much of the literature that discusses the relationship during the 1990s between the Chinese state on the one hand and society (intellectuals in particular) and culture on the other hand, there is a wide agreement on several points. First, the control of the state over society and culture has weakened compared with the 1980s. This weakening is commonly understood as a result of the intensification in market activity and the increased interaction with the capitalist, democratic West. The second point, which is intimately linked with the first, is that the state has withdrawn from most aspects of people's everyday lives, and that a kind of "true" nonpolitical popular culture independent of the state has emerged. Third, unlike some aspects of life, when it comes to politics and political challenge to the state, the state was certainly more aggressive in its suppression of such challenge than it had been during the 1980s. It is often suggested in connection with this point that some of the new liberties in other aspects of life are allowed so people will leave politics alone, that is, leave it to the government. The fourth and last point, which is a corollary of the second and third, is that contrary to the 1980s, with very few exceptions, there was very little resistance to the state during the 1990s, especially among intellectuals, and that culture was basically nonpolitical.

The following statements, from a recent article by Merle Goldman that summarizes the relations between the state and intellectuals in the 1990s, offer an example of this common characterization, despite the fact that the article actually focuses on the political activity of China's intellectuals during this decade:

> [In the 1990s] the party-state's further retreat from the cultural and intellectual realm in terms of censorship, financial support and tolerance of diversity and foreign influences sparked an explosion of artistic experimentation, a vibrant popular culture and non-political intellectual discourse. (1999, 702)

> By the mid-1990s, all public political dissent was suppressed once again. (703)

> Though party-state's control weakened further in the 1990s as a result of accelerating market reforms, growing involvement with the outside world and its continuing withdrawal from most areas of daily life, it continues to suppress any action that it considers a political threat. (710)

> The party-state has been successful so far in suppressing any intellectual and student challenges on sensitive anniversaries or during visits by Western leaders, by putting controversial intellectuals and students under surveillance, house arrest or detention, and preventing students from gathering outside their universities. (711)

Some of the points above were certainly implied and sometimes explicitly stated in this book. Yet, based upon the data that I present in this chapter in particular, I would like to conclude my book by proposing that such common characterizations should be qualified. Indeed, in much of the book I pointed to the new limits of state control and power and conversely to the new liberties and power that the general populace has started to enjoy since the beginning of reforms. However, the application of such characterizations is far from total. This chapter suggests that, in some respects at least, the state has actually improved its ability to control society compared with the 1980s. The best example of such improvement is Chinese MTV. Given the increasing importance of television in everyday life throughout China during the 1990s, as well as the wide appeal of Chinese MTV in particular, it could also be argued that, compared with the 1980s, the state has been able to penetrate deeper into people's everyday lives rather than withdrawing from them. During my stay in Beijing, in most cases when I encountered a television set turned on, it was Chinese MTV that people were watching. The popularity of Chinese MTV was obviously not limited to urbanites. Newcomers just arrived from the countryside generally mentioned Dong Wenhua and other state singers as their most favorite pop stars, something that indicated the influence of MTV programs in rural areas.

Though I don't recall a single urbanite with whom I spoke who mentioned any state singer as his/her favorite singer, the influence of Chinese MTV among urbanites was nevertheless also obvious. Some young urbanites, for example, mentioned Gao Feng and his "Great China" as their most favorite singer and song, respectively. A better example perhaps was the fact that on several different occasions I heard urbanites humming the tunes even of some of the most official MTV songs, like "Return Home Safely," which in the mid-1990s one could only hear on television.

Though it is certainly not only the result of the influence of television and certainly not only of the influence of Chinese MTV, it is difficult to explain the tide of nationalism that washed China in the 1990s without acknowledging the role of television in initiating and shaping this tide. Even though many rockers suggested to me that they avoid watching Chinese MTV because of its politicized nature, nonetheless this chapter showed that in the mid-1990s they too shared much with the state. This unity, which centers around nationalism, even if it is only partial, implies that the leadership has been able to exert some influence also on its most vocal opponents despite their repeated claims for independence and alienation from the state.

The widespread expressions of nationalism and traditionalism among Chinese rockers in the mid-1990s illustrates the complex dynamics of China's cultural politics and the fact that there were some contradictory trends working simultaneously in Chinese culture during this period. At the same time as some minority and women artists achieved a new public voice that was more independent of the state and official representation and discourse than ever before, many rockers seem to have moved during the same period in the opposite direction—that is, closer to the state, after at least a decade of radical split between China's intellectuals and the state.

The intense wave of popular nationalism in the 1990s, in which intellectuals played a most active role, appears almost paradoxical in light of the common statements in the academic literature about weakening state control and its withdrawal from people's daily lives, especially if one considers the fact that most scholars agree that this wave was initiated and inspired by the state.[54] The root of this contradiction, I believe, lies in the common habit in the literature about post-Mao China to assume a priori a split between the government and society and to discuss state control exclusively in terms of negative methods, such as censorship, imprisonment, and so on. Such emphasis tends to overlook the important fact that state control in China has never been limited to negative methods, and indeed the use of such methods during the 1990s, no matter how successful, falls short of offering a full explanation of the rise of popular nationalism during this decade.

Thus, this chapter suggests that in the mid-1990s the state was adopting new strategies, techniques, mediums, and styles of control rather than just watching its control dwindle. Chinese MTV is one such new form of control, which implies that new technologies are not necessarily only a threat to the state, but can also be used by it to exert control. Another form of control that I mentioned is the appropriation of the market. The market indeed weakened state control in many respects, as it is often argued, but by the mid-1990s the state had learned how to use it to consolidate its control. Maintaining tight control over television and large-scale concerts, two of the main sources of income for musicians in China's new capitalist environment, was one of the new techniques that the state applied in the 1990s to control even the most defiant of musicians.

If in previous chapters I focused on new voices, whose prime novelty was their independence from the state and their challenge to the orthodox style of representation, then this chapter suggests that in the 1990s the state itself, too, achieved a new voice, the main novelty of which was its relatively inclusive nature and the fact that it actually consisted of multiple voices and was not easily identified as the voice of the state. The point about the voice(s) of the state not being easily identified as such leads us back to the official-popular binary and again to the relationship between the state and people's everyday lives. The first quotation above from Goldman's article illustrates the persisting tendency among some China scholars to divide Chinese culture into official culture and popular culture and to view the two as mutually exclusive. Contrary to this view, this book shows that such division, especially where the 1990s are concerned, is problematic. In chapters 1, 2, and 3 I discussed several cases of popular cultural expressions that arose independently of the state but were nonetheless able to penetrate the most official sphere. This chapter challenged the problematic binary from the other direction, showing how the divide is constantly challenged by officialdom in its own efforts to be as popular as possible. The result is that a significant portion of culture today in China cannot really be divided into "popular" as opposed to "official," or vice versa, because the two are often mixed together and overlapping. Popular culture is not an object over which a single force or social group has exclusive ownership. Rather it is a site where many different forces and groups meet, and the state certainly participates in much of popular culture today in China.

Finally, in the mid-1990s there was indeed much less overt politics and resistance to the state in popular music culture than in the preceding years. The most powerful manifestation of this trend was the decline of rock as a coherent popular movement and subculture of resistance. However, despite this general trend, this book suggests that public dissent and resistance were far from nonexistent. Cui Jian's 1994 album *The Egg under the Red Flag* is a case in point. Another example is Zang Tianshuo's 1995 album *My Last Ten Years*. No less important, however, are the new, autonomous voices of minority and women musicians that I described in chapters 2 and 3. These, together with the ambivalent voices of Zang Tianshuo and other rockers, suggest that resistance, like state control, did not necessarily weaken, certainly did not disappear, but rather assumed different forms. The most important characteristic of resistance during the 1990s, as opposed to the 1980s, was its more fragmented nature (e.g., gendered, ethnic, and so on). This fragmentation, however, does not necessarily imply that resistance during the 1990s was less effective in bringing about change.

Notes

INTRODUCTION

1. It is important to emphasize that I speak here about what James Scott has labeled "public transcripts" and defined as the "open interaction between subordinates and those who dominate" (1990, 2). Other voices that did exist in China during this period were normally in the form of "hidden transcripts," a term used by Scott to denote the "critique of power spoken behind the back of the dominant" (xii). Indeed, as Rubie Watson reminds us, "[The socialist state] was never as omnipotent as the cold war warriors of the 1950s claimed it to be . . . [and] it is important that we do not credit [it] and its agents with too much power" (1994, 2). Although relatively little research has been done on the "hidden transcripts" of the Maoist period, we nevertheless have some evidence that even during the Cultural Revolution people in some cases resisted the policies of the party and spoke in different voices. See, for example, Perry Link's essay in his 1989 edited volume on unofficial literature during the Cultural Revolution. Another example is provided in *Chen Village*, by Chan, Madsen, and Unger (1984).

2. For an extensive theoretical discussion of the decentralizing and democratizing effects of cassette technology, see Manuel (1993, 1–20).

3. One of the most notable advocates of this view is Theodor Adorno (1990), who also happens to focus in much of his discussion on music.

4. See, for example, John Fiske, who defines popular culture as "the culture of the subordinated and disempowered . . . [and that which] shows signs of resisting or evading . . . [dominant] forces" (1989, 4). In contrast to Adorno, Fiske argues that although the subordinated create their culture with objects and resources produced and provided by the dominant forces in society, "popular culture is made by the people, not imposed upon them" (25). Something can become popular, according to Fiske, only if it provides an opportunity for resisting or evasive uses or meanings (34).

5. See, for example, Hall (1981) and Middleton (1985a). "Popular culture,"

Hall suggests, "is neither, in a 'pure' sense, the popular traditions of resistance . . . nor is it the forms which are superimposed on and over them. It is the ground on which transformations are worked. In the study of popular culture, we should always start here; with the double-stake in popular culture, the double movement of containment and resistance, which is always inevitable inside it" (228).

6. This point is also made by Middleton (1985b, 26). The point is relevant, especially in view of the fact that all the theoretical studies on popular culture that I mention here treat the phenomenon in the context of the democratic, capitalist West.

7. Fiske, for example, suggests that "popular culture always bears traces of the constant struggle between domination and subordination," and adds that "popular culture . . . [is] a site of struggle" (1989, 19–20). Hall's emphasis on structurally fixed, hierarchical, binary, and conflict-oriented power relationships is illustrated in the following passage: "There is a continuous and necessarily uneven and unequal struggle, by the dominant culture, constantly to disorganize and reorganize popular culture. . . . There are[, however, also] points of resistance: there are also moments of supersession. This is the dialectic of cultural struggle. . . . The field of culture [is] a sort of constant battlefield" (1981, 233).

8. See, for example, Jin (1989c), on Cui Jian.

CHAPTER 1. CHINA DIVERSIFIED

1. Romantic love, however, did not completely disappear from public culture during the Maoist period, at least not before the Cultural Revolution. Colin Mackerras (1975, 197–200), for example, reports that despite official efforts to popularize new operas with collective, militant, revolutionary themes, one of the most popular operas in major cities until the very eve of the Cultural Revolution was none other than the famous traditional love story *Liang Shanbo and Zhu Yingtai*. Love songs circulated publicly even during the Great Leap Forward (1958–60), one of the most radical leftist campaigns of the Maoist period, during which they were used by the party for propaganda purposes (Blake 1979).

2. Li Jinhui was one of the first composers in China to combine elements of Western popular music with elements of Chinese music. During the 1920s and 1930s he wrote hundreds of songs that were popularized in mass quantities in printed collections, films, records, and performances. For a book-length study of Li Jinhui, see Sun Ji'nan (1993).

3. *Tongsu yinyue* is a broad and rather loose category that generally denotes popular music. Nevertheless, the term is often used to denote specifically soft or more lyrical pop, as opposed to rock, disco, and other rhythm-oriented styles. *Gangtai* music may be considered a substyle within *tongsu* associated with a particular geographical origin. The meanings of all these terms, however, are far from definite.

4. Another famous controversial song was "Night at a Naval Port" *(Jungang zhi ye*, lyrics by Ma Jingxing, music by Liu Shizhao, performance by the female singer Su Xiaoming), which depicted a night at a navy port in a soft, gentle voice.

5. Jin Zhaojun (1996a) notes that the word "star" *(mingxing)* itself appeared in China only in 1980, after a large-scale pop concert entitled "New Stars Concert" was organized in Beijing by *Beijing Evening Newspaper (Beijing wan bao)*.

6. The tenth anniversary of *liuxing/tongsu* music was celebrated in 1996 in Beijing in another large-scale pop concert.

7. Hou, the author of the famous pan-Chinese nationalistic ballad "Heir of the Dragon" *(Long de chuanren)*, defected from Taiwan to the mainland in June 1983, defying the Nationalists' ban on visits to the mainland. He explained that he always felt himself a "guest" in Taiwan and wanted to go "home" to get in touch with his roots. The Taiwanese-turned-Chinese musician, however, was expelled from China back to Taiwan several years after his defection because of his involvement in the 1989 democracy movement (Jaivin 1990b).

8. Jiangnan is the Chinese name of the region south of the Yangtze River.

9. In another version of the song it is "struggle and produce."

10. For a translation and discussion of the *Talks*, see McDougall (1980).

11. For a book-length study of *Yellow Earth*, see McDougall (1991). See also Rayns (1987, 37–39).

12. I am grateful to Jin Zhaojun for pointing out this aspect of the Northwest Wind (Jin, interview with the author, Beijing, 8 June 1996).

13. The song's lyrics were written by Mo Yan, the author of the book on which the movie was based. The tune was composed by Zhao Jiping.

14. For more discussion of Zhang Yimou's *Red Sorghum* as "national allegory," see Zhang Yingjin (1990). For discussion of Root-Seeking literature and writers, including Mo Yan and his *Red Sorghum*, see Feuerwerker (1998, 188–237).

15. Chi's most famous song was entitled "Tears of Remorse" *(Huihen de lei)*.

16. The only exception, in fact, is the Mao fad songs, which are discussed later. Wang Xiaofeng suggests that both sold about three million copies. Sales figures throughout this study, however, should be treated with caution because of the widespread practice of cassette pirating in China.

17. Translated by Jones (1992a, 154). "Transform the earth" and "Change the sky" were Maoist slogans popular during the years of the Cultural Revolution.

18. For more details on the *getihu* during the 1980s, see Gold (1989).

19. According to Wang Xiaofeng, the ban started only in 1987, after Cui Jian performed his rock version of "Nanniwan" in one of Beijing's parks (Wang Xiaofeng, interview with the author, 1 June 1996).

20. For a video recording of "Having Nothing" being performed in the square during the 1989 movement, see Sue Williams' documentary film *Born under the Red Flag* (1997).

Another important rock/Northwest Wind song that was popular around that time is "Follow Your Feelings" *(Genzhe ganjue zou)*, sung by the Taiwanese female singer Su Rui (Gold 1993). For a discussion of other songs that were sung during the movement, see Samson (1991). In her article Samson examines the efficacy of very different songs (communist, patriotic, and children's songs) as well as Western classical music and traditional Chinese instrumental music as a protest medium. She suggests that the most important song during the protest movement was the "Internationale."

21. Both in his article and in an interview that I had with him (Zhang Guangtian, interview with the author, Beijing, 24 June 1996), Zhang has suggested that rock is a "colonialist weapon" used by the West to advance its economic and political interests.

22. The link between rock and student protests did not go unnoticed by officials. In one of the earliest reports on Cui Jian, Linda Jaivin suggests that "one reason for Cui's troubles was an internal document linking the student movement of late 1986 with the growing popularity of rock 'n roll" (Jaivin 1988, 84).

23. Wayhwa's name should be transliterated according to the *pinyin* romanization system as "Weihua." The musician, however, writes her name in English in the way it appears in the text. In a personal communication (February 2001), she told me that she invented this spelling and that it does not have any special meaning. She added, however, that "way" is more meaningful in English. Wayhwa's original name is Wang Wayhwa, but she decided to omit her family name (Wang) when she started to work at the CCTV.

24. See *Yaogun Beijing* in the discography.

25. Half of this song, including the opening recited line, is performed in English.

26. Zhao Jianwei's 1992 book on Cui Jian, for example, is entitled *Cui Jian zai Yiwusuoyou zhong nahan (Cui Jian Cries Out in Having Nothing)*.

27. The word *nahan* invokes Lu Xun's famous 1922 compilation of short stories of the same title.

28. The cover of the band's album features both Chinese and English names of the band. Most people with whom I spoke, including the band members themselves, however, seem to prefer the English name.

29. It is important to note, however, that *xibeifeng*, though nostalgic, did not celebrate a return to Confucianism. Rather it shared much of the disdain toward Confucianism that is found in rock, albeit in a more subtle way, by articulating a romantic desire to return to and revive an imagined extra-/pre-Confucian, primordial Chineseness, which was less culturalized and tame, more forceful, free, and vital. "Young Sister Go Boldly Forward," discussed earlier, nicely illustrates this ethos. Northwest Wind, not incidentally, was also referred to as Northwest rock *(xibei yaogun)*. Rock and *xibeifeng*, however, still differ significantly from each other in the fact that *xibeifeng* drew inspiration from and symbolically located itself in rural China and in the past, while rock has been since its inception in China a purely urban phenomenon that cel-

ebrated Westernization and modernization and often tended to be explicitly elitist.

30. For a discussion of the sociocultural aspects of the movement, see Perry (1992).

31. See *Yaogun Beijing II* in the discography.

32. For a detailed discussion of the economic difficulties faced by Chinese rockers, see Efird (2001). Efird suggests that another reason for these difficulties is the government-mandated price of music cassettes (10 RMB, approximately $1.20) and that the policy of governing cassette prices is "an attempt to control the profits of bands and producers" (79).

33. For an article that deconstructs the boundaries between pop and rock in China, see Jeroen De Kloet (2000). Claire Huot (2000, 154–56) also presents a critique of the pop-rock dichotomy at the very beginning of her chapter on popular music, suggesting that it was not tenable in the 1990s.

34. I talk about the "traditional Hong Kong model" because a lot of popular political activity started to take place in Hong Kong during and immediately after the 1989 democracy movement and later, in the mid-1990s, in connection with the 1997 return to the mainland. For two articles that discuss the rise of politicized popular music in Hong Kong as a response to 1989 and 1997, see Joanna Ching-Yun Lee (1992a, 1992b).

35. For a discussion of the viability of the rock subculture in Beijing of the mid-1990s, see Efird (2001). Efird depicts rock activity mainly at the club level in areas with significant presence of foreigners in the context of the café/bar boom during that period.

36. One example of this influence manifests itself in the extreme popularity that the notion of "uniqueness" (*yu zhong bu tong*, which literally means to be different from the majority or crowd) enjoys in various cultural domains, ranging from popular commercials to mainstream art critiques.

37. For a short article on the mid-1980s revival of revolutionary opera arias, see Barmé (1987).

38. For a book-length study of the "Mao craze," see Barmé (1996).

39. For a discussion of the impact of *The Red Sun* in remote areas in Yunnan Province, see Rees (2000: 135–36).

40. For a theoretical discussion of the *re* phenomenon in China that focuses on the stock market but also considers the "Mao craze," see Hertz (1998). Hertz nevertheless perpetuates the top-bottom binary, making a distinction between *re*, which she suggests is usually a "popular" bottom-up movement, and *yundong* (lit. "movement" or "campaign"), which she considers a kind of "official *re*" (81), and thus a top-down mobilization. The "Mao fever," according to her, in contrast to the "stock fever" *(gupiao re)*, falls into the first category.

41. For more details on Cui Jian's rendition of "Nanniwan" and other musical manifestations of the "Mao craze," see Huot (2000, 160–61). Cui's "Nanniwan" appears on his 1991 album, *Jiejue (Solution)*.

42. The desire to achieve such a liberation was illustrated during the 1989

demonstrations, when some demonstrators damaged the huge portrait of Mao that hangs north of Tiananmen Square.

CHAPTER 2. THE NEGOTIATION OF MINORITY/
MAJORITY IDENTITIES AND REPRESENTATION
IN POPULAR MUSIC CULTURE

1. The negotiation and representations of ethnic identities in the context of Chinese popular music have been studied only recently. The few studies on the subject include Rachel Harris's studies of Xinjiang popular music (forthcoming [a], [b]) and Janet Upton's study of Han-produced "Tibetan" popular music (forthcoming).

2. One exception is Dru Gladney's (1991) discussion of the China Salman Rushdie protest of 1989, in which thousands of Muslim Chinese held an officially approved and partly sponsored demonstration in the streets of Beijing to express their anger with a publication in Chinese called *Sexual Customs* (*Xing fengsu;* Ke and Sang, 1989), which they considered to be offensive to Islam.

3. In his article on the minority films of Tian Zhuangzhuang, for example, Gladney writes that in these films: "[The minorities] have no 'voice,' literal or otherwise, of their own" (1995, 170). A similar observation is made in a more recent article by Zhang Yingjin, who writes that "minority people hardly if ever occupy the subject position in minority films" (1997, 90).

4. For studies of officially unrecognized minority groups and the problems involved in some minority classifications, see Harrell (1990, 1996b) and Cheung (1996).

5. For more general details on the socioeconomic, cultural, and political situation of minorities in China, see Mackerras (1994, 1995).

6. Besides the Yuan (1264–1368) and the Qing, there were also the Liao (912–1125) and the Jin (1115–1234), two foreign dynasties, established by the Khitans and the Jurchens, respectively, that controlled parts of northern China.

7. Gladney (1994a) and Schein (1997) have referred to this phenomenon in the Chinese context as "oriental orientalism" and "internal orientalism," respectively.

8. For a discussion of the Nationalists' policy toward minorities, see Dreyer (1976, 15–41).

9. Most documents of the Nationalists mentioned by name only the Han, Hui, Tibetan, Manchu, and Mongol, and generally played down the differences even among these five ethnic groups.

10. Minority rights are similarly protected in all later PRC constitutions.

11. For a general discussion of the treatment of minorities during the 1950s, 1960s, and early 1970s, see Dreyer (1976).

12. Han (1980, 6, 8) transliterates this Mongolian name into English in two different ways: twice as "Meiliqib" and once as "Meiliqig." My transliteration of the name is based on the Chinese characters used to write the name in Chinese.

13. In another version of the song the lyrics read: "They sing about the leader Chairman Mao."

14. The *dongbula* is the Chinese name of a two-string lute popular among the Kazaks (Han 1980, 3).

15. The negative otherness of minorities is depicted most forcefully in minority films. In many of these films there are references to extreme violence and oppression, which the films suggest are characteristic of traditional minority culture. For more details on revolutionary minority films, see Clark (1987a).

16. Chinese Music Television *(Zhongguo yinyue dianshi)* was established in 1993. It is a body within the CCTV (China's Central Television) in charge of production and presentation of video clips of popular Chinese songs for daily broadcast nationwide. In late 1995 Music Television expanded significantly when a new art channel was established in the CCTV. In the mid-1990s this new channel (CCTV-3) broadcasted clips of popular songs for several hours daily, and according to my observations, it was one of the most popular television channels, at least in Beijing.

17. This collection appears in the videography under *Zhongguo min'ge jingdian (2), MTV 42 shou (Chinese Folksongs Classics 2, 42 Songs with MTV).*

18. For more details on these practices, see Han (1980, 2) and Mackerras (1984).

19. According to Han (1980, 6) the prize was won in 1952.

20. See the video collection *Zhongguo min'ge jingdian.*

21. I refer here to the Xinjiang Villages in Weigongcun and Ganjiakou. These Villages were demolished between 1998 and 1999 to provide space for massive construction projects. Around the same time, municipal authorities in Beijing started to prosecute street vendors, and this policy resulted in the disappearance from the capital of most of the Uyghur shish-kebab vendors. However, despite this blow or perhaps because of it, Uyghur culture started to thrive around the same time in other parts of the city, where many Xinjiang restaurants started to pop up like mushrooms after the rain. For a discussion of the Uyghur community in Beijing, see Baranovitch (forthcoming).

22. The change in attitude, however, was not always for the better. For one example of the increase in tension and alienation because of the new contact, see Baranovitch (forthcoming).

23. For more details on the desertification of former grasslands, see Khan (1996, 130) and Dee Mack Williams (1996a, 1996b). Khan points to the migration of Han farmer-settlers as the main cause for the process of desertification. Williams's studies offer another perspective, focusing on the negative impact of the grassland enclosure policy initiated by the central government since decollectivization and implemented among pastoral Mongols.

24. For more details on the official pressure that has caused many Mongols to shift to agriculture, see Khan (1996, 140).

25. Teng Ge'er was first introduced to me as a "rocker." While discussing Chinese rock in one of the small restaurants at the Central Conservatory of

Music in Beijing, a Mongolian student approached me and said proudly that there is a "Mongolian rocker" I should hear.

26. The official compromise in Teng Ge'er's case is not uncommon in post-Mao China. For other examples of a positive official response to minority demands and protest, see Gladney (1991).

27. Despite its focus on Han peasant culture, the Root-Seeking movement of the 1980s also included appropriations of minority culture. For a discussion of one such appropriation in the domain of literature, see Louie (1992).

28. The appropriation of minorities to assert Han modernity and superiority in the context of a century-long inferiority complex vis-à-vis the West is not completely new either. The following comment made by Lu Xun in the early 1930s on an early minority film entitled *Romance in the Yao Mountains* (1932) provides an example of similar uses of minority culture earlier in the twentieth century:

> The idea of this film is to enlighten the Yao minority. Nowadays one rarely hears big talk about Chinese civilization controlling the whole world. So when we have the urge to enlighten others, we have to resort to Yaos and Miaos. And to accomplish this great deed, we must first marry them. The descendants of the Yellow Emperor cannot possibly marry the princesses of Europe, so we have to propagate our spiritual civilization nearer home. (Quoted in Leyda 1972, 78)

29. For more details on *Sister Drum*, see Upton (forthcoming). The album appears in the discography under Dadawa.

30. Lolo was born in Kunming, Yunnan Province. His family is originally from the Yunnan Chuxiong Yi Autonomous Prefecture.

31. For a discussion of the importance of surnames in defining and articulating Han identity, see Ebrey (1996).

32. See, for example, Wu Jingrong (1979). By contrast, many dictionaries published outside of China still bear traces of the traditional pejorative attitude. One widely used Chinese-English dictionary, for example, still has the name Lolo written with the dog radical and defines it as "a primitive tribe" (Liang Shiqiu 1987).

33. "The Love of the Boat Tower" is a folksy Han pop song sung in duet style by a male singer and a female singer, which became extremely popular all over China in 1993. I discuss this song in the next chapter.

34. The Jingpos are a small minority group who live in Yunnan Province.

35. *Man* is the ancient Chinese name for non-Han ethnic groups in southern China.

36. Huang Liaoyuan has written numerous articles on Chinese popular music, and he is also the editor of a comprehensive book on the subject. See Huang Liaoyuan et al. (1997).

37. According to Lolo, *wu wei* means in his native language something similar to "oh, God!"

38. For details on the festival, see Zhang Weiwen and Zeng Qingnan (1993, 151–53).

39. The *bawu* is a wind instrument that many consider today to be a traditional Chinese instrument. It originated, however, with the minority groups of southwest China.

40. The discographic details of this album appear in the discography under *Shan ying* (1993).

41. Esther Yau (1994, 283) has elaborated this point, suggesting that minority films from the revolutionary period were both escapist and didactic, depending on who was watching them. She argues that while for most Han audiences they probably fulfilled escapist functions, they were didactic for minority audiences.

42. See, for example, the discussions by Clark (1987a), Yau (1994), Gladney (1994a), and Zhang Yingjin (1997) of *Sacrificed Youth (Qingchun ji)*, a 1985 film by the late female director Zhang Nuanxin. The discussions by Clark (1987a), Rayns (1991), and Gladney (1995) of Tian Zhuangzhuang's minority films, which I mention later, also follow a similar approach.

43. For a discussion of minority religion between 1949 and 1979, see Heberer (1989, 107–10).

44. This applies especially to those minorities who are associated with Buddhism, as opposed to Islam, perhaps because Buddhism is perceived as more indigenous and less exclusionary.

45. Zheng translates this word on his album as "nothing with."

46. Although an increasing number of Chinese of mixed ethnic origin have chosen recently to be registered as minorities because they are thus eligible for important privileges, the idea of becoming an ethnic minority would probably still be inconceivable for most Han Chinese, even on a symbolic level. So deep-rooted was and still is the notion that the minorities are inferior, and the implication that crossing the lines should be avoided, that it did not even escape from modern academic publications. In one study of the Yis from the early 1940s, the Chinese anthropologist Lin Yueh-hua writes: "There are . . . Han Chinese who . . . are . . . captives and slaves [of the Lolo] and considered by [them] as part of their property. They have to wear Lolo costumes and change to Lolo names: they have thus degenerated into Lolo ways of life" (1961, 19). This traditional sense of superiority and "alienation" was perpetuated in literary references to minority culture during the Root-Seeking movement of the 1980s, despite the fact that this literature paradoxically aimed to represent minorities as part of the Chinese self (see Louie 1992). It is against such a background that Zheng Jun's desire to be transformed into the minority other becomes meaningful, even if the desire is only on a symbolic level. The 1980s, nevertheless, also saw several artistic articulations of a desired minoritization. One early articulation of such desire, which like Zheng's song challenges the traditional view of the Han majority/minorities relationship as assimilating/assimilated, or superior/inferior respectively, is found in the film *Sacrificed Youth*.

47. Tony Rayns, for example, has observed that *On the Hunting Ground* is "a devastating critique of China's traditional 'national minority' films" (1991, 108). For more details on Tian Zhuangzhuang's minority films, see Clark (1987a); Rayns (1991); and Gladney (1995).

48. Other important musicians in the mid-1990s who had a minority background and who were associated with rock, besides Cui Jian, Teng Ge'er, and Lolo, include Zang Tianshuo (half Manchu), the late Zhang Ju (Tujia), Ai Jing (half Manchu), Wu Tong (Manchu), Cheng Jin (half Korean), Askar (Uyghur), and Siqingerile (Mongol).

49. The rocker, however, was also told that he would have to perform without a band and somehow hide his long hair (Zheng Jun, personal communication, 1995). Long hair and a band have come to symbolize rock culture in China, and it is these two features that state officials find most disturbing when they have to deal with rockers.

50. The "state" and "officialdom," of course, are complex categories in their own right. It may have also been the case that some reform-minded officials who appreciate and even sympathize with Zheng Jun's alternative agenda found in the above-quoted line about Lhasa being home a source of legitimization for approving the broadcast of this otherwise forbidden song. Robert Efird offers a more materialistic explanation, suggesting that "it apparently required a great deal of financial persuasion [by Zheng Jun's company, Red Star] to secure official permission for long-haired Zheng Jun to appear on TV," and that "the ability to broadcast Chinese rock music on state-owned television and radio unquestionably reflects the latter's increasing dependence on advertising revenue in order to turn a profit" (2001, 80).

CHAPTER 3. NEGOTIATING GENDER IN POST-REVOLUTIONARY POPULAR MUSIC CULTURE

1. The custom of footbinding was officially banned in 1902 by the Anti-footbinding Edict issued by Empress Dowager Ci Xi. It quickly declined in cities but persisted for decades in the countryside. For a book-length study of the practice, see Levy (1967).

2. See *Qianfu siji diao* in the discography.

3. One notable exception is Honig and Hershatter (1980, 308–33), which includes a discussion of feminist voices in widely distributed magazines and newspapers.

4. The first characterization is suggested in relation to women's representation both on television and in films. For a discussion of the representation of women on television, see Notar (1994), Rofel (1994b, 710–12), Brownell (1999), and Erwin (1999). For a discussion of the representation of women in films, see Rayns (1987), Mayfair Yang (1993), and Cui (1997). The second characterization is offered particularly in relation to the domain of film, where women are conspicuously active in China. See Dai (1995), and Dai and Yang (1995).

5. For a book-length study of the masculinity crisis among Chinese male writers during the 1980s, see Zhong's *Masculinity Besieged?* (2000).

6. The *Romance of the Three Kingdoms (Sanguo zhi yanyi)* and *Water Margin (Shui hu zhuan)* are centuries-old popular militaristic novels.

7. In his critique of the lack of masculinity among Chinese men, Zhao seems to echo an earlier and better-known but similar critique by Sun Longji, who concluded that Chinese men are eunuchs. See Sun Longji (1983).

8. Wang refers here to Sha Yexin's play from 1986, *Xunzhao nanzihan,* the title of which could also be translated as "looking for a real man."

9. Emily Honig and Gail Hershatter, nevertheless, also acknowledge the fact that dressing up and adornment are regarded as a "liberating act" (Honig and Hershatter 1988, 43). Women's adornment and sexuality will be discussed in length later in this chapter.

10. The Spring Festival Party *(chunjie lianhuan wanhui)* is an impressive, diverse, and colorful television variety show that is broadcast live on CCTV once a year on the eve of the Chinese New Year and features the nation's most famous stage artists. As far as I know, very few people would give up watching this highlight program, which lasts from 8 P.M. to well after midnight.

11. For results of a statistical survey among 650 Chinese youngsters that supports this observation, see Jeroen De Kloet (2000, 260–62).

12. Unlike rock music and much of its concomitant ethos, however, the idealized concept of a brotherhood that excludes women has a long history in China. The popular novel *Water Margin,* which I mentioned earlier in relation to Zang Tianshuo, and the origins of which could be traced back to at least the sixteenth century, provides one example of such a history. The idea of brotherhood is so central in this novel that it has also been translated into English as *All Men Are Brothers.* In the context of the search for real manhood in the 1980s and 1990s, the concept of brotherhood was also revived in literature (Louie 1991).

13. Dai Jinhua suggests that this marginalization of women, which she calls "the exile of women from history" (1999, 196) was not limited only to the late 1980s but was rather an important characteristic of the entire decade.

14. Discussing the films by Chen Kaige, Wendy Larson suggests that in all of his films, including those that he produced in the 1980s, the male character is feminized. She observes, however, that this feminization has become more conspicuous in his later films, culminating in *Farewell My Concubine* of 1993. Dai Jinhua also notes the obvious feminization of the male character (Cheng Dieyi) in *Farewell My Concubine,* but she extends the notion of the feminized male also to Zhang Yimou's *Raise the Red Lantern* (1991), in which there is actually no visible male character at all. Dai's argument is that in both cases the male directors assume the position of a female or a feminized male to cater to the masculine gaze of the Western audience in the context of a Western-dominated cultural market.

15. See Mao Ning (1995) in the discography.

16. An example of this shift in the taste of China's intellectuals was mentioned in chapter 1, where I noted how even in Beijing University, once a

stronghold of rock, in the mid-1990s many showed obvious preference for soft songs by *gangtai* superstars.

17. The Confucian classics talk about five cardinal relations in society, called *wulun* (literally meaning "five human relations"). These are ruler-subject, father-son, husband-wife, elder brother-younger brother, and friend-friend. With the exception of the last, all are hierarchical, and they are generally perceived as parallel at least to some degree. In other words, according to Confucian philosophy a subject is to his ruler not only like a son is to his father but also as a wife is to her husband. As Dorothy Ko notes, "The husband-wife bond had served as a metaphor for ruler-subject ties and a model for all political authority since the Warring States period (fifth century to 221 B.C.)" (1994, 5). Ko correctly observes that "we cannot conceive of the history of gender in isolation from political history, and vice versa" (6).

18. One example of the ruler-subject/husband-wife parallel that explicitly highlights the value of loyalty is the saying, often used in texts since the early Han (second and first centuries B.C.), "a loyal official does not serve two rulers, a faithful wife does not marry a second husband" (Sima Qian 1996, 2457).

19. For discussions of how women's patronage of culture since the sixteenth century on did nevertheless exert some influence, albeit limited, on the male-dominated public cultural sphere, see Handlin (1975) and Ko (1994).

20. According to the statistical survey conducted by De Kloet among 650 Chinese youngsters, "Pop stars such as Jacky Cheung and Leon Lai appeal significantly more to a female audience" (2000, 261). Elsewhere, De Kloet suggests that "the aethetics . . . of Leon Lai negotiate notions of Asian masculinity that, from a Western perspective, are very gay" (2000, 270).

21. Changing costume several times during a performance is a common practice today in China among female singers and other performers.

22. The identity of the critic was revealed to me by Wang Xiaofeng (personal communication).

23. This encroachment manifests itself in various ways, including pressures to conform to a timetable for conceiving and a quota for the number of children that they can have, both of which are set by others, the imposed use of contraceptives, routine physical checks to verify compliance with a decision to insert an intrauterine device (IUD), pressures in cases of unapproved pregnancy, imposed abortions, and imposed sterilization. For more details and particular case studies, see Croll, Davin, and Kane (1985), Potter and Potter (1990, 225–50), Huang Shumin (1989, 175–85), and Evans (1997, 156–60).

24. I am grateful to Nicole Constable for this observation.

25. For a discussion of the parallel between the treatment and position of China's minorities and Chinese women in popular Chinese culture, see Gladney (1994a). The link between ethnicity and gender, specifically between minorities and the feminine, is elaborated upon by Schein (1996, 1997, 2000).

26. The term *shili pai*, however, sometimes means something completely different: namely, singers who have a unique, powerful voice (as opposed to the sweet voice used in mainstream). Sun Yue, nonetheless, made it clear in her in-

terview that she used the term *shili pai* to denote musicians who, in addition to singing, also write lyrics and compose tunes.

27. According to the music critic Wang Xiaofeng, "The Love of the Boat Tower" sold over two million copies between 1993 and 1997 (personal communication).

28. Ai Jing's 1993 album features two versions of "My 1997," one referred to as "original," which concludes the album, and a shorter one, which opens the album. I chose to translate the former because it includes important elements that, I believe, help to gain a better understanding of Ai Jing's voice.

29. Mei Yanfang is the Mandarin name of Hong Kong superstar Anita Mui.

30. The printed lyrics of this song in Ai Jing's album are identical to what she actually sings except for this part. The line "Give me this big red stamp" is altered in the printed lyrics to "give me a stamp," which looks a bit less negative. This is another example of how artists work in China to avoid censorship, and how censorship in China operates in relation to albums of popular music; that is, focusing mainly on the printed lyrics and ignoring the actual singing.

31. Hung Hom Coliseum is where Hong Kong's most important pop concerts are held.

32. Ai Jing and her song "My 1997" have been discussed in several studies (Jones 1994; Zha 1994, 1995; Mayfair Yang 1997). Yet in none of these studies was any serious attention paid to her gender and the significance of her song in the context of China's male-dominated pop scene.

33. According to Wang Xiaofeng, Ai Jing was, in fact, the first female musician to sing her own songs (personal communication).

34. In 1995, Anita Mui was allowed to launch an impressive concert tour in China, but after performing her provocative "Bad Girl" in one of the early concerts, despite an official request not to do so, the tour was cancelled. Ai Jing's reference to Anita Mui invokes subversive sentiments also because the latter helped to raise millions of dollars for the 1989 pro-democracy movement. For more details on Anita Mui, see Lawrence Witzleben (1999).

35. For a discussion of an earlier example of this practice, see Liu (1994).

36. According to Wang Xiaofeng, by May 1997, "My 1997" had sold about 300,000 copies in China alone, whereas *The Story of Yanfen Street* had sold only 11,000 (personal communication). When I asked the music critic Jin Zhaojun to provide me with some sales figures for Ai Jing's albums, he refused because of the unreliable nature of published sales figures in China but did comment, nevertheless, that *The Story of Yanfen Street* "was not successful" (personal communication).

37. I am grateful to Nicole Constable for this observation.

38. One conspicuous exception to this rule, however, is found in Tang Dynasty's "Nine Beats" *(Jiu pai)*, a song that depicts a dance with the moon.

39. The word used by Cheng Lin for "bitterness" is *youyuan*. One mainland dictionary indicates that this word refers specifically to the bitterness "of a young woman thwarted in love" (Wu Jingrong 1979).

40. The engagement with breathing here and in the next stanza invokes the name of Wayhwa's former rock band. In both cases this engagement communicates a state of suffocation, oppression, and death from which Wayhwa wishes to be liberated.

41. For a detailed study of Wang Shuo that examines this manipulation of language, see Barmé (1992b, esp. 57–60).

42. The use of the word "modernization" itself, of course, could also be interpreted along similar lines.

43. I am grateful to Gillian Rodger for suggesting this point to me.

44. According to Wang Xiaofeng, Wayhwa's album, as of May 1997, had sold only 40,000 copies (personal communication). Jin Zhaojun again was unwilling to mention any figure, but he nonetheless suggested that Wayhwa's album was not commercially successful.

CHAPTER 4. POPULAR MUSIC AND STATE POLITICS

1. For another recent study that seeks a more "fluid approach" and questions many of the dichotomies used or implied in earlier studies of popular Chinese music, such as pop-rock, high-low, commercial-alternative, East-West, local-global, and subversive subcultures–dominant culture, see De Kloet (2000).

2. One important exception to this generalization is found in Johnson, Nathan, and Rawski (1985), where unity is actually overstressed. This exception seems to be related to the fact that this edited volume on popular culture deals with imperial China.

3. The entire *Book of Music* has been lost. Parts of it, however, were gathered to make the nineteenth chapter in the *Book of Rites (Liji)*, an ancient encyclopedia of ceremonial regulations, sociopolitical institutions, and religious and philosophical creeds, which was compiled during the first century B.C. from documents of various periods.

4. The film has been translated into English as *The Emperor's Shadow*.

5. For a book-length study of Chinese television, see Lull (1991).

6. These types of music were, however, available on television in urban areas through local television and cable television stations, which naturally have smaller audiences compared with the CCTV, which broadcasts nationwide.

7. For another discussion of patriotic songs, see Micic (1995, 84–86). In line with my own observations, Micic concludes the discussion by suggesting, "It would be naive to suggest that only party elders and hard-line party apparatchiks constituted the fans of these songs" (86).

8. This was not the case for BCTV (Beijing Cable Television) channels.

9. The other major type of event that can still draw a large crowd of people in China today is sports events. The notion that such events, and mass events in general, are potentially dangerous, not only physically but also politically (for the state and its representatives) has been suggested by Susan Brownell, who wrote: "Several thousand students braved the infield crush to watch the

ceremonies. The situation was potentially dangerous, as the crowd was nearly out of control. . . . A meeting between representatives of the state and society in China is a dangerous thing. Hence it is not surprising that the culturally demarcated realm in which it takes place is highly choreographed" (1995, 87).

10. A recording of "The East Is Red" played on Marquis Yi's Bells has even been shipped to space and broadcast from a satellite. I am grateful to Joseph Lam and Bell Yung for pointing out to me the identity and importance of the instruments that play the prelude in Gao's song.

11. *Shan'ge* refers in Chinese to a whole type of folksongs that is explicitly associated with peasant life. Songs belonging to this category are generally characterized as improvised songs in free rhythm, sung loudly during work outdoors. For a book-length study of *shan'ge*, see Schimmelpenninck (1997). The problem of definition of this type and other types of folksongs is discussed on pp. 16–22, 308–21.

12. See *Yaogun Beijing II* in the discography.

13. Wayhwa was asked to serve as an anchor in a concert that was given in Beijing by Julio Iglesias because she knows him and knows English, and was promised that in return she would be allowed to sing two of her own songs during the concert. Minutes before the concert started, however, the rocker was notified by officials that she could not sing her songs. The musician, nevertheless, did manage eventually to sing her songs after she threatened that she would not anchor the concert and argued that allowing her to anchor the show was at least as risky as allowing her to sing her songs and that it did not make any sense (Wayhwa, interview with the author, 25 June 1996). This incident serves as another example of the symbiotic relationship between officialdom and self-employed musicians. It also serves as a good example of how matters in China are often negotiated at low levels and how, despite everything that is described above, there is still significant space for negotiation. I discuss this space later on.

14. Hall does speak elsewhere (e.g., in his 1981 article) about a dialectical relationship between hegemony and resistance, but there, too, as I suggest in the introduction, he nevertheless implies a fixed structural view of the two. I refer particularly to his 1980 article because the model that he proposes in this article was adopted by Pratt (1990) and, more importantly, by Jones (1992a), who produced the only book-length study in English of popular music in China to date.

15. Lu Xun devoted a whole essay to the Wall ("Changcheng") in which he condemned it as a symbol of enclosure and political oppression. The Wall was also condemned by Huang Xiang during the Democracy Wall Movement of the late 1970s and criticized once again a decade later in the controversial television series *River Elegy* (see Jing Wang 1996, 132–33). Later in this chapter I also discuss criticisms of the Wall in rock music.

16. "The Great Wall Is Long" won the gold medal in the 1994 annual CCTV video competition.

17. For more about the switch during the Cultural Revolution from the

traditional emphasis on form to an emphasis on content, see James L. Watson (1992, 79).

18. For an exploration of some post-revolutionary manifestations of the traditional tension between center and periphery, see Friedman (1994).

19. The decision of the local television station in Hangzhou to broadcast this rock song was probably related to the fact that its lyrics, which I discuss later in this chapter, were written during the Song Dynasty (960–1279), when Hangzhou served as the capital. The broadcast in Hangzhou is yet another manifestation of the tension between center and periphery that has always existed in China. The band members also recalled, however, that those who approved the broadcast were later criticized by their superiors.

20. One notable exception is Dadawa's 1995 *Sister Drum (A jie gu)*. Non-mainland labels involved in the production of mainland rock albums include Taiwan's Magic Rock *(Mo yan)* and Rolling Stones *(Gun shi)*, Hong Kong's Red Star *(Hongxing)* and Mother Earth *(Dadi)*, and Japan's JVC.

21. For a detailed account of Cui Jian's 1995 U.S. concert tour, see Cynthia P. Wong (1996).

22. For a more detailed discussion of this topic, see ibid.

23. *Zhongguo ren* can mean both ethnic Chinese and of PRC nationality. Ethnic Chinese who live outside of China often identify their Chinese ethnicity using the term *Hua ren*. People from Hong Kong and Taiwan often also identify themselves as *Xianggang ren* and *Taiwan ren*, respectively. Thus, by identifying himself as *Zhongguo ren* rather than *Hua ren*, Wu was trivializing nonmainland Chinese identities and asserting the centrality of mainland China to all Chinese identities.

24. For another critique of the transnationalism versus nationalism binary, which draws upon the domain of sports in China, see Brownell (1999). Brownell writes:

> At first glance, television would appear to be the mass medium that most transcends national boundaries, and telecasts of international sporting events would appear to be the most remarkable example.... However, it is not clear that sports telecasting is at the leading edge of the emergence of a transnational public sphere, because its technological infrastructure as well as its content tend to reinforce distinctions between nations at the same time that they create new inter-connections between them.... Nationalism is built into the very structure of international sports and sports ritual. The Olympic Games and other major events actually require athletes to represent particular nations, marking their representation in rituals such as the awards ceremonies and parade of athletes, and in symbols such as uniforms, flags, and anthems. (210–12)

25. The official interference with Gao Feng's original title is, of course, another form of censorship. As a result of this interference, Gao's song appears

today in many collections under two titles: "China" *(Zhongguo)* and "Great China" *(Da Zhongguo)*, the latter often placed in parentheses.

26. Gao Feng told me that in June 1996, for example, he earned approximately 100,000 *yuan*, which is equal to about 12,000 U.S. dollars. For comparison, the average salary of a senior university professor at that time was between 1,000 and 1,500 *yuan*.

27. See Gao Feng (1996) in the discography.

28. For another discussion of the phenomenon, see Schell (1994, 320–27).

29. This negative and tragic view of red is also powerfully communicated in "Maple," a famous, controversial story that was published after the Cultural Revolution and made into a film in late 1980. The story was among the first cultural expressions to deal with armed conflict and violence in general during the Cultural Revolution, a subject that was taboo for several years. See Link (1984, 57–73).

30. This interpretation derives from the fact that in a traditional Chinese wedding the face of the bride is covered with a piece of red cloth.

31. *Lao Gugong* is also referred to in English as the Imperial Palace. My translation of the title of the song follows Wayhua's translation as it appears in her album. Wayhwa obviously chose the other English name—that is, "Forbidden City"—to enhance her negative view of the place.

32. This song is written and sung in English.

33. He Yong's attribution of the practice of footbinding to Ci Xi is erroneous. As a Manchu, Ci Xi did not have bound feet.

34. The album features two versions of "Garbage Dump," but both are significantly different from the earlier version that is quoted above, which is cited in Zhao Jianwei's book (1992, 291–92).

35. See Jones (1992a, 131–32). Jones's translation of the song is based on a 1990 live performance. The version he translated is slightly different from the one published in Zhao Jianwei's book.

36. In the printed lyrics attached to the cassette, this line starts with the words *wei shenme bu neng.* . . . In the recording, however, Dai Bing uses the colloquial word *ganma*. I discuss the meaning of the difference later in this chapter.

37. In the printed lyrics this line is somewhat unclear and can perhaps be translated as follows: "I only want to say what I know." My translation follows the singing.

38. See Wu Jingrong (1979).

39. I talk specifically about Zang's rock music because the musician also wrote music for a television series that was considerably different and did make its way to the screen.

40. I am grateful to Gao Feng for pointing out to me the relationship between the two songs.

41. The meaning of this appropriation, like that of many of Cui's songs, however, is far from unequivocal. As many people suggested to me, in wearing an old army jacket, Cui may equally have been articulating his nostalgia for the idealistic revolutionary past.

42. Translated by Xianyi Yang and Gladys Yang (1984, 308–9). All notes to the poem are by the translators.

43. A third-century king who reigned in Jingkou.

44. The first ruler of the Southern Song Dynasty in the fifth century and a native of this city, who led successful expeditions against the northern Tartars.

45. A.D. 424–453.

46. In Inner Mongolia, reached by the Han army after defeating the Huns in 119 B.C.

47. In 1161 the Nuzhen Tartars [Jurchens] occupied Yangzhou.

48. When Northern Wei, a Tartar Dynasty, defeated the Southern Song troops in the fifth century, their emperor built a temple near Yangzhou.

49. A brave general of the Warring States period (475–221 B.C.), who to prove his ability to lead an army in his old age rode out in full armor after a hearty meal.

50. The "Four Great Heavenly Kings" is the popular name of Hong Kong's most famous four male pop idols, Jacky Cheung (Zhang Xueyou in Mandarin), Aaron Kwok (Guo Fucheng), Andy Lau (Liu Dehua), and Leon Lai (Li Ming).

51. He Yong's comments led to a fierce reaction from the Hong Kong media and from several Hong Kong pop musicians, who immediately asserted their superiority and revealed how the mainland is perceived in Hong Kong. Jacky Cheung (Zhang Xueyou), for example, was quoted as saying the mainland musicians were "primitive people who come from a cave" (quoted in Yi 1995, 1).

52. The few exceptions include Jones (1994), De Kloet (2000, 256–58), and Gregory Lee (1995).

53. For a video and audio recording of the 1994 rock concert in Hong Kong, see *Zhongguo yaogunyue shili* in the discography and videography.

54. Merle Goldman, for example, writes that young intellectuals and urban youth "readily embraced the leadership's reinvigorated nationalism" (1999, 704).

References

A Se. 1996. "'China Girl' gui 'guli': Björk Beijing xing" ("China Girl" Returns to Her "Native Place": Björk's Beijing Tour). *Yinxiang shijie* 4: 16–17.

Adorno, Theodor W. 1990. "On Popular Music." In *On Record: Rock, Pop, and the Written Word*, edited by Simon Frith and Andrew Goodwin, 301–14. New York: Pantheon Books.

"Ai Jing: Lianjie Shenyang he Dongjing, qishi niandai he jiushi niandai min'ge de jingshen" (Ai Jing: Linking Shenyang and Tokyo, and the Spirit of the Folksongs of the 1970s and the 1990s). 1995. *Zhongguo bailaohui* 7: 31.

"Ai Jing Dongjing gechanghui jishi" (A Record on Ai Jing's Solo Concert in Tokyo). 1995. *Zhongguo bailaohui* 7: 13.

Attali, Jacques. 1985. *Noise: The Political Economy of Music*. Translated by Brian Massumi. Manchester: Manchester University Press.

Bakhtin, Mikhail. 1984. *Rabelais and His World*. Translated by Helene Iswolsky. Bloomington: Indiana University Press.

Baranovitch, Nimrod. 2001. "Between Alterity and Identity: New Voices of Minority People in China." *Modern China* 27 (3): 359–401.

———. Forthcoming. "From the Margins to the Centre: The Uyghur Challenge in Beijing." *The China Quarterly* 175.

Barlow, Tani E., ed. 1993. *Gender Politics in Modern China: Writing and Feminism*. London: Duke University Press.

Barmé, Geremie. 1987. "Revolutionary Opera Arias Sung to a New, Disco Beat." *Far Eastern Economic Review*, February 5: 36–38.

———. 1992a. "The Greying of Chinese Culture." In *China Review 1992*, edited by Kuan Hsin-chi and Maurice Brosseau, 13–13.52. Hong Kong: Chinese University Press.

———. 1992b. "Wang Shuo and *Liumang* ('Hooligan') Culture." *The Australian Journal of Chinese Affairs* 28: 23–64.

———. 1996. *Shades of Mao: The Posthumous Cult of the Great Leader*. New York: M. E. Sharpe.

Barmé, Geremie, and John Minford, eds. 1988. *Seeds of Fire: Chinese Voices of Conscience.* New York: Hill and Wang.

Bernoviz (Baranovitch), Nimrod. 1997. "China's New Voices: Politics, Ethnicity, and Gender in Popular Music Culture on the Mainland, 1978–1997." Ph.D. diss., University of Pittsburgh.

Blake, Fred. 1979. "Love Songs and the Great Leap: The Role of a Youth Culture in the Revolutionary Phase of China's Economic Development." *American Ethnologist* 6 (1): 41–54.

Brace, Timothy. 1991. "Popular Music in Contemporary Beijing: Modernism and Cultural Identity." *Asian Music* 22 (2): 43–66.

———. 1992. "Modernization and Music in Contemporary China: Crisis, Identity, and the Politics of Style." Ph.D. diss., University of Texas at Austin.

Brace, Timothy, and Paul Friedlander. 1992. "Rock and Roll on the New Long March: Popular Music, Cultural Identity, and Political Opposition in the People's Republic of China." In *Rockin' the Boat: Mass Music and Mass Movements,* edited by Reebee Garofalo, 115–28. Boston: South End Press.

Brownell, Susan. 1995. *Training the Body for China: Sports in the Moral Order of the People's Republic.* Chicago: University of Chicago Press.

———. 1999. "Strong Women and Impotent Men: Sports, Gender, and Nationalism in Chinese Public Culture." In *Spaces of Their Own: Women's Public Sphere in Transnational China,* edited by Mayfair Mei-hui Yang, 207–31. Minneapolis: University of Minnesota Press.

Calhoun, Craig C. 1994. "Science, Democracy, and the Politics of Identity." In *Popular Protest and Political Culture in Modern China,* 2nd ed., edited by Jeffrey N. Wasserstrom and Elizabeth J. Perry, 93–124. Boulder, Co.: Westview Press.

Chai, Chu, and Winberg Chai, eds. 1967. *Li Chi: Book of Rites: An Encyclopedia of Ancient Ceremonial Usages, Religious Creeds, and Social Institutions.* Translated by James Legge, vol. 2. New York: University Books.

Chan, Anita, Richard Madsen, and Jonathan Unger. 1984. *Chen Village: The Recent History of a Peasant Community in Mao's China.* Berkeley: University of California Press.

"Chen Ming—*Jimo rang wo ruci meili*" (Chen Ming—*Loneliness Makes Me So Beautiful*). 1995. *Yinxiang shijie* 9: 18.

Cheng Chibing. 1993. "Xiao yanzi de aoxiang: Ji qingnian geshou Ai Jing" (The Soaring of the Little Swallow: Reporting on the Young Singer Ai Jing). *Yinxiang shijie* 1: 4.

Cheung, Siu-woo. 1996. "Representation and Negotiation of Ge Identities in Southwest Guizhou." In *Negotiating Ethnicities in China and Taiwan,* edited by Melissa J. Brown, 240–73. Berkeley: Institute of East Asian Studies, University of California.

Chiu, Randy. 1985. "*Disike* Takes the Floor as Youth Culture Takes the Stage." *Far Eastern Economic Review,* May 9: 61.

Chong, W. L. 1989–90. "Su Xiaokang on His Film 'River Elegy.'" *China Information* 4 (3): 44–55.

Chow, Rey. 1990–91. "Listening Otherwise, Music Miniaturized: A Different Type of Question About Revolution." *Discourse* 13 (1): 129–48.

———. 1993. "Against the Lures of Diaspora: Minority Discourse, Chinese Women, and Intellectual Hegemony." In *Gender and Sexuality in Twentieth-Century Chinese Literature and Society,* edited by Lu Tonglin, 23–45. Albany: State University of New York Press.

Clark, Paul. 1987a. "Ethnic Minorities in Chinese Films: Cinema and the Exotic." *East-West Film Journal* 1 (2): 15–32.

———. 1987b. *Chinese Cinema.* Cambridge: Cambridge University Press.

Croll, Elisabeth. 1995. *Changing Identities of Chinese Women: Rhetoric, Experience and Self-Perception in Twentieth-Century China.* New Jersey: Zed Books.

Croll, Elisabeth, Delia Davin, and Penny Kane, eds. 1985. *China's One-Child Family Policy.* London: Macmillan Press.

Cui, Shuqin. 1997. "Gendered Perspective: The Construction and Representation of Subjectivity and Sexuality in *Ju Dou.*" In *Transnational Chinese Cinemas: Identity, Nationhood, Gender,* edited by Sheldon Hsiao-peng Lu, 303–29. Honolulu: University of Hawaii Press.

Dai Jinhua. 1995. "Invisible Women: Contemporary Chinese Cinema and Women's Film." *Positions* 3 (1): 255–80.

———. 1999. "Rewriting Chinese Women: Gender Production and Cultural Space in the Eighties and Nineties." In *Spaces of Their Own: Women's Public Sphere in Transnational China,* edited by Mayfair Mei-hui Yang, 191–206. Minneapolis: University of Minnesota Press.

Dai Jinhua and Mayfair Yang. 1995. "A Conversation with Huang Shuqing." *Positions* 3 (3): 790–805.

Dalsimer, Marlyn, and Laurie Nisnoff. 1984. "The New Economic Readjustment Policies: Implications for Chinese Working Women." *Review of Radical Political Economics* 16 (1): 17–43.

"Daoban—Guoyu Rap zhuanji" (*Pirated Version*—Mandarin Rap Album). 1995. *Yinxiang shijie* 3: 18.

De Jong, Alice. 1989–90. "The Demise of the Dragon: Backgrounds to the Chinese Film 'River Elegy.'" *China Information* 4 (3): 28–43.

De Kloet, Jeroen. 2000. "'Let Him Fucking See the Green Smoke Beneath My Groin': The Mythology of Chinese Rock." In *Postmodernism and China,* edited by Arif Dirlik and Xudong Zhang, 239–74. Durham, N.C.: Duke University Press.

Diamond, Norma. 1988. "The Miao and Poison: Interactions on China's Southwest Frontier." *Ethnology* 27 (1): 1–25.

———. 1995. "Defining the Miao: Ming, Qing, and Contemporary Views." In *Cultural Encounters on China's Ethnic Frontiers,* edited by Stevan Harrell, 92–112. Seattle: University of Washington Press.

Dreyer, June T. 1976. *China's Forty Millions*. Cambridge, Mass.: Harvard University Press.

Duke, Michael S., ed. 1989. *Modern Chinese Women Writers: Critical Appraisals*. New York: M. E. Sharpe.

Eberhard, Wolfram. 1982. *China's Minorities: Yesterday and Today*. Belmont, Calif.: Wadsworth.

Ebrey, Patricia. 1996. "Surnames and Han Chinese Identity." In *Negotiating Ethnicities in China and Taiwan*, edited by Melissa J. Brown, 19–36. Berkeley: Institute of East Asian Studies, University of California.

Efird, Robert. 2001. "Rock in a Hard Place: Music and the Market in Nineties Beijing." In *China Urban: Ethnographies of Contemporary Culture*, edited by Nancy Chen, 67–86. London: Duke University Press.

Erwin, Kathleen. 1999. "White Women, Male Desires: A Televisual Fantasy of the Transnational Chinese Family." In *Spaces of Their Own: Women's Public Sphere in Transnational China*, edited by Mayfair Mei-hui Yang, 232–57. Minneapolis: University of Minnesota Press.

Evans, Harriet. 1997. *Women and Sexuality in China: Female Sexuality and Gender Since 1949*. New York: Continuum.

"Fang Fang—*Lan tian shang*" (Fang Fang—*In the Blue Sky*). 1996. *Yinxiang shijie* 4: 22.

Fang Mengyin. 1995. "Chen Ming—Yi zhi wenrou de yeying" (Chen Ming—Gentle and Soft Nightingale). *Yinyue shenghuo bao*, May 19.

Feigon, Lee. 1994. "Gender and the Chinese Student Movement." In *Popular Protest and Political Culture in Modern China*, 2nd ed., edited by Jeffrey N. Wasserstrom and Elizabeth J. Perry, 125–35. Boulder, Co.: Westview Press.

Feuerwerker, Yi-tsi Mei. 1998. *Ideology, Power, Text: Self-Representation and the Peasant "Other" in Modern Chinese Literature*. Stanford, Calif.: Stanford University Press.

Fiske, John. 1989. *Understanding Popular Culture*. London: Routledge.

Foucault, Michel. 1980. *The History of Sexuality*. Translated by Robert Hurley, vol. 1. New York: Vintage Press.

Friedlander, Paul. 1991. "China's 'Newer Value' Pop: Rock-and-Roll and Technology on the New Long March." *Asian Music* 22 (2): 67–81.

Friedman, Edward. 1994. "Reconstructing China's National Identity: A Southern Alternative to Mao-Era Anti-Imperialist Nationalism." *The Journal of Asian Studies* 53 (1): 67–91.

Frolic, B. Michael. 1980. "Frontier Town." In *Mao's People: Sixteen Portraits of Life in Revolutionary China*. Cambridge, Mass.: Harvard University Press.

Gilmartin, Christina, Gail Hershatter, Lisa Rofel, and Tyrene White, eds. 1994. *Engendering China: Women, Culture, and the State*. Cambridge, Mass.: Harvard University Press.

Gladney, Dru C. 1991. *Muslim Chinese: Ethnic Nationalism in the People's Republic*. Cambridge, Mass.: Harvard University Council on East Asian Studies.

———. 1994a. "Representing Nationality in China: Refiguring Majority/ Minority Identities." *The Journal of Asian Studies* 53 (1): 92–123.

———. 1994b. "Ethnic Identity in China: The New Politics of Difference." In *China Briefing 1994*, edited by William A. Joseph, 171–92. Boulder, Co.: Westview Press.

———. 1995. "Tian Zhuangzhuang, the Fifth Generation, and Minorities Film in China." *Public Culture* 8 (1): 161–75.

Gold, Thomas B. 1989. "Guerrilla Interviewing Among the *Getihu*." In *Unofficial China: Popular Culture and Thought in the People's Republic*, edited by Perry Link, Richard Madsen, and Paul G. Pickowicz, 175–92. San Francisco: Westview Press.

———. 1993. "Go With Your Feelings: Hong Kong and Taiwan Popular Culture in Greater China." *The China Quarterly* 136: 907–25.

Goldman, Merle. 1999. "Politically Engaged Intellectuals in the 1990s." *The China Quarterly* 519: 700–11.

Greenhalgh, Susan. 1993. "The Peasantization of the One-Child Policy in Shaanxi." In *Chinese Families in the Post-Mao Era*, edited by Deborah Davis and Stevan Harrell, 219–50. Berkeley: University of California Press.

Gulik, Robert H. van. 1961. *Sexual Life in Ancient China: A Preliminary Survey of Chinese Sex and Society from ca. 1500 B.C. till 1644 A.D.* Leiden: E. J. Brill.

Guo Jun. 1995. "Geshou zhuanfang: *Lolo yao*" (A Special Interview with a Singer: *Lolo's Swing*). *Yanyiquan* 11: 44.

Hall, Stuart. 1980. "Encoding/Decoding." In *Culture, Media, Language: Working Papers in Cultural Studies, 1972–79*, edited by S. Hall, D. Hobson, A. Lowe, and P. Willis, 128–38. London: Hutchinson.

———. 1981. "Notes on Deconstructing 'The Popular.'" In *People's History and Socialist Theory*, edited by Raphael Samuel, 227–40. London: Routledge & Kegan Paul.

Han, Kuo-huang. 1980. "Introductory Notes." In *Vocal Music of Contemporary China: Volume 2—The National Minorities* (LP record). Folkways Records.

Handlin, Joanna F. 1975. "Lü Kun's New Audience: The Influence of Women's Literacy on Sixteenth-Century Thought." In *Women in Chinese Society*, edited by Margery Wolf and Roxane Witke, 13–38. Stanford, Calif.: Stanford University Press.

Hansen, Mette Halskov. 1999. *Lessons in Being Chinese: Minority Education and Ethnic Identity in Southwest China.* Seattle: University of Washington Press.

Harrell, Stevan. 1990. "Ethnicity, Local Interests, and the State: Yi Communities in Southwest China." *Comparative Studies in Society and History* 32 (3): 515–48.

———. 1995a. "Introduction: Civilizing Projects and the Reaction to Them."

In *Cultural Encounters on China's Ethnic Frontiers,* edited by Stevan Harrell, 3–36. Seattle: University of Washington Press.

———. 1995b. "The History of the History of the Yi." In *Cultural Encounters on China's Ethnic Frontiers,* edited by Stevan Harrell, 63–91. Seattle: University of Washington Press.

———. 1996a. "Introduction." In *Negotiating Ethnicities in China and Taiwan,* edited by Melissa J. Brown, 1–18. Berkeley: Institute of East Asian Studies, University of California.

———. 1996b. "The Nationalities Question and the Prmi Problem." In *Negotiating Ethnicities in China and Taiwan,* edited by Melissa J. Brown, 274–96. Berkeley: Institute of East Asian Studies, University of California.

Harris, Rachel. Forthcoming (a). "Cassettes, Bazaars and Saving the Nation: The Uyghur Music Industry in Xinjiang, China." In *Global Goes Local: Popular Culture in Asia,* edited by Tim Crage and Richard King. Vancouver: University of British Columbia Press.

———. Forthcoming (b). "Wang Luobin: 'Folksong King of the Northwest' or Song Thief?: Copyright, Representation and Chinese 'Folksongs.'" In *Consuming China: Approaches to Cultural Change in Contemporary China,* edited by Kevin Latham and Stuart Thompson. N.p.: Curzon Press.

He Li. 1996. "Jizhe yaogun: Jizhe gei guo tamen jiqing de yinyue—Jiushi niandai yaogun fengjing" (Reporting on Rock: Reporting on the Music That Once Provided Them with Intense Emotion—The Rock Scene in the 1990s). *Xiju dianying bao,* no. 797.

Heberer, Thomas. 1989. *China and Its National Minorities: Autonomy or Assimilation?* New York: M. E. Sharpe.

Hertz, Ellen. 1998. *The Trading Crowd: An Ethnography of the Shanghai Stock Market.* Cambridge: Cambridge University Press.

Holm, David. 1984. "Folk Art as Propaganda: The *Yangge* Movement in Yan'an." In *Popular Chinese Literature and Performing Arts in the People's Republic of China 1949–1979,* edited by Bonnie S. McDougall, 1–35. Berkeley: University of California Press.

Honig, Emily, and Gail Hershatter. 1988. *Personal Voices: Chinese Women in the 1980's.* Stanford, Calif.: Stanford University Press.

Hooper, Beverley. 1984. "China's Modernization: Are Young Women Going to Lose Out?" *Modern China* 10 (3): 317–43.

Huang Liaoyuan et al., eds. 1997. *Shi nian: 1986–1996 Zhongguo liuxing yinyue jishi (Ten Years of Chinese Pop Music, 1986–1996).* Beijing: Zhongguo dianying chubanshe.

Huang, Shu-min. 1989. *The Spiral Road: Change in a Chinese Village Through the Eyes of a Communist Party Leader.* Boulder, Co.: Westview Press.

Hung, Chang-tai. 1985. *Going to the People: Chinese Intellectuals and Folk Literature 1918–1937.* Cambridge, Mass.: Harvard University Council on East Asian Studies.

———. 1994. *War and Popular Culture: Resistance in Modern China, 1937–1945.* Berkeley: University of California Press.

Huot, Claire. 2000. *China's New Cultural Scene: A Handbook of Changes.* London: Duke University Press.

Jaivin, Linda. 1988. "Blowing His Own Trumpet." *Far Eastern Economic Review,* March 24: 84–87.

———. 1990a. "Cultural Purge Sweeps Clean." *Far Eastern Economic Review,* August 23: 47–48.

———. 1990b. "Dragon's Disowned Heir: Joyless Homecoming for Taiwan Popstar-Turned-Mainland-Dissident." *Far Eastern Economic Review,* September 13: 36–37.

Jankowiak, William. 1993. *Sex, Death and Hierarchy in a Chinese City: An Anthropological Account.* New York: Columbia University Press.

Jin Zhaojun. 1988. "Feng cong nali lai?: Ping getan 'xibeifeng'" (Where Is the Wind Coming From?: Commenting on the Pop Scene's Northwest Wind). *Renmin ribao,* August 23.

———. 1989a. "Yi zhong dute de wenhua xianxiang: 'Qiu ge' manyi zhi yi" (A Unique Cultural Phenomenon: Casual Discussion on 'Prison Songs' 1). *Renmin ribao,* March 3.

———. 1989b. "Lianjia de ganshang: 'Qiu ge' manyi zhi er" (Cheap Sentimentality: Casual Discussion on 'Prison Songs' 2). *Renmin ribao,* March 4.

———. 1989c. "Cui Jian yu Zhongguo yaogun yue" (Cui Jian and Chinese Rock). *Renmin yinyue* 4: 32–33.

———. 1990a. "Yaogun zai Jingcheng" (Rock in Beijing). *Beijing qingnian bao,* March 23.

———. 1990b. "Lai ye congcong fengyu jian cheng: Tongsu yinyue shi nian guan" (Arriving Hastily in Wind and Rain: A View of a Decade of *Tongsu* Music). *Renmin yinyue* 1: 30–33.

———. 1991. "Zuo ye xingchen, jin ye xingchen, xilie zhi si: Zhongliu ji shui jin feng liu: Wei Wei yu Liu Huan" (The Stars of Yesterday's Night, the Stars of Tonight 4: Elegant Performance in Midstream: Wei Wei and Liu Huan). *Beijing qingnian bao,* February 15.

———. 1992. "Zai huishou huangran ru meng zai huishou wo xin yijiu: Wo dui yindai *Hong taiyang—Mao Zedong songge* de sikao" (Looking Back Again It Seems Like a Dream, Looking Back Again My Heart Is Like Before: My Reflections on the Cassette *Red Sun—Praise Songs for Mao Zedong*). *Xinwen chuban bao,* February 24.

———. 1993. "Youzhe dian, Zhongguo yaogun" (Chinese Rock, Take It Easy). *Jinrong shibao,* January 16.

———. 1995a. "Huidao minjian—Ting *Luoluo yao* you gan" (Back to the Folk—My Feelings after Listening to *Lolo's Swing*). *Yanyiquan* 11: 43.

———. 1995b. "Mao Amin: Xiwang wei ziji gechang" (Mao Amin: Hoping to Sing for Herself). *Yanyiquan* 9: 1–4.

———. 1996a. "Getan huixiang lu (2): Dianzi biao, taiyang jing, zhedie san, yu 'Xianglian'" (Pop Scene Recollection Record [2]: Electric Watch, Sunglasses, Folding Umbrella, and "Longing for Home"). *Yinyue shenghuo bao,* April 12.

———. 1996b. "Getan huixiang lu (3): Zouxue jianghu xing" (Pop Scene Recollection Record [3]: *Zouxue* Is Reaching All Corners of the Country). *Yinyue shenghuo bao*, April 19.

———. 1996c. "'Ba daizi'—qian chuangzuo shidai: Getan huixiang lu (4)" ("Stripping off Cassettes"—The Pre-Creativity Era: Pop Scene Recollection Record [4]). *Yinyue shenghuo bao*, April 26.

———. 1996d. "Shi nian fengyu shi nian ge" (Ten Years of Wind and Rain, Ten Years of Songs). *Yinyue shenghuo bao*, April 5.

Johnson, David, Andrew Nathan, and Evelyn S. Rawski, eds. 1985. *Popular Culture in Late Imperial China*. Berkeley: University of California Press.

Jones, Andrew F. 1992a. *Like a Knife: Ideology and Genre in Contemporary Chinese Popular Music*. Ithaca, N.Y.: East Asian Program, Cornell University.

———. 1992b. "Beijing Bastards." *Spin*, October 1992: 80–90, 122–23.

———. 1994. "The Politics of Popular Music in Post-Tiananmen China." In *Popular Protest and Political Culture in Modern China*, 2nd ed., edited by Jeffrey N. Wasserstrom and Elizabeth J. Perry, 148–65. Boulder, Co.: Westview Press.

Kaup, Katherine Palmer. 2000. *Creating the Zhuang: Ethnic Politics in China*. Boulder, Co.: Lynne Rienner.

Ke Lei and Sang Ya, eds. 1989. *Xing fengsu (Sexual Customs)*. Shanghai: Shanghai wenhua chubanshe.

Khan, Almaz. 1995. "Chinggis Khan: From Imperial Ancestor to Ethnic Hero." In *Cultural Encounters on China's Ethnic Frontiers*, edited by Stevan Harrell, 248–77. Seattle: University of Washington Press.

———. 1996. "Who Are the Mongols? State, Ethnicity, and the Politics of Representation in the PRC." In *Negotiating Ethnicities in China and Taiwan*, edited by Melissa J. Brown, 125–59. Berkeley: Institute of East Asian Studies, University of California.

Ko, Dorothy Y. 1994. *Teachers of the Inner Chambers: Women and Culture in China, 1573–1722*. Stanford, Calif.: Stanford University Press.

Larson, Wendy. 1997. "The Concubine and the Figure of History: Chen Kaige's *Farewell My Concubine*." In *Transnational Chinese Cinemas: Identity, Nationhood, Gender*, edited by Sheldon Hsiao-peng Lu, 331–46. Honolulu: University of Hawaii Press.

Lee, Coral. 2000. "From Little Teng to A-Mei: Marking Time in Music." *Sinorama* 25 (3): 33–44.

Lee, Gregory. 1995. "The 'East Is Red' Goes Pop: Commodification, Hybridity and Nationalism in Chinese Popular Song and Its Televisual Performance." *Popular Music* 14 (1): 95–110.

Lee, Joanna Ching-Yun. 1992a. "All for the Music: The Rise of Patriotic/Pro-Democratic Popular Music in Hong Kong in Response to the Chinese Student Movement." In *Rockin' the Boat: Mass Music and Mass Movements*, edited by Reebee Garofalo, 129–47. Boston: South End Press.

———. 1992b. "Cantopop on Emigration from Hong Kong." *Yearbook for Traditional Music* 24: 14–23.

Levy, Howard. 1967. *Chinese Footbinding: The History of a Curious Erotic Custom.* New York: Bell Publishing Company.

Leyda, Jay. 1972. *Dianying: An Account of Films and the Film Audience in China.* Cambridge, Mass.: M.I.T. Press.

Li Fan. 1996. "'Xin min'ge' san bu qu huigu: Cong 'Qianfu de ai,' 'Tian bu xiayu, tian bu guafeng' dao 'Tou yi ke yueliang zhaoliang tian' de chuangzuo licheng" (Looking Back on Three "New Folksongs": The Course of Creation from "The Love of The Boat Tower" and "There Is No Rain and Wind," to "Stealing a Moon to Illuminate the Sky"). *Yinxiang shijie* 4: 4–6.

Li Xi'an. 1995. "Luoluo he ta de *Luoluo Yao*" (Lolo and His *Lolo's Swing*), *Yanyiquan* 11: 43.

Li Xiaojiang. 1994. "Economic Reform and the Awakening of Chinese Women's Collective Consciousness." In *Engendering China: Women, Culture, and the State,* edited by Christina Gilmartin, Gail Hershatter, Lisa Rofel, and Tyrene White, 360–82. Cambridge, Mass.: Harvard University Press.

Liang Maochun. 1988. "Dui wo guo liuxing yinyue lishi de sikao" (Reflections on the History of Our Country's Popular Music). *Renmin yinyue* 7: 32–34.

Liang Shiqiu, ed. 1987. *A New Practical Chinese-English Dictionary.* Taipei: Far East Book Co.

"Lin Yilun—*Huo huo de geyao*" (Lin Yilun—*Fire Hot Songs*). 1995. *Yinxiang shijie* 6: 18.

Lin Yueh-hua. 1961. *The Lolo of Liang Shan.* Translated by Ju-shu Pan. New Haven, Conn.: Hraf Press.

Ling Ruilan. 1994. *Zhongguo xiandai youxiu gequ jingcui jicheng: Tongsu gequ 1978–1990 (A Pithy Collection of Modern Chinese Excellent Songs: Tongsu Songs 1978–1990).* Shenyang: Chunfeng wenyi chubanshe.

Ling Xuan. 1989. "'Xibeifeng' yu 'qiu ge'" ("Northwest Wind" and "Prison Songs"). *Renmin yinyue* 5: 37–38.

Link, Perry. 1981. *Mandarin Ducks and Butterflies: Popular Fiction in Early Twentieth-Century Chinese Cities.* Berkeley: University of California Press.

———, ed. 1984. *Stubborn Weeds: Popular and Controversial Chinese Literature after the Cultural Revolution.* London: Blond and Briggs.

Link, Perry, Richard Madsen, and Paul G. Pickowicz, eds. 1989. *Unofficial China: Popular Culture and Thought in the People's Republic.* San Francisco: Westview Press.

Litzinger, Ralph A. 1995. "Making Histories: Contending Conceptions of the Yao Past." In *Cultural Encounters on China's Ethnic Frontiers,* edited by Stevan Harrell, 117–39. Seattle: University of Washington Press.

———. 1998. "Memory Work: Reconstituting the Ethnic in Post-Mao China." *Cultural Anthropology* 13 (2): 224–55.

Liu, Lydia H. 1994. "The Female Body and Nationalist Discourse: Manchuria in Xiao Hong's *Field of Life and Death.*" In *Body, Subject and Power in China,* edited by Angela Zito and Tani E. Barlow, 157–77. Chicago: University of Chicago Press.

Louie, Kam. 1991. "The Macho Eunuch: The Politics of Masculinity in Jia Pingwa's 'Human Extremities.'" *Modern China* 17 (2): 163–87.

———. 1992. "Masculinities and Minorities: Alienation in *Strange Tales from Strange Land.*" *The China Quarterly* 132: 1119–35.

Louie, Kam, and Louise Edwards. 1994. "Chinese Masculinity: Theorizing *Wen* and *Wu.*" *East Asian History* 8: 135–48.

Lu, Tonglin, ed. 1993. *Gender and Sexuality in Twentieth-Century Chinese Literature and Society.* Albany: State University of New York Press.

Lull, James. 1991. *China Turned On: Television, Reform, and Resistance.* New York: Routledge.

Mackerras, Colin. 1975. *The Chinese Theatre in Modern Times: From 1840 to the Present Day.* Amherst: University of Massachusetts Press.

———. 1984. "Folksongs and Dances of China's Minority Nationalities: Policy, Tradition, and Professionalization." *Modern China* 10 (2): 187–226.

———. 1994. *China's Minorities: Integration and Modernization in the Twentieth Century.* New York: Oxford University Press.

———. 1995. *China's Minority Cultures: Identities and Integration since 1912.* New York: St. Martin's Press.

Manuel, Peter. 1993. *Cassette Culture: Popular Music and Technology in North India.* Chicago: University of Chicago Press.

"*Mao Amin—Mao Amin*" (Mao Amin—Mao Amin). 1995. *Yinxiang shijie* 4: 18.

McClary, Susan. 1991. *Feminine Endings: Music, Gender, and Sexuality.* Minneapolis: University of Minnesota Press.

McDougall, Bonnie S. 1980. *Mao Zedong's "Talks at the Yan'an Conference on Literature and Art": A Translation of the 1943 Text with Commentary.* Ann Arbor: Center for Chinese Studies, University of Michigan.

———. 1991. *The Yellow Earth: A Film by Chen Kaige: With a Complete Translation of the Filmscript.* Hong Kong: Chinese University Press.

———, ed. 1984. *Popular Chinese Literature and Performing Arts in the People's Republic of China 1949–1979.* Berkeley: University of California Press.

McMahon, Keith. 1994. "The Classic 'Beauty-Scholar' Romance and the Superiority of the Talented Woman." In *Body, Subject and Power in China,* edited by Angela Zito and Tani E. Barlow, 227–52. Chicago: University of Chicago Press.

Micic, Peter. 1995. "'A Bit of This and a Bit of That': Notes on Pop/Rock Genres in the Eighties in China." *Chime Journal* 8: 76–95.

Middleton, Richard. 1985a. "Articulating Musical Meaning/Re-Constructing Musical History/Locating the 'Popular.'" *Popular Music* 5: 5–43.

———. 1985b. "Popular Music, Class Conflict and the Music-Historical Field." In *Popular Music Perspectives,* edited by David Horn, 24–46. Salisbury: May & May.

———. 1990. *Studying Popular Music.* Philadelphia: Open University Press.

Nonini, Donald M., and Aihwa Ong. 1997. "Introduction: Chinese Transnationalism as an Alternative Modernity." In *Ungrounded Empires: The Cultural Politics of Modern Chinese Transnationalism,* edited by Aihwa Ong and Donald Nonini, 3–33. New York: Routledge.

Notar, Beth. 1994. "Of Labor and Liberation: Images of Women in Current Chinese Television Advertising." *Visual Anthropology Review* 10 (2): 29–44.

Oaks, Timothy S. 1995. "Tourism in Guizhou: The Legacy of Internal Colonialism." In *Tourism in China: Geographic, Political, and Economic Perspectives,* edited by Alan A. Lew and Lawrence Yu, 203–22. Boulder, Co.: Westview Press.

Ong, Aihwa. 1997. "Chinese Modernities: Narratives of Nation and of Capitalism." In *Ungrounded Empires: The Cultural Politics of Modern Chinese Transnationalism,* edited by Aihwa Ong and Donald Nonini, 171–202. New York: Routledge.

Ortner, Sherry B. 1995. "Resistance and the Problem of Ethnographic Refusal." *Comparative Studies in Society and History* 37 (1): 173–93.

Perry, Elizabeth J. 1992. "Casting a Chinese 'Democracy' Movement: The Roles of Students, Workers, and Entrepreneurs." In *Popular Protest and Political Culture in Modern China: Learning from 1989,* edited by Jeffrey N. Wasserstrom and Elizabeth J. Perry, 146–64. Boulder, Co.: Westview Press.

Potter, Sulamith H., and Jack M. 1990. *China's Peasants: The Anthropology of a Revolution.* Cambridge: Cambridge University Press.

Pratt, Ray. 1990. *Rhythm and Resistance: Explorations in the Political Uses of Popular Music.* New York: Praeger.

Qiu Zi. 1996. "Chen Ming—*Jimo rang wo ruci meili*" (Chen Ming—*Loneliness Makes Me So Beautiful*). *Fuzhuang shibao,* no. 97.

Rayns, Tony. 1987. "The Position of Women in New Chinese Cinema." *East-West Film Journal* 1 (2): 32–44.

———. 1991. "Breakthroughs and Setbacks: The Origins of the New Chinese Cinema." In *Perspectives on Chinese Cinema,* edited by Chris Berry, 104–10. London: BFI Publishing.

Rees, Helen. 2000. *Echoes of History: Naxi Music in Modern China.* Oxford: Oxford University Press.

Robinson, Jean C. 1985. "Of Women and Washing Machines: Employment, Housework, and the Reproduction of Motherhood in Socialist China." *The China Quarterly* 101: 32–57.

Rofel, Lisa. 1994a. "Liberation Nostalgia and a Yearning for Modernity." In *Engendering China: Women, Culture, and the State,* edited by Christina Gilmartin, Gail Hershatter, Lisa Rofel, and Tyrene White, 226–49. Cambridge, Mass.: Harvard University Press.

———. 1994b. "Yearnings: Televisual Love and Melodramatic Politics in Contemporary China." *American Ethnologist* 21 (4): 700–22.

Said, Edward. 1978. *Orientalism.* New York: Random House.

Samson, Valerie. 1991. "Music as Protest Strategy: The Example of Tiananmen Square, 1989." *Pacific Review of Ethnomusicology* 6: 35–64.

Schein, Louisa. 1996. "Multiple Alterities: The Contouring of Gender in Miao and Chinese Nationalism." In *Women Out of Place: The Gender of Agency and the Race of Nationality,* edited by Brackette F. Williams, 79–102. London: Routledge.

———. 1997. "Gender and Internal Orientalism in China." *Modern China* 23 (1): 69–98.

———. 2000. *Minority Rules: The Miao and the Feminine in China's Cultural Politics.* London: Duke University Press.

Schell, Orville. 1988. *Discos and Democracy: China in the Throes of Reform.* New York: Pantheon Books.

———. 1994. *Mandate of Heaven: A New Generation of Entrepreneurs, Dissidents, Bohemians, and Technocrats Lays Claim to China's Future.* New York: Simon & Schuster.

Schimmelpenninck, Antoinet. 1997. *Chinese Folk Songs and Folk Singers: Shan'ge Traditions in Southern Jiangsu.* Leiden: CHIME Foundation.

Scott, James C. 1990. *Domination and the Arts of Resistance: Hidden Transcripts.* New Haven, Conn.: Yale University Press.

Sha Yexin. 1986. "Xunzhao nanzihan" (Looking for a Real Man). *Shiye* 3: 115–76.

Sima Qian. 1996. *Shiji (Historical Records).* Beijing: Zhonghua shuju.

Song He and Tie Cheng. 1987. "Ye Shanghai tiaodong de xin yinfu: Manbu zai Shanghai yinyue chazuo" (The New Notes That Beat in Shanghai at Night: Strolling among Shanghai's Music Teahouses). *Yinxiang shijie* 12: 14–15.

Song Wei. 1992. "Teng Ge'er, kan yaogun shuo Cui Jian hua Taibei" (Teng Ge'er Speaks about Rock, Cui Jian, and Taipei). *Zhongguo wenhua bao,* October 25: 4.

Song Xiaoming. 1995a. "Chang gei yueliang de ge" (A Song Sung for the Moon). *Yanyiquan* 11: 42.

———. 1995b. "Youli, youli, youjie" (Reasonable, Profitable, Elegant). *Yanyiquan* 8: 40.

Su Xiaokang and Wang Luxiang. 1991. *Deathsong of the River: A Reader's Guide to the Chinese Series Heshang,* introduced, translated and annotated by Richard W. Bodman and Pin P. Wan. Ithaca, N.Y.: East Asia Program, Cornell University.

Sun Ji'nan. 1993. *Li Jinhui pingzhuan (Annotated Biography of Li Jinhui).* Beijing: Renmin yinyue chubanshe.

Sun Longji. 1983. *Zhongguo wenhua de "shenceng jiegou" (The "Deep Structure" of Chinese Culture).* Hong Kong: Jixianshe.

Swain, Margaret Byrne. 1990. "Commoditizing Ethnicity in Southwest China." *Cultural Survival Quarterly* 14 (1): 26–30.

———. 1995. "A Comparison of State and Private Artisan Production for Tourism in Yunnan." In *Tourism in China: Geographic, Political, and Economic Perspectives,* edited by Alan A. Lew and Lawrence Yu, 223–33. Boulder, Co.: Westview Press.

Thierry, François. 1989. "Empire and Minority in China." In *Minority Peoples in the Age of Nation-States,* edited by Gerard Chaliand, 76–99. London: Pluto Press.

Turner, Victor. 1969. *The Ritual Process: Structure and Anti-Structure.* Chicago: Aldine Publishing.

Tyson, James L. 1991. "Rock-and-Roll Feminists Defy Tradition in Mainland China." *The China News,* October 20.

Upton, Janet. Forthcoming. "The Poetics and Politics of *Sisterdrum:* 'Tibetan' Music in the Global Cultural Marketplace." In *Global Goes Local: Popular Culture in Asia,* edited by Tim Crage and Richard King. Vancouver: University of British Columbia Press.

Wang, Jing. 1996. *High Culture Fever: Politics, Aesthetics, and Ideology in Deng's China.* Berkeley: University of California Press.

Wang Pingping. 1995. "Chuangzuo geng duo geng hao de yinyue dianshi jingpin: Zhongyang dianshitai Zhongguo yinyue dianshi chuangzuo guihua hui zai Jing juxing" (Create More and Better MTVs: A Production Planning Meeting of CCTV's Music Television Held in Beijing). *Zhongguo dianshi bao,* June 12.

Wang Xiaofeng. 1995a. "He Yong nao Xianggang" (He Yong Stirs Hong Kong). *Yinxiang shijie* 3: 2–3.

———. 1995b. "Shenme shi chengshou nüxing?" (What Is a Mature Woman?). *Yanyiquan* 12: 49.

———. 1996. "Xinxian de Wayhwa" (A New Wayhwa). *Yinxiang shijie* 2: 4–5.

Wang, Yuejin. 1989. "Mixing Memory and Desire: *Red Sorghum,* A Chinese Version of Masculinity and Femininity." *Public Culture* 2 (1): 31–53.

Watson, James L. 1992. "The Renegotiation of Chinese Cultural Identity in the Post-Mao Era." In *Popular Protest and Political Culture in Modern China: Learning from 1989,* edited by Jeffrey N. Wasserstrom and Elizabeth J. Perry, 67–84. Boulder, Co.: Westview Press.

Watson, Rubie S., ed. 1994. *Memory, History, and Opposition under State Socialism.* Santa Fe, N.M.: School of American Research Press.

Wheeler-Snow, Lois. 1972. *China on Stage: An American Actress in the People's Republic.* New York: Random House.

Williams, Dee Mack. 1996a. "Grassland Enclosures: Catalyst of Land Degradation in Inner Mongolia." *Human Organization* 55 (3): 307–13.

———. 1996b. "The Barbed Walls of China: A Contemporary Grassland Drama." *The Journal of Asian Studies* 55 (3): 665–91.

Williams, Raymond. 1977. *Marxism and Literature.* New York: Oxford University Press.

Witzleben, Lawrence. 1999. "Cantopop and Mandapop in Pre-Postcolonial Hong Kong: Identity Negotiation in the Performances of Anita Mui Yim-Fong." *Popular Music* 18 (2): 241–58.

Wong, Cynthia P. 1996. "Cui Jian, Rock Musician and Reluctant Hero." *ACMR Reports* 9 (1): 21–32.

Wong, Isabel K. F. 1984. "*Geming Gequ:* Songs for the Education of the Masses." In *Popular Chinese Literature and Performing Arts in the People's Republic of China, 1949–1979,* edited by Bonnie S. McDougall, 112–43. Berkeley: University of California Press.

Wong, Yu. 1996. "Wang's World." *Far Eastern Economic Review,* August 8: 46–49.

Woo, Margaret Y. K. 1994. "Chinese Women Workers: The Delicate Balance between Protection and Equality." In *Engendering China: Women, Culture, and the State,* edited by Christina Gilmartin, Gail Hershatter, Lisa Rofel, and Tyrene White, 279–95. Cambridge, Mass.: Harvard University Press.

Wu Jingrong, ed. 1979. *The Pinyin Chinese-English Dictionary.* Hong Kong: The Commercial Press.

Wu Xiaoying. 1995a. "Cheng Lin: Xianzai shi wo fahui gexing de shihou le!" (Cheng Lin: Now I Start to Bring My Individual Character into Play!). *Yinxiang shijie* 4: 2–3.

———. 1995b. "Li Chunbo: zai Guangzhou meiyou jia, zai Beijing you ge gongzuoshi" (Li Chunbo: I Do Not Have a Home in Guangzhou, but I Have a Studio in Beijing). *Yinxiang shijie* 6: 4–5.

Xu Tian. 1996. "Ai yo yinyue, women zai chengzhang" (Ai! Music, We Are Growing Up). *Yinyue shenghuo bao,* April 12.

Xue Ji. 1993. *Yaogun meng xun (Rock's Search for Dreams).* Beijing: Zhongguo dianying chubanshe.

Yang, Mayfair Mei-hui. 1993. "Of Gender, State Censorship, and Overseas Capital: An Interview with Chinese Director Zhang Yimou." *Public Culture* 5 (2): 297–313.

———. 1997. "Mass Media and Transnational Subjectivity in Shanghai: Notes on (Re)Cosmopolitanism in a Chinese Metropolis." In *Ungrounded Empires: The Cultural Politics of Modern Chinese Transnationalism,* edited by Aihwa Ong and Donald Nonini, 287–319. New York: Routledge.

———. 1999. "From Gender Erasure to Gender Difference: State Feminism, Consumer Sexuality, and Women's Public Sphere in China." In *Spaces of Their Own: Women's Public Sphere in Transnational China,* edited by Mayfair Mei-hui Yang, 35–67. Minneapolis: University of Minnesota Press.

Yang, Mu. 1994. "Academic Ignorance or Political Taboo? Some Issues in China's Study of Its Folk Song Culture." *Ethnomusicology* 38 (2): 303–20.

Yang, Xianyi and Gladys Yang, trans. 1984. *Poetry and Prose of the Tang and Song.* Beijing: Panda Books.

Yang Xiaolu. 1990. "Zhongguo dangdai tongsu gequ gaishu" (A General Description of Contemporary Chinese *Tongsu* Songs). In *Zhongwai tongsu gequ jianshang cidian (An Appreciation Dictionary of Chinese and Foreign Tongsu Songs),* edited by Yang Xiaolu and Zhang Zhentao, 225–27. Beijing: Shijie zhishi chubanshe.

Yang Xiaolu and Zhang Zhentao, eds. 1990. *Zhongwai tongsu gequ jianshang cidian (An Appreciation Dictionary of Chinese and Foreign Tongsu Songs).* Beijing: Shijie zhishi chubanshe.

Yau, Esther C. M. 1994. "Is China the End of Hermeneutics?; or Political and Cultural Usage of Non-Han Women in Mainland Chinese Films." In *Multiple Voices in Feminist Film Criticism*, edited by Diane Carson, Linda Dittmar, and Janice R. Welsch, 280–92. Minneapolis: University of Minnesota Press.

Yi Zhou. 1995. "Shen chu lishi zhi zhong" (Placed in the Midst of History). *Yanyiquan* 3: 1–3.

You Wei. 1996. "Tang chao: Jiezhu xifang zhaodao dongfang" (Tang Dynasty: Finding the East with the Aid of the West). *Yinxiang shijie* 4: 6–7.

"Yu Wenhua, Yin Xiangjie—Tian bu xiayu tian bu guafeng tian shang you taiyang" (Yu Wenhua, Yin Xiangjie—There Is No Rain and Wind, and the Sun Is Shining). 1995. *Yinxiang shijie* 3: 18.

Yung, Bell. 1984. "Model Opera as Model: From *Shajiabang* to *Sagabong*." In *Popular Chinese Literature and Performing Arts in the People's Republic of China 1949–1979*, edited by Bonnie S. McDougall, 144–64. Berkeley: University of California Press.

Zeng Yi. 1988. "Qiu ge de fengxing shuoming le shenme?" (What Does the Popularity of Prison Songs Mean?). *Guangming ribao*, October 19.

Zha, Jianying. 1994. "Beijing Subnotebooks." *Public Culture* 6 (2): 397–406.

———. 1995. *China Pop: How Soap Operas, Tabloids, and Bestsellers Are Transforming a Culture*. New York: New Press.

Zhan Hao. 1995a. "Zhang Guangtian: Rang liuxing yinyue shuo Hanyu" (Zhang Guangtian: Let Pop Music Speak the Han Language). *Yinxiang shijie* 11: 16.

———. 1995b. "Ai Jing bu ai ti minyao" (Ai Jing Does Not Like to Mention Folk Rhymes). *Yinxiang shijie* 6: 2–3.

Zhang Guangtian. 1996. "Miao wu qing ge, chun lai hu? Guanyu 'liuxing yinyue' de ji dian sikao" (Good Songs and Wonderful Dances, Has Spring Arrived? Some Thoughts about "Popular Music"). *Bailaohui* 1: 50–51.

Zhang Peiren. 1995. "Zhongguo yaogun yue shili: Xianggang yanchu houji" (The Power of Chinese Rock: Hong Kong Performance Postcript). *Yanyiquan* 3: 4.

Zhang Weiwen and Zeng Qingnan. 1993. *In Search of China's Minorities*. Beijing: New World Press.

Zhang Xianliang. 1989. *Half of Man Is Woman*. Translated by Martha Avery. London: Penguin Books.

Zhang, Yingjin. 1990. "Ideology of the Body in *Red Sorghum*: National Allegory, National Roots, and Third Cinema." *East-West Film Journal* 4 (2): 38–53.

———. 1997. "From 'Minority Film' to 'Minority Discourse': Questions of Nationhood and Ethnicity in Chinese Cinema." In *Transnational Chinese Cinemas: Identity, Nationhood, Gender*, edited by Sheldon Hsiao-peng Lu, 81–104. Honolulu: University of Hawaii Press.

Zhang Zhentao. 1990. "Zhongguo san si shi niandai liuxing gequ, qunzhong gequ gaishu" (A General Description of Mass and Pop Songs in China

During the 1930s and 1940s). In *Zhongwai tongsu gequ jianshang cidian (An Appreciation Dictionary of Chinese and Foreign Tongsu Songs)*, edited by Yang Xiaolu and Zhang Zhentao, 1–5. Beijing: Shijie zhishi chubanshe.

Zhao Jianwei. 1992. *Cui Jian zai Yiwusuoyou zhong nahan: Zhongguo yaogun beiwanglu (Cui Jian Cries Out in "Having Nothing": A Memorandum on Chinese Rock)*. Beijing: Beijing shifan daxue chubanshe.

Zheng Chunhua. 1993. "Cang lang dadi de lantian: Ji Mengzu geshou Teng Ge'er" (The Blue Sky of the Land of the Blue Wolf: Reporting on the Mongolian Singer Teng Ge'er). *Yinxiang shijie* 1: 2–3.

Zhong, Xueping. 1994. "Male Suffering and Male Desire: The Politics of Reading *Half of Man Is Woman*." In *Engendering China: Women, Culture, and the State*, edited by Christina Gilmartin, Gail Hershatter, Lisa Rofel, and Tyrene White, 175–91. Cambridge, Mass.: Harvard University Press.

———. 2000. *Masculinity Besieged? Issues of Modernity and Male Subjectivity in Chinese Literature of the Late Twentieth Century*. London: Duke University Press.

Zhou You, ed. 1994. *Beijing yaogun buluo (Beijing's Rock Tribe)*. Tianjin: Shehuike xueyuan chubanshe.

Zhu, Ling. 1993. "A Brave New World? On the Construction of 'Masculinity' and 'Femininity' in *The Red Sorghum Family*." In *Gender and Sexuality in Twentieth-Century Chinese Literature and Society*, edited by Lu Tonglin, 121–34. Albany: State University of New York Press.

DISCOGRAPHY

Ai Jing. 1993. *Ai Jing: Wo de 1997 (Ai Jing: My 1997)*. Dadi changpian / Magic Stone / Shanghai yinxiang chubanshe, CD021.

———. 1995. *Ai Jing: Yanfen jie de gushi (Ai Jing: The Story of Yanfen Street)*. Dadi changpian / Zhongguo luyin luxiang chuban zongshe, ISRC CN–A12–94–316–00/A. J6. (JS009).

Chen Ming. 1994. *Chen Ming: Jimo rang wo ruci meili (Chen Ming: Loneliness Makes Me So Beautiful)*. Zhongguo changpian Guangzhou gongsi, ISRC CN–F13–94–384–00/A. J6.

Cheng Lin. 1995. *Cheng Lin: Hui jia (Cheng Lin: Returning Home)*. Dianyin chuanbo qiye youxian gongsi, ISRC CN–F12–94–432–00/A. J6. (P–2529).

Cui Jian. 1989. *Cui Jian: Xin changzheng lu shang de yaogun (Cui Jian: Rock and Roll of the New Long March)*. Zhongguo lüyou shengxiang chubanshe, BJZ01.

———. 1991. *Cui Jian: Jiejue (Cui Jian: Solution)*. Zhongguo beiguang shengxiang yishu gongsi, BSL 029.

———. 1993. *Cui Jian: Beijing yanchanghui (Cui Jian: The Beijing Concert)*. Zhongguo lüyou chubanshe, ISRC CN–M29–93–0009/A. J6.

———. 1994. *Cui Jian: Hongqi xia de dan (Cui Jian: The Egg under the Red Flag)*. Shenzhenshi jiguang jiemu chuban faxing gongsi, ISRC CN–F27–94–361–oo/A. J6.

Dadawa (Zhu Zheqin), He Xuntian, He Xunyou, and Lu Yimin. 1995. *A jie gu (Sister Drum)*. Taipei: Feidie changpian.

Dengdai na yi tian (Waiting for That Day). 1996. Zhongxin chubanshe, ISRC CN–X48–96–0001–o/A. J6.

Dou Wei. 1994. *Dou Wei: Hei meng (Dou Wei: Black Dream)*. Shanghai shengxiang chubanshe/Gunshi yousheng chubanshe youxian gongsi, ISRC CN–E04–94–325–oo/A. J6.

Gao Feng. 1994. *Gao Feng: Tian na bian de ai (Gao Feng: Love Over There in the Sky)*. Baidai changpian (EMI)/Zhonghua wenyi yinxiang lianhe chubanshe, ISRC CN–A49–94–349–oo/A. J6.

———. 1996. *Gao Feng: Fengshou (Gao Feng: Bumper Harvest)*. Zhonghua wenyi yinxiang lianhe chubanshe, ISRC CN–A49–95–336–oo/A. J6.

He Yong. 1994. *He Yong: Lajichang (He Yong: Garbage Dump)*. Shanghai shengxiang chubanshe/Gunshi yousheng chubanshe youxian gongsi, ISRC CN–E04–94–326–oo/A. J6 (Y–1132).

Hong taiyang: Mao Zedong songge xin jiezou lianchang (The Red Sun: Praise Songs for Mao Zedong Sung in Succession to a New Beat). 1991. Zhongguo changpian zonggongsi Shanghai gongsi, L–133.

Lin Yilun. 1995. *Lin Yilun: Huo huo de geyao (Lin Yilun: Fire Hot Songs)*. Guangzhou xin shidai yingyin gongsi, ISRC CN–F21–95–303–oo/A. J6. (MTS–9503).

Lolo. 1995. *Lolo yao (Lolo's Swing)*. Guoji wenhua jiaoliu yinxiang chubanshe/Guangzhou xin shidai yinxiang faxing gongsi, ISRC CN–A26–95–315–oo/A. J6. (IAM94011).

Lunhui/Again. 1995. *Lunhui/Again: Chuangzao (Lunhui/Again: Creation)*. Zhongguo changpian Shanghai gongsi, ISRC CN–E01–94–0088–o/A. J6. (CL–105).

Mao Amin. 1994. *Mao Amin*. Beijing dongfang yingyin gongsi/Huaxing changpian, ISRC CN–A13–94–382–oo/A.J6. (CAL–33–1158M).

Mao Ning. 1995. *Mao Ning: '95 zui xin jinqu da fengxian (Mao Ning: The Newest Golden Hits of 1995)*. Guangdong wenhua yinxiang chubanshe/Gunshi yousheng chubanshe, ISRC CN–H03–94–328–oo/A.J. (MG–415).

Na Ying. 1994. *Na Ying: Wei ni zhaosi muxiang (Na Ying: I Yearn for You Day and Night)*. Fumao changpian (DECCA)/Zhongguo kangyi yinxiang chubanshe, ISRC CN–A53–94–301–oo/A. J6.

Qianfu siji diao (Four Season Songs of the Boat Tower). Zhongguo zhigong yinxiang chubanshe, ISRC CN–A47–94–313–oo/A. J6.

Shan ying (Mountain Eagle). 1993. *Shan ying yanchang zhuanji (1): Wo ai wo de jiaxiang (Mountain Eagle, Singing Album [1]: I Love My Hometown)*. Sichuan wenyi yinxiang chubanshe, ISRC CN–G12–93–305–oo/A.J6.

————. 1994. *Shan ying: Zouchu Daliangshan (Mountain Eagle: Getting Out of Daliangshan)*. Guangzhou taipingyang yingyin gongsi, ISRC CN–F12–94–415–oo/A. J6. (P–2522).

Tang chao (Tang Dynasty). 1992. *Tang chao yuedui (Tang Dynasty)*. Gunshi yousheng chubanshe youxian gongsi/Zhongguo yinyuejia yinxiang chubanshe, Z421 Ho62.

Teng Ge'er. 1994. *Teng Ge'er: Meng sui feng piao (Teng Ge'er: Dreams Float with the Wind)*. Baidai (EMI)/Zhonghua wenyi yinxiang lianhe chubanshe, ISRC CN–A49–94–348–oo/A. J6. (94Coo9).

————. 1996. *Hei junma (Black Steed)*. Xueyuan yinxiang chubanshe, ISRC CN–A56–96–0001–o/A. J6.

Tian Zhen. 1996. *Tian Zhen*. Hunan wenhua yinxiang chubanshe. ISRC CN–F37–96–301–oo/A.J6.

Wayhwa. 1995. *Wayhwa: Xiandaihua (Wayhwa: Modernization)*. Zhongguo guoji wenhua jiaoliu yinxiang chubanshe, ISRC CN–A26–95–334–oo/A. J6. (Hong Kong edition: 1996 by Dim Sum Records, DSCD WHo1–96).

Yaogun Beijing (Beijing Rock). 1993. Beijing wenhua yishu yinxiang chubanshe/Yongsheng yinyue changpian youxian gongsi, ISRC CN–Co2–93–308–oo/A. J6.

Yaogun Beijing II (Beijing Rock II). 1994. BMG Music Taiwan Inc., 9022–4/74321225664 (ISRC CN–A13–94–316–oo/A. J6).

Zang Tianshuo. 1995. *Zang Tianshuo: Wo zhe shi nian (Zang Tianshuo: My Last Ten Years)*. Shanghai yinxiang gongsi, ISRC CN–Eo2–95–305–oo/A. J6.

Zhang Guangtian. 1993. *Zhang Guangtian: Xiandai gequ zhuanji (Zhang Guangtian: Album of Modern Songs)*. Zhongguo yinyuejia yinxiang chubanshe, ISRC CN–A50–93–0008/A. J6.

Zheng Jun. 1994. *Zheng Jun: Chiluoluo (Zheng Jun: Naked)*. Zhongguo yinyuejia yinxiang chubanshe/Hongxing shengchanshe, ISRC CN–A50–94–306–oo/A. J6.

Zhongguo huo (Chinese Fire). 1992. Gunshi yousheng chubanshe youxian gongsi/ Zhongguo yinyuejia yinxiang chubanshe, Z427 Ho64.

Zhongguo ju xing shouchang yuanban (Original Edition of Original Renditions of Songs by China's Giant Stars). 1996. Zhongguo changpian zonggongsi, ISRC CN–Ao1–96–0120–o/A. J6. (EL–721).

Zhongguo yaogun 1 (Chinese Rock 1). 1994. Beijing beiying luyin luxiang gongsi, ISRC CN–Ao8–94–319–oo/A. J6.

Zhongguo yaogun 2 (Chinese Rock 2). 1994. Beijing beiying luyin luxiang gongsi, ISRC CN–Ao8–94–320–oo/A. J6.

Zhongguo yaogunyue shili (The Power of Chinese Rock Music). 1995. Gunshi yousheng chubanshe youxian gongsi/Shanghai shengxiang chubanshe, ISRC CN–Eo4–95–358–oo/A. J6. (Y–1175) (MSC–002).

VIDEOGRAPHY

Williams, Sue, dir. 1997. *Born under the Red Flag*. Ambrica Productions.

Zhongguo min'ge jingdian (2), MTV 42 shou (Chinese Folksongs Classics 2, 42 Songs with MTV). Heilongjiang yinxiang chubanshe, ISRC. CN–D10–95–355–00/ V.J6.

Zhongguo yaogunyue shili; Dou Wei, Zhang Chu, He Yong, Tang chao yuedui, MTV yanchanghui (The Power of Chinese Rock: Dou Wei, Zhang Chu, He Yong, Tang Dynasty, MTV Concert). 1995. Guizhou guangbo dianshi daxue yinxiang jiaocai chubanshe. ISRC CN–G09–95–0322–0/ V.J6.

Index

Page numbers in italics refer to illustrations.

Text: 10/13 Aldus
Display: Aldus
Compositor: G & S Typesetters, Inc.
Printer and Binder: Thomson-Shore, Inc.